BTEC national
2nd Edition

Sport
Book 2

Ray Barker • Wendy Davies
Chris Lydon • Rob Saipe
Phil Smith • Nick Wilmot

Series editor: Mark Adams

www.harcourt.co.uk

✓ Free online support
✓ Useful weblinks
✓ 24 hour online ordering

01865 888118

Heinemann

Heinemann is an imprint of Harcourt Education Limited, a company incorporated in England and Wales, having its registered office: Halley Court, Jordan Hill, Oxford OX2 8EJ. Registered company number: 3099304

www.harcourt.co.uk

Heinemann is the registered trademark of Harcourt Education Ltd

Text © Ray Barker, Wendy Davies, Chris Lydon, Rob Saipe, Phil Smith and Nick Wilmott

First published 2007

12 11 10 09 08 07[1]
10 9 8 7 6 5 4 3 2 1

British Library Cataloguing in Publication Data is available from the British Library on request.

ISBN 9780435465155

Edited by Anne Sweetmore, Oxon, UK
Typeset by Techtype, Oxon, UK
Illustrated by Tek-art, Surrey, UK
Cover design by Pentacor Ltd
Picture research by Kath Kollberg
Cover photo/illustration © Superstock
Printed at Scotprint Ltd

Websites
The websites used in this book were correct and up-to-date at the time of publication. It is essential for tutors to preview each website before using it in class so as to ensure that the URL is still accurate, relevant and appropriate. We suggest that tutors bookmark useful websites and consider enabling students to access them through the school/college intranet.

This material has been endorsed by Edexcel and offers high quality support for the delivery of Edexcel qualifications.

Edexcel endorsement does not mean that this material is essential to achieve any Edexcel qualification, nor does it mean that this is the only suitable material available to support any Edexcel qualification. No endorsed material will be used verbatim in setting any Edexcel examination and any resource lists produced by Edexcel shall include this and other appropriate texts. While this material has been through an Edexcel quality assurance process, all responsibility for the content remains with the publisher.

Copies of official specifications for all Edexcel qualifications may be found on the Edexcel website – www.edexcel.org.uk

Contents

Acknowledgements Sport Book 2

The authors and publisher would like to thank Mark Adams for his help and support in developing the BTEC National Sport resources.

Ray Barker would like to thank Rob Saipe for his contribution to Unit 24.

The authors and publisher would like to thank the following individuals and organisations for permission to reproduce photographs:

Front cover: Superstock
Feature icons: Getty Images / PhotoDisc, Jupiter Images / Photos.com, Corbis

Front cover: © Superstock
Feature icons: Getty Images / PhotoDisc, Photos.com, Corbis

PA Photos / Joel Ryan – page 2
The Bridgeman Art Library / Private Collections – page 4
Alamy / Popperfoto – page 4
Alamy / Vic Pigula – page 5
Alamy / Vario Images GmbH & Co. kg – page 19
PA Photos / AP / Daniel Maurer – page 29
Getty Images / AFP / John MacDougall – page 31
Corbis / EPA / Bartolmeij Zborowski – page – page 34
Getty Images / Richard Heathcote – page 39
iStockPhoto / Tyler Stalman – page 46
Getty Images / Hassan Ammar – page 48
Corbis – page 49
PA Photos / AP / Steve Mitchell – page 54
iStockPhoto / Eliza Snow – page 62
PA Photos / Tom Hevezi – page 64
Corbis / Ariel Skelley – page 66
iStockPhoto / Rene Mansi – page 69
Action Plus / Neil Tingle – page 70
Corbis / Duomo – page 80
iStockPhoto / Nico Smit – page 90
Science Photo Library – page 93
Corbis / Xinhua Press / Qi Heng – page 94
Action Plus – page 108
Corbis – page113
Corbis / FURGOLLE / Imagepoint FR – page 117

Corbis / Randy Faris – page 124
PA Photos / AP / Mary Ann Chastain – page 126
PA Photos / AP / Martin Meissner – page 127
Corbis / Reuters / Patrick Price – page 131
Corbis / Louie Psihoyos – page 133
PA Photos / Peter Byrne – page 135
Corbis / EPA / CJ Gunther – page 138
PA Photos / Empics Sport / Adam Devy – page 141
Beehive Systems Limited – page 146
Action Plus – page 152
Corbis / Reuters / Eddie Keogh – page 160
Popperfoto – page 162
PA Photos / Empics Sport / Adam Devy – page 175
Alamy / George S deBlonsky – page 177
PA Photos / AP / Marc Bence – page 183
PA Photos / AP / Alessandro Trovati – page186
Harcourt Education Ltd / Trevor Clifford – page 196
Science Photo Library / Biophoto Associates – page 199
Harcourt Education Ltd / Trevor Clifford – page 201
Science Photo Library / Faye Norman – page 195
Corbis / Fotostudio FM / sefa – page 206
Harcourt Education Ltd / Trevor Clifford (x7) – page 219/220/221
Action Plus / Glen Kirk – page 228
Alamy / Rick Decker – page 236
Getty Images / Scott Boehm – page 237
Getty Images / Hrvoje Polan – page 238
Action Plus / Steve Bardens – page 240
Action Plus / Neil Tingle – page 243
Getty Images / Stu Foster – page 238
Alamy / China Photo World – page 249
Corbis – page 253
Getty Images / PhotoDisc – page 260
Crown Copyright – page 263
Alamy / Mark Baynes – page 266
Still Pictures / Ron Gilling – page 267
Corbis / Brand X / Dinodia Photo Library – page 270
Corbis / Gideon Mendel – page 272

Action Plus / Glyn Kirk – page 274
Alamy / David Anthony – page 282
Getty Images / AFP / Dibyangshu Sarkur – page 283
Alamy / Paul-Hill.co.uk – page 290
Alamy Images / NRT – page 294
Getty Images / Photonica – page 295
Alamy / John Powell Photographer – page 299
Photolibrary / Flirt – page 307
Getty Images / Altrendo – page 313
Rex Features – page 324
Alamy / Roy Lowe – page 332
Corbis / David Katzenstein – page 342
Alamy / Dennis MacDonald – page 355
Rex Features – page 359
Getty Images / Stone – page 366

The authors and publisher would like to thank the following individuals and organisations for permission to reproduce copyright material:

1. Unit 23 pg 263 Crown Copyright (front page of green paper) http://www.everychildmatters.gov.uk/
2. Unit 24 page 296, Evolution Group annual report 2006 – front page
3. Unit 24 page 306 (Village Hotels customer feedback sheet) www.village-hotels.co.uk
4. Unit 24 page 311 (Newcastle Utd FC, events and merchandise leaflets) www.nufc.co.uk
5. Unit 24 page 316 (Wet 'n' Wild, promotional leaflets) www.wetnwild.co.uk
6. Unit 24 page 318 (Doncaster Dome promotional leaflet) www.the-dome.co.uk
7. Unit 24 page 321 (Freetown Sports promotional leaflet) www.freetownsports.co.uk

Every effort has been made by the publisher to contact copyright holders of material reproduced in this book. Any omissions will be rectified in subsequent printings if notice is given to the publishers

Introduction

Welcome to this BTEC National Sport Book 2, specifically designed to support students on the following programmes (with the number of units required to gain the qualification identified):

- BTEC National Award in Sport
  3 core and 3 specialist units
- BTEC National Award in Sport (Performance and Excellence)
  3 core and 3 specialist units
- BTEC National Certificate in Sport (Performance and Excellence)
  8 core and 4 specialist units
- BTEC National Certificate in Sport (Development, Coaching and Fitness)
  7 core and 5 specialist units
- BTEC National Diploma in Sport (Performance and Excellence)
  8 core and 10 specialist units
- BTEC National Diploma in Sport (Development, Coaching and Fitness)
  7 core and 11 specialist units

It is important to highlight the fact that some of units you will study on your course are included in BTEC National Sport Book 1. The following table shows the units included in Sport Book 1 and Sport Book 2. The table indicates whether it is a **core (bold)** or *specialist (italic)* unit. Those units in green appear in this title, those in blue are covered in BTEC National Sport Book 1.

If nothing is indicated in a box, that means the unit is not included in your qualification.

Unit	BTEC National Award in Sport	BTEC National Award in Sport (Performance and Excellence)	BTEC National Certificate in Sport (Performance and Excellence)	BTEC National Certificate in Sport (Development, Coaching and Fitness)	BTEC National Diploma in Sport (Performance and Excellence)	BTEC National Diploma in Sport (Development, Coaching and Fitness)
1 The Body in Action	**1**	**1**	**1**	**1**	**1**	**1**
2 Health and Safety in Sport	**1**	**1**	**1**	**1**	**1**	**1**
3 Training and Fitness for Sport	**1**	**1**	**1**	**1**	**1**	**1**
4 Sports Coaching	*1*		*1*	**1**	*1*	**1**
5 Sports Development	*1*			**1**		**1**
6 Fitness Testing for Sport and Exercise	*1*	*1*	**1**	**1**	**1**	**1**
10 Sports Nutrition		*1*	**1**	*1*	**1**	*1*
11 Sport and Society			*2*	*2*	*2*	*2*

Unit	BTEC National Award in Sport	BTEC National Award in Sport (Performance and Excellence)	BTEC National Certificate in Sport (Performance and Excellence)	BTEC National Certificate in Sport (Development, Coaching and Fitness)	BTEC National Diploma in Sport (Performance and Excellence)	BTEC National Diploma in Sport (Development, Coaching and Fitness)
12 Instructing Physical Activity and Exercise				2	2	2
16 Psychology for Sports Performance		1	1	1	1	1
17 Sports Injuries			2	2	2	2
18 Analysis of Sports Performance			2		2	2
19 Talent Identification and Development in Sport					2	2
20 Sport and Exercise Massage			2	2	2	2
21 Rules, Regulations and Officiating in Sport			2	2	2	2
23 Working with Children in Sport				2	2	2
24 Sport as a Business				2	2	2
25 Work-based Experience in Sport			2	2	2	2
26 Technical and Tactical Skills in Sport		1	1		1	
27 The Athlete's Lifestyle		1	1		1	

The revised specification has been structured to allow learners maximum flexibility in selecting specialist units, so that particular interests and career aspirations within sport can be reflected in the choice of unit combinations. This series of books effectively reflects the specification and will help the tutor and student successfully to direct their learning along a specific path, enabling them to develop essential skills required for gaining employment or securing career progression.

You should also note that Exercise, Health and Lifestyle in addition to Exercise for Specific Groups are included in the BTEC National Sport and Exercise Sciences Book.

The aim of this book is to provide a comprehensive source of information for your course. It follows the BTEC specification closely, so that you can easily see what you have covered and quickly find the information you need. Examples and case studies from sport are used to bring your course to life and make it enjoyable to study. We hope you will be encouraged to find your own examples of current practice too.

You will often be asked to carry out research for activities in the text, and this will develop your research skills and enable you to find many sources of interesting sports information, particularly on the internet. The book is also a suitable core text for students on HND, foundation degree and first-year degree programmes. To help you plan your study, an overview of each unit and its outcomes is given at the beginning of each unit.

Features of the book

This book has a number of features to help you relate theory to practice and reinforce your learning. It also aims to help you gather evidence for assessment. You will find the following features in each unit.

Case studies

Interesting examples of real situations, for example, laboratory data are described in case studies that link theory to practice. They will show you how the topics you are studying affect real people and businesses.

Theory into practice

These features allow you to consider theoretical knowledge and relate this to Sport and Exercise Science tasks or research.

Taking it further

Facilitating the knowledge from each unit and extending your thinking is what Taking it further is all about. Questions will be posed that will stretch the learning and build on what has already been explained.

Knowledge checks

At the end of each unit is a set of quick questions to test your knowledge of the information you have been studying. Use these to check your progress, and also as a revision tool.

Case study

Title

A basketball coach wants to measure the overall flexibility of the team's players and has decided to use the sit-and-reach test to measure this. However, although this test is a measure of flexibility, it would not be valid.

1   Explain to the coach why the sit-and-reach test is not a valid measure of overall flexibility.

2   The coach needs some advice about fitness testing with his players. He has come to you for some advice. Your job is to suggest a more appropriate method of testing the players' overall flexibility. Make sure you can explain why your suggestions will increase the validity of testing.

Reliability

Reliability relates to whether, if you carried out the research again, you would get the same results. However, reliability can be claimed without the results being correct. For example, if you always ask the wrong questions in research, you would always get the same wrong answers. This would mean the test would be reliable because you have received the *same* wrong answers, even though they are not the ones you have been wanting.

In quantitative research, reliability can be one researcher conducting the same test on the same individual on a number of occasions, and getting the same (or similar) results. Alternatively, it can be different researchers conducting the same test on the same individual and getting the same (or similar) results.

In qualitative research, reliability relates to the same researcher placing results into the same categories on a number of different occasions, or different researchers placing results into the same or similar categories.

Remember!

You need to be careful, as reliability can be claimed without the results being correct!

There are certain factors you need to take into account that can affect reliability. For example:

* errors can happen when researchers don't know how to use the equipment correctly
* the equipment is poorly maintained
* the wrong type of equipment is selected.

There are two main types of reliability.

* Inter-researcher reliability: This looks at whether different researchers in the same situation would get the same (or similar) results. An example of when inter-researcher reliability is a problem comes through body composition assessment. When people are learning to use the skinfold calliper technique (see page 129) of assessing body composition, it is sometimes difficult to take accurate measurements from the correct sites. Researchers often come up with different values. When this happens, you cannot claim to have achieved inter-researcher reliability.
* Test-retest reliability: This relates to doing the same test on a number of different occasions and getting the same (or similar) results. An example of a test-retest reliability issue in sport or exercise research is the measurement of heart rate. Heart rate can be affected by a number of factors, such as temperature, time of day, diet, sleep patterns, physical activity levels and alcohol. Therefore, if you were to measure heart rate on the same person at the same time of day, but on different days, it is likely you would get different measurements.

Your tutor should check that you have completed enough activities to meet all the assessment criteria for the unit.

Tutors and students should refer to the BTEC standards for the qualification for the full BTEC grading criteria for each unit (www.edexcel.org.uk).

I do hope that you enjoy your course and find this book an excellent support for your studies. Good luck!

Graham Saffery

Assessment practice

A newly-qualified fitness instructor has been asked to measure the body fat percentage of a client. They are a little unsure of how to use the skinfold callipers, but take the measurements anyway. However, they take the measurements in the wrong places and record the results. The results of the tests are shown below.

Site	Measurement 1 (mm)	Measurement 2 (mm)	Measurement 3 (mm)	Mean (mm)
Biceps	7	7	7	7.0
Triceps	7	6	7	6.6
Subscapular	8	11	6	8.3
Suprailiac	13	6	7	8.6
				30.5

1 What validity issues can you identify? **P2**
2 What reliability issues can you identify? **P2**
3 Which results in the table do you think are unreliable? Explain your answer. **M2**

grading tips

Grading Tip P2
Say how you know when something is not valid or reliable.

Grading Tip M2
Give examples from the case study and data that you have been provided with, to show where the validity and reliability issues are.

Think it over

Can something be valid without being reliable? Can something be reliable without being valid?

Accuracy

Accuracy relates to how close your measurement is to the 'gold standard', or what you are actually intending to measure. Imagine you are looking at the weight of a boxer before a fight. If the boxer had an actual weight of 100 kg and your weighing device showed him to weigh 100.1 kg, you could say this is accurate. However, if the measuring device showed him to weigh 103 kg, you would say this is not accurate as it is not close to their actual body weight.

Key Term

Gold standard The norm value closest to what you are actually intending to measure. For example, in darts if you wanted to hit the bulls eye, the gold standard would be hitting the bulls eye.

Precision

When working in a research setting, any measurement you take will have some unpredictability about it. This degree of unpredictability relates to the amount of precision the tool selected for measurement has. Precision is related to the refinement of the measuring process. It is mainly concerned with how fine or small a difference the measuring device can detect. Precision is closely related to repeatability/reliability (see page 128).

An example involves measuring the bowling speed of Steve Harmison in the Ashes series using a speed gun and light gates. The speed gun gives you three speeds, all to the nearest mile per hour (e.g. 80mph, 81mph,

Assesment practice/Activities

Activities are also provided throughout each unit. These are linked to real situations and case studies and they can be used for practice before tackling the preparation for assessment or completing your own actual assessment.

Think it over

These are points for individual reflection or group discussion. They will widen your knowledge and help you reflect on issues that have an impact on Sport and Exercise Science.

Key terms

Issues and terms that you need to be aware of are summarised under these headings. They will help you check your knowledge as you learn, and will prove to be a useful quick-reference tool.

Preparation for assessment

Each unit concludes with a suggested full unit assessment which, taken as a whole, fulfils all the unit requirements from Pass to Distinction.

Each task is matched to the relevant criteria in the specification.

If you are aiming for a Pass, make sure you complete all the Pass (P) tasks.

If you are aiming for a Merit, make sure you complete all the Pass (P) and Merit (M) tasks.

If you are aiming for a Distinction, you will also need to complete all the Distinction (D) tasks. P1 means the first of the Pass criteria listed in the specification, M1 the first of the Merit criteria, D1 the first of the Distinction criteria, and so on.

Sport and society

Introduction

Sport makes many contributions to our society in Britain today, providing jobs, entertainment and the opportunity for great endeavour, and doing much good for our health, fitness and wellbeing. It has grown in scale over the past 100 years, but in a fairly fragmented way. Sport has become a sector with impacts on, and importance for, all communities in UK society.

Sport in our society has many far-reaching agendas, such as the need for higher levels of participation and more resources – and, of course, Olympic success. All these issues are constantly under the scrutiny and influence of the media. Sport is not free of problems either, regularly bringing racism, sexism, corruption, drugs, inequality and commercialism to the fore.

In this unit you will gain an understanding of the historical development of sport in society, and be brought up to date with the contemporary issues that surround many sports bodies and drive many sports organisations' strategic plans.

After completing this unit you should be able to achieve the following outcomes:

- Understand how the development of sport has influenced how it is organised.
- Know about the sports industry in the United Kingdom today.
- Understand how contemporary issues affect sport.
- Understand cultural influences and barriers that affect participation in sports activities.

Think it over

In a 2005–06 participation survey called 'Active People' (conducted by MORI for Sport England), the general levels of participation in sport around the UK reached only 18–20 per cent. This is not a very high percentage – why do you think this is so?

Do you think it's because too many people are 'couch potatoes' now, just playing computer games and not taking exercise or eating a good diet? Could it be because doing sport today means you have to spend money, and some people can't afford it? Does everyone have the same chance to participate, such as those from ethnic minorities or single-parent families?

The development of sport

Countryside, leisure and military activities give us many of the origins of sport as we know it today, but the development of sports has taken place slowly over a number of centuries. In this section we investigate different historical periods and social developments that played a role in forming sport in our society today.

Pre-industrial leisure

The term 'pre-industrial' means the period before machinery and factories were common, and before large towns and cities were established, when most people lived in small communities (villages and hamlets).

First let's consider the largely agricultural society of the Tudor and Stuart period (1600–1700). The lifestyle was mainly 'subsistence' – living off the land to survive. Life hinged on good harvests and being able to trade goods or produce, and this basically agricultural lifestyle is referred to as the agrarian period. Leisure was an intrinsic part of life, not a separate activity as it tends to be today. Work focused on making goods to sell, or growing crops to eat and sell at markets. People were tied to work the land, with little machinery to help them, and did so to survive and pay their rent, rather than for leisure. But on market days, or at fairs, there would also be an opportunity to take part in some 'leisure' activities. Picture a busy market square with beasts and goods for sale, but also scenes of people being enthralled by the tricks of street entertainers, music being played for dancing, and of course gambling and drinking in the local hostelries.

The rich were able to travel locally, and may have hunted on neighbouring estates or travelled to the coast to sail. For the poorer peasants there were local 'folk games', which would include events of skill along the lines of today's sports such as archery. But many country folk would not have the skills, time or energy to take part. The church did not look favourably on any kind of sport, and put pressure on King James to tone down the games and encourage people to worship more.

▲ Archery could be considered as a historical folk game

The puritan period of Cromwell's Protectorate was followed by the restoration of the monarchy in 1660. The new King, Charles II, resurrected sports, and tennis, yachting and hunting grew in popularity again. Other sports, such as early forms of cricket, skating and fishing, were followed by the rich. Life for the poor in these times still had its leisure element though, with parlour games such as draughts, dice, dominoes and cards, and festivals (many of which were religious). Some traditional events that took place are still represented today by surviving country shows and county fairs. We still celebrate harvest festival, and go to shows to watch ploughing matches and bale-tossing competitions, and to view the best animals and birds.

The pre-industrial period (1700–1800) brought many changes, with more travel becoming possible, although roads were muddy and fraught with dangers such as highwaymen. But no-one travelled to matches as they do today.

Not all sports were kind – consider bull- and bear-baiting, and dog- and cock-fights, some of which persist today around the world, which fostered a lot of gambling. Hard physical work continued for many, including children, and sport was represented by sword-fighting, duelling and bare-knuckle fighting. Much physical activity had traditionally been for military purposes – getting fit to fight, and building strength to wield swords, pikes and axes. On the other hand, cricket was born in the early 1700s, and in 1744 a Kent side beat an All-England one 111 to 110. Meanwhile, spa towns such as Bath encouraged bathing, dancing and taking walks in the park, and the rich continued with their equestrian sports on their private estates.

Activity

Discuss what other agricultural or animal-based sports and military activities you can think of that have carried on through the centuries.

Case study

One example of these traditions is the Great Yorkshire Show, held in Harrogate every July at the agricultural showground. In 2006 the gate figure was 135,111 – an all-time high in the show's 148-year history, showing how popular this type of show still is. You can still see some traditional sports and pastimes in the country pursuits and forestry events arena, such as pole-climbing, sheep-shearing, wood-turning and falconry.
See www.greatyorkshireshow.com

1   Why do you think there are still some enduring country sports?

Taking it further

Find out if any traditional events, fairs, shows or markets have survived in your area, and try to discover when they originated.

Early nineteenth century

The Victorian period of the 1800s brought more mechanical inventions, and businesses such as mills were set up to produce and trade goods within the British Empire. New jobs became available in factories in towns, which attracted poorer country people to move to the towns in search of paid work, rather than subsistence farming. The cities grew, but life was hard and certainly not as healthy as country life – conditions were often cramped and unsanitary, the absence of electricity, running water or an inside toilet being made worse by overcrowding. Work was physically demanding (e.g. mining or labouring on building sites), and there was little time off, and little or no additional earnings available for sport and leisure activities. In cities, sport and leisure opportunities were fewer, and very different from country sports, with activities for the working classes being more informal, or spectator sports oriented to watching rather than participating, such as boxing, wrestling and rowing. Many activities also had a gambling dimension or were blood sports brought in from country pursuits, such as dog-fighting. Market towns and market days were probably the most active, and some still retain their traditional street football matches, such as Duns in the Scottish Borders.

Many people with strong religious beliefs saw sport and leisure activities as wasteful of time and effort, which meant that churchgoers opposed activities, especially on Sundays. They also objected to children working.

Think it over

How does organised religion's influence on sporting activity in the nineteenth century contrast with today?

Aristocratic sports flourished among the richer classes, who were benefiting from trade and land ownership. They had leisure time and were able to follow pursuits such as hunting, riding and shooting on estates – hence their love of equestrianism today. In towns, they would have larger houses with gardens, and played croquet and bowls. The inequality between classes (and genders) was becoming very apparent in income, time and access to leisure pursuits.

Industrialisation of the mid-nineteenth century

The invention of steam power brought better transport and much industrial change. In addition, sport was influenced by the growth of the new public schools.

■ Influence of public schools

'Public' schools – which in fact were for 'private' fee-paying students – blossomed in the early nineteenth century as the wealth gained by many merchants and other business people allowed the richer classes to pay for their children's education. Sports flourished within their walls, especially rugby, cricket, tennis and some soccer. Rules were made to help structure the sports, and these form the basis of rules and regulations today. So the public schools made a great contribution to sport.

■ Work versus leisure

But it was not 'sport for all' – meanwhile, in the poorer Victorian slums, factory workers and their children had little to speak of other than street and pub games such as darts. Their working week would be close to 70 hours. However, there were many more public holidays than now, with saints' days and church festivals providing the excuse for some time off.

These holidays were gradually suppressed by hard-nosed businessmen and factory-owners who promoted a hard-working ethic. This tide of capitalism was opposed over the years by working-class people, who fought for a shorter working day and week, higher wages, and time off work for leisure in return for their labour.

Late nineteenth century

This period saw a change in attitudes and the right to time off – the 'weekend' was born, which gave sport and leisure a chance to flourish. The new-found leisure of the working classes, often just a Saturday afternoon off, was quickly filled with amusements and entertainment, but also with some sports matches taking on the more commercial approach that we see today. Music hall flourished, as did opportunities to play and watch football, cricket and golf and, for some, ballooning and flying. Sunday remained the day of worship, but this was often followed by home-based leisure pastimes and hobbies.

▼ Timeline – the development of sports

1600s	1700s	1800s	1900s	2000s
game fairs; military-type skills; working life and leisure not separate	festivals and fetes; country sports flourish	some free time; all popular sports develop	transport allows travel to matches and big games	sport modernises, hallmark events feature
local	district	regional	national and international	global
folk games	equestrianism	teams, clubs and leagues	associations begin to run sports	world championships in all sports

Olympics revived 1896

pre-industrial		industrial	modernising era	technological era
1600s	**1700s**	**1800s**	**1900s**	**2000s**
Tudors and Stuarts	Georgian	Victorian	Modernising	Current
agricultural lifestyle, sport and leisure mainly for wealthy	more activities for poor in towns and country, but blood sports common	structure and rules for sports developed along with more opportunities for both rich and poor	diversity of sport builds up, along with policies for equal access and participation	globalisation and commodification of sport, plus health drives

▲ Timeline – the growth of sports and leisure

Many groups of employees still worked long hours – such as shop-workers, who still often worked an 80-hour week. Drinking in public houses and 'gin palaces' grew as a social habit, while certain workers followed specific pursuits, such as miners who often kept racing pigeons. Some people regarded these leisure habits as not sufficiently constructive, and a drive resulted to try and create sporting and leisure habits with 'proper rules'.

A crucial event for children was the Elementary Education Act of 1870, which made it compulsory for children aged 5–13 to go to school, where play was encouraged.

■ Rationalisation

In this period, rationalisation of sport and leisure meant encouraging more organised, structured and 'wholesome' recreation – sports and games with a healthy purpose, as opposed to drinking, gambling and blood sports such as bare-knuckle fights. The YMCA, created in 1844 as the Young Men's Christian Association, combined Christian values with healthy sports. Several other motives could be found in the 'rational recreation' philosophy:

- keeping people healthier so they could work harder
- giving them challenging leisure experiences to help them forget the drudgery of work
- compensating them for hard physical labour
- helping them to get some fresh air and escape poor working conditions.

■ Regulation

At this time, the influence of the public schools created a general trend towards regularising how sports were played – for example, boxing adopted the Queensberry rules in 1867. Sports associations, leagues and clubs began to form too, many being 'works teams' such as

Case study

As early as the sixteenth century, the public schools had been instrumental in taking football away from its violent 'mob' form and turning it into an organised team sport. The Victorians brought to the sport a uniform, national set of rules and a degree of organisation previously missing. A desire for consistency among the many public schools playing the game culminated in a coming together of the different codes in October 1863 at London's Freemasons' Tavern. A set of rules based on Harrow School's understanding of the game was adopted, and the Football Association was formed.

1 Investigate your favourite football team – when was it formed and what were its origins?

Arsenal, the football team formed in 1886 by workers at the Woolwich Arsenal Armaments Factory.

Sports venues also began to spring up – football grounds, tennis clubs, public baths (although these were mainly provided to get people clean), parks and gardens. So the development in this period gave much more structure and fabric to sport, laying down the modern foundations. The beginnings of professionalism were laid down too.

A key feature late in this period was the reintroduction of the Olympic Games by Baron de Coubertin in 1896.

City councils also played an active role in providing sports venues for their communities, often in conjunction with wealthy benefactors such as Andrew Carnegie.

Early twentieth century

The early years of the twentieth century saw much more mechanisation of all aspects of work, with steam-driven engines and belt-drive machinery in mills, so although it became noisier, the hard physical labour for some began to ease.

■ Better working conditions

Hours of work shortened a little, giving more leisure time, and wages increased a little, giving more disposable income. Sports and leisure activities became more accessible for some, though not generally for women yet.

■ Outdoor activities

In contrast to urban sport and leisure, there was also growing interest in the outdoors, as transport had improved and people could get to the coast or into the hills for recreation. Some richer people made the 'grand tour' of spas and resorts in Europe, spreading their sports and health interests such as skiing, climbing and simply 'taking the waters'. There was sufficient interest in winter sports activities for the Winter Olympics to be created in 1924.

Countryside equestrian activities had always been popular among the landed gentry. This was superseded to some extent by racecourses being built on the edges of towns and cities. This encouraged large numbers of working class to travel out of town to bet on the horses, still an attractive day out today.

Notable events that were squeezed in between the two World Wars and the economic depression of the 1930s were:

- motor racing at Monza in Italy
- Davis Cup tennis
- the first soccer World Cup
- the Olympics hosted by Hitler in Nazi Germany.

Sport began to take on new roles of helping the economy, promoting national pride, and bringing in new technology. Sport's mantle of being 'time-wasting' was truly cast off.

Case study

Sporting London

By the early 1900s, some spectator sports already held major organised events during the year in or near London – such as the Oxford and Cambridge Boat Race on the Thames, Epsom Derby horse racing and the Wimbledon Lawn Tennis Championships. These are all still part of the sporting calendar today. At the start of the twentieth century, the leading national sport in England (though not the rest of the UK) was cricket. It was already organised on a county basis, which in London meant Middlesex County Cricket Club at Lord's in St John's Wood and Surrey County Cricket Club at the Kennington Oval. The 1901 FA Cup Final, played at Crystal Palace, was the first ever football match to be filmed and drew an unprecedented crowd of 110,820, probably because London's top club at the time, Tottenham Hotspur, was playing Sheffield United. The city also hosted the third modern Olympics at White City in 1908.

(Source: www.20thcenturylondon.org.uk)

1 **Compare what went on in the White City Olympics with what is being prepared for the 2012 Games in London.**

Late twentieth century

Sadly, the First and Second World Wars disrupted the growth pattern of sport and leisure activities, and after the wars a period of rebuilding began. This was accompanied by the 'baby boom', which gave us our massive population of over-55s today (more than 50 per cent of the population).

Influence of war

Although the wars affected the population of males and the pursuit of sport, they did help the progress of technology and bring in new capabilities after the wars. Also, after going through such hard times people seemed more determined to enjoy themselves. Women had proved themselves in the war effort, and now had a vote, so opportunities began to open up for their participation as well, although conflict and inequality were still apparent, with most sports still being male-dominated.

Commercialisation and social change

Jet-plane travel allowed the sports industry to become fully globalised. Sport entered the era of big business, with more sporting commodities being created, opportunities for wealthy businessmen to commercialise aspects such as clothing, and scope for agents to pursue high fees for the top players.

In some cases, sport also became a political tool. By the late twentieth century, black athletes were more able to assert their rights to play at all levels as their physical prowess was recognised and equality of opportunity improved. Women also began to achieve equality in many sporting domains that had previously been male-only, including some Olympic sports such as middle-distance running, and club competitions such as rugby and cricket. Top athletes of both sexes and all colours have become 'sports commodities' – consider Michael Jordan and Maria Sharapova, who command large fees for matches and endorsing goods. These are the top stars, but at grassroots level women and ethnic minorities still lag behind in participation rates. A study carried out at the end of the twentieth century by Sport England reported that the overall participation rate by ethnic minorities in the UK was 40 per cent compared with a national average of 46 per cent, and the participation rate for female ethnic minorities was 32 per cent compared with a national average for all women of 39 per cent. So clearly, issues remain.

General affluence in the later twentieth century swelled the middle classes of Europe, bringing in new customers and new players, and broadening the scope and range of activities on offer as commercial packages.

But as sport became a commodity with a high value, it became less accessible to poorer people.

Think it over

What has been achieved in the twenty-first century in terms of equality and participation? One example might be that at Wimbledon in 2007, women players received the same prize money as the men for the first time.

Influence of media and technology

The ability of people and organisations to communicate received a massive boost in the late twentieth century, with mobile phones, satellite TV, DVDs, the internet, and so on. This represented new technology that could be a product in itself (computer games, music players), but also brought in new ways to advertise sports-related services and products. Events, clothing, courses and adventure travel were all boosted by electronically driven promotion.

Television is worth considering further as it has had a huge impact (see page 27). The power of TV over sport is immense in terms of when it is played (at times to suit key audiences), opinions on top participants (bad press can ruin the careers of both managers and players), and sponsorship demands running into millions. Some top football clubs in the premiership (such as Chelsea and Manchester United) have a global presence in countries as far away as the USA and China through TV, fan websites and merchandising.

Think it over

Sponsorship figures for matches, teams and leagues have reached multi-million pound levels. For example, in 2005 Chelsea Football Club signed a £50 million 5-year shirt-sponsorship deal with Samsung, and 2007–08 accounts will show the benefits of its £13 million-a-year kit deal with Adidas. Some would say this is too much power, too much greed, and an unfair distribution of wealth. Do you agree? What other negative effects of media influence can you identify?

The research company Sports Revolution has found that an average football fan spends over £1000 supporting his or her club in a season, and may spend as much as £4500.

Premiership fans spend up to this much per year on:	
	£
supermarket shopping	1987
petrol	878
clothing	748
mobile phones	528
health and beauty products	214
CDs and DVDs	126
books	99
cinema	68
total	4648

Table 11.1 The average fan spends over £1000 supporting his or her club – Barclays fans spending report, 2004–05 (source: www.sportsrevolution.co.uk)

Assessment practice

Prepare a session for your class on the development of sport from pre-industrial times to the present day. You should do the following tasks.

1 Prepare a one-page handout showing the different historical periods, briefly describing or explaining what each is called. **P1 M1**

2 Prepare three presentation slides to describe or explain the key features of the different historical periods, showing factors aiding growth and defining key terms. **P1 M1**

Grading tips

Grading Tip P1

It will help to create a timeline to illustrate the key points and events, such as the impact of transport improvements or increased income. Describe main organisations and how they work together.

Grading Tip M1

Ensure that you explain how events had an impact on society, and how people spent their work and leisure time. Describe the main organisations and explain how they developed.

11.2 Know about the sports industry in the United Kingdom today

In the late 1890s, sports governing bodies were set up to organise, control and develop individual sports – including the Rugby Football Union (RFU), the Football Association (FA), the Lawn Tennis Association (LTA) and many others. They have guided their sports for over 100 years.

In the 1990s, some new bodies were set up to control and develop sport in a more strategic way (including the English Institute for Sport, UK Sport and Sports Coach UK). Most sports governing bodies had tended to 'do their own thing' without a joined-up strategy, which the government really wanted, especially after some poor Olympic performances.

Web links

Sports governing bodies

Rugby Football Union	www.rfu.com
Football Association	www.thefa.com
Lawn Tennis Association	www.lta.org.uk
Irish Football Association	www.irishfa.com
Welsh Bowling Association	www.welshbowlingassociation.co.uk
British Canoe Union	www.bcu.org.uk
Scottish Hockey Union	www.scottish-hockey.org.uk
England Basketball	www.englandbasketball.co.uk

Strategic organisations

DCMS	www.culture.gov.uk
UK Sport	www.uksport.gov.uk
Sport England	www.sportengland.org
Sport Scotland	www.sportscotland.org.uk
Sports Council Wales	www.sports-council-wales.org.uk
Sport Northern Ireland	www.sportni.net
English Institute for Sport	www.eis2win.co.uk
Sports Coach UK	www.sportscoachuk.org
Engllish Federation of Disability Sport	ww.efds.net
Women's Sport Foundation	www.womenssportsfoundation.org

Key organisations

This section gives brief overview of some key organisations that have been set up to organise sport throughout the UK.

The DCMS (www.culture.gov.uk) has a very broad range of sectors under its wing, not just sport, but also government policy on the arts, the National Lottery, tourism, libraries, museums and galleries, broadcasting, creative industries including film and the music industry, press freedom and regulation, licensing, gambling and the historical environment.

In the area of sport, it offers funding for sports provision and aims to improve the quantity and quality of sporting opportunities. The DCMS funds Sport England and supports UK Sport. Along with the National Lottery, DCMS has committed over £1 billion to the development of sports facilities. In addition, it supported the new Wembley Stadium project, is trying to get more 5–16-year-olds to take up sport, and is aiming to reduce obesity in young people under 11 and to increase activity rates to 30 minutes, three times a week across society in general by 2020.

The DCMS aims to:

- encourage wider participation in sport
- help create a more active nation
- improve sports performance
- make the UK a world-class sports power.

Activity

Review the aims of the DCMS and try to identify weaknesses in this strategy.

Think it over

Why have some young people fallen into such a lethargic lifestyle?

Central Council of Physical Recreation

The CCPR (www.ccpr.org.uk) is the oldest sporting body (other than governing bodies), formed in 1935 in response to concern that PE was a low priority and children were not healthy enough. At that time, few stayed on at school after 14. The CCPR was set up by the efforts of a single-minded woman called Phyllis Colson. Her aims – still important nearly 80 years later – were to:

- encourage as many people as possible (male and female) to participate in all forms of sport and physical recreation
- provide the separate governing bodies of the individual sports with a central organisation to promote their individual and collective interests
- increase public knowledge and awareness of the importance of sport.

During its history the CCPR has helped to create several national centres around the country for sport – Bisham Abbey, Lilleshall, Plas y Brenin, Crystal Palace and Holme Pierrepont. It has helped to shape policy on women's sport, brought in sport leaders' awards, created sports trusts, staged conferences, had VAT reduced for sports clubs, and helped the Royal Family

Taking it further

Visit the website of CCPR. How is it structured? Identify its six divisions and see what role they play in delivering sport in this country.

host sportspeople from all over the Commonwealth. Its overall aim today is to represent all national sports organisations, acting to 'promote, protect and develop the interests of sport and physical recreation at all levels'.

UK Sport

This is one of the UK's newest sports organisations, formed in 1996. UK Sport aims to work in partnership with the home-country sports councils (Scotland, England, Wales and Northern Ireland) and with other agencies to try and attain world-class success. It is responsible for managing and distributing public

investment, and is a distributor of funds raised by the National Lottery through the DCMS. UK Sport's work is directed by a Board, which meets every two months, and several sports panels that make strategic decisions on support for sports organisations.

UK Sport's mission is: 'to work in partnership to lead sport in the UK to world-class success'. Its goals are to:

- develop UK experts to support our athletes on the road to the Beijing and London Olympics
- bring best practice in other sporting nations to the UK
- provide clear strategic support to win bids for holding major events in the UK
- promote the highest standards of sporting conduct
- be responsible for improving the education and promotion of ethically fair and drug-free sport.

Activity

Consider each of UK Sport's goals, and try to identify two barriers to each being achieved.

UK Sport guides the overall strategy for the whole of the UK. Within this, each country has a sports organisation (previously called a sports council) that is responsible for implementing plans, funding development and supporting all kinds of sports initiatives.

Sport England

Sport England's mission is 'Working with others to create opportunities to get involved in sport, to stay in sport and to excel and succeed in sport at every level.' To achieve this, Sport England's goals are:

- taking the lead in sport in England
- finding funding partners to invest in sport throughout England
- providing advice, support and knowledge to English sports organisations
- trying to influence politicians to make good decisions for sport
- trying to encourage people to get involved in sport, and stay in it.

Activity

How many regions does Sport England cover, and do you think there are enough? Visit the Sport England website (www.sportengland.org) to answer this question.

Taking it further

There are a number of regional teams at work within Sport England – can you find out more about their roles? (Visit www.sportengland.org)

Case study

Sport England sets out some 'business objectives' for itself, which you could use to judge its effectiveness – its starting power, staying power and power to succeed, while running itself efficiently.

- Start – increase participation in sport in order to improve the health of the nation, with a focus on priority groups.
- Stay – retain people in sport and active recreation through an effective network of clubs, sports facilities, coaches, volunteers and competitive opportunities.
- Succeed – achieve sporting success at every level.
- Internal efficiency – ensure that we operate and allocate our resources with maximum effectiveness.

1 **How can you judge if Sport England has been effective and successful in its stated business objectives?**

Sport Scotland

Sport Scotland's mission is 'to encourage everyone in Scotland to discover and develop their own sporting experience, helping to increase participation and improve performances in Scottish sport'. It works closely with public, private and voluntary organisations to achieve this ambitious goal. As a public body, it also works closely with the Scottish Executive, advising Scottish Ministers on the best policy for Scottish sports issues.

As well as running the Scottish Institute of Sport (www.sisport.com) to support the development of high-performance sport in Scotland, Sport Scotland runs three national sport centres:

- Inverclyde, a residential training centre
- Cumbrae, a water-sports centre
- Glenmore Lodge, Europe's leading outdoor centre.

It also distributes National Lottery and government money for sports development, makes awards to help create links between schools and communities, and supports areas and groups deprived of sporting opportunities.

Sport Scotland has announced a new national strategy, 'Reaching Higher – Building on the Success of Sport 21'. The revised strategy continues the aims of the earlier 'Sport 21', but specifically defines roles and responsibilities for Sport Scotland's key partners – the Scottish Executive, local authorities and sports governing bodies.

It has an ongoing goal of 60 per cent of adult Scots taking part in sport at least once a week by 2020, and will continue to develop the following:

- an Active Schools network
- sustainable club structures
- a coaching network
- regional sports partnerships
- the institute network
- a network of national, regional and local facilities.

Taking it further

Visit the Sport Scotland website (www.sportscotland.org.uk) to assess if it has any new priority areas or issues in its plans for 2007 onwards.

Sports Council Wales is the national organisation responsible for developing and promoting sport and recreation. It was set up in 1972, and is the main advisor to the Welsh Assembly Government on all sporting matters. It is also responsible for distributing lottery funds to sport in Wales.

Its 'vision' is to increase participation and performance through a strategy for Welsh sport that puts young people first. The main aims of the strategy are:

- creation of sporting opportunities for children
- recruitment and development of coaches, administrators and officials
- raising standards of performance and achieving excellence
- effective distribution of SPORTLOT funds (the Welsh version of the lottery funds for sport)
- addressing issues of inclusion through sport
- increasing participation by women and girls.

To achieve its overall aim of developing sport from grassroots to elite standard, Sports Council Wales works closely with other organisations such as schools, clubs, local authorities and the private sector.

Taking it further

Evaluate Sports Council Wales' plans for children, women and girls, and its future plans, by visiting its website. (www.sports-council-wales.co.uk)

Sport Northern Ireland

Sport Northern Ireland describes itself as the 'lead facilitator' (helper) for sport in Northern Ireland, so aims to increase and sustain its commitment to participation in the province, and to:

- raise the standards of sporting excellence
- promote the good reputation and efficient administration of sport
- develop the competencies of its staff.

It has a strong drive to improve leadership skills among coaches and helpers so that they can work more effectively in the community, and much emphasis is placed on young people. Performance-level athletes are not forgotten, with a range of support and advice available – coaching, facilities, lifestyle, finance, medical and scientific.

Its interim plan for 2005–08 emphasises closing gaps in provision, addressing access problems and boosting participation for health benefits.

In 2004 Sport Northern Ireland was awarded £90 million from UK Sport to initiate a 'modernisation programme' with the sports governing bodies, as described on its website (www.sportni.net).

Activity

Using material from the text and your own research, identify and describe the main similarities and differences of the strategies and goals of the four sports councils.

National governing bodies (of sport)

These organisations usually aim to promote and develop a particular sport. Almost all types of sport have one. It is not possible to cover all of them here, but a few popular examples from each country in the UK are described to show the typical range, scope and work that they carry out.

■ Basketball

Each country in the UK has its own organisation. Collectively, they make up the British Basketball Federation (www.british-basketball.co.uk), and from this the Great Britain team is chosen.

The English organisation, England Basketball (www.englandbasketball.co.uk), typifies the work of the country organisations, with a mission to:

- increase access to regular participation in basketball
- develop a structure for all players to achieve their full potential in basketball
- improve international performance.

■ Hockey

The Scottish Hockey Union (www.scottish-hockey.org.uk), which celebrated its 100th anniversary in 2000, is the recognised governing body for the sport in Scotland, providing for the development, management and promotion of hockey across all ages and abilities. Scotland has a proud international heritage in hockey, dating back to its first internationals against Ireland in 1901 (women) and 1902 (men). In 1908 Scotland played in the first hockey match at the Olympic Games.

Strong links exist between the governing body and the districts, clubs, players and officials within Scotland, while the Union also has important affiliations to the European Hockey Federation (www.eurohockey.org) and the International Hockey Federation (www.fihockey.org).

The Scottish Hockey Union's operating plan for 2004–07, 'Scottish Hockey – Managing the Business', includes aims to:

- give members the opportunities and skills to allow them to participate in the sport of hockey at the level or area they wish
- be a major force in European hockey
- have a thriving district and club structure that is at the heart of communities throughout Scotland
- ensure the delivery of quality hockey programmes throughout Scotland
- deliver quality services and administration to and for hockey in Scotland.

Think it over

Why do you think the Scottish Hockey Union operates as a limited company and has a business plan?

■ Canoeing

The British Canoe Union (www.bcu.org.uk), set up in 1936 to send a team to the Berlin Olympics, is the lead body for canoeing and kayaking in the UK. It has divisions in all four countries of the UK. An estimated 2 million people take to the water in a canoe each year, the vast majority under the watchful eye of one of 10,500 British Canoe Union qualified coaches, or as part of

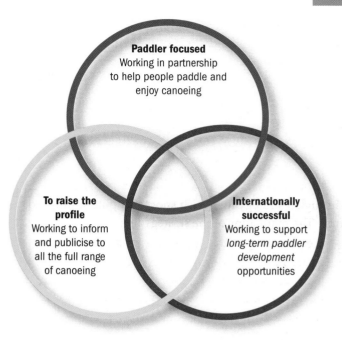

Paddler focused
Working in partnership to help people paddle and enjoy canoeing

To raise the profile
Working to inform and publicise to all the full range of canoeing

Internationally successful
Working to support *long-term paddler development* opportunities

▲ Objectives of the Britiish Canoe Union

an affiliated organisation. Its mission of 'helping and inspiring people to go canoeing' is supported by a plan with three interlinked overall objectives above:

■ Bowls

The Welsh Bowling Association (www.welshbowlingassociation.co.uk) is the governing body for many of the outdoor bowling clubs in Wales. Its website carries reports on matches, officials and events, international teams and leagues.

Activity

Identify the similarities and differences between the five national governing bodies described here, and draw conclusions about how effective their websites are in promoting sport and supplying information.

■ Football

The Irish Football Association (www.irishfa.com) was founded in November 1880, and is the fourth oldest governing body in the world, behind the other three home football associations. The aims of the association then were to promote, foster and develop the game throughout the island; now the IFA looks after the interests of the game in the six northern counties of Northern Ireland.

The game in Ireland wasn't just a male preserve in its early days. The first recorded game between women took place in 1895, and soon crowds approaching 50,000 were not uncommon for games between women. This has carried forward into the IFA's current philosophy:

'The IFA respects and values diversity, endeavouring to provide an environment which values and enables the full involvement of all people, in all aspects and at every level, regardless of cultural identity, political affiliation or religious beliefs. ... We believe in the philosophy of football for all and have a vision statement which reads: "By 2007 football will be the most popular and inclusive sport in Northern Ireland, in which all are encouraged to participate and realise their full potential, led by a dynamic and outward looking governing body with successful International teams". (Source: www.irishfa.com)

Assessment practice

Prepare four presentation slides showing the roles of:

1 the Department for Culture, Media and Sport

2 the Central Council of Physical Recreation

3 UK Sport

4 the four home country sports councils.

Select two sports governing bodies and produce a summary report describing and explaining how they organise themselves and develop their sport.

Grading tips

Grading Tip

Describe what the main organisations are, and how they work together.

Grading Tip

Describe the main organisations and explain how they have developed.

Scale, structure and provision

This section focuses on deepening your understanding of the scale, structure and provision that exist at present, in terms of people, organisations, importance to the UK economy, and delivery by many types of provider.

The scale of an industry can be judged by the degree of products or services it offers, the extent of the activities of its providers, and measurable quantities such as jobs, economic value and participants.

Think it over

How many people do you think currently work directly or indirectly in the sports industry, and how could you find out? Can you give some good examples?

Economic importance

This is the value of sport to the country in terms of its earnings and job potential. Sport England (based on research carried out by the Sport Industry Research Centre in Sheffield in 2001) states that in 2000, 450,000 people were employed (directly or indirectly) in the sports industry, with that figure likely to grow steadily in the run-up to the 2012 Olympics. The gross value to the economy in 2000 was around 1.6 per cent (probably nearer 2 per cent today), and additional sports-related activity was around £12,000 million. Targets for 2020 are higher as we try to move towards a more active nation, with over 500,000 people employed in sport. If the current government and Sport England targets (70 per cent of us participating regularly) are met, this could leap to over a million employed in sport. With a boost to government income (through corporation tax and income tax plus VAT), and government savings as we get healthier, this is an attractive proposition. But all this is based on the premise of more government investment in sport, higher participation rates, and a healthier population.

Think it over

How important do you think the 2012 Olympics will be to the government and to Sport England, bearing these figures in mind?

Participation

We have seen how, over time, leisure activities and sports came first for the rich, and later for the working class. Today, participation in active sport is a very desirable aim for everyone in society as it has so many benefits:

- it keeps us healthier and fitter
- it builds up confidence for some, and leadership for others
- it uses leisure time constructively, and might relieve stress
- we can learn new skills and meet new people.

Not everyone can participate in sport as much as they would like – or, in some cases, at all (see page 38). There may be barriers to participation as family, job and other duties cut into available leisure time. We also have a highly technological society, with people increasingly enjoying electronic forms of leisure, further reducing the scale of active sports participation.

■ Rates of general participation

Rates of participation in sport are difficult to measure. This is done through the General Household Survey for the UK (although there are also some smaller regional surveys, with more detail).

The General Household Survey is an inter-departmental, multi-purpose, continuous survey carried out by the Office for National Statistics, collecting information on a range of topics gathered from people living in private households in Great Britain. The trend in sports participation between 1996 and 2002 is shown in Table 11.2.

Gender	Percentage of GB population participating in sports	
	1996	2002
Males	54	38
Females	51	36

 Table 11.2 Declining participation in sport (source: General Household Survey, 2002)

These figures are based on questions asked about physical and leisure activities in the four weeks before the survey. Walking, swimming and cycling are the most popular activities, and the 16–19 age group is the most active.

Think it over

Study the data in Table 11.2. Do they indicate that we are moving towards the targets set by Sport England and the government? What factors could be affecting participation rates?

The more recent 'Active People Survey', carried out in 2005 and 2006, reports on participation by district in England – a few examples are given in Table 11.3.

Location	Location type	Percentage of population regularly participating in sports*
Alnwick	Rural area in the north	23.9
Barnet	London borough	22.5
Sheffield	City in the north	18.2

*'Regular participation' defined as 30 minutes' moderate intensity, 3 days a week.

▲ Table 11.3 Participation in sport by location (source: Active People Survey, 2006)

Case study

General participation rates in our society are not as good as in many other Scandinavian countries, for example Finland (Table 11.3).

Type of participation	Percentage of Finnish population participating in sports		
	Male	Female	Both genders
Competitive, organised, intensive	7	4	6
Intensive	27	38	33
Regular, competitive and/or organised	7	4	5
Regular, recreational	29	26	29
Irregular	8	4	6
Occasional	3	1	2
Non-participants	17	22	19

▲ Table 11.4 Participation in sport in Finland (source: http://w3.uniroma1.it/compass/finland.htm)

1 Use the figures for regular participation and compare them with the figures for Great Britain in Table 11.1, suggesting reasons for the differences.

Taking it further

You can do some more detailed research at www.sportengland.org (Get Resources, Research, Active People Survey) to find out about your own area. Or use www.statistics.gov.uk/lib2002/tables/#sport

■ Professional participation

Over the past 20 years, the scale of professional sport has grown immensely, to some extent modelled on American society. Now talented athletes and players can earn a very good living, at least during the period of their playing career (if they don't get injured). Some go on to be superstars, such as David Beckham or Michael Jordan. But to meet the salaries of these stars, many clubs are put under great financial pressure. Well paid professionals are icons and sources of inspiration for young people, so they do contribute indirectly to participation rates. Consider how many young people pick up a tennis racket when Wimbledon is on and Andy Murray is playing.

Many sports in the UK have professional leagues and circuits – football, rugby, golf, tennis, cricket and basketball, for example – but beyond the most popular games, the scale of professional participation rapidly drops away. In smaller sports, such as canoeing, curling or diving, top performers may never be able to turn professional.

Activity

The pressure to succeed or win can bring out the worst in some professionals – can you list three negative aspects of professionalism?

Taking it further

Suggest some disadvantages of being a professional player.

■ Amateur participation

Amateurism is at the heart of sport in the UK – the largest proportion of participation is based in amateur sport (sometimes called the grassroots). The scale of amateur clubs and participants is hard to quantify – every town and village will have teams, individuals and clubs turning out every weekend and some week nights to play friendlies, competitive matches and tournaments in every sport in the land. It may not be an exaggeration to say that 80 per cent of sport in society takes place in an amateur context. Today, the term amateur means 'one who does sport for interest not for money', but in nineteenth-century England it was used by upper-class Englishmen to define their higher social status.

Most amateur sport goes on in the voluntary part of the industry – the not-for-profit sector. Many people volunteer to run amateur clubs for nothing other than the satisfaction of doing a good job and seeing other people enjoy their sport. Sport England estimates that there are over 6 million people giving 1 billion hours to sport every year – coaches, officials, mini-bus drivers, match secretaries, umpires, treasurers, stewards, and countless other helpers sustain over 100,000 affiliated clubs with over 8 million members.

Case study

In a famous incident in 1912, Olympic officials stripped American decathlete Jim Thorpe of two gold medals, because he had once accepted money – only amateurs were allowed to compete in those days.

1   **What other issues do you think exist between amateur and professional status, and what sort of barriers prevent some people from turning professional?**

The UK sportswear market is worth over £4 billion ▶

Manufacturing

■ Retail

The retail sector for sports mainly consists of shops and websites selling sports goods and clothing (merchandising sales). This sector of the sports industry has enjoyed quite a boom time, with buoyant sales of trainers, shirts and equipment – one of the biggest contributors has been fans buying their favourite team shirts. Figures for 2002 showed that the UK sportswear market was worth £4.05 billion, of which £2.9 billion was accounted for by clothing and £1.15 billion by footwear. Sportswear is worth just over 10 per cent of the total UK clothing and footwear market. (source: www.bized.co.uk/current/leisure)

Consumers in the UK spent £4.48 billion on sportswear in 2004, and this represented just over 10 per cent of their total spending on clothing and footwear (only 8.5 per cent of the clothing market, but a 22 per cent share in footwear). The spend was split between £3.15 billion on sports clothing and £1.33 billion on sports footwear.

Sportswear is a global industry, with production mainly located in the Far East. Three large brands dominate: Nike, Reebok and Adidas. Below these are a number of highly specialised brands in the UK, for example Umbro and Hi-Tec Sports.

■ Sports equipment

The manufacturing side of sports equipment has seen growth based on the health and fitness boom. Data produced in 2004 by a market research company, Keynote, show good sales for golf, home fitness, fishing, rackets and indoor sports and boards. Key factors in growth are fashion, demographics, the influence of the media, and the fitness trend.

Among the market leaders are Acushnet Europe, Amer Sports UK, Callaway, Dunlop Sport, Salomon, Pentland, and Blacks. Some specific manufacturers of cricket, hockey, tennis and watersports kit have also done well, such as Dunlop Slazenger.

The consumer market for sports equipment was estimated by Keynote in 2005 to be worth £1 billion.

■ Consumer spending

Consumer spending on sport and leisure goods or activities has grown gradually since the mid-1990s as people have become more affluent, but also because of powerful marketing campaigns that tempt us with new products and services.

Sport and leisure spending should be dependent on our disposable income after all bills have been paid, but with our credit-oriented society many people put their consumer spending on a credit card, and may run up massive debts enjoying themselves. This is a very negative aspect of consumer spending.

Employment

About 450,000 people are employed in the sports industry. Here we consider the diversity of jobs in the industry, to show the scope and scale – a typical range of jobs is shown in Table 11.4 (see also Chapter 25).

Employment	Type	Example*
Coach	Part-time	Kids' club
Teacher	Full-time	School, further education, higher education
Physiotherapist	Consultant	Professional club
Player	Self-employed (via agent)	Footballer
Administrator	Volunteer or professional	Local amateur club
Event organiser	Freelance	Large professional club
Scientist (e.g. dietician)	Full-time	Large professional club
Technician (e.g. equipment)	Full- or part-time	Skiing
Developer	Full-time	Local authority
Recreation assistant	Casual	Multiplex
Commercial manager	Full-time	Rugby club
Instructor (indoor/outdoor)	Seasonal	Adventure holidays
Facility manager	Working shifts	Swimming pool

▲ Table 11.5 A range of sporting jobs and their likely working patterns

Activity

Using the list in Table 11.5, identify three common skills that would be needed for each employment type, and two specialist skills. You could visit some online jobs sites (e.g. www.jobswithballs.com, www.kingswoodjobs.co.uk, www.jobs1.co.uk) to assess these more accurately.

Taking it further

Discuss the problems that may exist for employers in terms of skills needs, recruitment and vacancies for both paid and voluntary staff.

Structure

The sports industry is made up of three main sectors – public, private and voluntary – according to the type of provider. The three sectors are increasingly working

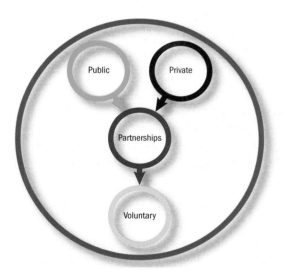

▲ The sectors of the sports industry linked in partnership

together to give the best benefit for communities and sports, so partnerships are often at the core of developments.

■ Public sector

The public sector includes all organisations from government departments down to local, district or city authorities. Some other government-funded organisations make an indirect contribution to our sports pursuits, such as the Environment Agency looking after waterways and lakes. Local councils are responsible for one of the largest areas of provision, meant to benefit all sectors of society.

Local authorities

Local authorities in England do not have to provide sport and leisure opportunities – this is a 'discretionary service' for the public. So provision can vary from town to town or from city to city. It depends both on what local councillors want to provide, and also on how much money is available for sports provision. The structure of provision is very varied, from pools to pitches, parks to putting, halls to courts and playgrounds. These are usually subsidised from the council tax to help make access more affordable for poorer people. Many facilities built in the 1970s are now ageing and need renewing – an issue for local authorities, which generally do not have the large capital sums needed to build new facilities.

Case study

Here is one example of a city authority's aims and provision.

The City of Liverpool aims to provide:

- sports development opportunities to all sectors of the community in a wide range of sporting choices from athletics to tennis
- a range of special sporting and cultural events through the sports events unit
- the management of the city's municipal golf courses, allotments and public football pitches
- a policy and development team which manages capital grants from the sports lottery fund and other agencies and new leisure projects
- management and operation of the city's indoor sports centres, swimming pools and lifestyle gyms.

(Source: www.liverpool.gov.uk/Leisure_and_culture/ Sports)

1 **Make a list of your own local authority's provision for sport. How diverse is it, and how old are the facilities?**

In terms of structure, each council will have a different arrangement depending on its politics and dynamics. Local authorities have full-time professional officers who control, manage and organise for the council – which is run by locally elected councillors, who in many ways are amateurs. The officers will advise councillors on the best decisions to make, but these may not always be followed because of power and funding issues, and whether the action will help win votes for the councillor.

■ Private sector

These are commercial operators who offer sport opportunities for profit, unlike the other two sectors, which operate at a subsidy (local authorities) or not for profit (voluntary sector). Many have become household names (brands) due to the health and fitness boom, such as Virgin Active Health Clubs and David Lloyd Leisure.

Health clubs

The growth in health clubs has been meteoric in the past 10 years, not just the large chains such as Bannatyne's Health Clubs, but also smaller local clubs as enthusiasts set up their own gym, or small businesses or hotels incorporate a pool and spa with a fitness suite to make a health club complex. Some health and fitness clubs are also situated in public sector facilities.

This sector is dominated by a number of top providers who cover the whole country. At the beginning of 2006 (although consolidation has seen some brand name changes) these were (by turnover):

- Cannons
- D C Leisure Management
- David Lloyd Leisure
- De Vere Group
- Esporta
- Fitness First
- Holmes Place
- Kunick (now owned by Danoptra Ltd)
- L A Fitness
- LivingWell (now Bannatynes)
- Virgin Active Health Clubs.

A recent market report by AMA Research suggests that the boom may have peaked in some ways, but is still growing in others, with:

- consolidation within the private health and fitness club market (those with a membership base)
- continuing growth in the corporate health and fitness market (gyms created by companies solely for their staff)
- investment in refurbishment and upgrading of local authority leisure facilities
- increasing competition and price pressures within the market
- growth in niche market segments, e.g. children's fitness.

(Source: www.amaresearch.co.uk)

Activity

Working with a partner, decide what you think are the main challenges for health club operators.

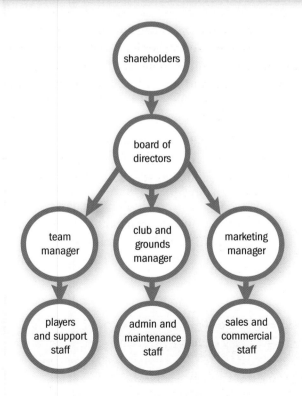

▲ A sample club structure

Professional sports teams and clubs

This is a large section of the professional segment of the sports industry, and is represented by the many professional leagues that are run in the UK, with the Football Premiership the most famous. A few other examples include:

- county cricket teams
- rugby league and rugby union clubs
- ice hockey
- speedway.

These will have a formal structure with boards, managers and shareholders in some cases – more like the commercial sector.

Below this highly structured set-up, other professional sports people will belong to a club, but may compete as individuals (e.g. golfers, runners or tennis players).

In the UK we have very modest range of sports that are professionally structured, compared with the USA with its range of tennis, baseball, basketball, American football, soccer and ice hockey. Other countries have different types of professional structure depending on their sporting history (e.g. cycling in France and the Netherlands). These are also professionally managed.

Activity

Discuss in class why there are differences in large-scale professional sports in the UK and those in the USA or Europe. Identify some barriers and issues.

■ Voluntary sector

The voluntary sector is the largest source of participants in sports. The structure of organisations in this sector will normally be committee-based.

Organising committee member:	Looking after:
chairperson	meetings and public image
treasurer	finance
secretary	communications and administration

Some of the larger organisations, such as the YMCA, The Guide Association or The Scout Association, have a central HQ (often in London) and a team of professional managers. The YMCA, formed in 1844, is the largest voluntary sector provider of health and fitness services that promotes physical activity and healthy living. YMCA International is a worldwide movement, represented in over 45 countries with approximately 60 million members.

Youth hostels

The Youth Hostel Association (YHA; www.yha.org.uk) has a central HQ in Matlock, Derbyshire, and is one of the leading budget accommodation providers in the UK. It functions to help everyone, especially young people of limited means, to explore, travel and discover England and Wales by providing cheap, safe and secure accommodation in coastal, countryside and city locations. There are more than 200 youth hostels to choose from in the UK, catering for all travellers from the globetrotting backpacker to family groups, schoolchildren or friends. Most are run by a small team of paid staff, or a couple who are accommodated on site and act as hosts.

One of YHA's latest activities is undertaking 'challenges', which are fund-raisers for disadvantaged children. In 2006 a team from YHA successfully completed the Great Wall of China Challenge. Their fundraising efforts raised a spectacular £27,468.74 for 'Breaks 4 Kids', which will enable hundreds of disadvantaged children to enjoy a break at a youth hostel with their friends.

Sports clubs

Sports clubs abound in the UK – they are the grassroots of sport, and at the heart of any community's sports provision. Most clubs are small and have a simple constitution laying out their set-up and aims. Most have a committee structure (captain or chairperson, treasurer and secretary). Most belong to a larger association, which governs them, for example a national governing body (NGB) such as the All England Netball Association. Most have range of teams of different age groups, and most are run by volunteers.

Case study

Holt Football Club in Scarborough is run by three volunteer coaches. It has three teams, under-9s, under-11s and under-12s. Parents act as the treasurer, secretary and chairperson. The club has around 40 members and plays in the local leagues every Sunday. Two local businesses (Care Micro Systems and Inventair Ltd) sponsor the teams, and parents transport the players to matches and training, making their contribution. Such clubs are often the springboard for new talent to develop.

1 **You probably knew of a similar set up to Holt FC when you were younger – but what problems do you think small, local sports clubs have?**

Larger sports clubs are much in evidence, too, with more teams, permanent facilities and a more extensive structure. For example, Cambridge Lawn Tennis Club is the biggest club in Cambridgeshire, with around 650 members and 17 courts. The club was voted Best Club in the East Region by the LTA, and was runner-up in the national finals 2006. There are junior, adult and over-50s sections, regular coaching, tournaments, matches, and social and fund-raising activities. It was the first club in the region to be awarded the coveted Clubmark quality award.

(Source: www.cambridgeltc.com)

Activity

Use the internet to find some similar examples of successful local sports clubs in your favourite sports.

■ Partnerships

When major expansion or coverage is needed, partnerships are the answer – today partnerships are at the core of many large schemes. The usual structure is that the private sector provides the funding, and receives returns over future years through rental or fees. The public sector (local authority) provides the land and planning permissions or favourable conditions, while the voluntary sector provides the participants or customers. These schemes are called public–private partnerships (PPPs) or private funding initiatives (PFIs). Examples include:

- London Borough of Elmbridge – in September 2004, a new leisure facility was planned to be owned and funded by Elmbridge Borough Council, but designed, built, operated and maintained by DC Leisure Management. This was one of the first PPPs of its nature in the UK.
- Caludon Castle School – health club operator Attiva is opening a PFI health club in a school – thought to be the first such development in the UK. The health club will be operated by a franchisee and will be open to the public at heavily subsidised prices. Attiva has been working together with the Coventry Education Partnership and Active Leisure Management on the project.

Activity

As a class, debate whether you think that partnerships of this sort are good for sport – what might go wrong with partnership arrangements?

Provision

The sports industry, in its many forms and through many agencies, tries to provide sport at several different levels to serve all sections of society – the young, families, males and females, ethnic minorities and older people, sometimes described as 'sport for all'. Over the years, a model of sports development has evolved that depicts each of the key stages (see Unit 18, page 144).

The sports development continuum, as it is often called, has four levels.

Foundation

Provision at this level is mainly aimed at young participants – primary school children or complete beginners in an activity. They generally aim to provide basic skills education, such as catching or throwing, or simple rules, with an emphasis on fun so that participants will enjoy their sessions and hopefully continue the activity. Sport England's strategy includes an 'Active Schools' approach focusing on learning for this level.

Participation

This level comprises diverse participants of all ages and types, and many types of scheme. These are structured to focus mainly on community participation, to try and get people to play more regularly, especially those who don't take exercise or play sport much at all. Sport England has one scheme aimed at this level, called 'Active Communities', mainly delivered by local authorities.

Performance

This level of the continuum emphasises improvement, perhaps through regular practice, competition or skills training. Participants may be selected to go on a course, take up a place at an academy, or even receive sponsorship. Courses may help with skills and an athlete's knowledge of their sport, as well as nurturing talented players – for example, a county scheme to identify players who can gain representative honours and possibly move on to the next level.

Excellence

This is national level, leading to becoming an international, which might involve preparation for competition at championship levels around the world. From April 2006, UK Sport took over running this for a range of sports, at least up to the 2012 London Olympics. It has set out three new aspects of the World Class Programme, which supports top athletes in training and funding: the talent stage, to support athletes with potential; the development stage, to support athletes building up to podium level; and the podium stage, to support athletes with realistic medal potential.

Theory into practice

Select four different sports, and for each identify a strategy to achieve each of the four headings given in the continuum – foundation skills, participation habits, higher performance and creating excellent competitors. Use the internet to help with your research.

Grading tip

Grading Tip P2

Make sure you cover a good range of key agencies and organisations from each sector to gain an overall picture.

Assessment practice

Imagine you are a newly employed graduate working for a sports goods company. You need to carry out some market research before you assess which new sector might provide your company with good returns. These are the tasks that will give you the best information:

1 Assess the scale of the British sports market.

2 Assess the structure of the industry.

3 Assess how sports provision is made in the UK.

4 Reach some conclusions on which area to invest in.

Create a report with four sections corresponding to the tasks above   P2

11.3 Understand how contemporary issues affect sport

Sport in society has come a long way since the eighteenth century. But, as in the past, its development is affected by the context – the society of the day. Some issues are as old as sport itself (racism, sexism); others reflect our technological age (media, globalisation) and market systems (materialism).

Contemporary means 'current', and an issue can be described as a topic of discussion about which people have different views. A range of issues will be uncovered in this section, but to create evidence for your assessment you will have to do a good deal more reading to get a deeper understanding of each issue.

Media

The media – means of communication – have many dimensions in this electronic age. Each medium will raise certain issues, some with positive outcomes for sport in society, others with negative outcomes, while media induce change that not everyone likes. Some brief notes on the main media follow.

■ Internet

The internet is possibly the biggest and most negative influence, attracting young people away from active sports to more sedentary solo activities. This may be why we have such low levels of participation in sports in the UK. However, it does offer real-time viewing of sport and global coverage, making events more accessible to more people.

Radio

Radio generally has a positive influence on sport in society – it is an excellent medium for reaching national audiences (e.g. BBC Radio 1–5), but also offers great value for local teams and clubs, as local matches can be reported direct to their community via local radio stations. Radio reports can be listened to by people on the move. They also offer the medium of local advertising for sports retailers and sponsors. Digital radio has improved quality, but may not yet be accessible to all.

Television

Terrestrial TV

Television which comes to us via cable or signals from masts is classed as terrestrial (ground-based). This has been with us for over 50 years, but recently has lost many of the traditional sports event transmissions to satellite broadcasters, who have outbid them. Traditionally the BBC showed all the classic British events, but today many are seen live only by those who can afford Sky TV (e.g. the football premiership, cricket and some rugby matches). This excludes those who can't afford the dishes and monthly subscriptions. Most channels are now being transmitted digitally (e.g. Freeview, which has increased the range and quality), but are still not accessible to all. Some football clubs have their own TV station – for example, Manchester United's MUTV in conjunction with Sky.

Satellite TV

This is an exciting dimension in the viewing of sport, as global live transmissions are now possible. This has made some events very valuable as they command the largest audiences, and satellite companies pay very big fees for the rights to many top events. Governments usually sell licences to transmit and make a good income from these. This is a massive commercial sector.

Some might argue that the fees and income are ridiculously high. In 2000, the Football Association sold the TV rights for English football for over £1 billion to a variety of TV companies, for example, Sky and NTL paid for the right to show live games and to offer pay-per-view games, while ITV paid to show the highlights of games on a Saturday evening. Ten years previously, the combined package had cost the BBC and ITV only £1 million.

Domination by British Sky Broadcasting (BSkyB) may not be healthy for the game, as too much influence can be applied to make commercial targets (see Unit 24) – and not everyone can afford pay-per-view TV. And ITV Digital's pay-TV services collapsed in 2002, causing major financial problems for some football clubs, which suffered a severe loss of expected revenue.

Activity

Table 11.6 shows the share of sport broadcasting by the different channels in 2001.

Channel	Duration of sport broadcasting (minutes)
BBC	80
Eurosport	360
ITV Sport	1460
ITV 1	445
Sky Sports ppv	165
Sky Sports 1	1765
TOTAL	4275

Table 11.6 Minutes of sport broadcast by the major UK channels over one weekend (18–19 August 2001) (Source: *The Guardian*, 20 August 2001)

Over a selected weekend, try and assess what is happening this year.

You can also view the share of audiences by the different channels, to get an idea if trends have changed – try www.bbc.co.uk and www.barb.co.uk, Viewing Summaries, or look at dtg.org.uk for trends.

Presenting national events

Some national events have had their transmission times and formats changed to suit wider TV audiences, such as:

- Sunday or mid-week soccer matches beamed around the world to global fan clubs
- boxing matches held late at night to suit the prime-time US TV market
- Formula 1 racing interrupted by car-related advertisements.

Any sponsors keen to have their advertisements shown in the breaks pay large sums to do so. Sport is influenced by the power of the media.

In its portrayal of football, television has a tendency to focus on, and isolate, players on the screen in an attempt to create a sense of dramatic impact (theatre) and increase the 'human' element. But this presents the viewer with a selective and limited view that deprives them of a perception of the game as a whole.

Influence on rules of the game

With media pressure to sell TV subscriptions and sponsor events, some sports (such as rugby Super League and bowls) have amended their rules and leagues to make them more acceptable to TV viewers. Some sports have allowed video and webcams to be used or worn to give camera-eye views for audiences (Formula 1 and cricket), and the use of video playbacks is now more common in rugby and tennis (Hawk-Eye, see page 232).

In the USA, American football and basketball are so reliant on TV coverage for their funding that they have adapted and changed their rules and competitions in order to suit TV scheduling. In both sports, time-outs and official game stoppages have been built in to allow the TV companies to show adverts. A TV representative tells the officials when to restart play, once the adverts are over. In other sports, such as baseball and golf, the commentators simply read out adverts during their commentaries.

Participating versus spectating

It is easy to argue that, with the coverage of and access to viewing sport, fewer people will actually be playing. This may be borne out by the fact that participation rates have actually dropped (see page 17). And some argue that programming of games has helped to convert followers of the sport into 'consumers' (commodification of the game) rather than supporters.

But TV offers ways of seeing events that would otherwise be impossible to attend, and reaching a larger audience than could fit into a stadium.

■ Local press

Local newspapers are very good at supporting the grassroots. Pick up any local or regional newspaper and you will find reports and scores for everything that happens locally, from under-11s football and cricket, to the achievements of individuals in cross-country or swimming. These stories and photos are essential to sell newspapers locally.

■ National press

The national press has a much more powerful influence, including the power to damage individuals' careers as journalists and newspapers make comments on performances which then go out to millions of people. Examples include the departure of the England Rugby Union coach Andy Robinson, or the negative press England's cricketers received in Australia while trying to defend the Ashes in 2006 – and in the Cricket World

Cup of 2007. Examples can be picked out weekly. Some would argue that the press are deliberately controversial, sensationalising stories to sell their papers.

Activity

Using recent national newspaper stories, compile two examples of the negative press that a sportsperson can receive.

▲ Some feel there is a danger of the sponsors taking over the sport

Abject England roll over

FRIDAY JANUARY 5, 2007

The inevitable happened 12 minutes before lunch this morning when Matthew Hayden hit the run that gave Australia victory by 10 wickets in the final Test and the 5–0 whitewash they have craved for the last 16 months. Set to score 46, Justin Langer and Hayden took just one ball shy of 11 overs to complete England's biggest humiliation in 86 years....

 The power of the press

Sponsorship does bring in much-needed cash to a club – but in football, for example, there never seems to be enough sponsorship money filtering down to lower league sides, so that they can survive and develop new talent for the bigger clubs.

Other issues include: What happens when the sponsorship stops? What happens if a team does not perform well? What happens if the sponsor buys the club?

Advertising

Advertising is a necessity for many professional sports – without it they would not exist, for it brings in cash to pay players, and to run clubs and stadiums. Teams and players wear their sponsors' names on their shirts in return for the funding. TV cameras pick up and highlight sponsors' logos plastered across and around the playing areas. Some of these logos appear in 3D on the pitch.

Issues include: Why are adverts for cigarettes and alcohol no longer allowed in sports broadcasts?

■ Magazines

Sport-related magazines proliferate at the moment, covering health, fitness, exercise, diet and the body beautiful. They can have a positive influence, with good guidance and interesting articles or programmes to follow. However, many images of slim, fit people create pressures on others to mimic their shape, causing dietary and emotional problems in the process. Bulimia and anorexia cases are often the result.

Sponsorship

Sponsorship is said to have a symbiotic relationship with sport – one can't live without the other.

Think it over

How do you think the use of mobile phones to view, catch up with or record sports will influence sport in society?

Deviance

Deviant behaviour is behaviour that is a recognised violation of social norms – such as hooliganism, violent behaviour or abuse. When it occurs in communities, it presents itself as a social problem that needs solutions. Sport has been able to provide a potential solution, or at least a pathway to conformity and citizenship for some examples of deviance. Many sport development schemes have been used to try and help change negative behaviour.

A further dimension of deviance is seen in the desire to win or succeed at all costs – some athletes will cheat or use drugs to enhance their performance and become winners.

■ Anti-crime initiatives

Playing sport is seen as good way to help mainly young people become involved in more purposeful activities than crime. Sport can help people understand discipline and rules, and may help to build confidence and other skills.

Sports development schemes often adopt an anti-crime agenda – it has been shown that crime rates drop when more constructive sports are available, especially in deprived areas of major cities. Voluntary organisations and police forces have been using this tool for inclusion for many years.

■ Social exclusion

'Exclusion' in this context means being somewhat detached from normal society. Sport has again been used successfully to draw people back into normal, healthy habits. So sport clearly has value a social tool.

Think it over

The social and economic cost of crime to the nation is enormous – over a quarter of the working-age population has a previous conviction, and the annual cost of crime is £50 billion.

(Source: http://sportdevelopment.org.uk/ Everybodywins.pdf)

Discuss in groups how you think sport might be used in a positive way to reduce crime levels.

■ Gamesmanship

This is sometimes seen as the cynical side of sport – gamesmanship has been defined as:

'The use in a sport or game of aggressive, often dubious tactics, such as psychological intimidation or disruption of concentration, to gain an advantage over one's opponent.'

Case study

Testway Housing, in partnership with Hampshire Police and Andover Rugby Club, and with Sportsmatch funding, involved many of the most difficult juveniles from local housing estates in playing rugby during the summer holidays. The local Police Superintendent confirmed that the scheme had contributed to a 46 per cent reduction in vandalism.

(Source: http://sportdevelopment.org.uk/ Everybodywins.pdf)

1   What do you think are the main reasons for young people turning to crime and vandalism in the first place, and why do you think sport is seen as such a good solution?

'Get Hooked on Angling' is run with Durham Police, and is designed to give young people at risk of social exclusion the opportunity to go angling for free. The scheme promotes social inclusiveness and dissuades young people from anti-social behaviour. It aims to engage groups that hang around on street corners to become actively involved in fishing. This successful scheme is being expanded across the UK and is now running in America.

2   What other benefits to society will there be if people are more included and have better access to sport?

With the pressure to win in many modern sports, gamesmanship (and gameswomanship) has become all too frequent. Perhaps the best example in 2006 was the French footballer Zinedine Zidane being sent off during the World Cup final after an Italian player made a cynical remark designed to antagonise him, which caused him to react aggressively.

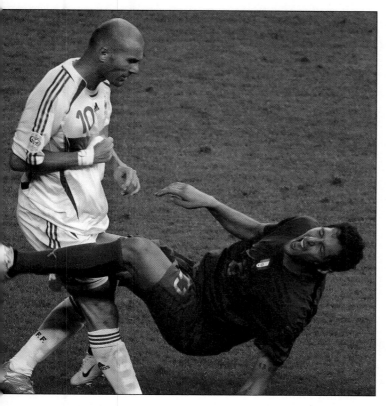

▲ Was Zidane's famous headbut in the World Cup final a response to gamesmanship?

Activity

For each of three different sports, describe three different types of gamesmanship such as trying to influence the referee in soccer.

■ Drugs and banned substances

Another example of deviance is taking drugs to improve performance. We tend to think of the high-level athletes who have been caught taking drugs – but there are many other players who want to build strength or body mass. There are many issues here: how it is unethical to enhance performance using drugs; how it breaks rules and codes of conduct; what the long-term effects might be on the players; and what the costs of policing it are. Can you think of others?

There are many banned substances, and thus many tests that have to be taken to ensure athletes are drug-free. The drug manufacturers are becoming more sophisticated every year in what they put on the market, so the temptation may be very strong. The list of banned drug classes comprises:

- stimulants
- anabolic agents
- diuretics
- peptide hormones and analogues.

Some supplements and medicines contain banned substances, which has caught out some athletes who have tested positive after unknowingly taking medication. Examples include the Olympic skier Alain Baxter, who claimed that a tiny trace of methamphetamine had originated from a Vicks inhaler; and two Pakistani test cricketers, Shoaib Akhtar and Mohammad Asif, who tested positive in drugs tests but still defend their innocence.

Activity

Can you list five other athletes, each in a different sport, e.g. cycling, running or football, who have tested positive? What were the consequences in each case?

Education and sport in schools

Physical education (PE) and sport in schools has become a key issue for everyone in education, from the government downwards. The government has set targets for schools in terms of allowing more time for PE in the curriculum – for primary schools, the Department for Children, Schools and Families (formerly the Department for Education and Skills) and the Qualifications and Curriculum Authority (the organisation that oversees the curriculum) both recommend at least 75 minutes of curriculum time per week to deliver the PE programme at Key Stages 1 and 2, and 90 minutes at Key Stage 3. At Key Stages 3 and 4 (secondary schools), the amount of time and range of activities are more flexible, to allow local schools to adopt what they can do best, but most aim for a minimum of 2 hours' PE per week. Pupils should learn a variety of activities, including dance, games and gymnastics at Key Stage 1. During Key Stages 2–4, tutors must offer two other areas selected from swimming and water safety, athletics, and outdoor and adventurous activities. The standard types of PE and sport on offer during Key Stages 3 and 4 are likely to be from:

- dance
- gymnastics
- invasion games
- net and wall games
- striking and fielding games.

The overall aims of this range are quite complex:

- to give pupils skills and confidence
- to create a lifelong learning attitude/interest in sport
- to give regular activity and exercise sessions
- to help with working in a team
- to learn to follow rules and play fair
- to give pupils a chance to take part in activities away from home and out of doors.

All of this links into the Physical Education, School Sport and Club Links Strategy, which includes links to local clubs to allow for out-of-school progression.

Taking it further

You can learn more about the government's strategy for sport in schools by visiting a number of websites: www.qca.org.uk, www.teachernet.gov.uk, www.dfes.gov.uk.

Child protection

The safety and security of children in general has become a major issue for our society, and unfortunately there are some horror stories of children in the care of sports coaches being abused. However, sports governing bodies and clubs are among the most proactive in terms of child protection (see Chapter xx). Most clubs now have to have a child protection policy in place before they can become affiliated. Sport England and the National Society for the Prevention of Cruelty to Children (NSPCC) have long been cooperating in putting out guidelines for clubs to follow. Additionally, every person working with children in a sports context has to have a Criminal Records Bureau check to determine whether they have a criminal past or record that would make them unsuitable to work with, or even pose a threat to, children.

The guidelines suggest:

- screen carefully everyone who might work with children in a club or schools set-up
- adopt and implement the sports governing bodies' guidelines
- don't allow any adults to be on their own with children – always have two on duty
- avoid physical contact with children, except in specific coaching situations
- listen to language and watch behaviour.

(Source: www.sportengland.org.uk)

Each school or club needs to have a procedure to follow if any of the following happens:

- a child or young person alleges that abuse has taken place, or that they feel unsafe
- a third-party or anonymous allegation is received
- a child or young person's appearance, behaviour, play, drawing or statements cause suspicion of abuse and/or neglect
- a child or young person reports an incident(s) of alleged abuse that occurred some time ago
- a report is made regarding the serious misconduct of a worker towards a child or young person.

Where there are grounds for concern that a child or young person could be at risk of abuse or neglect, the key tasks for any sports organisation are observing, reporting, recording, and cooperating with the child protection agencies.

(Source: www.crbs.org.uk)

Health initiatives

Recently a great deal of attention has been paid to the health risks of obesity in young people, with TV

Case study

The calendar of campaigns planned for 2007 by Liverpool Health Promotion Service gives a good idea of the range you might find in your area.

1   **What underlying agendas are being covered by these campaigns, and what benefits might they bring?**

5-a-Day Healthy Eating Week	www.5aday.nhs.uk
No Smoking Day	www.nosmokingday.org.uk
Let's Get Active Week	www.liverpoolactivecity.net
Child Safety Week	www.capt.org.uk
Sun Safety Month	www.sunsmart.org.uk
Sexual Health Week	www.fpa.org.uk
World Mental Health Day	www.wmhday.net
World AIDS Day	www.worldaidsday.org
Alcohol Awareness Week	www.drinkaware.co.uk

(Source: www.lhps.org.uk/health_campaigns.html)

programmes such as Jamie Oliver's highlighting bad eating habits and lack of exercise as the main causes. As a result, there have been campaigns to try and encourage young people to eat healthier school meals and take more exercise. There are many other types of health campaign, regarding smoking, alcohol and sexual health, for example.

Taking it further

Try to identify your local health promotion service, and assess what unhealthy issues and habits it is trying to tackle, and how.

Racism

Racism, according to the Commission for Racial Equality, means holding biased or unfair views about other nationalities or ethnically different people, and treating them as inferior.

Incidents of racism in sport and our modern multi-cultural society are, fortunately, becoming less common – for example, racist comments at football matches directed at non-white or non-UK players have been the focus of campaigns and legislation that promise to punish those who make them. The Football Association has been running a strong campaign for number of years, called 'Let's Kick Racism Out of Football' (www.kickitout.org). Racism in any form is really unacceptable in sport, and most governing bodies have a code to be followed. In 2000 a Racial Equality Charter for Sport was launched to try and banish racial harassment altogether. The charter was drawn up by Sporting Equals (www.sportingequals.com), a partnership project set up by Sport England and the Commission for Racial Equality, and is backed by seven national sports governing bodies, including UK Athletics and the Rugby Football Union.

Think it over

In small groups, discuss what harm racial taunts and comments can cause at sporting events. As a class, debate what the outcomes might be.

Sexism

Sexism, like racism, has connotations of treating people unfairly or in a biased way. Gender differences in sport have long historical roots – sport was (some would argue still is) a male-dominated sector. Women have had to fight their corner to win the right to compete in many sports. For too long, most men held the opinion that women were either too weak or frail to compete in (men's) sports – or should be at home looking after house, children and the kitchen! The Victorians typified this with attitudes that saw women as objects of beauty who should not expose flesh, perspire or be exposed to contact sports. Compare that attitude with modern women players on the tennis circuit or rugby pitch, and we have come a long way in the UK in 100 years. However, this is not the case in every country in the world, as there are many countries where women still do not have equal rights or opportunities.

In spectating as well as participating, the advent of a new (sometimes global) fan base appears to have encouraged a more cosmopolitan audience, including more active support from young, female and ethnic minority fans, and this may have helped to undermine the traditional masculine (and often hostile) environment of many top sports events in England. It certainly has not affected the sales of merchandise adversely.

Commercialisation

This means making sports into a more marketable 'commodity' that can be sold to audiences, spectators or participants, usually for a profit. (Sometimes this is called 'commodification'.) Example include:

- selling the TV rights to a big match – e.g. the UEFA Champions League
- selling of official team strips and other merchandising
- package deals to travel to a big event – e.g. the Winter Olympics
- the chance to gamble – e.g. online betting.

Activity

Using the following examples, and working with partner, decide how these sporting events or individuals are commercialised or 'commodified' today:

- Olympic Games
- European swimming championships
- David Beckham
- Wimbledon.

Now, as a class, take some of the examples of commercialisation put forward, and debate the issues for sport – both positive and negative.

Globalisation

▲ Sport is now a global spectacle

Globalisation is a result of a number of factors – commercialisation and also professionalism, which allows players to compete around the world in their sport or to play for teams in any country. Two other factors are global communication and travel capabilities – the sports landscape, and in some cases seascape, takes in the whole globe, and we are now able to watch sport 24/7.

Think it over

Who do the profits from global sports events go to?

Does globalisation mean that we need huge international federations to run our sports?

Do the TV channels show us everything we want to see – or just what they want us to see?

Are sports interests really at the heart of it all?

Grading tips

Grading Tip P3

In completing this task you may wish to use previous newspaper articles to help you.

Grading Tip M2

Ensure you give good detail here and show your understanding of the cultural role that sport plays in society today.

Grading Tip D1

Make sure you describe the issues with examples.

Grading Tip M3

Make sure you try to explain how cultural influences can cause barriers to participation.

Assessment practice

Imagine you are a trainee sports reporter for a local newspaper, eager to make a splash with a series of articles over the next few weeks. The two major areas you have decided to investigate and expose are:

(a) the influence of the media – on air and in print – on games and events

(b) deviance in sport (e.g. drugs, exclusion, gamesmanship).

1   Prepare two 800-word articles for your paper, including the main issues and giving your views.

2   Select two issues to write about from the following: child protection, racism, sexism, commercialisation and globalisation. Create two short feature articles (500 words each) under the series headline 'Issues in Sport'.

3   Prepare three short articles (400 words each) on 'factors that cause cultural influences on sports participation', for example one replying to a reader's letter about lack of time for PE in school; one as an editorial piece on keeping healthy through sport; and one giving your opinion on drugs in sport.

Over the centuries, differences in culture have influenced what sport is played, how sport is played, and why sport is played. It has not been a case of 'sport for all' throughout its development in society, either – there are many reasons why some people cannot play, some personal, some material. To help redress this imbalance, many agencies have derived strategies and initiatives to help encourage and give access to sporting opportunities in our society.

In this section we investigate three main areas – cultural influences, barriers to participation, and strategies and initiatives to give more equality of access.

Cultural influences

The influences and differences in our society relating to sports participation stem from four main areas.

Gender

The difference between the sexes has produced inequality in terms of access to and participation in sport (see page 34). Women have been stereotyped by men into domestic, child or work roles for many years (and still very much so in some cultures), leaving few opportunities or activities suitable for women to participate in. The dominant culture in the UK has been male, and masculinity in sport and male pursuits predominated until perhaps the 1990s, when a more enlightened equal approach allowed women's participation in sports to blossom.

Activity

Identify four sports in which women have made a breakthrough in participation, which were originally a male domain. Identify four sports where women predominate. What reasons can you think of for this?

Ethnicity

This term refers to a population whose members identify with each other, usually on the basis of a common genealogy or ancestry, and are united by common cultural, linguistic or religious traits. It has many influences on sport:

- it may influence whether we play or succeed in sport
- it can influence what sports we play – North American culture favours games such as baseball and American football, while 'Australian rules football' is very different again
- it may limit our opportunities to progress in sport, such as routes into professional football for African players
- it may influence other people's or players' attitudes to us – racist views.

Think it over

Where poor attitudes to other cultures are found, we also often find discrimination and racial groups clustering together – how do you think that might affect a multicultural society in a city, for example, when it comes to sport?

Age

In 2006, new legislation came in making it illegal to discriminate against anyone on the basis of age – usually because they are older. For older people working in the sports industry, this means they should be able to stay on at work longer if they wish, be just as eligible for promotion as someone younger, and have the same terms and conditions of contract.

In terms of participation, age can create problems for participation – a person may be too young, and may not be able to afford access fees; or may be too old or on a low income and so unable to pay playing costs. Older people from different cultures may struggle to find those from their own culture to play with, or may feel too 'different' to try and join a club at all.

Activity

What do you suggest would be good ways to help integrate those of different cultures earlier in life, to help them have friends they can play with regularly and create an attitude of lifelong participation?

Socio-economic group (class)

Socio-economic groups were created in the twentieth century to help classify society into different types. This is basically a crude measure, based on income, which produces six categories (Table 11.7). These class groupings have traditionally been used by advertising agencies, but have become less useful in recent decades, especially the distinction between clerical workers and manual workers in education and disposable income. Four decades ago, when these groupings were first widely used, the numbers in each of the main categories (C, D and E) were reasonably well balanced, today the C group in total forms such a large sector that it dominates the whole classification system. These groups can, however, be useful in considering participation rates and reasons.

Taking it further

With a partner, identify the participation rates, frequency and spending for these groups, using the Sport England website, the Office of National Statistics website, and material from the General Household Survey on spending (www.sportengland.org.uk, www.statistics.gov.uk, www.esds.ac.uk).

Socio-economic group	Example	Effect on participation	Rate of participation
A	Doctor, solicitor, barrister, accountant, company director	High income, good education, lifetime player	Highest
B	Teacher, nurse, police officer, probation officer, middle manager	Good income, education, health awareness	High
C1	Junior manager, clerical/office worker, supervisor	Good income and education, enjoy exercise	Medium
C2	Foreman, agricultural worker, bricklayer	Less to spend on leisure, may not have learned many sports at school	Modest
D	Manual worker, fisherman, apprentice	Less to spend on leisure, may not have learned many sports at school	Low
E	Casual labourer, state pensioner, unemployed	Poor diet, low income and motivation	Lowest, if at all

Table 11.7 Socio-economic groups and their rates of participation in sport

Barriers to participation

Not everyone can access and play sport, and there are many possible reasons for this, including those discussed below.

Time

Lack of time is the most frequently used excuse for not participating or taking exercise. Time for leisure or sport is an important issue for those who wish to take part, for they have to juggle priorities such as work, parenting and domestic duties to create enough time to participate in their chosen activities. Others may have too many time pressures (such as homework, a paper round, family to look after) to participate at all, although they might wish to. These are the people who may become unhealthy due to lack of exercise. This creates a spectrum with dedicated people at one end and non-participants at the other, all wishing to play but some with no free time.

Activity

Conduct a survey of your class – how much time is dedicated to sport and activity by each person in a typical week? What are the time barriers they have to overcome? Then use the same survey with another class who are not studying sport, and compare the results.

Resources

Resources fall into three main groups: people, finances, and physical things – so for someone struggling to participate in sport, scarce resources may mean:

- too little money, or none at all
- too few, or no, suitable facilities
- no-one or no team to play for;

whereas someone better off may have:

- choice in what they spend on
- ability to travel to whatever facility they prefer
- a range of friends or club mates to play with.

Fitness

Lack of fitness is often an excuse given by people who say they are unable to take part. They probably need to build up their fitness to help them take part. Initially, the problem is finding the motivation to do so.

Ability

Lack of ability can prevent someone from taking part at a higher level, but it should not be allowed to prevent them from finding a sport at a level where they can play. Getting some coaching to improve ability, or joining a class, is a good start-up strategy.

Lifestyle

A busy lifestyle is often an excuse again for not taking part in exercise or sport. We have a 'long-hours culture' in the UK, where people eager to impress, or to get on, stay late at work to get more done in a day. This eats into their spare time and often leaves them none at all for activities by the time they get home, eat and take care of household duties. Prioritising areas other than work might help to achieve a work–life balance.

Medical conditions

People with genuine medical conditions need to take exercise under supervision or guidance. Many do so under GP referral schemes, where a trained instructor looks after their needs, perhaps at a local gym, after being referred by their doctor.

Activity

For each of this list of 'excuses' for not taking part in sport, add one new practical idea to help overcome the reasons for not participating.

Strategies and initiatives

Over and above personal approaches to overcoming inactivity and encouraging participation, a number of sports-related agencies have designed a range of strategies and initiatives to help people participate. Some are general schemes across the country, stemming from government. Others are more targeted or locally aimed at certain groups of low-level participants. Some of these schemes are described below.

National and local

■ 'Game Plan'

This was a national government plan for sport, created in 2002, produced jointly by the government's Strategy Unit and the DCMS. It details the government's vision and strategy for sport from both a mass participation and a performance perspective up until 2020 (but note that it was published before the awarding of the 2012 Olympic Games to London). The report has sections on comparative participation and sports performance data, research statistics, and theories underpinning the value of sport.

Taking it further

Do some further research on this document to assess what it has to say about improving participation and overcoming the barriers that exist: see www. culture.gov.uk and www.sportdevelopment.org.uk/ gameplan2002.pdf

■ 'Every Child Matters'

This was a second government strategy, which proposed a range of measures to reform and improve children's care nationally (see page 256). The aim is to protect children, but also to go beyond this and maximise the opportunities open to young people to improve their life chances and fulfil their potential, particularly through sport and out-of-school activities.

■ 'Sporting Equals'

This is a national initiative, which is working towards creating a society where:

- people from ethnic minorities can influence and participate equally in sport at all levels, as players, officials, coaches, administrators, volunteers and decision-makers
- awareness and understanding of racial equality issues that impact on sport is high
- providers of sport work towards a fully integrated and inclusive society, and a sporting environment is established where cultural diversity is recognised and celebrated.

Kiran Matharu is not just an unlikely golfer – she is also the first female British Asian sports champion ▶

■ Talented Athlete Scholarship Scheme

This is a national DCMS (government)-funded programme that is a partnership between sport and higher and further education. The programme distributes awards to talented athletes who are committed to combining sport and education. It aims to reduce the number of talented athletes dropping out of sport, and supports and develops the talent of today for sporting success in the future. Other major bodies behind the scheme are the English Institute of Sport, Sport England and UK Sport.

■ Coaching Task Force 2002

The Coaching Task Force was set up by the DCMS to look into ways of improving coaching. It published a report in July 2002, with targets as follows:

- 31 sports to implement a UK Coaching Certificate by January 2007
- 45 Coach Development Officers in post by April 2005
- 3000 Community Sports Coaches in post by the end of 2006
- research to be produced on 'Sports Coaching in the UK'.

The government promised to invest more than £25 million over the following three years to implement these goals.

■ Plan for Sport 2001

This document is the 2001 action plan based on the document *A Sporting Future For All*, published by the government in 2000. This action plan deals with initiatives to develop sport in education, community and the modernisation of organisations involved in sport. This is an ongoing strategy, and the DCMS website gives regular updates on its progress – however, it has been overshadowed by the 2012 Olympics, also reported on the DCMS website.

■ 'Girls First'

This scheme is applied locally to secondary schools in Wales, giving £1000 to each qualifying school to provide after-school activities, specifically targeting girls' participation. It is hoped that by providing enjoyable activities on a regular basis, more girls will be encouraged to form positive habits about exercising and keeping healthy.

Think it over

Why do you think encouraging girls to take up active participation in sport is so important to the Welsh Government? What would you do with the £1000?

■ TOP Programmes

This is probably the best known scheme to help develop sport across England. The initiative, by the Youth Sports Trust, aims to supply schools with a sports bag and trained leaders, giving them ready access to resources for sport.

Theory into practice

Visit the Youth Sports Trust website at www. youthsporttrust.org, where you can update yourself with current progress with the scheme (e.g. statistics on schools taking part, bags given out and leaders trained). Assess what the aims are for 2008, and how many pupils they want to be doing sport by then.

■ Active Sports

This is an ongoing national development programme, supported by Sport England, that aims to help young people get more from their participation in sport – from grassroots to high-level young performers. The programme is based around targeted sports, including basketball, cricket, girls' football, hockey, netball and rugby union. Each local area is encouraged to devise its own content to suit local needs and facilities.

Think it over

Why do you think the work of Active Sports (www.sportengland.org/index/get_active.htm) will be important before the next Commonwealth Games or the 2012 Olympics?

■ Sportsmark

This is an award made to outstanding schools for sports provision.

Case study

Thomas Telford School achieved a Sportsmark Gold with Distinction Award in May 2003, in recognition of the outstanding quality of the sports provision provided by the school. Sportsmark Gold is awarded to schools that provide a well balanced and wide-ranging physical education and sports programme both during and after school. The award was extended for another year in May 2006.

- Each student receives at least three hours' PE each week, and everyone is encouraged to participate in numerous inter-house competitions organised after school.
- Competitive sport against other schools is fully encouraged.
- Over 120 students are involved in the Duke of Edinburgh Award Scheme.

Students can study a wide variety of courses, including GCSE and GCE Physical Education, BTEC Sport in Key Stage 4 and in the Sixth Form, GCE Leisure Studies as well as Sports Leaders Awards at Junior and Community levels together with a variety of sports coaching qualifications.

(Source: www.ttsonline.net)

1 **Do you think this success will also make the school an attractive place to study at?**

Assessment practice

Imagine you have recently been employed as a sports development officer for a local authority. You have been asked to put together some plans for the multicultural borough that you look after. Carry out the following tasks to help you with this.

1   Summarise three cultural influences that exist in your area.   **P4**

2   Explain the full range of barriers to participation in sports that people of all abilities, age groups, income groups, genders and ethnic types experience in your area.   **P5 M4**

3   Evaluate three strategies you could use in your area to help overcome barriers.   **P6 M5 D3**

Grading tips

Grading Tip   P5 P6

Mind maps, diagrams, tables and charts might help you present some of the information.

Grading Tip   M4 M5

Good explanations will be needed here.

Grading Tip   D2 D3

An in-depth analysis will be important here.

Knowledge check

1   What was sport in pre-industrial society generally like?

2   How important were the public schools in helping to develop sport for society?

3   Can you explain 'rationalisation' and 'regulation' developments in sport?

4   Give names in full for the following – DCMS, CCPR, NGB.

5   Why is sport often called 'big business' these days?

6   Name the three main sectors in the sports industry.

7   What are the four levels of sports development and provision that are commonly used?

8   Give four ways in which the media can affect sports.

9   Explain how racism and sexism can affect participation in sports, giving examples of each.

10 List five barriers to participation in sports.

Preparation for assessment

Imagine you are new journalist, just taken on by a magazine called *Sporting Issues*. Your editor has commissioned you to write a comprehensive series of articles about sport and society. It will run over six weeks, and deal with the following subjects. Write at least 500 words for each article, with an appropriate headline, covering the main issues but making them interesting and contemporary for your readers.

1 'Sport from pre-industrial times to the present day': this needs to describe or explain the development and organisation of sport over that period. **P1 M1**

2 'Provision of sport in the UK today': this should describe the scale, structure and provision we have today. **P2**

3 'Contemporary issues in sport': describe, explain or evaluate the effects of your four chosen issues. **P3 M2 D1**

4 'Cultural influences on sports participation': this must describe or explain three influences that you select. **P4 M3**

5 'Barriers to sports participation': try to describe, explain or analyse a range of several barriers as they apply to different types of people. **P5 M4 D2**

6 'Schemes for the promotion of sports': try to describe, explain or evaluate at least three different strategies or schemes. **P6 M5 D3**

Grading tips

Grading Tip **M1 M2 M3 M4 M5**

An **explanation** will need to use examples to help show understanding.

Grading Tip **D1 D2 D3**

An **analysis** or **evaluation** will need to do the same, but also should show a deeper understanding, and make comparisons or recommendations of alternative approaches.

Examples will help bring interest to your articles and show your real understanding

Pictures or photos may enhance your explanation or analysis (but don't rely entirely on these).

To achieve a pass grade the evidence must show that the learner is able to:	To achieve a merit grade the evidence must show that, in addition to the pass criteria, the learner is able to:	To achieve a distinction grade the evidence must show that, in addition to the pass and merit criteria, the learner is able to:
P1 describe the development, and organisation, of sport from pre-industrial origins to the present day **Assessment practice pages 10 and 16**	**M1** explain the development, and organisation, of sport from pre-industrial origins to the present day **Assessment practice pages 10 and 16**	
P2 describe the scale, structure and provision of the sports industry in the United Kingdom today **Assessment practice page 26**		
P3 describe the effects of four contemporary issues on sport **Assessment practice page 35**	**M2** explain the effects of four contemporary issues on sport **Assessment practice page 35**	**D1** evaluate the effects of four contemporary issues on sport **Assessment practice page 35**
P4 describe three cultural influences on sports participation **Assessment practice pages 35 and 42**	**M3** explain three cultural influences on sports participation **Assessment practice page 35**	
P5 describe the barriers to sports participation **Assessment practice page 42**	**M4** explain the barriers to sports participation **Assessment practice page 42**	**D2** analyse the barriers to sports participation **Assessment practice page 42**
P6 describe three strategies or initiatives which relate to sports participation **Assessment practice page 42**	**M5** explain three strategies or initiatives which relate to sports participation **Assessment practice page 42**	**D3** evaluate three strategies or initiatives which relate to sports participation **Assessment practice page 42**

14 Instructing physical activity and exercise

Introduction

This unit introduces you to the theories and practices required to instruct physical activity and exercise. You will learn how to improve people's health and personal fitness through physical activity. Activities are included to assist you in planning and preparing for clients, along with advice on how to explain and demonstrate key skills and techniques.

Ensuring that clients have a detailed and suitable training programme is essential for their sporting success. It is vital that such programmes are devised and instructed in a clear, safe and professional manner. Improving people's health and personal fitness through instructing physical activity remains a primary goal throughout the ever-changing fitness industry.

This unit will help to develop your knowledge, skills and understanding required to successfully plan, deliver and evaluate a range of exercise programmes. You will explore the principles behind planning a safe and effective exercise session. This includes the use of pre-screening questionnaires, and planning activity sessions to meet individual clients' needs.

Having explored the principles of training and exercise, you will learn how to deliver a safe and healthy session. Activities will help develop practical skills, including group teaching, enhancing communication skills, and being aware of different ability levels. Finally, you will investigate the importance of reviewing personal performance and identifying strengths and areas for improvement.

This unit is assessed internally. After completing this unit you should be able to achieve the following outcomes:

- Understand the principles of safe and effective exercise sessions.
- Be able to design an exercise programme.
- Be able to plan and lead an exercise session.
- Be able to review design of an exercise programme and leading of an exercise session.

Think it over

An understanding of anatomy and physiology is essential for designing safe and effective training programmes for individuals and groups. It is also important to be able to communicate ideas so that the sessions you design are safe and enjoyable.

In small groups, discuss what you think are the key components of a safe exercise session. Consider what skills are needed to lead a session, and how you can develop your own skills to meet these demands.

Principles of fitness training

Before an athlete attempts to achieve personal sporting and training goals, it is important to understand the principles of a training programme. These are normally devised with the help of a personal trainer, who will identify areas for physical improvement. Many people will have simple targets, such as to lose weight or to gain muscle size. Some people will exercise just to feel better. So if you are acting as a personal trainer or instructor, it is vital that you both understand the principles of training, and can relate these to the particular client's personal targets.

Components of fitness

The five key components of fitness are:

- strength
- aerobic endurance
- muscular endurance
- flexibility
- body composition.

■ Strength

Strength can be thought of as the ability of a muscle – or group of muscles – to 'exert a maximal force' or 'overcome a maximal resistance' in a single contraction.

In general, the amount of strength that can be generated is in direct proportion to the size of the muscle or muscle group. Some sports require specific muscle training in order to improve muscle size and strength.

■ Aerobic endurance

Aerobic endurance can be thought of as the ability of the heart, lungs, blood vessels (arteries and veins) and skeletal muscle to take in, transport and use oxygen efficiently, and over a prolonged period.

Aerobic endurance is achieved as a result of continuous training. 'Aerobic' means that energy is produced with oxygen present, which allows long and steady physical activity. Activities such as swimming, cycling, jogging and exercising to music are all associated with aerobic endurance.

Key Terms

Skeletal muscle is used to create movement using contractions – the muscles are attached to the skeleton with tendons, and shortening of the muscles allows movement to occur.

Aerobic endurance is sometimes described as cardiovascular or respiratory fitness.

■ Muscular endurance

Muscular endurance is the ability of a muscle – or group of muscles – to make repeated contractions against light-to-moderate resistance over a prolonged period.

Strength refers to the amount of force exerted (or resistance overcome) in a single muscle contraction ▶

Muscular endurance is different from aerobic endurance as it depends on the ability of muscles to perform without oxygen present (anaerobically) for a few minutes.

Research indicates that the principal method of improving muscular endurance is to train at a medium intensity for a reasonable duration – more than ten repetitions. Muscular endurance can be improved using the same equipment as for strength training, to increase both muscular and cardiovascular endurance.

Boxing is an example of a sport where muscular endurance is important.

■ Flexibility

Flexibility can be thought of as a measure of the ability to move a joint through a complete – and natural – range of motion without discomfort or pain.

Many sports require great flexibility, not least to prevent injury. Sports such as gymnastics require the performer to have a wide range of movement.

Factors affecting flexibility include the condition of muscles, connective tissue, ligaments and tendons, the bones that form the synovial joint, and the amount of excessive body fat around the joint.

Key Terms

Connective tissue is used to attach muscles to bones, and is used for structure and support of the skeleton.

Key Terms

Synovial joints are freely movable joints that allow movement. A synovial capsule between the bones prevents bones rubbing together and lubricates the joint cavity.

Optimum flexibility, which allows muscles acting over a joint to be stretched through a full and wide range, can reduce the potential for injuries, especially when a high-speed movement occurs. However, it should be noted that flexibility beyond the natural range of the joint can result in short- and long-term injury – such as joint instability.

■ Body composition

Body composition is the body's physical make-up in terms of fat and non-fat (or 'lean') body tissue. It is measured as a percentage.

Body composition – particularly the fat percentage – can be measured in several ways.

- The most common method is to use a set of callipers to measure the thickness of fat in various places on the body. These include the abdominal area, the sub-scapular (shoulder blade) region, arms, buttocks and thighs. These measurements are then used to estimate total body fat.
- Another method is bioelectrical impedance analysis, which uses the resistance of electrical flow through the body to estimate the amount of body fat.

A person's weight is not a key consideration within the context of his or her body composition. It is possible for a person to be considered heavy according to standard guides, but to have only a moderate percentage of body fat. This is because lean muscle tissue weighs more than an equal volume of fat tissue.

◀ **Flexibility is the ability to move a joint through its complete, natural range of motion**

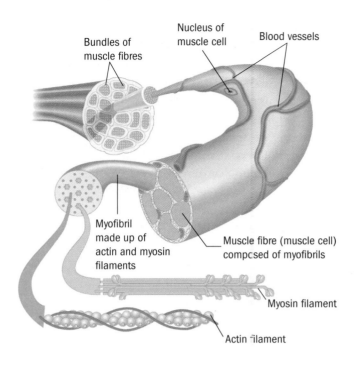

▲ **Cross-section of skeletal muscle**

Adaptations to training

The human body undergoes changes both during and after exercise. These changes can be described as:

- short-term – there is an immediate change, such as an increase in heart rate or breathing rate
- long-term – such as improved aerobic endurance or an increase in muscle size.

An understanding of why these changes happen will allow you to explain to a client their physiological responses to your prescribed training programme.

■ Hypertrophy

Hypertrophy is the term used to describe an increase in the size of individual muscle fibres (myofibrils). As you will have seen in Sport Book 1, Unit 1, skeletal muscle is composed of many individual fibres. These fibres are responsible for muscle contractions. Generally, the bigger the individual muscle fibres, the bigger the muscle and the greater the muscular strength.

For hypertrophy to occur, the muscle has to be actively stimulated. The easiest method of doing this is as part of a weight-training programme. This is most effectively done by undertaking resistance training – although

hypertrophy can also occur during other short-duration, high-intensity anaerobic exercises such as interval training, rowing, cycling and sprinting.

■ Increased muscle tone

Some people use the term 'muscle tone' to refer to how 'in shape' a person is. Health clubs, for example, might tell you they are 'improving muscle tone' when they are actually aiming to reduce the amount of fat in your body mass. Technically, what they are referring to is muscular strength, or a lower fat-to-muscle ratio. 'Toned' in this sense means 'fit' or 'trim'.

Generally speaking, the fat-to-lean body mass ratio can be improved by exercising both aerobically and anaerobically. It is recognised that by training using resistance at a moderate level while using more frequent repetitions, a client might be able to improve muscle definition. It is also important that dietary considerations be taken into account. The person needs to decrease his or her body fat percentage while increasing the lean body mass (body mass excluding fat).

■ Decreased resting heart rate (RHR)

One of the principal long-term adaptations to aerobic exercise is a decrease in a person's resting heart rate.

As we saw in Sport Book 1, Unit 1, the heart pumps blood around the body to deliver oxygen to working muscles and remove waste products such as carbon dioxide and water. The demand for oxygen increases during exercise, so the heart must work harder. After training aerobically over a period of time, the body will make physiological changes in order to improve its ability to transport and use oxygen.

- The heart muscles become larger and stronger (through hypertrophy), allowing it to pump greater amounts of oxygenated blood. Blood circulation to the muscles thus improves to meet the demand for oxygen.
- Haemoglobin – which is needed to transport oxygen in the blood – is produced in greater amounts.
- The skeletal muscles increase their ability to produce energy using oxygen and are therefore more efficient.

■ Increased stroke volume

Because the person's heart is now bigger and stronger, it has an increased stroke volume. This describes the amount of blood that can be pumped from the heart's ventricles in one contraction. Therefore, at rest the heart is able to pump more blood in one beat than in a person who is less aerobically fit.

Cardiac output is the amount of blood that is pushed out of the heart in one minute. It is defined as:

$$\text{cardiac output (CO)} =$$
$$\text{stroke volume (SV)} \times \text{heart rate (HR)}$$

Stroke volume is defined as the volume of blood ejected from a ventricle with each beat of the heart. Long-term aerobic exercise will increase the size and efficiency of the heart and the stroke volume, which in turn will result in a slower heart rate.

Activity

Consider how your body adapts to exercise.

Make a table or flowchart of the key changes that you experience during exercise, listing why these changes occur, and the likely benefits of these changes.

FITT principles

When designing any training programme, it is important that you consider the principal factors that will make it safe and effective. These are known as the principles of training, and you should follow them when devising any fitness or training programme.

FITT refers to:

- frequency
- intensity
- time
- type.

■ Frequency

Frequency refers to how often a person will train, for example twice a week. You must appreciate that exercise will be limited to the amount of time a person has available. Studies have shown that the average number of sessions per week is two or three. If an exercise plan is undertaken over a long period, then it is more likely to be included in a person's hectic lifestyle. Obviously results will be slower to appear, but they are still achievable.

Remember!

Be honest with clients about what to expect. Then they are less likely to be disappointed in the long run.

■ Intensity

Intensity in FITT refers to the level of effort required to perform an exercise session – in other words, how hard the exercises are. Exercise intensity can be measured in a number of ways for a variety of exercises.

Measurement techniques range from using equipment such as a heart-rate monitor (which can give a result in the form of a digital display on a watch), through to measuring pulse rate at given intervals, or the weight or resistance used in strength training, or the speed of completion of a run. Another method, the 'of perceived rating exertion', is described on page 62.

Simple equipment such as a heart-rate monitor can provide valuable information in measuring exercise intensity

Intensity is sometimes referred to as 'overload'. This means that for any improvements to be made, you must work the body beyond what it is normally used to. If overload is not achieved then the best a person can expect is to maintain his or her current level of fitness or health.

■ Time

Time in FITT refers to how long each session will last. Generally speaking, higher-intensity exercises can be performed for a short period, while lower or moderate levels of intensity can be maintained for longer. Either

Light	Moderate	Vigorous
Golf	Swimming	Squash
Fishing	Football	Football (if out of breath)
Darts	Tennis	Running
Bowls	Brisk walking	Swimming (if out of breath)
Slow walking	Cycling	Tennis (if out of breath)
Table tennis	Aerobics	Cycling (if out of breath)
Gardening		

▲ Table 14.1 Intensity of exercise

Variable	Fitness-related	Health-related
Frequency	3–5 days per week	Most days, preferably every day
Intensity	60–90% of maximum heart rate (MHR)	At least moderate intensity
Time (duration)	20–60 minutes continuously	At least 30 minutes
Type	Any aerobic activity	Not specified

▲ Table 14.2 Exercise recommendations for fitness and for general health

way, any form of exercise can have a beneficial effect on everyday health. However, for significant benefits to occur, a training session should be more than 30 minutes.

Tables 14.1 and 14.2 show categories of intensity as well as exercise recommendations for health and fitness, according to one survey.

■ Type

Type in FITT refers to the category of training that will be performed. This could be aerobic or resistance training, for example. Your proposed training programme for a client should have the correct exercises to achieve the client's goals. You should consider strength, flexibility, muscular endurance, aerobic endurance and body composition.

Key Terms

FITT stands for frequency (how often), intensity (how hard), time (how long) and type (how appropriate).

Health and safety

There are many possible reasons why a training programme might be unsafe. You must be especially aware of all of these factors:

- poor technique
- incorrect clothing or footwear
- poor or broken equipment
- medical conditions
- prior injury.

You must ensure that both yourself and your client are properly prepared before any training session commences. This will involve several things.

PAR-Q

One of the easiest ways to determine a client's background in terms of activity and fitness level is to use a Physical Activity Readiness Questionnaire (PAR-Q). Completion of a PAR-Q is a sensible first step to take if a client is planning to increase the amount of physical activity in his or her life.

For most people, extra physical activity should not pose a problem or hazard. The PAR-Q has been designed to identify the small number of adults for whom physical activity might be inappropriate, and those who should seek medical advice concerning the type of activity most suitable for them.

Contraindications

Key Term

A **contraindication** is a physical or mental condition or factor that increases the risk involved when engaging in a particular activity. *Contra* means 'against'.

You must be aware of a client's contraindications before he or she starts any exercise programme. This can be done by completing a short questionnaire or conducting a short, informal interview. This will ensure you are aware of any conditions that are likely to affect a person's ability to train safely.

Remember!
You are responsible for your client's health when you are devising a personalised training programme.

Some examples of contraindications are:
- asthma
- pregnancy
- a history of heart disease
- an injury
- operations
- diabetes.

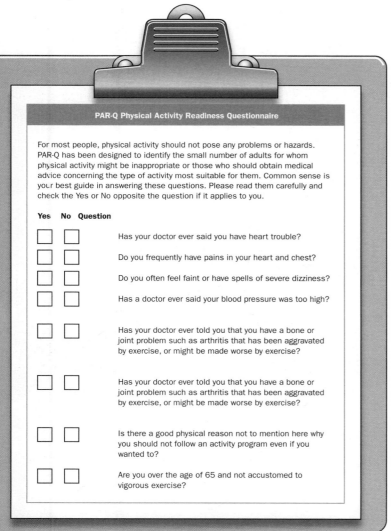

PAR-Q Physical Activity Readiness Questionnaire

For most people, physical activity should not pose any problems or hazards. PAR-Q has been designed to identify the small number of adults for whom physical activity might be inappropriate or those who should obtain medical advice concerning the type of activity most suitable for them. Common sense is your best guide in answering these questions. Please read them carefully and check the Yes or No opposite the question if it applies to you.

Yes	No	Question
☐	☐	Has your doctor ever said you have heart trouble?
☐	☐	Do you frequently have pains in your heart and chest?
☐	☐	Do you often feel faint or have spells of severe dizziness?
☐	☐	Has a doctor ever said your blood pressure was too high?
☐	☐	Has your doctor ever told you that you have a bone or joint problem such as arthritis that has been aggravated by exercise, or might be made worse by exercise?
☐	☐	Has your doctor ever told you that you have a bone or joint problem such as arthritis that has been aggravated by exercise, or might be made worse by exercise?
☐	☐	Is there a good physical reason not to mention here why you should not follow an activity program even if you wanted to?
☐	☐	Are you over the age of 65 and not accustomed to vigorous exercise?

▲ **A Physical Activity Readiness Questionnaire**

A risk assessment is performed to ensure that all facilities and equipment are safe for use. You should carry out a review of these before each training session. The risk assessment will identify the possibility of harmful effects to individuals from certain human activities or facilities.

Remember!

Poor behaviour can be a risk factor, and this must be taken into consideration when performing a risk assessment.

Risk assessment checklist

- [ ] Complete consent form ensuring the client understands the risk involved in exercise training.
- [ ] Check equipment is working properly.
- [ ] Ensure trainer is qualified and insured for personal injury.
- [ ] Perform induction to show how each piece of equipment should be used safely.
- [ ] Check client before every session for injuries or illness.
- [ ] Conduct a full warm-up and cool-down each session.

Warm-up

A warm-up is usually performed before participation in a sport or exercise. The warm-up generally consists of a gradual increase in intensity of physical activity. For example, before running or playing an intense sport, you might slowly jog to warm the muscles and increase the heart rate.

It is important that the warm-up should be specific to the activity that will follow, which means that warm-up exercises should prepare the muscles that are to be used and activate the energy systems required for that particular activity. Stretching the active muscles is also recommended after doing a warm-up.

Functions of a warm-up

▲ A sufficient warm-up is important to avoid injury

There are three main functions:

- to increase heart rate
- to raise body temperature
- to prepare the major joints of the body.

The warm-up should increase the heart rate in order to pump more blood around the body to the working muscles, in preparation for exercise. This, in turn, will allow more energy to be produced using oxygen, and increase the body and muscle temperature. Increasing muscle temperature will, in turn, improve the elasticity of the working muscles so that they are less likely to become injured. In addition, a warm-up should involve a wide range of movements that are specific to the exercise or sport to be undertaken.

For a warm-up to be most effective, it should be tailored to the individual client.

Components of a warm-up

The warm-up can comprise a variety of exercises. These can be categorised as either pulse-raisers or stretches.

■ Pulse-raisers

As the name suggests, a pulse-raiser is a simple cardiovascular exercise that will raise a person's heart rate (pulse) in readiness for further exercises. Pulse-raisers can involve general activities, or activities that incorporate movements specific to a particular sport.

The pulse-raiser should gradually increase in intensity as time goes on, and normally lasts 5–10 minutes. At the end of a pulse-raising warm-up, the heart rate should be near to the level that will be expected during the main activity.

Types of pulse-raiser commonly used as part of a warm-up include:

- walking and/or jogging
- swimming
- cycling
- rowing.

Each of these will increase not only heart rate, but also body temperature.

To include sport-specific exercises, the warm-up will start gradually and then include actions to be performed more vigorously later on.

■ Stretches

Stretches are used as part of a warm-up to improve joint mobility. Stretching will induce the body to produce more fluid in synovial joints, in readiness for more exercise. The joints will become warmer and allow a full range of motion to be achieved. Stretching should start with small movements and then progress to larger, full ranges of motion.

The main joints that should be mobilised by stretches are the shoulders, elbows, spine, hips, knees and ankles.

There are a number of different methods of stretching to improve flexibility and joint mobility:

- passive stretching
- static stretching
- dynamic stretching
- proprioceptive neuromuscular facilitation.

Passive stretching

This is one form of static stretching in which an external force acts on the body part to move it into a new position. The external force is often just the effect of gravity, but it can also be achieved with the help of a partner, stretch bands or other mechanical devices. The more force exerted on the body part, the less time it will take to develop further into the stretch, but this increases the potential for injury.

Static stretching

Static stretching is used to stretch muscles while the body is at rest. It uses various techniques that gradually lengthen a muscle to a point of mild discomfort, at which point the position is held for a period (10–30 seconds). During this holding period – or directly afterwards – participants may feel a mild discomfort or warm sensation in the muscle.

Static stretching exercises involve specialised tension receptors in muscles. When done properly, static stretching slightly lessens

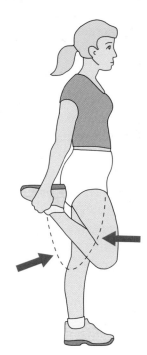

A static stretch

the sensitivity of these tension receptors, which allows the muscle to relax and to be stretched to a greater length.

Dynamic stretching

Dynamic stretching involves moving muscles through their full range of motion in a controlled manner. Dynamic stretching keeps the heart rate raised and makes the muscles ready for further exercise.

Dynamic stretching promotes a form of flexibility that is beneficial in sports using momentum from an effort to propel the muscle into an extended range of motion (not exceeding the static/passive stretching ability).

Proprioceptive neuromuscular facilitation

Proprioceptive neuromuscular facilitation (PNF) is a combination of passive stretching and isometrics, in which a muscle is first stretched passively and then contracted. The technique targets nerve receptors in the muscles to extend muscle length.

◀ **A PNF stretch**

- The athlete then contracts the stretched muscle for 5–6 seconds, and the partner must inhibit all movement. The force of the contraction should be appropriate to the condition of the muscle. For example, if the muscle has been injured, do not apply a maximum contraction.
- The muscle group is now relaxed, then immediately and cautiously pushed past its normal range of movement for about 30 seconds.
- Allow 30 seconds' recovery before repeating the procedure two to four times.

Key Terms

Isometrics is a contraction of the skeletal muscle where a muscle does not change length, nor does movement occur. This type of contraction is used to control a joint by keeping it static (e.g. the beginning movement of a press-up, where the body is supported by the arms and shoulders but no movement occurs).

PNF stretching was originally developed as a form of rehabilitation, and to that end it is very effective. It is also excellent for targeting specific muscle groups. As well as increasing flexibility and range of movement, it can also improve muscular strength.

- First the relaxed muscle is stretched by an external force, such as an exercise partner, or by the person's own body weight against the floor, wall or similarly resistant object. Where a partner is available, the athlete and a partner assume the position for the stretch, then the partner extends the body limb until the muscle is stretched and tension is felt (see diagram).

Duration of a warm-up

The warm-up should be customised to the physical capabilities of the client and the intensity of the activity. A brief warm-up of 10 minutes' jogging and stretching will adequately prepare a 'weekend' client for a run. In contrast, an athlete's preparation for a run might include 10–15 minutes' jogging, 5–10 minutes' stretching, 5–10 minutes' running with gradual increase to race pace, and finally 5–10 minutes' jogging.

A specific warm-up should be included in the programme for each activity that will follow. Experiment with various warm-ups to determine the amount, intensity and duration that will provide maximal preparation without fatigue.

Types of warm-up

A range of techniques can be used to raise heart rate and body temperature and prepare the body for further exercise.

■ Specific aerobic routines

Aerobic (cardiovascular) exercise is a good way of raising heart rate and body temperature, and increasing joint mobility.

- The first phase of the warm-up should raise the heart rate, leading to an increase in the speed of delivery of oxygen to the muscles and the temperature of the body. Performing a cardiovascular exercise such as jogging can easily increase the heart rate.
- The second stage should include mobility or stretching exercises. Press-ups, lunges and squat thrusts are good for this.
- The final stage of a warm-up should involve a sport-specific or skill-related component. This should work the neuromuscular mechanisms related to the activity. For example, if you were warming up to play soccer you might practise kicking a ball to a team-mate.

■ General routines

A general warm-up will still aim to raise heart rate, increase body temperature and improve joint mobility. However, the warm-up will not be specific and may simply include a combination of cardiovascular work and stretching. A general warm-up will start at low to medium intensity, with the intensity increasing after stretching. Warm-up time can be used to prepare mentally if playing a competition game.

Cool-down

The purpose of a cool-down is to return the body to its pre-exercise state.

Functions of a cool-down

There are three main objectives:

- to return the heart rate back to normal
- to remove any waste products that may have built up during exercise
- to return the muscles to their original state (or length if stretched).

A cool-down will also keep the metabolic rate high and capillaries dilated to enable oxygen to flush through the muscle tissue, which helps remove lactic acid waste created by the exercise. This should stop the blood from staying in the veins, which can cause dizziness if the exercise is stopped too quickly. A cool-down can also reduce the effect of delayed-onset muscle soreness, which often follows strenuous exercise that the body is not used to.

Key Terms

Delayed-onset muscle soreness is the pain or discomfort often felt 24–72 hours after exercising. It subsides generally within 2–3 days. It was once thought to be caused by lactic acid build-up, but a more recent theory is that it is caused by tiny tears in the muscle fibres caused by eccentric contraction such as downhill running, or unaccustomed training levels.

The final part of the cool-down should include stretching that is designed to facilitate and improve flexibility, as the muscles will be very warm at this stage.

Remember!

Clients may not feel like doing a cool-down after a strenuous workout, but they must understand that because of the possible benefits, it is worth doing. By getting into the habit from an early age, clients will be more disciplined about performing a cool-down.

Pulse-lowering

You should select cardiovascular exercises that involve all the major muscle groups. Start at a high intensity and slowly lower so that a drop in heart rate can be achieved. This normally lasts for approximately five minutes, and it is common to use an exercise bike as the client can sit down after strenuous exercise.

Stretches

Stretching as part of a cool-down will allow the muscles to return to their normal working length. It will also aid the removal of waste products that may have built up in the muscles. Stretching can be either maintenance or developmental:

- maintenance stretching allows the muscles to return to their normal length
- developmental stretching is used on muscles that may have become tight and shortened during exercise.

Developmental stretches involve stretching and holding the working muscle for about ten seconds until it relaxes. Following this, the muscle should be stretched again but at an increased level, and again held for ten seconds. This process should be repeated three times.

PNF is a more advanced form of cool-down flexibility training that involves both stretching and contraction of the muscle group being targeted (see page 54).

Activity

For the following sports, identify and explain the key components of fitness required to perform successfully. Using your knowledge of these, devise a short exercise programme that addresses how each of the components outlined can be improved:

- basketball
- tennis
- 100-metre sprinting.

A PNF cool-down exercise ▶

Athlete and partner assume position for the stretch, then the partner extends the body limb until the muscle is stretched and tension is felt.

The athlete then contracts the stretched muscle for 5–6 seconds and the partner must inhibit all movement. (The force of the contraction should be relevant to the condition of the muscle – e.g. if the muscle has been injured, don't apply maximum contraction).

The muscle group is relaxed, then immediately and cautiously pushed past its normal range of movement for about 30 seconds. Allow 30 seconds recovery before repeating the procedure two to four times.

Assessment practice

You have been asked by the local leisure facility where you work to prepare a presentation for a local athletics club describing the principles of fitness training. The presentation should include essential information on the components of fitness and the short- and long-term adaptations to exercise. To make the presentation interesting, valid sporting examples should be used to highlight key components of fitness training. **P1**

Some helpful hints:

- Describe all the key components of fitness and relate these to specific sports or exercises.
- Consider how your body changes immediately during exercise, and explain why this happens.
- Also consider how your body would change during longer, sustained periods of exercise.
- What are the long-term benefits of training to the components of fitness?
- Use a wide variety of sports or exercises to describe both the components of fitness and the adaptations to a training programme.

Assessment practice

Following your presentation, the head of the athletics club has asked you to prepare a document that describes the health and safety requirements an instructor must consider when planning and delivering an exercise programme or session. The document should clearly describe the importance of health and safety in exercise, and the ways in which an instructor can limit the risk of injury or illness. **P2 M1**

Both a warm-up prior to exercise and a cool-down post-exercise are vital in preventing injury. Design a suitable warm-up and cool-down for a sport of your choice. Remember that your warm-up should be specific to the exercise you are about to undertake, and contain a variety of stretches and pulse-raising exercises. Having designed the warm-up and cool down, demonstrate them to a small group, describing the need for each chosen exercise. **P3**

Grading tip

Grading Tip **M1**

You must further explain the health and safety considerations associated with exercise programmes and sessions. You could:

- prepare a PAR-Q form that can be used to identify health- and injury-related problems that may affect safe exercise
- outline and explain common contraindications and highlight why these must be considered
- prepare and conduct a risk assessment on a sports facility at your school or college – explain the purpose of a risk assessment and outline what you would do if a potential risk was identified.

Grading tip

Grading Tip **P1**

Consider how your body changes immediately during exercise, and during longer, sustained periods of exercise. Explain why this happens. What are the long-term benefits of training to the components of fitness? Refer to a wide variety of sports or exercises.

Structure

In your role as an effective professional trainer, you must be able to plan and deliver safe and appropriate training programmes. This section will give you an understanding of the key considerations and the processes you must follow in order to do that. It also outlines some of the common mistakes people make, and the reasons why training programmes are not always successful.

Introduction to a session

Remember!

At the start, it is always necessary to be aware of any medical issues you might need to take into consideration. This is especially important when a new client – or one who has not undertaken an activity programme recently – is involved. A simple medical screening questionnaire can be used in consultation with the client and a medical professional. This might result in ensuring that adequate facilities are available during training sessions (such as an asthma inhaler).

The first step in designing a programme is to gather as much information about your client as possible. This will allow you to build up a picture of the person's lifestyle and goals. At your first meeting, a short interview and completion of a pre-exercise questionnaire (or PAR-Q – see page 51) will give you the information needed to plan an individual training programme. You must take into account that not all clients will be the same as you in terms of their level of fitness or their exercise goals. You must identify relevant lifestyle factors before an accurate plan can be devised. Examples of factors that need to be considered include:

- current activity level
- occupation
- leisure activities
- diet
- smoking
- alcohol intake
- stress levels
- time available to train or exercise
- current and previous training history.

Some common reasons given for wanting to exercise include:

- cardiovascular fitness
- weight (fat) loss
- overcome injury (rehabilitation)
- improve flexibility
- muscular strength
- improved health
- muscle size
- power
- muscle tone
- muscular endurance.

A word of caution – if you ask a client what he or she wants to achieve, the answer will often be simply 'to get fit'. Make sure that you identify specific targets or goals.

The warm-up

Recall that the purpose of a warm-up is to increase heart rate, raise body temperature and prepare joint mobility (see page 52). Your proposed exercise programme must incorporate a range of suitable warm-up activities that involve both the cardiovascular system and stretching. Tailor warm-ups to meet the specific needs of the client.

Main components of sessions

■ Activities and their duration

A variety of training methods can be adapted to suit the individual client. They include:

- continuous training
- interval training
- Fartlek training
- resistance training.

Continuous training

This describes training that an athlete does in a steady, aerobic way. Continuous training involves comparatively easy work performed for a relatively long period – for example, cycling at a slow speed for 30 minutes or more. This helps to develop aerobic fitness and muscular endurance. Top athletes such as Lance Armstrong and Paula Radcliffe use continuous training.

Continuous training is one of the best ways to build a solid aerobic base on which to add more specific types of fitness. It is also one of the easiest types of training when it comes to monitoring your heart rate. Essentially, it involves running, cycling, swimming etc. at a set pace, usually for 30–45 minutes. Table 14.3 shows an example of a continuous training plan.

Element	Duration (minutes)	Intensity (% of MHR)
Warm-up	10	50–60
Workout	20–45	70–80
Cool-down	10	50–60

 Table 14.3 A continuous training programme for a hockey player

Interval training

Interval training is broadly defined as repetitions of work at high speed or intensity followed by periods of low activity or rest. For example, a runner will improve his or her workload by combining high-intensity bursts of fast running with recovery periods of slower jogging.

Interval training can be any cardiovascular workout (stationary biking, running, rowing, etc.) that involves brief bouts at near-maximum exertion interspersed with periods of lower-intensity activity.

One popular workout that incorporates this method of training is called 'walk-back sprinting'.

Walk-back sprinting

☐ Sprint 200 metres.

☐ Change direction and walk back to the starting point (recovery period).

☐ Repeat the sprint within three minutes.

☐ Repeat the whole process again five times.

Fartlek training

This is a form of interval training. Developed by Swedish coach Gösta Holmér, it is a form of conditioning that puts stress mainly on the aerobic energy system due to the continuous nature of the exercise.

The difference between this type of training and continuous training is that the intensity or speed of the exercise varies, meaning that aerobic and anaerobic systems can be put under stress. Most Fartlek sessions last a minimum of 45 minutes, and can vary from aerobic walking to anaerobic sprinting. Fartlek training is generally associated with running, but it can include almost any kind of exercise including cycling, rowing or swimming.

One of the main reasons for choosing Fartlek training is that it can be adapted to the needs of the individual. Unlike continuous training, Fartlek training can benefit participants in sports such as soccer, field hockey and rugby, as it develops aerobic and anaerobic capacities that are both used in these sports. To take this further, athletes can make the most of the flexibility of Fartlek training by copying the activities that would take place during their chosen sport or event.

Fartlek training

- [ ] Warm-up – light/easy running for 10–15 minutes.
- [ ] Steady, hard speed for 0.75 to 1.5 miles – like a long repetition.
- [ ] Rapid walking for about five minutes – recovery.
- [ ] Easy running interspersed with sprints of about 50–60 metres, repeated until a little tired – start of speed work.
- [ ] Easy running with three or four 'quick steps' now and then – simulating suddenly speeding up to avoid being overtaken by another runner.
- [ ] Full speed uphill for 175–200 metres.
- [ ] Immediately, fast pace for one minute.
- [ ] Repeat the whole routine until the total training period has elapsed.

Resistance training

Resistance training is often referred to as strength training, because it is used to develop the strength and size of skeletal muscles. It involves using resistance or weights during a muscular contraction. Resistance training may also be used to improve muscular endurance.

Resistance training can use the body's own weight to produce the resistance, or it can use fixed or free weights. Using such weights involves a number of repetitions and sets, with the following training principle applied:

muscular strength = high resistance and low repetitions

muscular endurance = lower resistance and high repetitions

Theory into practice

Research how the four types of training discussed here – continuous, interval, Fartlek and resistance training – might be used by a tennis player. Decide which would be the most beneficial, and discuss your results. Remember to consider what are the key fitness components of tennis.

▲ Muscular strength = high resistance, low repetitions; muscular endurance = low resistance, high repetitions

■ Exercise intensity

This refers to how hard you are exercising. It is often measured as a percentage of your MHR, with common applications being rated low, medium or high intensity.

- Low intensity – training at up to 70 per cent of MHR, used to improve general fitness.
- Medium intensity – up to 80 per cent of MHR, used to improve aerobic threshold or endurance.
- High intensity – up to 90 per cent of MHR, used by athletes to improve their strength or anaerobic threshold.

■ Training zones

Training zones are used to determine the level of intensity at which you are working. This is particularly important for cardiovascular training or exercise.

Heart-rate training zones are calculated by taking into consideration your maximum heart rate (MHR) and your resting heart rate (RHR). To work out your MHR you should subtract your age in years from 220:

$$\text{MHR} = 220 - \text{age}.$$

Your RHR can be measured by taking your pulse at rest, preferably before any form of movement or exercise.

Because it is difficult to exercise and measure your heart rate manually, it is useful to use a heart-rate monitor.

The four main training zones are described in Table 14.4.

Key Terms

Fast-twitch muscle fibres are fast-contracting and able to produce a great force; they may be more or less resistant to fatigue (see Sport Book 1, Unit 1).

■ The Karvonen formula

Knowing how fast your heart is beating is no help unless you know how fast it should be beating. The Karvonen formula is a method used to specify training intensities in relation to the heart-rate training zones explained in Table 14.4.

The Karvonen formula will allow you to determine how fast your heart should be beating when you are in one of the heart-rate training zones:

$$\text{desired heart rate (HR)}$$
$$= \text{RHR} + [(\text{MHR} - \text{RHR}) \times \% \text{ intensity}].$$

Consider an example of a client with an MHR of 180 beats per minute (bpm) and an RHR of 70 bpm. So:

for 60% intensity: $70 + [(180 - 70) \times 0.60] = 136$ bpm

for 85% intensity: $70 + [(180 - 70) \times 0.85] = 163$ bpm

Using a heart-rate monitor, the client will be able to exercise using cardiovascular training at the correct level, not allowing his or her heart rate to exceed the required level or zone.

Zone	Percentage of MHR	Training
Fitness	60–70	Develops basic endurance and aerobic capacity – all easy recovery running should be completed at a maximum of 70% MHR
Aerobic	70–80	Develops your cardiovascular system – the body's ability to transport oxygen to, and carbon dioxide away from, the working muscles is developed and improved; as fitness improves it will be possible to run at up to 75% MHR and get the benefits of fat-burning and improved aerobic capacity
Anaerobic	80–90	High-intensity – your body cannot use oxygen quickly enough to produce energy so relies on energy that can used without oxygen, namely glycogen stored in the muscles. This can be used for only a short period – a build-up of lactic acid will rapidly cause fatigue
Red line	90–100	Maximum level of exercise – training possible only for short periods, effectively trains fast-twitch muscle fibres and helps develop speed. This zone is reserved for interval running – only for the very fit

▲ Table 14.4 The four training zones

■ Rating of perceived exertion

Another method of describing exercise intensity levels uses the so-called Borg rating of perceived exertion (Table 14.5). Perceived exertion is how hard you feel your body is working. It is based on physical sensations during activity, including increased heart rate, increased respiration or breathing rate, increased sweating and muscle fatigue.

Through experience of monitoring how your body feels, it becomes easier to know when to adjust your exercise intensity. For example, a walker who wants to engage in moderately intensive activity would aim for a Borg scale level of 'somewhat hard' (12–14). If she described her muscle fatigue and breathing as 'very light' (9 on the Borg scale) she would want to increase the intensity. On the other hand, if she felt her exertion was 'extremely hard' (19 on the Borg scale), she would need to slow down her movements to achieve the moderate intensity range.

6	No exertion at all
7	Extremely light
8	
9	Very light – easy walking slowly at a comfortable pace
10	
11	Light
12	
13	Somewhat hard – quite an effort, you feel tired but can continue
14	
15	Hard (heavy)
16	
17	Very hard – very strenuous, you are very fatigued
18	
19	Extremely hard – you cannot continue for long at this pace
20	Maximal exertion

▲ Table 14.5 The Borg rating of perceived exertion

▲ This boat-race crew have been through all of the levels of perceived exertion

The cool-down

A cool-down should be included in all training programmes and must be designed to lower heart rate, decrease body temperature and return the muscles to their original state (see page 57). It also helps to remove waste products that have built up during exercise. A combination of reduced-intensity cardiovascular exercise and stretching will help a client recover. A minimum of ten minutes should be allocated at the end of a session for an effective cool-down, although this time can be increased if necessary.

Factors to consider when designing an exercise programme

Screening clients

Each client should complete a screening session with you. This may involve a short, informal interview and the completion of a pre-exercise questionnaire (such as the PAR-Q, see page 53). The questionnaire should include questions about the client's medical history and exercise history. This should give you a clear picture of the exercise that will be safe to undertake.

Remember!

If, at any point, you are unhappy with the responses the client has made, then you should get the approval of a qualified doctor first. Never take chances.

■ The client's motives

Clients are motivated to exercise for a variety of reasons. They include losing weight, health benefits, preparation for a competitive activity or sport, or recommendation by a doctor. It is important that you understand why a particular client wants to exercise, or why he or she may need an individual fitness programme. Understanding their motives will allow you to get a picture of your client's short- and long-term aims or goals.

■ Barriers

Why people don't exercise, or why they drop out of exercise programmes, is an area that all instructors need to understand. Having knowledge of common barriers to participation will allow you to address these and overcome them.

One of the most common reasons for not exercising is lack of time. People have busy lives with work, education and family commitments, and fitting in exercise can often be difficult. Therefore you must consider how and when a client can exercise, and adapt the proposed programme to their life.

Another barrier is a general lack of motivation. This can be addressed by making a programme varied and interesting.

■ The client's current physical activity level

The pre-exercise questionnaire and interview will allow you to determine the client's current level of activity.

This is important, so that you do not prescribe exercises that are too easy, so that little progress is likely to be achieved. And you must never prescribe exercise that is too hard for the client, as this can be dangerous and cause discomfort or injury. Each client must be comfortable with his or her exercise programme, and you should fully understand their individual exercise needs, taking into account current level and ability.

■ Short- and long-term goals

A client should identify specific goals, with your help. What goals are to be achieved in the long term, and how will they be approached in the short term?

Goal-setting can follow the SMARTER principle. Goals should be:

- Specific
- Measurable
- Adjustable
- Realistic
- Time-constrained
- Exciting and challenging
- Recorded.

Short-term goals are used as 'stepping stones' to achieve the final goal. An example is a client who wishes to lose five kilograms in weight. His long-term goal would be to lose this total weight, while his short-term goal might be to lose 0.5 kilos per week over a ten-week period.

Who are the clients?

There are many different types of client for whom you might have to write exercise programmes – individuals, groups, adults or children.

Remember!

Each of these clients will have specific reasons for exercising. Any programme that is written must reflect his or her individual needs or goals.

■ Various abilities

Some clients may be highly experienced athletes, while others will be undertaking exercise for the first time. You must be aware of the different levels in ability and adapt training programmes accordingly. You must ensure that each client is safe when exercising, and your recommended programme must be suitable to his or her ability and fitness level.

■ Individuals and groups

Training programmes can be set in the form of individual or group exercise. Group training can prove challenging, as there is likely to be a wide range of abilities within the group. Exercises must be adapted so that individuals are able to exercise at their specific level.

Group exercise can be a good motivator, as other people encourage the individual who may be struggling within the session. Group activities are also a good way of meeting people, and are commonly used as a social experience.

■ Specific groups

Groups that may wish to exercise together can include the elderly, children or those who are obese. Again, it is important that any programmes are adapted to meet the needs of the group and the individuals, so that training is safe.

The elderly will generally undertake programmes that are low in intensity, with little resistance and several repetitions. This is aimed at achieving a good level of general fitness.

Children should not undertake any weight training exercise as it can cause permanent damage, especially to the skeletal system that is still growing. Children should undertake exercise that is low in resistance and high in repetitions (such as aerobic exercise). This can be used to improve general health and fitness as well as improve aerobic capacity.

Excess weight and obesity are increasing in the population. Table 14.6 has some alarming statistics.

Year	Age	Percentage overweight		Percentage obese	
		Boys	Girls	Boys	Girls
1984	4–12	5.4	9.3	0.6	1.3
1994	4–12	9.0	13.5	1.7	2.6
1997	5	18.2	19.3	8.1	6.1
2001	6			8.5	8.5

▲ Table 14.6 Growing numbers of overweight and obese children in the UK

Therefore a training programme might have to be designed to incorporate weight loss. This will be based predominantly on aerobic, low-resistance activities that will improve the client's ability to exercise over a period of time. Gentle walking or slow jogging can be recommended – although it is important that the client be given a full health check prior to any exercise, especially if he or she has not exercised for some time.

For any exercise programme to be effective, lifestyle and dietary advice may also be given so that any goals outlined are realistically achievable.

Code of ethical practice

A code of ethical practice is a set of guidelines that exercise professionals should follow to ensure they are working at the highest standards. The Register of Exercise Professionals (www.exerciseregister.org) describes such a code as 'good practice for professionals in the fitness

◀ Aerobic exercise is good for children – high-resistance exercise is not

industry by reflecting on the core values of rights, relationships and responsibilities.'

People who work in the exercise profession must accept their responsibility to those who participate in exercise, to other fitness professionals and colleagues, to their respective fitness associations, professional bodies and institutes, to their employer, and to society. They should follow the four main principles of ethical practice:

- rights
- relationships
- personal responsibilities
- professional standards.

■ Rights

An exercise professional will promote the rights of every individual, and recognise that every person should be treated as an individual. Professionals must treat all clients equally regardless of race, gender, age, disability, religion, ethic background or sexual orientation, and should keep all client information confidential.

■ Relationships

Exercise professionals should develop a rapport with their clients based on openness, trust, honesty and respect. They must always promote the welfare and best interests of their clients, and encourage them to accept responsibility for their own behaviour and actions during training sessions. An exercise professional will also be aware of the physical needs of clients, especially those with injuries or those still growing, to ensure training is appropriate.

■ Personal responsibilities

Exercise professionals should agree to demonstrate proper behaviour at all times. They should be fair, honest and considerate to all clients and others working in the fitness industry, and display control, respect, dignity and professionalism.

They should also ensure that they do not over-train clients or undertake any practices that are likely to result in injury.

Think it over

If members of the public or customers come to your premises, or you go to theirs, you should think about taking out public liability insurance.

This type of insurance covers awards of damages given to a member of the public because of injury or damage to their property caused by you, or your business. It also covers any related legal fees, costs and expenses.

Why should you take out public liability insurance, and what are the consequences of not having this if an accident were to occur?

■ Professional standards

The exercise professional will ensure that he or she is suitably qualified and undertake regular, up-to-date retraining. The professional will accept responsibility for his or her actions and continuously evaluate personal performance with the aim of improving.

Web links

Further information on the Register of Exercise Professionals Code of Ethical Practice can be found at: www.exerciseregister.org/JoinCode.htm

Activity

Design a pre-exercise screening questionnaire that would be suitable to use in the sport of your choice. Ensure the questions are relevant and cover areas such as illness, disease and injury. Ask your fellow students to fill in the form, then check if you have managed to gather all the information you need. What questions could you add?

Understanding the needs of a client means that you must take into account a variety of factors, such as his or her likes or dislikes, accessibility, culture, commitments, personal goals and time. This will both allow you to devise a programme that is suitable for the individual, and allow the individual to maintain a high level of commitment.

■ Guidelines

Not everybody wants to go to a gym to gain muscle strength or muscle size. The Health Education Authority gives the following general guidelines which can be adapted to individual clients.

- To improve health, an individual needs to exercise at a rate that will make him or her slightly out of breath and warmer than usual. This may involve light exercise for 30 minutes, and can be repeated five or six times per week. Activities may include walking, gentle swimming or gardening.
- To improve cardiovascular fitness, an individual can exercise at between 70 and 90 per cent of his or her MHR three times per week. The exercise should increase and maintain a higher heart rate and may include jogging, swimming, cycling or rowing.

(The Health Education Authority has now been replaced by NICE, www.nice.org.uk – but these guidelines are still currently in use.)

■ The client's likes and dislikes

These influence what activities the client will be prepared to undertake. However, there may be some exercises that the client needs to do in order to achieve specific goals. You must ensure that he or she recognises the importance of exercising using a variety of methods.

■ Accessibility of facilities

Provision varies from place to place, so activity sessions may be limited by a lack of facilities and the ease of reaching them. A client who has a long distance to travel to a session may drop out because of the inconvenience – the time commitment and possibly the cost of transport. This should be discussed with the client at the beginning, and exercises that can be adapted may be considered. Price is also a consideration – low-income groups may have access to only the cheaper sessions or facilities.

■ Cultural issues

Some cultures experience barriers due to social or religious taboos or traditions, different attitudes to sport, little experience of structured sport, or a lack of role models. An exercise professional must consider how to overcome these barriers and adapt programmes accordingly.

Case study

In 2004, the Yorkshire Dales National Park Authority developed a new initiative called 'Beyond the Boundary' that uses cricket as a means of engaging with the Asian community of the Bradford Metropolitan Council area. Through sport, it was realised that the community could be brought together regardless of race or background and given the opportunity to experience different environments, such as cities and the Yorkshire Dales. The initiative involved organising a series of cricket matches between youth teams from urban Bradford and the rural Yorkshire Dales. Players' families were also encouraged to attend, to watch the matches and to take part in visits to local tourist attractions together.

The initiative had two main aims:

- to give families from urban Bradford the opportunity to experience and visit the Yorkshire Dales National Park and be encouraged to undertake future visits
- to give urban and rural communities in Yorkshire an opportunity to meet and form relationships around a shared interest.

1 **What do you think is the importance of sport in a community?**

2 **What are social barriers, and can sport be used to overcome these?**

For more information regarding equal opportunities and sport see www.sportingequals.com

■ Other commitments

A client's other commitments tend to come in the form of either work or family, and generally these will take precedence over formal exercise. Sessions must be fitted around these commitments, so the ideal exercise programme may have to be adapted.

■ Goals

All goals must be realistic and achievable, and clearly time-defined. This will help the client to decide whether the goals are truly realistic over a given period. The programme should ideally outline short-, medium- and long-term goals so that continuous evaluation of the programme's effectiveness is possible.

■ Time

Probably the most quoted reason for not exercising – or dropping out – is lack of time. Time can be swallowed up by work, family duties and social preferences.

You can encourage clients to incorporate exercise into a busy lifestyle by walking rather than using the car, or getting off the bus one stop earlier than usual. Using the stairs instead of lifts or escalators can also contribute to improving health.

▲ People with busy lives need to incorporate exercise – such as walking or climbing stairs – into their daily routine

Think it over

Working together in small groups, identify types of people who may wish to attend an exercise session. List their likely goals, and how you would design a programme to accommodate their needs.

Web links

www.publichealth.nice.org.uk – the National Institute for Health and Clinical Excellence (NICE) is responsible for providing national guidance on promoting good health and preventing and treating ill health.

www.sportengland.org – Sport England (supported by the National Lottery) advises, invests in and promotes community sport, and aims to get two million people more active in sport by 2012 (see page 12).

Assessment practice

So far, the athletics club has been impressed by your knowledge of instructing physical activity. They are now keen to appoint a fitness instructor on a part-time basis who can work with the emerging young athletes. As part of the interview process for this post, you are required to design a six-week exercise programme for the following two athletes:

100-metre sprinter
1500-metre runner. **P4 M2 D1**

Some helpful hints:

- Identify the components of fitness for each athlete.
- Consider the key requirements of fitness for each, and design your programme accordingly.
- Think about how the body will adapt to the exercise you recommend over the six-week period.
- Make sure your programme is varied and progressive.
- Ensure you consider warm-up and cool-down exercise to reduce the chance of injury.
- Remember to consider any health and safety factors.

grading tips

Grading Tip M2

Explain why you have chosen each of the different exercises outlined in your six-week training plan. This must be done for each of the athletes concerned. You should also explain the key differences between the exercises you have chosen.

Grading Tip D1

Justify why you have chosen each of the exercises for the two athletes. You should explain the purpose of each exercise, highlighting the component/s of fitness it is designed to train. You should then give examples of other exercises the athletes may wish to undertake so that the sessions are varied and enjoyable.

14.3 Be able to plan and lead an exercise session

We have seen that a number of factors must be considered when planning and delivering an effective exercise session. Apart from the all-important health and safety, an exercise professional has also to consider the venue, equipment and personal communication skills. You must understand the importance of each of these if you are to be successful.

Plan an exercise session

Health and safety

The fitness and health club sector has grown in recent years. It has seen the development and enhancement of facilities and services, and one of the key areas of improvement is the necessity to deliver safe, well structured practice.

Before you start any exercise programme, it is essential that health and safety has been fully considered. Before the session starts, you must check the equipment that is to be used, and the facility. The following lists the principal points that must be considered:

The health of each individual client must be determined before they take part in exercise ▶

- is the equipment suitable and in full working order?
- are there suitable amounts of equipment?
- is the area to be used free from cables or wires?
- does the area have good ventilation?
- is the temperature suitable for physical activity?

Health screening

Health screening must take place before any exercise or testing is performed by the client, and must be

administered by the sports practitioner. Screening usually takes the form of a questionnaire, and its aim is to identify any medical condition that would prevent the client from exercising safely.

Screening and testing are normally carried out before induction, or during the induction process. At this stage, the practitioner will complete the relevant paperwork, taking down personal details.

A high-quality health screening programme should involve a number of health checks, which may include the following components:

- taking the client's past medical history
- taking the family medical history
- recording blood pressure
- measuring lung function
- checking cholesterol level
- measuring body composition.

The screening process essentially seeks to identify individuals who:

- have a medical risk
- require special attention in their programme
- require a doctor's referral
- have other special needs (such as visual impairment).

The lifestyle questionnaire should also be about:

- diet
- alcohol and tobacco use.

After the interview, you should explain the proposed training programme, how the client will be inducted into exercise, and the safe use of equipment.

Remember!

Following your discussions with the client, you should outline safety aspects such as fire exits and first aid, as well as the availability of drinking water.

Aims and objectives

■ Determining the aims of a session

The success of a session has to be judged against a set of aims. These are the principal targets. The aims must be achievable, but they must not be too easy so that the participants are not challenged at all. If that happens, the individuals or team will fail to improve.

There should also be a time constraint attached to the aims. For example, a marathon runner might set an aim of being able to run 10 kilometres at four months prior to the event – to allow for progression to be made to complete the full distance of just over 42km (26.2 miles).

■ Determining the objectives

Objectives will accompany the session's aims – these refer to how the aims will be achieved. The objectives will outline very specific goals, which may be short- or medium-term goals. For example, an objective of a marathon runner may be to identify suitable training methods to improve muscular and cardiovascular endurance. Another client may simply wish to get fit. His or her objectives will identify the specific ways in which to get fit – such as cardiovascular fitness, weight loss or improved muscle strength or endurance.

Determining the structure of sessions

Structure is very important if the client is to enjoy the exercise and avoid injury. In general terms, a session will follow the order: warm-up, main activity, cool-down (or 'warm-down').

■ The warm-up

A warm-up generally consists of a gradual increase in intensity in physical activity. For example, before running or playing an intense sport you might slowly jog to warm muscles and increase heart rate. It is important that warm-ups should be specific to the exercise that will follow, which means that exercises should prepare the muscles to be used and to activate the energy systems that are required for that particular activity. Stretching the active muscles is also recommended after doing a warm-up (see page 54).

■ The main activity

It is important that a number of rules are followed.

Rule 1: Exercise major muscles in pairs

When using resistance training, it is important that corresponding muscles be trained equally. Muscles help stabilise a joint, so if one is stronger than another this may cause joint instability and injury. It can also cause long-term problems with posture and may affect sporting performance. The main pairs of muscles are:

- pectorals and trapezius
- bicep and tricep
- latissimus dorsi and deltoid
- abdominals and erector spinae
- quadricep and hamstring.

Rule 2: Do the difficult exercises first

A simple exercise will involve only one joint (e.g. bicep curl), whereas a more difficult exercise will involve two or more joints (e.g. chest press). The more difficult exercises will need more focus, so they should be done early on before the onset of fatigue.

Rule 3: Train the large muscles first

The large muscles of the body are:

- trapezius
- lattisimus dorsi
- pectorals
- quadriceps
- hamstrings
- gluteus maximus.

The main reason for exercising these muscles first is that they will require the most effort, so they should be exercised before they start to fatigue. The smaller muscles of the body help the larger muscles work, so should remain relatively fresh when exercising.

Rule 4: Exercise the abdominal muscles last

The abdominal and muscles of the lower back are used to provide support to the main core of the body. These should remain free from fatigue so that injury to the back can be avoided and correct posture can be maintained.

▼ The main pairs of muscles

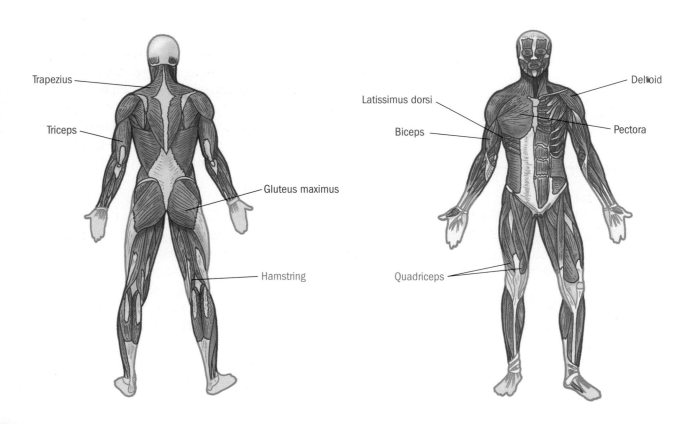

Activity

In pairs or small groups, identify the major skeletal muscles that are being used for each phase of the following simple exercises:

1   press up
2   tricep dip
3   step up
4   chest press.

■ The cool-down

The purpose of the cool-down is to return the body to its normal level. This will involve light exercise to lower the heart rate and body temperature, whilst stretching is used to prevent muscle soreness (see page 57).

The venue

Being able to lead an effective session will depend on the venue used. Is it the correct size for the number of people, and is it suitable for exercises? You should also consider whether the venue will provide the necessary equipment. If clients have to provide their own, this will have a financial implication and may prevent some people from taking part.

The venue must be safe. A full health and safety check should be conducted prior to all sessions.

Marketing your services

Marketing can be broadly defined as the need to identify, anticipate and satisfy customers' needs. It is particularly important if you are to run a successful business. It will be vital to promote your service in a way that attracts clients, makes them want to return in the future, and recommend it to their friends and family.

The way in which you perform during sessions will also help. You must be professional and competent at all times, and be clearly willing to help people achieve their fitness goals.

Risk assessment

A risk assessment is used to evaluate the chances of an accident occurring during a session. It will identify the factors that are likely to cause an injury or illness. An exercise practitioner should conduct a risk assessment before any session. At the very least, the following should be considered:

- is the venue the correct size, with adequate heating and ventilation?
- is the floor free from obstructions and obvious dangers?
- is the equipment (whether provided by the venue or the clients) sufficient and suitable, and free from damage?
- is clients' clothing appropriate, including footwear? Are they wearing jewellery?
- is any client suffering from an illness or injury that will make exercising dangerous?

A record form should be used to note down all risk assessments conducted. Keep them for easy referral later.

Setting up a session

To present a professional image, all sessions should be planned in advance. You must identify the venue, the time of the session and the equipment needed. In advance of the session, you should set up the equipment to be used so that it is ready when the clients arrive. The equipment should be checked for damage, and not used if you are unsure.

■ Checking and maintaining equipment

Equipment should be checked for damage before and after a session. Any damaged equipment should be either repaired or replaced before the next session.

Remember!

You should *never* allow exercise using broken or damaged equipment. It could result in serious injury.

All equipment should be stored correctly, and in a way that helps to set up the next session quickly and safely. Records of any maintenance work should be kept to ensure repairs have taken place or equipment has been replaced.

Activity

You have been asked by your teacher to organise an exercise session for a group of local league football players. This session will be conducted outside. Complete a table outlining what factors you must consider when planning this session. Why are these factors so important, and what do you think could happen if they are not checked?

Assessment practice

Having designed a successful six-week training programme for the two contrasting athletes, you have been shortlisted for an interview at the athletics club. The club manager has decided that the best way of recruiting a suitable exercise instructor is to see them perform a practical exercise session. You are required to plan a one-hour, safe and effective exercise session for a group of young athletes. **P5 M3 D2**

The session plan should include the following information:

- aim and objective of the session
- health and safety considerations
- risk assessment
- equipment required
- warm-up and cool-down
- structure of the session.

Grading tips

Grading Tip **M3**

Within your plan, explain the exercises you have chosen for the proposed session. It is worth considering what each chosen exercise actually trains – what component of fitness is being addressed?

Grading Tip **D2**

Justify why you have chosen the exercises outlined in your proposed session plan. Think about why these exercises are beneficial to the athletes, and what alternative activities you could choose if you needed to.

Deliver an exercise session
Your introduction to a session

All participants should be aware of several key factors:
- what is expected of them
- how the exercises should be completed
- health and safety issues
- variations of activities for male and female participants
- ability levels or factors that may affect existing/past injuries.

In order to communicate these messages, time should be taken to determine how people learn best, and how they will be able to replicate movements that in some cases are new to them and complex in nature. To demonstrate a session effectively, the acronym IDEA presents a natural progression suitable for exercise classes, gym inductions, coaching sessions or on a one-to-one personal training basis. IDEA stands for introduction, demonstration, explanation, application.

- Introduction – of the exercise, its purpose, its benefits and basic technique.
- Demonstration – this should be non-verbal, allowing participants to observe the movements without

a spoken message that might detract from their observation.

- Explanation – of the basics of the exercise: mention perhaps two or three technique-related points, but avoid information overload.
- Application – give participants an opportunity to practise the movements and gauge whether there are any potential problems or areas for improvement – it is essential to ensure correct technique, so this is a key phase in the introduction to a session.

Instruction delivery

When clients begin to exercise, they will need ongoing support to ensure correct technique and avoid injury. This support from you will come in a number of forms.

■ Communication

Communication is an essential tool for developing relationships and interacting. The key to good communication is to provide the amount of information the receiver can use effectively, rather than the amount the exercise leader would like to give.

Your message should be transmitted in a clear voice and be free from jargon. The use of jargon and slang terms is commonplace, but they can often cause 'grey areas' and be the cause of real confusion. The acronym KISS provides a simple guide to follow when delivering information: keep it simple, stupid!

Ensure the information you provide allows enough guidance for individuals to take part safely and to establish good technique performance. Further information can be delivered over time when the basic principles have been mastered.

■ Technique correction

The correction of technique must be addressed early. Leaving small errors to develop will result in serious problems later, which will take valuable time to correct. Poor technique will often fail to deliver the preferred results. People engaging in weight-training programmes are a prime example of this, because they tend to fail to target the desired muscle regions and see little or no improvement.

Correction is best developed using mirroring techniques. The individual completes the movement while looking in a mirror, or copies the instructor who completes the movement opposite them. Either way, the movement needs to be completed correctly a number of times before it becomes second nature to the client.

■ Correct body alignment

The development of 'core stability' is a fairly new phenomenon in the fitness world. It basically seeks to develop an equilibrium or balance throughout the skeletal and muscular systems. Body alignment will target areas of posture and balance as fundamental factors to ensure the body remains functional and efficient. Core stability achieves this by highlighting the core (abdominal and lower back regions) as the framework to generate a solid platform to work from. You should be aware of the benefits of developing this platform, not only in the core region, but also throughout the body.

Body alignment also deals with creating a balance between muscle groupings. For example, the quadriceps are capable of producing substantial power output but should not be too powerful for the opposite muscles – the hamstrings – to deal with, otherwise one of the hamstrings is likely to sustain damage. Also, men targeting only their biceps and chest and ignoring their legs and back is common in gym work.

▲ A stability ball pike – for developing core stability and upper body strength

■ Modification of exercises

Not everyone is built the same way. Some people will find an exercise easily achievable, while others might have difficulty with it. As an exercise professional you should always have contingency plans available to ensure everyone has an opportunity to attempt the activity. The art of modification of exercises is an essential tool.

Introducing variety for more experienced individuals will keep training interesting for them in the long term. For example, the common press-up can be tailored for a variety of competencies, as shown below.

Press-ups – the beginner	
1	Full press-up
2	Half-press performing the exercise on the thigh
3	Box press-up performed on the knees

Press-ups – the advanced exercises	
1	Full press-up
2	Full press-up with hands together
3	Full press-up with feet raised onto a bench or bed

■ Observation

When leading an exercise session, you will be able to gauge levels of experience and potential from simply watching. With experience, technique correction can be completed by studying running styles, arm positioning, foot strike on the floor or head position – to name but a few – during a phase of movement.

■ Motivation

A common reason why people leave exercise and training programmes is a drop in motivation. This may be caused by previous poor experience, lack of enjoyment, or failure to achieve aims and objectives. You must motivate your client, especially when the going gets tough.

Imparting motivation will involve verbal encouragement as well as considering your own body language. You must be positive at all times to make sure that you are pushing the client into working as hard as is reasonable to achieve his or her goals safely.

■ Rapport with clients

Having a friendly and open rapport with clients will help you to produce effective training programmes. Being honest and respectful will keep up the clients' motivation. Clients should feel that they are able to discuss their programmes with you, and feel comfortable in trying to achieve their targets.

Activity

Make a list of five key skills that you feel are essential to lead an effective exercise session. Then, in small groups, compare your lists and debate the differences – decide which are the most important, and why.

Remember!

It is important to be friendly and patient, especially when the client is struggling.

Activity

In small groups, explore the importance of non-verbal communication (body language). Try and communicate a common phrase or expression without using any gestures. For example, you may wish to describe a recent sporting performance that you have witnessed. Your group should list examples of body language that you used, highlight any positive and negative examples, and compare them.

1 List examples of positive/negative body language.

2 What are the problems of displaying negative body language?

3 Why must a leader be enthusiastic and confident?

Ending a session

Once the session has been completed (including the cool-down), you have the opportunity to ask clients how they feel it went. This time is important, as it gives you valuable feedback as part of your own personal evaluation. Through discussion with your clients, you can amend their programme(s) as well as improve areas of your delivery.

This time should also be spent giving the clients feedback. Explain how you thought they did.

Checking and setting down of equipment

Check all equipment for damage, and arrange for repair or replacement as necessary. Store it in a manner that is likely to prevent accidents or damage. The setting down of equipment should be performed efficiently and safely. In particular, heavy items should be carried correctly.

Assessment practice

Having prepared a suitable one-hour session as part of your job interview, you are now required to deliver the session. The session must be safe and effective, and you may seek support if you need to. **P6 M4**

Some helpful hints:

- Ensure you have checked for any injuries and illnesses.
- Are there any reasons why anybody should not participate?
- Have you checked the facilities and equipment prior to the session?
- Ensure you clearly outline the aims of session at the beginning of the session.
- Don't forget your verbal and non-verbal language (body language) – be enthusiastic!
- Remember to encourage and motivate all the participants during the session.
- Be confident!

14.4 Be able to review design of an exercise programme and leading of an exercise session

After any exercise programme, it is important that you review your own performance as well as that of your clients. There are many different ways of doing this, including peer evaluation, questionnaires and self-evaluation. Each method should be understood and used if you are to improve your sessions in the future.

Methods of evaluation

Peer evaluation

You can gain information from your peers about your performance. This evaluation can be in the form of interviews or questionnaires. Peer observations are useful because they highlight strengths and weaknesses of performance and give valuable information on how to improve.

Remember!

What works for one client may not always work for another, as different people have different needs.

Questionnaires

Questionnaires can be given to clients after sessions have been completed. Again, valuable information can be gained about what they enjoyed or disliked. This information can then be applied in future sessions.

Here are some examples of questions that can be asked:

- Did the session meet your original objectives?
- Did you enjoy the session, and if not, why not?
- Did you feel safe throughout the session?
- In what ways would you like to see future sessions developed?

Self-evaluation

You should always ask yourself questions after each session, and you must answer these honestly, even if the answers are likely to identify weaknesses in your performance. Self-evaluation is an important tool as it means future sessions will be safe and effective, and clients will remain motivated and make targeted progression. Self-evaluation will also help you to identify any future training needs you have to update your skills.

■ Performance

By reviewing performance, you can identify whether your selected activities are fit for their purpose. This means making sure the exercises used are actually addressing the long-term and short-term goals of the client. Ask yourself 'Are these goals being achieved, and if not, why not?'

■ Progression

Have clear targets that are measurable, so that any improvements can be tracked. If a specific aspect of the programme is not effective, then changes can be made and the session adapted.

■ Adaptation and modification

Perform regular session reviews. If the client's goals are not being met, then it is important that the session be amended. Such adaptations should take into account the client's needs, and may address whether a client has become demotivated. Adaptations will also allow variety, which can further enhance enjoyment.

Activities may be modified to take into account factors such as injury, illness, unexpected changes to the length of sessions, and client demotivation. Modifications should be discussed fully with clients so that they are aware of what to expect in the future.

■ Improve your own performance

Conduct a full personal performance review to identify areas of strength and weakness. This may include whether you can improve your clients' motivation, and the way in which you instruct them. Remember that you may have to adapt your approach and instructor skills for each individual – what works for one client may not work for another.

■ Development needs

It is important that an instructor identifies his or her areas of weaknesses and addresses these through continued professional development (see page 79).

Codes of practice

A code of practice should be a clear set of rules that identifies how you and your clients should behave before, during and after each session. Exercise and fitness professionals should follow the four main principles of ethical practice: rights, relationships, personal responsibilities and professional standards. An understanding of each of these will ensure that you remain professional throughout your work and that clients can expect the highest level of commitment from you.

A code of practice will also clearly define safe behaviour, which will help reduce the risk of injury to clients and others.

Modifying a programme you have designed

When modifying a programme, it is important to be specific in the changes you make and to outline why they are being made. There are a number of reasons why changes are made. They may include FITT progression, increased motivation and the achievement of goals.

FITT progression

As you read earlier (see page 51), FITT refers to frequency, intensity, time and type of exercise within a training programme. You should be able to modify these specific aspects in order to achieve a client's outlined goals. For example, the intensity may be too high, so that a client struggles to complete a session. Training at too high an intensity can also result in injury, so should be addressed immediately.

Here are some questions to ask yourself and each of your individual clients:

- Is the frequency of each session too high or too low? In other words, can the clients commit to each session?
- Is the intensity or level of work too easy or too hard for the clients?
- Is the time allocated for each session too long or too short? In particular, do the clients struggle to complete the sessions fully?
- Are the types of exercise used appropriate and effective?
- Do the clients enjoy the range of exercises used?

Changes to maintain interest and motivation

Each training session should involve a variety of exercises. Too much repetition can cause boredom and may demotivate the client. Through talking to the client, find out what he or she is enjoying, and what is boring or disliked. Regular modifications can help enhance commitment by the client.

At the beginning of any programme, you will have found out what a particular client wishes to achieve. However, it is common for initial goals to be unrealistic. Through review, you should identify whether the original targets are being met and, if not, how they should be changed.

Remember!

If a client does not achieve any of his or her goals because they are too difficult, they are likely to become demotivated and lose interest. But goals should not be too easy, so that there is a lack of a challenge.

Continued professional development (CPD)

The health and fitness industry is a fast-moving and changing area, which means that an instructor must have an understanding of up-to-date practices and knowledge (see Web links). As sport and exercise sciences develop, we are able to gain better insight into how the body functions and how it changes during and after exercise. New training courses will give you knowledge and skills that can be used with confidence in future sessions. In addition, clients will have confidence in the training programmes you provide.

Through reviews, you should be able to identify any personal training weaknesses you may have and then undertake additional courses or qualifications. This will ensure your skills remain at the high level demanded by the health and fitness industry.

Web links

www.leisureopportunities.co.uk
www.premierglobal.co.uk
www.who.int (World Health Organization)
www.uksca.org.uk (UK Strength & Conditioning Association)
www.saqinternational.com (SAQ)

Setting targets or goals

Any targets that you set should follow the SMARTER principle that you read about on page 65 – they should be specific, measurable, adjustable, realistic, time-constrained, exciting/challenging and recorded. By following this principle, you and your clients can conduct continuous reviews of performance and ensure that identified goals are achievable. This will also allow you to make any modifications as necessary.

Activity

In small groups, research on the internet an exercise evaluation form. Following an exercise session, attempt to complete this form and evaluate how valid this is. In your group, make changes that you feel are relevant and explain why these changes have been made.

Assessment practice

Having successfully completed your session, it is essential that you evaluate how it went. As part of your interview you are likely to be asked about your instructing performance. Review your own performance in designing, planning and delivering the exercise session, in preparation for the interview process. Remember – you must be honest in your evaluation, and you should be able to identify both your strengths and weaknesses, so that further areas for improvement can be identified. **P7**

Some helpful hints:

- Prepare an evaluation sheet for participants to complete at the end of the session.
- Be honest in your personal performance evaluation.
- List the strengths of the session – what went well?
- List the weaknesses of the session – what would you change next time?

Knowledge check

1 What are the principles of training?

2 When planning an exercise or training programme, outline and explain the main health and safety considerations.

3 Warm-ups and cool-downs are an important part of any exercise programme. Describe why these must be used, and their purpose.

4 Using your knowledge of exercise programmes, design a six-week training programme for a client of your choice. Then select a different client and design an individual programme for them.

5 Having previously designed a six-week programme, explain why you selected your outlined activities and suggest alternative exercises that may be used.

6 What factors must you consider when delivering a safe and effective session?

7 What is the purpose of a performance review?

8 How can a performance review be conducted?

9 What is a risk assessment and why should it be performed?

10 What is screening, and what information should be collected?

Preparation for assessment

You have recently been employed to help a local cricket club improve their players' fitness. The role will involve developing specific training programmes, devising and implementing these, and evaluating sessions.

1   Design a six-week exercise programme for each of the players that includes and describes the principles of fitness training. You may wish to consider the specific needs of a batsman, bowler and the fielders. This programme must also describe and explain the importance of health and safety within your designated programme. Your programme must also describe the importance of a warm-up and cool-down as part of your planned sessions.   **P1 P2 M1 P3 P4**

2   Using the devised six-week session, explain and justify your choice of activities. To help you with this, you may wish to consider the nature of cricket and the specific needs and differences of a batsman and a bowler. Also consider how fielding may use a variety of fitness principles.   **M2 D1**

3   The cricket club has asked you to undertake an exercise session for the team as part of its pre-season preparations. Plan a single session from your designed six-week programme, ensuring that you emphasise safety.   **P5**

You must also explain your choice of activities for the players, and suggest possible alternatives   **M3 D2**

If possible, you should undertake the exercise session including a full warm-up and cool-down. As part of this, you must describe how you would deliver the session   **P6 M4**

4   Following your session, you feel it is important to review your performance so that you can identify your strengths and areas for improvement. Use an appropriate evaluation sheet to review the session, explaining what went well and what areas you feel may need addressing in order to improve.   **P7**

To achieve a pass grade the evidence must show that the learner is able to:	To achieve a merit grade the evidence must show that, in addition to the pass criteria, the learner is able to:	To achieve a distinction grade the evidence must show that, in addition to the pass and merit criteria, the learner is able to:
P1 describe the principles of fitness training **Assessment practice page 59**		
P2 describe the health and safety considerations associated with exercise programmes and sessions **Assessment practice page 59**	**M1** explain the development, and organisation, of sport from pre-industrial origins to the present day **Assessment practice page 59**	
P3 describe the importance of warm-up and cool-down in exercise programmes and sessions **Assessment practice page 59**		
P4 design a six-week exercise programme for two selected contrasting clients **Assessment practice page 69**	**M2** explain choice of activities for exercise programmes for selected clients **Assessment practice page 69**	**D1** justify choice of activities for exercise programmes for selected clients, suggesting alternative activities **Assessment practice page 69**
P5 plan a safe and effective exercise session **Assessment practice page 74**	**M3** explain choice of activities for the planned exercise session **Assessment practice page 74**	**D2** justify choice of activities for the planned exercise session and suggest alternative activities **Assessment practice page 74**
P6 deliver a safe and effective exercise session, with support **Assessment practice page 77**	**M4** deliver a safe and effective exercise session **Assessment practice page 77**	
P7 review own performance in the designing of exercise programmes and the planning and delivery of the exercise session, identifying strengths and areas for improvement **Assessment practice page 80**		

17 Sports injuries

Introduction

Taking part in sport and exercise has numerous benefits. These can be health-related, psychological, social and also, on a wider scale, economic. The physical aspect of sport and exercise is potentially the most beneficial. The exercise component of most sports activities is known to be valuable in preventing disease and disability.

Despite the benefits, the stress that sport and exercise activity puts on the human body inevitably causes physical problems from time to time. Due to the increasing range of activities available, and the number of participants in sporting and exercise activities, the range and types of injury are diverse.

Sports injuries can be a major cause of physical pain, frustration, heartache and financial loss for players of all sporting disciplines and at a variety of performance levels. In this unit you will investigate the identification of risks and the prevention of injuries. You will also examine the types, causes and symptoms of a range of injuries and the treatments available, identifying which methodologies are applicable. Putting into practice the knowledge that you will develop, you will produce an initial treatment plan, along with a long-term rehabilitation programme for two commonly occurring sports injuries.

This unit is internally assessed. On completion of the unit you will have achieved the following learning outcomes:

- Understand how common sports injuries can be prevented by the correct identification of risk factors
- Know about a range of sports injuries and their symptoms
- Know how to apply methods of treating sports injuries
- Be able to plan and construct treatment and rehabilitation programmes for two common sports injuries.

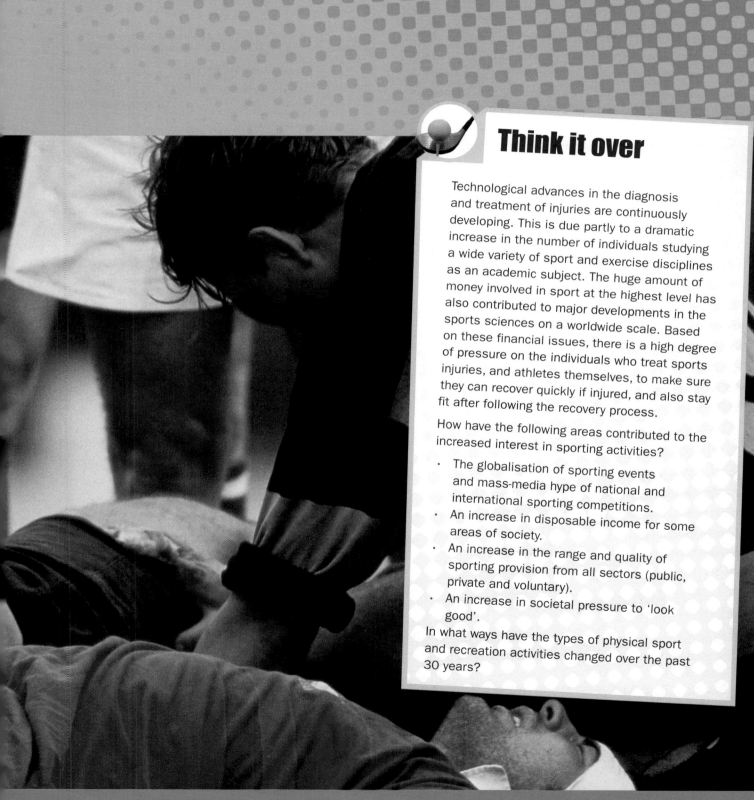

Think it over

Technological advances in the diagnosis and treatment of injuries are continuously developing. This is due partly to a dramatic increase in the number of individuals studying a wide variety of sport and exercise disciplines as an academic subject. The huge amount of money involved in sport at the highest level has also contributed to major developments in the sports sciences on a worldwide scale. Based on these financial issues, there is a high degree of pressure on the individuals who treat sports injuries, and athletes themselves, to make sure they can recover quickly if injured, and also stay fit after following the recovery process.

How have the following areas contributed to the increased interest in sporting activities?

- The globalisation of sporting events and mass-media hype of national and international sporting competitions.
- An increase in disposable income for some areas of society.
- An increase in the range and quality of sporting provision from all sectors (public, private and voluntary).
- An increase in societal pressure to 'look good'.

In what ways have the types of physical sport and recreation activities changed over the past 30 years?

The pressure to perform and succeed, particularly at the highest level, is extremely high. The risk of injury can be a cause of stress for a sportsperson. Athletes performing in a range of sports are concerned about injury – studies on professional rugby union players, for example, found that the most frequently cited stressors were injury concerns, mental errors and physical errors.

It could be argued that the most important issue surrounding sports injuries is how to prevent them occurring, or minimise the severity if they do. The high-impact nature of many contact sports, particularly at high level, will cause many minor injuries (such as cuts and bruises) in virtually all games that are played. The development of some knowledge regarding various simple tasks that are important when taking part in all sport and exercise activities will help to prevent many niggling injuries that can inhibit us taking part in the activities we enjoy.

The frequency, severity, type, location and various other elements of sports injuries vary dramatically between sporting disciplines. Other aspects, such as playing position and even style of play, can be determining factors in the common injuries that can occur. For example, the frequency of traumatic injuries varies greatly between sports, with contact sports such as soccer, ice hockey, wrestling, American football and rugby having higher rates of traumatic injury.

Various individuals, as well as athletes themselves, help to reduce the likelihood of accidents taking place.

Activity

Consider how those in different roles – sportsmen or women themselves, and those supporting them – can decrease the likelihood of injury for athletes. Complete Table 17.1.

Tip – think about the types of injuries sports players may be prone to.

People	Actions/roles to prevent risk of injury	
	Injuries due to overuse of a body part	Injuries that occur in one particular instant (trauma)
Long-distance runner	Analyse running style	
Ground staff/ event organiser		
Coach	Qualifications, knowledge, age, ability	Qualifications, knowledge of players' fitness level
Cricketer		
Sprinter		
Football player		Using correct equipment

▲ Table 17.1 How can each person involved in sport decrease the likelihood of injury?

Sports injury risks

Sports injuries can be caused by a wide variety of different factors, and are divided into categories on this basis. Injuries are caused by forces acting on the body – these can be external forces, such as from objects or other individuals making contact with someone; or internal forces, which are stresses from within the body. Identifying the risk factors can dramatically reduce the chances of someone developing the different types of injury. Whether the risk is from outside or inside the body is termed either extrinsic or intrinsic.

Key Terms

Extrinsic A risk or force from outside the body.

Intrinsic A risk or force from within the body.

Extrinsic risk factors

A sports coach plays a major role in developing the skills of athletes. If incorrect/contraindicated exercises are advised, or inappropriate coaching techniques are utilsed, these can be an intrinsic injury risk factor to athletes. If a coach demonstrates poor communication and leadership methods, this can also pose risks for sports players.

The rules of sport have many roles – from making a game an interesting spectacle, to protecting players from injury. The governing bodies of sports set out specific rules, and non-adherence to these will involve risks for both the player breaking the rules, and other players participating.

Using inappropriate or incorrect techniques is a real injury risk. As well as poor sports techniques, improper methods of setting up and handling equipment will cause risks to those involved.

Weather conditions are a major factor influencing sport performance, potentially increasing the risk of injury. The effect of many different types of weather on playing surfaces will increase the risks of injury, for example:

- slips and falls from slippery surfaces
- falling on uneven ground
- cold conditions make playing surfaces harder and potentially dangerous
- poor conditions may mean the style of play may change, and create further risks to players via the movements that they carry out.

Not wearing the correct equipment for your sport will create major extrinsic risk factors. Examples of incorrect use are:

- wearing the wrong footwear for the activity or playing surface
- wearing incorrect, damaged, or too much or too little protective equipment.

The process of risk assessment is covered in detail in Sport Book 1, Unit 2. It is important for coaches, support staff and players to be aware of hazards and risks associated with the activities being undertaken. Various health and safety considerations must be applied for all activities both before and during participation.

- Environment checks – it is extremely important that a safety check of sporting environment is carried out before a game or training. It is vital to remove any dangerous objects, or any slippery or uneven areas of a playing surface, along with a general consideration of potential risks.
- Sports equipment – the equipment we use as training aids, for protection, and to enhance performance can also act as a potential extrinsic risk factor, and it is essential that equipment is checked by players and coaches before use. A referee should also check equipment before the players enter the playing area (for example, checking studs before a rugby or football match). The misuse and abuse of sports equipment can also act as a risk factor.
- Misuse of equipment will cause risks to sports players – equipment is specifically designed to do a particular job. Tampering with or modifying equipment will cause it to be less useful and often dangerous.
- A lack of preparation for any accidents that could occur on the sports field may also cause undue risks to sports players. Experienced first-aiders and/or medical professionals and, crucially, a fully equipped first-aid kit should be present at all sports sessions. A safety checklist is a useful tool to make sure all activities and equipment are safe.

Intrinsic risk factors

The adaptations to the body (training effects) due to sport and exercise are generally beneficial to our health and wellbeing. However, due to anatomical differences and abnormalities (such as muscle imbalance), undue stresses can be placed on different parts of the body, potentially causing injuries.

Inadequate or poor preparation for sports training and competition will place risks on sportsmen and women. It is essential to prepare for sport both mentally and physically before participating. Warm-up is an essential aspect of any preparation for sport (see page 54). Appropriate flexibility for your chosen discipline is also an important component of fitness, and a lack of flexibility will place risk on an athlete.

Insufficient sleep before training and competition is another potential risk – being alert and refreshed for sport is a key ingredient for focus and success in both training and competition. A further crucial method of preparing for physical activity is sufficient nutrition (including hydration). Insufficient food and water before an activity will cause serious risks to the body.

Having the correct fitness levels to play the sport you participate in is very important to minimise the risks of injury. Playing at an appropriate level is also critical, as playing sport with individuals of either superior or inferior fitness levels will involve risk to yourself and others. The internal stresses on the body when participating with inadequate fitness levels act as an intrinsic risk factor. Particularly for youth sport players, it is important that players of similar age and physical development play against each other, rather than competing against less (or more) physically developed players.

The correct amount of training will have many skill and fitness benefits. Finding the balance between a well planned regime and overuse is something to consider when developing a training plan (see Unit 14). Too much intensity or frequency of exercise poses an intrinsic injury risk to an athlete.

A person's anatomy can predispose them to certain injuries – and on the other hand, a history of certain injuries can make a person more susceptible to anatomical abnormalities. A history of injury also increases the intrinsic risk of that injury reoccurring during future sports participation. Differences or problems associated with the anatomy of an individual are classed as an intrinsic risk factor.

For example, abnormal curvature of the spine is a potential risk that can become degenerative and inhibit sporting potential. Examples of such malalignment of the vertebrae include scoliosis, kyphosis and lordosis.

- **Scoliosis** is a lateral imbalance or sideways bending of the spine.
- **Kyphosis** is an excessive arching of the upper part of the spine.
- **Lordosis** is an excessive inward curve at the lower part of the spine.

These problems can occur independently, or sometimes together to a certain degree.

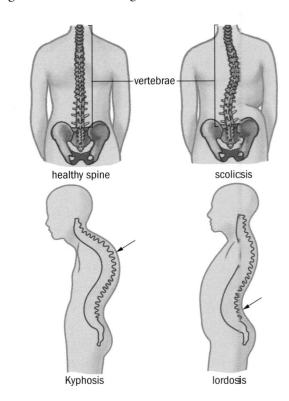

healthy spine   scoliosis

Kyphosis   lordosis

▲ **Malalignment of the vertebrae**

Activity

Complete Table 17.2 to check your understanding of categorisation of risk factors

Risk factor	Intrinsic (I) or extrinsic (E)
Lack of organisation for an event	
Inadequate preparation for a game	
Muscular imbalance	
Postural defects	
Poor technique	
Poor coaching and/or leadership	
Rules and regulations (governing bodies)	
Playing surfaces	
Poor preparation	
Age	
Inadequate fitness levels	
Overuse	
Growth and development	
Environment (weather)	
Insufficient flexibility	
A history of previous injury	
Nutrition	
Sleep disturbances	

▲ Table 17.2 Categorisation of risk factors

- be able to adapt coaching style based on ability, age, fitness, gender and motivation of the athletes being coached
- be able to stress the importance of health and safety in well planned training sessions and match situations – communication skills are vital for all coaches
- check that all equipment is safe to use, that it is being used correctly, and that the environment is safe for the activity being undertaken
- ensure that players are aware of all governing body guidelines and adhere to the rules and regulations that have been set out
- ensure sufficient first-aid provision is available for all training and competition scenarios – this is critically important
- make a detailed assessment of the risks of all activities.

Activity

In small groups, produce a fact sheet explaining the different types of risks associated with sporting activity. Include a section indicating the roles of different individuals in minimising extrinsic and intrinsic risk factors.

Preventive measures

Many of us may know – or know of – a sports player who seems to be injured for the majority of the time. It could be argued that some people are predisposed to (more likely to suffer from) injuries, compared with others playing the same sports. As well as specific actions by the athletes themselves, the coach will play a major role, particularly for younger athletes, in preventing mishaps on the playing field. Key considerations for a physical trainer or sports coach are as follows:

- have up-to-date knowledge of all players' abilities, including strengths and weaknesses in their physicality and skills
- have up-to-date and relevant knowledge and qualifications in the sport that they are coaching

Protective equipment

In many sports, the protective equipment available has changed dramatically over the years. Technological advances in the materials available and biomechanical analysis techniques (research and analysis of movement) have allowed dramatic improvements in the quality of protective equipment available. Advances have been in both specific protection of body parts, and limiting the negative impact of the protection on playing performance (such as excess weight and decreased range of movement).

The purpose of equipment is to help reduce the likelihood of injuries, and limit their severity if they do occur. Mouth guards and gum shields, for example, are

More protective equipment for cricketers has become available in recent decades

- government agencies (e.g. Department of Culture, Media and Sport)
- national medical organisation (e.g. National Health Service)
- public health professionals (e.g. GPs, medical specialists)
- sports associations (e.g. sports councils, Central Council of Physical Recreation).

It is the obligation of the sports player to ensure that specialist protective equipment is used correctly. Protective equipment can be used in the wrong manner, and this can be a hazard, potentially putting yourself and other players at risk. The reduction in sporting injuries due to direct trauma in recent years has been influenced by both the improved design of protective equipment, and the obligation on wearers to comply with the regulations of sports associations.

Some sports require only small, relatively insignificant protection, whereas others (e.g. ice hockey) need equipment that covers nearly the entire body.

When using different types of protective equipment, you should:

- use the equipment only for the sport it is designed for
- use only the correct size
- not share your personal equipment (e.g. boots, pads etc.) with other people
- not use damaged equipment
- not make modifications to equipment
- be aware that protective equipment does not make you invincible!
- use the equipment for both practice and competition
- be aware that some equipment can protect both you and other players.

common in many sports, and are generally successful in preventing both minor and more serious injuries. The use of a mouth guard for contact sports can decrease the risk of an athlete needing dental surgery. Research has strongly advocated their use for a range of sports, and this can be even more important for young and developing athletes.

Research by health professionals often highlights the need for safety equipment in a particular sport or recreational activity, based on whether particular activities are high-risk. Safety equipment is often advocated by various organisations promoting its quality. By advocating sports equipment, organisations help manufacturers sell more products, and also ensure appropriate safety equipment is being used by athletes throughout the country. Organisations that may support equipment development include:

- national governing bodies of sports (e.g. Football Association, Rugby Football Union)

Think it over

What factors will determine the amount of protective equipment needed for a particular sport?

Activity

Consider the types of sports-related protective equipment listed in Table 17.3. In which specific sports are they used? What different parts of the body are they protecting? A few sports have been added for you – add more to these lists, and fill in the empty areas.

Equipment	Relevant sports	Part of the body protected
Mouthguard	Boxing, ...	
Eyewear		
Headgear		Ears, ...
Footwear		
Bracing and taping	Football, ...	Wrists, ...
Padding	Rugby, ...	

▲ Table 17.3 Uses of protective equipment

Taking it further

Which specific types of injury will the examples of protective equipment in Table 17.3 protect you from?

Theory into practice

Being aware of the risks, and following some simple guidelines when participating, can dramatically reduce the likelihood of injuries occurring. Here is a simple set of instructions on how to minimise the likelihood of common injuries.

A general guide to injury prevention in sport

Ensure you have sufficient rest periods.

Be aware of even small/minor injuries, to avoid exacerbating any problems.

If you experience pain when training, make sure you stop immediately.

Pay attention to hydration (more so when in high temperatures).

Use the right equipment – using damaged or incorrect equipment can injure yourself and others.

Use the correct training surface for the activity.

Use the correct footwear in relation to the playing surface.

Consume more carbohydrate during periods of heavy training – this will ensure you have sufficient energy stores to participate in intense exercise.

Ensure you consume an adequate healthy meal after exercise to replenish your energy stores.

Know your limits – know what you are capable of, and seek advice if you are unsure.

Check that training and competition areas are clear of any potential hazards.

Check that equipment is appropriate for the activity, and not damaged in any way.

When undertaking new activities, make sure these are done gradually.

Allow sufficient time for an appropriate warm-up and cool-down that is specific to the activity.

Use the right technique – incorrect techniques can place undue stress on different parts of the body, and increase the likelihood of injury.

Pay particular attention to the weather conditions when involved in intense activity.

How can the injury prevention guidelines be applied and/or adapted to your specific sport?

Think it over

The protective equipment for many sports has changed dramatically over the years. Choose three sports and highlight the developments in equipment.

Remember!

Many individuals can play a role in preventing injuries – including players, coaches, support staff and parents, among others.

Assessment practice

You are a trainee working with the coach of a local youth sports team (pick a sport that is relevant to your background). Considering all the various risk factors associated with sports injuries, describe the range of measures you could put in place to prevent injuries to players in your team. **P1 P2 M1**

Grading tips

Grading Tip P1

Breaking down your answers into a table, explain (extrinsic and intrinsic risk factors) why different risk factors can lead to sports injuries.

Grading Tip P2

Highlight the different individuals involved, and explain their role in injury prevention.

Explain the different tasks that should be done before a sporting activity (e.g. equipment and playing area checks).

Grading Tip M1

Write a detailed explanation of the relationship between the specific preventive measures and the risk factors they relate to.

17.2 Know about a range of sports injuries and their symptoms

Some knowledge regarding the specific signs and symptoms of different sports injuries is vital to ensure the correct treatment is applied from the onset of the problem. Although initial treatments can be very similar, it is important to try and gain as much knowledge as possible about the injury, as early as possible. If this is done, hopefully the best possible care can be implemented at each stage of treatment. This section addresses a range of common sports injuries and

highlights signs, symptoms and the body's physiological and psychological responses.

It is important to have a good basic knowledge of human anatomy. To work with specific injuries, it is necessary to understand the different body tissues that have been damaged. With a reasonable understanding of human anatomy, a more detailed understanding of your injury can be developed, and therefore the best way to treat it.

From the time of injury, and for a period of time after it has taken place, various bodily changes occur. These can be classified as physiological and psychological responses. The body's response to sports injuries will depend on the type and severity of the injury.

In the majority of injuries, specific physiological body reactions will take place to protect and help heal the injured part.

Physiological responses

As soon as an injury takes place, the body will respond in a number of ways. Damage to body tissue will initiate the primary damage response mechanism, the two main signs and symptoms being pain and inflammation. Causes such as external trauma, overload (excessive use of one or more of the FITT principles – see page 51), repeated load, pressure and friction can cause inflammation, which is associated with the majority of sports injuries. Inflammation is caused by a number of factors, which will also trigger other signs and symptoms:

- accumulation of fluid surrounding the injury
- redness due to an increase in blood flow
- tenderness to touch
- impaired functioning and range of motion (ROM).

Blood clotting

When an injury occurs, and we bleed, the blood must clot to initiate the healing process. Platelets, which are cells within the blood, are activated by chemical reactions when trauma causes blood loss. These platelets then make the blood sticky, and within a short period of time will cause a clot as they stick to the surface of the blood vessels. The clotting mechanism is particularly important, as this process acts as a preliminary phase of the healing process.

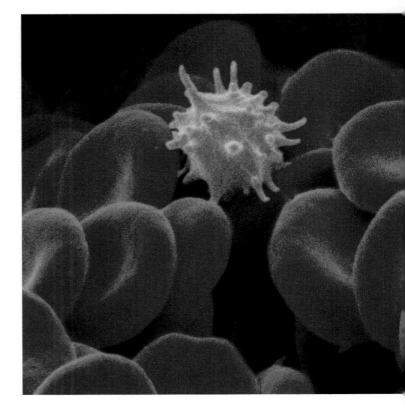

▲ Scanning electron micrograph of an activated blood platelet among red blood cells (unactivated platelets are smooth and oval-shaped) – platelets clump together to prevent bleeding and assist in clot formation (magnification: × 10,2000)

Scar tissue

The development of scar tissue is particularly important in healing of injuries. The remodelling process is concerned with restoring the tissue at the site of an injury as close as possible to its original state. From the time when an injury takes place, scar tissue will start to form, and it is crucial that the correct treatments are applied to regain the original functioning of the body part.

The more severe an injury, the more difficult it will be to restore damaged tissue to its original state. For example, the signs and symptoms of first-, second- and third-degree sprains and strains will be different, and the physiological responses will be more pronounced.

A more detailed explanation of the remodelling process is described on pages 1102–112.

Haematomas

Bleeding is a major physiological response to all injuries. When an acute injury occurs to the body, the damaged tissue will bleed into the surrounding tissues. The amount of bleeding that takes place will be specific to the type and severity of injury. There are two types of haematoma:

- intermuscular haematoma – bleeding occurs within the compartment of the muscle, but does not seep into the surrounding tissue
- intramuscular haematoma – blood escapes into the surrounding tissue (e.g. different muscle compartments).

The different types of haematoma are described in more detail on pages 102–103.

Pain

Many free nerve endings are situated between tissue cells, the number varying depending on the part of the body (for example, there are a large number in the skin). These pain receptors are part of the nervous system and transmit information, via neurons, through the spinal cord to the brain. The function of pain is critical in highlighting damage, preventing further injury to a person. It is essential that pain is interpreted as a warning

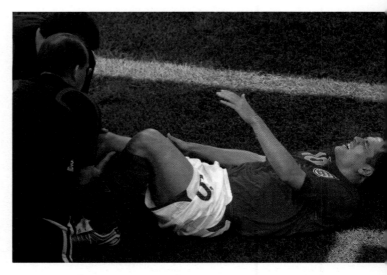

▲ England's Michael Owen, injured at the start of the 2006 FIFA World Cup match with Sweden

sign and the injured tissue should be rested. Depending on the problem, many different pain sensations can be experienced:

- acute (from many trauma injuries)
- aching
- continuous (e.g. heartburn)
- pounding
- burning.

The most prevalent types of pain for sports injuries are acute pain, and a dull ache associated with many overuse injuries. Isolating the type of pain sensation being experienced can help with the swift diagnosis and application of treatment for a sports injury.

Psychological responses

As well as the physiological responses of the body to injury, psychological responses can also cause stress to an athlete. The way a person deals with an injury can vary between individuals, and can either hinder or assist the healing and rehabilitation processes. Some potential negative psychological responses are listed below.

- Fear – can take many forms, including the fear of reoccurrence of an injury, and fear of not returning to full fitness.
- Stress and anxiety – can be felt by an athlete during competition. If the athlete then suffers an injury, these feelings will be increased. As an injury

progresses, concerns regarding the athlete's long- and short-term sporting prospects can become a psychological issue.

- Motivational issues – some injuries can take a long time to heal. As the duration of an injury increases, an athlete's motivation towards their sport may decrease.
- Depression – some athletes may demonstrate symptoms of clinical depression, such as decreased energy levels, constant sadness, withdrawal from social contact, etc.
- Anger – can be towards oneself, the injury, and also other people (particularly if the injury is the fault of another individual).
- Decreased confidence – very common for athletes returning to training and competition. An athlete may suffer from a lack of confidence in their own skill levels, and decreased confidence in their fitness and ability to push their body physically.
- Denial – sometimes an athlete may try to deny the severity of an injury, and try to return to their sport too quickly. It is important that those supporting sports players (e.g. coaches and family) are aware of the nature of the injury and take guidance from medical professionals.
- Frustration – a common issue for many athletes, particularly for long-term injury. The majority of sports players will crave to return to competition, and become frustrated by a lack of physical exercise and/or their specialist sport.
- Isolation from team mates: many team sports players' frustration can be exacerbated by the fact that they will not be involved in competition and training. This can lead to players becoming mentally withdrawn from their team.

The psychological responses to a sports injury will vary dramatically between individuals. Some may suffer no or few negative responses, whereas others may experience a number of psychological issues.

Key Terms

Physiological response The initial response of the body following a sports injury, specific to the injury.

Key Terms

Psychological response The mental aspect of how an athlete copes and comes to terms with their injury and treatment.

Taking it further

Design a questionnaire, and carry out some research looking at the psychological issues surrounding youth sports players, and how suffering an injury has affected them.

Chronic and acute injuries

Often, when we consider sports injuries, we think of the traumatic injuries that occur due to a mishap on a specific occasion, in a game or in training. But many injuries are caused by an accumulation of stress over a period of time, or overuse of a body part. High-level athletic performers are particularly susceptible to such injuries due to the intense training demands. Individuals with anatomical abnormalities or poor techniques are also at risk. Because of the demands of training, overuse injury is becoming endemic in modern sport.

An important way of categorising sports injuries is considering whether they are long-term or short-term. Chronic injuries are long-term injuries that have developed slowly. Acute or traumatic injuries occur suddenly through instant trauma to the individual. Examples could be:

- chronic – a runner develops a stress fracture due to repetitive overloading
- acute – an individual suffers a sprained ankle when cockling over while playing badminton.

Remember!

The main injury categories are:

- extrinsic – caused by forces/risks outside the body
- intrinsic – caused by forces/risks within the body
- chronic – develop when playing sport or exercising over a long period (often overuse injuries)
- acute – occur suddenly when exercising or playing sport.

Note: the severity of the injury is not determined by any of these categorisations.

Activity

Using your prior knowledge, and by researching the different types of injury that can occur, categorise different injuries into the types in Table 17.5.

Chronic intrinsic	Chronic extrinsic
Acute intrinsic	Acute extrinsic

 Table 17.5 Types of injury

Do any trends occur in the types of injury that fall into the different categories?

Injuries common to different parts of the body

Some parts of the human body are more susceptible to sporting injury than others. The joints and limbs are particularly vulnerable, and the head and neck can be susceptible depending on the activity. Parts of the human body can be categorised in a number of ways, including:

- by specific area (e.g. foot, abdomen or shoulder)
- by bodily system (e.g. muscular system or skeletal system).

Note: many injuries can be to more than one area or body system. In sport, the most common types of injury are musculoskeletal (injuries to the muscular or skeletal system, or a combination of both).

Assessment practice

Produce a written report describing how the body responds to a sports injury. Specifically

1. Describe the physiological responses common to most sports injuries. **P3**

2. Describe the psychological responses common to sports injuries. **P4**

3. Explain the physiological and psychological effects common to most sports injuries. **M2**

Grading tips

Grading Tip **P3**

This criterion requires you to describe each physiological change that occurs to the body following a sports injury. You could include some specific examples of sports injuries you are familiar with.

grading tips

Grading Tip **P4**

For this criterion you need to describe some of the typical psychological issues that an athlete may experience in the time following an injury, such as:

- anger
- anxiety
- depression
- frustration
- isolation from team mates
- response to treatment and rehabilitation
- need for motivation
- use of goal-setting.

Grading Tip **M2**

For this criterion you should explain why the physiological responses are taking place and their role in the healing process following an injury. You should also explain why any psychological issues occur, and the short- and long-term effects they may have on the athlete. Make sure you provide a full explanation of both physiological and psychological issues!

How do the psychological and physiological factors interact when a sports player suffers an injury?

Which individual characteristics may contribute to psychological effects of sports injuries in the long and short term?

How can the body's physiological and psychological responses change during the different stages of the healing process?

17.3   Know how to apply methods of treating sports injuries

Some common trends have emerged regarding the types of sporting injury that are prevalent. Collisions with other performers or objects, and twists or turns beyond the body's capabilities, are common causes of acute injury; continued excessive force on a specific body part (e.g. the knee) is associated with chronic injuries. This section details the anatomy and physiology of some common sports injuries. It is important that you are aware of the types of sport that may cause the different injuries outlined, and the specific preventive measures that can be taken.

Types of sports injury

Some minor injuries

■ Abrasion

An abrasion is superficial damage to the skin. In the majority of cases, abrasions (often friction burns) are relatively minor and cover a small area of skin. Many abrasions are caused by contact with a playing surface (e.g. falling and slipping), or clothing rubbing on the body.

Think it over

Which playing surfaces are more likely to cause abrasions when players fall on them?

How can governing bodies find the balance between quality of game play and risks associated with playing surfaces?

■ Cramp

Cramp is an involuntary contraction of muscles. Muscles that are particularly susceptible are the gastrocnemius (calf), the quadriceps (thigh), the hamstrings, the abdomen, the feet and hands, depending on the type of activity.

Cramp is caused by a lack of oxygen to the muscles, or a lack water or salt. Deep breathing can alleviate cramp if poor oxygen supply is the cause. In the case of a lack of water and salt, stretching, taking on more fluids and gentle massage can reduce the problem.

■ Blisters

Blisters are caused as a defence mechanism to help repair damage to the skin. They are a response to a burn or friction, and are fluid that develops under the upper layers of the skin. Avoid popping a blister, as this will make it more susceptible to infection.

■ Stitch

A stitch (exercise-related transient abdominal pain) is an intense, stabbing pain that occurs under the lower rib cage when exercising. Different theories exist as to the cause of a stitch – one theory is that, when completing exercises involving up-and-down motions (such as running), internal organs pull on the diaphragm, causing the pain. To get rid of a stitch when exercising, lean forward pushing your hands against the site of the pain. When you breathe out, do not expel all the air from your lungs, closing your mouth.

Key Terms

Oedema Swelling of any organ or tissue.

Abrasion Damage to the surface of the skin.

Activity

Working in groups, discuss the nature of the following sporting activities and suggest (with appropriate reasons) the types of injury that might be prevalent:

- field hockey
- football
- boxing
- netball
- cricket
- equestrian.

Based on the injuries you have highlighted, suggest strategies to decrease the risk/likelihood of such injuries taking place. Consider the following:

- protective equipment
- specific rules and regulations
- possible future schemes that could be implemented.

Make a table of your suggestions based on Table 17.6.

Sport	Common injuries	Protective equipment	Governing body guidelines	Future schemes
Field hockey				
Netball				
Football				
Cricket				
Boxing				
Equestrianism				

 Table 17.6 Strategies to reduce the risk of sports injuries

Taking it further

'In addition to each sport possessing a specific injury profile, even within a sport it is quite common for different playing positions to be susceptible to different injuries.'
Bird, N. Black and P Newton (1997) *Sports Injuries: Causes, Diagnosis, Treatment and Prevention.* Stanley Thornes, Cheltenham.

Some sports will inevitably result in more injuries to participants; and within a specific sport, some individuals will be more susceptible than others. What factors contribute to the frequency of injury in a particular sport? Why might some individuals playing the same sports be more prone to injuries than others?

Hard and soft tissue injuries

The type of body tissue that is damaged dictates whether it is a soft or hard tissue injury. Hard tissue injuries are to bones, joints and cartilage, whereas soft tissue injuries are to muscles, tendons, ligaments, internal organs and the skin. A combination of both hard and soft tissue injuries can occur, and this must be taken into consideration during the treatment and rehabilitation processes.

■ Hard tissue injuries

Hard tissue injuries are particularly prevalent in contact sports such as football, and in individual sports such as skiing, gymnastics and riding. Hard tissue injuries include fractures, dislocations and cartilage injuries. Although sport can cause skeletal injuries, as with other parts of the anatomy, exercise can result in strengthening and thickening of bone, making injury less likely.

Key Terms

Hard tissue injury Injury to bones, joints and cartilage.

Soft tissue injury Injury to muscles, tendons, ligaments, internal organs and skin.

Fractures

A fracture is a partial or complete break in a bone – a common form of hard tissue injury. Fractures can be categorised into many different types.

Open and closed fractures

A closed fracture is one where relatively little displacement of bone has occurred, which therefore does not cause much damage to the soft tissue surrounding the injury. An open fracture is one in which the fractured ends of the bone/s break through the skin. Open fractures have a high risk of infection, so it is vital that they are dealt with immediately after injury occurs. All fractures are relatively serious injuries, and specialist professional attention should be sought in all cases.

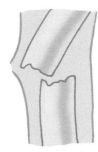 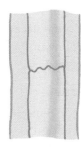

▲ **An open or compound fracture (left) and a closed or simple fracture (right)**

Complete and incomplete fractures

Some fractures do not crack the full length of the bone. This is an incomplete fracture. Fractures where a complete break in the bone occurs (when more than one fragment exists) are called complete fractures.

The way an injury takes place will cause bones to break in different ways. Most occur due to direct impact, but the site of the injury and how it occurs will mean different types of fracture are possible. The treatments for different fractures are slightly different, so it is important that the correct category of injury is diagnosed.

Greenstick fracture

The bone bends and splits without causing a full break in the bone (resembling a bending tree twig). This type of fracture is common among children, because children's bones are not fully developed and not as hard as fully matured bone.

Transverse fracture

A crack that is perpendicular (at right angles) to the length of the bone.

Oblique fracture

Similar to a transverse fracture, but the break occurs diagonally across the bone, resulting in sharp ends where the break occurred.

Spiral fracture

Very similar to an oblique fracture, but the break is in a spiralling motion along the bone. This often occurs due to a twisting motion accompanied by a high amount of stress to the bone.

Comminuted fracture

Produces multiple fragments of bone. With these types of injury, it is often necessary to use screws and wires to assist with healing of the bone, and long rehabilitation is also often required.

Impacted fracture

Both ends of the bone are forced together in a compression motion. Again, this type of fracture can be complicated, and rehabilitation is needed to restore normal functioning.

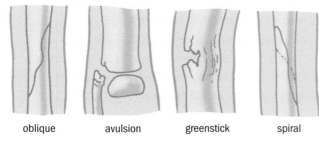

oblique   avulsion   greenstick   spiral

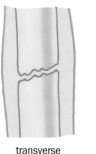  

transverse   comminuted   impacted

▲ The main types of fracture

Avulsion fracture

A fragment of bone becomes detached at the attachment point (either ligament, tendon or muscle).

Stress fracture

This is different from the other forms as it is not caused by a traumatic injury, but develops due to overuse or fatigue. A stress fracture can also be called a fatigue or insufficiency fracture, and generally occurs in weight-bearing bones

Stress fractures can be particularly difficult to spot using traditional X-ray equipment, particularly at the early stages of development.

Think it over

Of the different types of fracture, which are more likely to produce an open fracture, and why?

Activity

Produce a poster that describes the different types of fracture and gives information on the types of accident that may cause them.

Cartilage injuries

Cartilage comes in different forms, serving various purposes in the body. Cartilage acts as ossification (bone growth) sites, acts as the skeleton for a foetus, keeps tubes of the body open (such as the epiglottis), supports areas of the body requiring tensile strength (such as between the ribs), and lines adjoining bones.

Cartilage is vitally important in minimising the impact of internal skeletal forces during sports and general life activities. During intense exercise such as running, the forces on the knee, for example, can be huge. Cartilage absorbs the impact of bones while reducing the friction. Damage to cartilage is often caused by wear and tear, and can be a chronic problem.

Cartilage damage is often due to a chronic problem resulting from a degenerative condition (often osteoarthritis), or overuse due to long-term sporting or exercise activity. Acute trauma can also cause damage to cartilage, which can occur alongside other injuries (such as a dislocation).

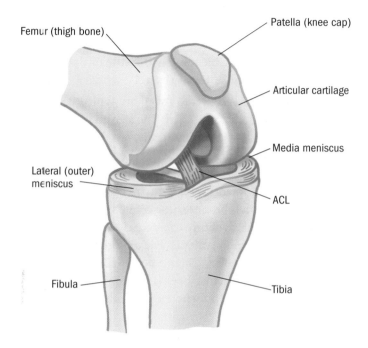

▲ The cartilage of the knee

Osteoarthritis can be broken down into three distinct phases:

1 the amount of cartilage decreases progressively
2 the body attempts to repair the cartilage
3 destruction of the bone occurs.

The exact causes of osteoarthritis are not fully understood. Contributory factors may include:

- long-term, high-impact sports participation
- a history of injury, particularly twisting injuries
- anatomical abnormalities in joints
- genetic predisposition
- poor muscular strength.

General cartilage damage can be common for long-term sports participants. Symptoms to be aware of include:

- stiffness of the affected area
- locking of a joint

- decreased ROM around a joint
- pain
- swelling around the joint.

Dislocation

A dislocation occurs when the correct alignment of bones becomes disrupted, moving them out of their normal position. Such injuries are often caused by impact with another player or object, or by a fall. Typical sites of dislocation due to sports are shoulders, hips, knees, ankles, elbows, fingers and toes.

If you suspect that a dislocation has occurred, it is important to seek medical attention to ensure the bones are replaced in correct alignment without damaging the joint. Very often, a dislocated joint will also result in ligament damage. The joints in the body are held together by ligaments – when a dislocation occurs they can become stretched, sometimes permanently. If this happens, a person becomes more susceptible to a reoccurrence of the same injury, particularly in joints such as the shoulder or kneecap.

Key Terms

Fracture A partial or complete break in a bone.

Dislocation A displacement of the position of bones, often caused by a sudden impact.

Subluxation An incomplete or partial dislocation.

■ Soft tissue injuries

Sprains and strains

Many people often find it difficult to differentiate between a sprain and a strain. It is quite simple, as long as you have a reasonable understanding of basic anatomy:

- a sprain is damage to ligaments (stretch or tear)
- a strain is damage to muscle or tendon.

Sprain

The causes of a sprain are generally due to a sudden twist, impact or fall that makes the joint move outside its normal range of movement. Sprains commonly occur to the ankle, wrist, thumb, knee, or generally the parts of the body that are at risk when involved in specific sporting activities.

The severity of sprains depends on different factors. More than one ligament can be damaged at the same time, and the more ligaments affected, the more severe the injury. Also, whether the ligament is stretched or torn (either partially or fully) determines how severe the injury is. Sprains can be categorised as either first, second or third degree, depending on severity:

- first-degree sprain – stretching of ligament (no tear)
- second-degree sprain – partial tear of ligament
- third-degree sprain – complete tear of ligament, or detachment of ligament from the bone.

Strain

A strain is damage to a muscle or tendon caused by overstretching that particular area. Similarly to a sprain, a strain can result in a simple overstretching of the muscle or, in more serious examples, partial or even complete rupture. Strains can be common in sports involving dynamic lunging, particularly when combined with sprinting activities, and in contact sports (e.g. tackling in football).

The severity of a strain is determined by a three-grade categorisation system:

- grade 1 – relatively minor damage to the muscle fibres (cells) – less than 5%
- grade 2 – the muscle is not completely ruptured, but more extensive damage to the fibres has occurred
- grade 3 – a complete rupture of the muscle has occurred – in most cases this will require surgery and rehabilitation.

Key Terms

Sprain A stretch or tear of ligaments.

Strain An injury to muscle or tendon.

Haematoma

A haematoma is a pocket of congealed blood that is often caused by bleeding to a specific area of the body. Haematomas may be small bruises, or can be more

serious when they occur to different organs (such as the brain), or cause large amounts of blood flow disruption. The majority of haematomas caused by sports injuries occur to the muscles, and are caused by impact or rupture. When we exercise, blood flow to the working muscles increases dramatically; this ensures sufficient oxygen and nutrients are supplied to the muscles, while removing metabolic waste products. If damage occurs to the muscle, bleeding will occur. Due to the increased blood flow, much more bleeding within the muscle can take place during high-intensity exercise activity.

Muscular haematomas fall into two main types, intermuscular and intramuscular. The size and shape of skeletal muscles varies dramatically, but the general structure remains similar. Muscle fibres (cells) are bundled together in groups and surrounded by a membrane. These are grouped in further bundles, again surrounded by a membrane. These groups of muscle fibres mean that the structure of a muscle is broken down into a number of compartments. For a more detailed overview of the muscular system, see Sport Book 1, Unit 1. Whether a muscular haematoma is inter- or intramuscular depends on where the bleeding takes place.

An intermuscular haematoma is when damage to the muscle causes blood flow within the muscle belly. In this case, the bleeding does not seep into the surrounding tissues, but is restricted to specific compartments within the muscle. An intramuscular haematoma, in contrast, results in blood escaping to the surrounding tissue. With these types of injury, the resultant bruise can spread to areas where the injuries did not occur. Both intra- and intermuscular haematomas can be either superficial or deep (superficial being towards the surface and deep being further inside the muscle).

Key Terms

Contusion A bruise – often caused by impact. Damage to the capillaries allows blood to escape into the surrounding tissues.

Haematoma A collection of clotted blood due to bleeding in a specific area of the body.

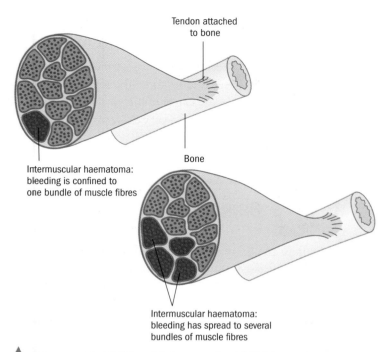

Tendon attached
to bone

Bone

Intermuscular haematoma:
bleeding is confined to
one bundle of muscle fibres

Intermuscular haematoma:
bleeding has spread to several
bundles of muscle fibres

▲ **Intermuscular (left) and intramuscular (right) haematomas**

■ Head injuries

Impact to the head – either a clash of heads between players, or a strike to the head of one individual – can be common in contact sports such as rugby. All head injuries should be treated as potentially serious, and some basic checks for specific symptoms must be carried out. Two distinct problems can develop due to blows to the head: concussion and compression.

Concussion

Concussion is caused by the brain shaking inside the skull. This causes a temporary loss of consciousness or functioning. Other signs and symptoms include:

- partial or complete loss of consciousness, usually of short duration
- shallow breathing
- nausea and vomiting can occur when the person starts to regain consciousness
- the injured person will often describe 'seeing stars'
- loss of memory of what has happened just before and immediately after the incident
- headache may occur.

Compression

Compression is bleeding within the skull, causing a build up of pressure on the brain. Compression is a very

serious condition, and has distinctly different signs and symptoms from concussion. Some of these include:

- decreasing level of consciousness as the condition worsens
- unconsciousness from the time of injury – the person may be deeply unconscious
- nausea and vomiting may occur
- the size of the pupils may be different
- one or both pupils may not respond to light
- deep, noisy, often slow breathing
- dry and flushed skin
- an intense headache is also common.

It helps to be able to pick up on the signs and symptoms of both injuries, to be able to inform the medical services. For both concussion and compression, it is important to seek medical attention.

■ Tendonitis

The repetitive and high-impact nature of sporting activity involves continued muscle actions, pulling on tendons, resulting in movement of the skeleton. Tendons will normally glide smoothly with the contraction of the muscles, allowing efficient movements. The varied and dynamic movements involved in sports can, from time to time, place friction on the tendons causing irritation and inflammation. This inflammation is called tendonitis, and is generally caused by overuse, particularly with increased or different training demands. As well as overuse, anatomical abnormalities and age can increase the possibility of developing tendonitis. The sites of the injury will generally be related to a person's sport. Common susceptible areas include the rotator cuff (shoulder), wrist extensor tendon, patellar tendon, and achilles tendon. The symptoms normally subside within a few days, but without care the problem can last weeks or even months.

■ Bursitis

An injury that occurs in relation to tendonitis is bursitis. Bursae (singular: bursa) are small, fluid-filled sacs scattered around the body, which act as cushions for the tendons, preventing friction with the bone. With repeated movements or impact, bursae can become swollen, and this swelling is called bursitis. Common sites are the shoulder, elbow, hip, knee and ankle. The severity of bursitis can vary, with healing time being as long as a year in some cases, although more minor cases can be rectified in a matter of weeks.

Tendonitis and bursitis can be treated using the PRICED procedure (see page 108). Some cases may be treated with corticosteroid injections to reduce the swelling. Anti-inflammatory drugs can also reduce the symptoms.

Key Terms

Tendonitis Inflammation of the fibres within a tendon.

Bursitis Inflammation of the bursa (sack of synovial fluid).

Think it over

Which sports will cause inflammation of different parts of the body?

■ Shin splints

Shin splints is a painful condition, commonly developing in runners, caused by overuse. Severity can be from mild to severe, as the pain often develops in the inside (medial) edge of the tibia. Inflammation of the sheath that surrounds the tibia, due to the forces of muscle actions of the lower leg, is a major cause of shin splints.

■ Back pain

Back pain is a very common problem for many individuals in society, as well as sports players. The back is central to the posture and movements in the majority of sports skills, so pain can cause major disruptions to performance. Due to the complex nature (in terms of the number of different structures) and size of the back, problems can be caused by various factors and are potentially difficult to treat. 'Four out of five adults have at least one bout of back pain sometime during life. In fact, back pain is one of the most common reasons for

health care visits and missed work.' (www.mayoclinic.com/health/back-pain/DS00171)

Treatment may involve anti-inflammatory drugs, physiotherapy, massage and many other approaches, depending on the specific cause of the pain. Sometimes the actual cause of pain can be very difficult to pinpoint, increasing the difficulty of treatment.

Remember!

Injuries can be to either hard body tissue (bones, joints, cartilage) or soft body tissue (muscles, tendons, ligaments, internal organs, skin). Some injuries can damage both hard and soft tissue.

First aid

The severity of sporting injuries can vary hugely, from minor cuts and bruises to life-threatening problems. Some are serious enough to need medical attention and specialist treatment; others are relatively minor and can be treated with simple home care. Some knowledge of first aid can potentially save a person's life, and can also help with minor problems to speed the recovery process and limit potential complications.

First aid is the care given immediately to an injured person. The advised procedures are to minimise the impact of an injury and reduce the risk of future complications. Due to the continuous developments in our knowledge of anatomy and physiology, advances in first aid procedures are continually being made. For this reason, the protocol for treating different injuries can change from time to time. For detailed, up-to-date information on first aid principles, a first aid manual should be available, also various training courses are available, many of which will need updating on a regular basis.

With potentially serious accidents, a specific primary survey should be carried out. This is to ensure that a patient is breathing, so it is of paramount importance that it is carried out first.

Primary survey

Danger – check the area for potential danger to yourself. Another casualty will worsen the problem. Also remove any potentially hazardous objects from around the casualty.

Response – check if there is any response from the injured person. If not, call for help immediately. Do not leave the injured person.

Airway – be aware of potential neck injuries. Gently tip the head backwards and check if there are any foreign objects in the person's mouth, blocking the airway.

Breathing – check to see if the person is breathing (up to 10 seconds). If not, send someone for an ambulance (dial 999).

Circulation – check for signs of circulation. If not, cardiopulmonary resuscitation (CPR, see below) should commence.

Secondary survey

A secondary survey should be carried out if an unconscious person is breathing. This is done to check all areas of the body for damage. The process should be carried out quickly and in a systematic way.

Bleeding – check the area, and check the patient head-to-toe for blood.

Head and neck – check for bruising and/or deformity. Gently feel the back of the neck for damage.

Shoulders and chest – compare the shoulders; feel for fractures in the collar bones and ribs.

Abdomen and pelvis – feel around the abdomen for abnormalities and to see if the person feels any pain.

Legs and arms – check legs, then arms, for fracture and any other clues.

Pockets – check the pockets of the person to make sure that when you roll them into the recovery position, items do not injure them. Be very cautious of sharp objects (e.g. needles). Have a witness if you remove anything from their pockets.

Recovery – making sure that you don't cause further damage to the person, place them in the recovery position (see below). If a neck injury is suspected, this should be done with the assistance of other people supporting the casualty's whole body.

Be aware of jewellery to make sure it is not worsening the problem – remove it in such cases. Also look for medic alerts (such as diabetes bracelets/necklaces).

Make a mental and/or written note of anything you have observed during the primary and secondary surveys. This information should be passed on to the emergency services to help with treating the patient.

The recovery position is a way of positioning an unconscious casualty, minimising the risk of their airway becoming compromised. Two potential dangers that are overcome are:

- the tongue relaxing and blocking the airway
- the patient vomiting and the vomit blocking the airway.

▲ The recovery position – turn the casualty onto their side; lift their chin forward in the open airway position and adjust their hand under their cheek as necessary; check the casualty can't roll forwards or backwards

Cardiopulmonary resuscitation

CPR is performed when a person is not breathing and does not show any signs of circulation. This process is carried out to keep the vital organs alive until help arrives. An oxygen supply to the brain is needed to sustain life, and this is done via inhaled air and the movement of blood in the body. If a person is not breathing and their heart is not beating, this will need to be done for them.

■ The CPR process

- If a casualty is not breathing, make sure you get someone to call for the emergency services immediately.

- Check for signs of circulation (10 seconds) – if there is no sign, begin CPR.
- Provide 30 chest compressions (at a rate of 100 per minute) followed by two rescue breaths. This should continue until the casualty recovers or the emergency services arrive.

Chest compressions
- Locate the base of the breast bone (sternum). Place heel of your hand in the centre of the chest.
- Interlock your fingers with your other hand.
- Compressions are completed with locked elbows, with shoulders vertical.
- The chest should be compressed 4–5cm (1.5 to 2 inches).

Rescue breaths
- Tip the casualty's head backwards.
- Nip the person's nose, and make a seal with your mouth around their mouth.
- Breathe slowly, making the person's chest rise.

(a)

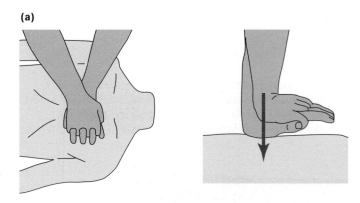

(b)

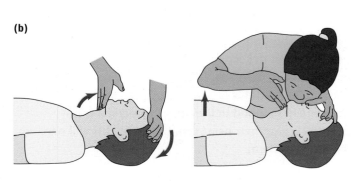

▲ The CPR process: (a) chest compressions, (b) rescue breaths

For children under 8 years old, chest compression should be carried out with one hand and rescue breaths should be gentle.

For babies (under 1 year old), chest compressions should be given with two fingers and rescue breaths carried out to mouth and nose very gently.

For a more detailed explanation of the CPR process, an up-to-date first-aid manual should be referred to, and ideally a first-aid course completed.

Shock

Shock is caused by a drop in blood pressure or blood volume. Shock can be a secondary reaction to many serious injuries (for example with major blood loss). There are three classifications:
- cardiogenic shock – the most common type, caused by the heart not pumping effectively
- hypovolaemic shock – caused by a loss in bodily fluids resulting in low blood volume, can be common for traumatic injuries such as major sports injuries
- anaphylactic shock – caused by a severe allergic reaction.

Signs and symptoms of shock:
- increased pulse rate (can become weaker as the condition worsens)
- pale and clammy skin, sweating as shock worsens (lips can become blue)
- fast, shallow breathing
- nausea or vomiting
- dizziness
- feelings of weakness
- with severe shock, deep breathing can develop, with confusion, anxiety and possibly aggression
- casualties can become unconscious.

■ Treatment of shock
- The cause of shock must be addressed (e.g. a fracture must be immobilised).
- Lay the person down and, if possible, raise the legs (keeping the flow of blood to the vital organs).
- Keep the person warm.
- Loosen any tight clothing.

With all cases of shock, the emergency services should be contacted immediately. The casualty should be monitored continuously (breathing, pulse and response).

Bleeding

Loss of blood is very common in many sports. Causes of blood loss can vary from very minor scratches to serious lacerations and puncture wounds. With all cases of blood loss, it is important to prevent infection in both the casualty and the person treating the wound. Disposable gloves should be worn at all times when dealing with blood. The main priorities of blood-loss treatment are to stop the bleeding, prevent the person from going into shock, and reduce the risk of infection to a wound.

■ Treating bleeds

Direct pressure should be applied to the site of bleeding using an appropriate bandage or gauze. Do not remove any large, impaled objects from a person. If an object is imbedded in a person, pressure can be applied at either side of the object. An absorbent, sterile dressing large enough to cover the wound completely should be applied firmly without restricting blood flow to the rest of the body.

Activity

With all first-aid procedures, there is a risk of infection to those carrying out the procedures. For the scenarios in Table 17.7, indicate what can cause infection, and the method of minimising risk. Try to think of more than one method of protection.

First-aid treatment	Potential hazards	Protection/action by first-aider
Bleeding		
CPR		
Shock		
Unconscious casualty		

▲ Table 17.7 Treatments, infection risks, and actions to minimise risk

Note: the completion of this unit does not qualify you as a first-aider. To perform any first-aid procedure correctly, it is advised that you complete a recognised first-aid qualification. If you do witness a serious accident, the most qualified and experienced individual should be the one who carries out the first-aid procedures. Do not crowd the injured person, and assist in any way that the first-aider asks.

Fortunately, the majority of sports injuries are not serious enough to require CPR or treatment for shock. However, appropriate treatment is required for all injuries – if in any doubt, a professional opinion is required. The correct treatment of injuries is critical to ensure that the healing process can occur without complications (further problems).

Key Terms

First aid Care given to an injured person immediately following an injury or accident.

Range of treatments

In assessing sporting injuries, you are likely to have seen the accident take place, and you will already have a reasonable understanding of the specific body part that may be damaged. In this context, some aspects of the primary and secondary survey can become obsolete, and a more specific sports-related assessment is more relevant. One such technique is performed by using the acronym SALTAPS.

To ensure the best efforts are made to carry out an accurate assessment of the signs and symptoms, and hopefully diagnose the injury itself, the following specific guidelines are used to assess injured people at the point of occurrence.

- **See** – observe the injury taking place.
- **Ask** – ask questions about the injury, where it hurts, type of pain, etc.
- **Look** – for specific signs, e.g. redness, swelling, foreign objects.
- **Touch** – palpate the injured part to identify painful areas and swelling.

- **Active movement** – ask the injured person if they can move the injured part of the body without help.
- **Passive movement** – if the person can move the injured part, gently move it through a full ROM.
- **Strength testing** – can the player stand or put pressure on the injury? Can they resume playing? If so, make sure you continue to observe them.

Note: with increasingly serious injuries, it is important to stop the SALTAPS process at an appropriate stage.

In the treatment of all sports-related injuries, the most appropriate individuals to give treatment are the most experienced. The aim of the SALTAPS process is to make an accurate assessment of the type, severity and location of an injury. This can be difficult for some sports injuries – even the most experienced practitioners can find an initial on-site diagnosis very difficult.

Case study

You are a first-aider on work experience alongside the sports therapist for a youth football team. During a match, two players collide in a tackle. After the incident, one of the players clutches their leg and is clearly in substantial pain. Following the SALTAPS procedure, highlight some typical responses that you may encounter, and the possible injuries. For the injuries you identify (e.g. strains, sprains, fractures, bruises), highlight the point at which you should stop the SALTAPS procedure.

For acute but less severe traumatic injuries, the initial treatment should involve the PRICED procedure. When soft tissues are injured they become inflamed, and the purpose of treatment is to reduce swelling prevent further damage and ease pain.

- **Protect** – the person and injured part of the body, to minimise the risk of further injury.
- **Rest** – to allow healing and prevent any further damage.
- **Ice** – stops the injured area from swelling.
- **Compression** – acts as support and also prevents swelling.
- **Elevation** – reduce blood flow to the area, reducing swelling with the aid of gravity.
- **Diagnosis** – needs to be done by a professional.

The treatment of chronic injuries will depend on the type and cause. In many cases, the cause of such injuries can be difficult both to diagnose and to treat. Anatomical problems such as muscular imbalance or leg malalignment (intrinsic factors; see page 87) can be a common cause of chronic injury. Extrinsic factors can also play a part, such as incorrect equipment, poor conditions, inappropriate playing surfaces and incorrect technique. These factors, which will have developed over time, will need to be corrected to prevent reoccurrence of the injury.

Key Terms

PRICED Procedure for the treatment of acute injuries – Protect, Rest, Ice, Compression, Elevation, Diagnosis.

SALTAPS Procedure for the assessment of an injured person – See, Ask, Look, Touch, Active movement, Passive movement, Strength testing.

Assessment practice

Working in a coaching, teaching or performance environment will expose you, or other participants, to sports injuries from time to time. In your role as first-aider on work experience alongside a sports therapist, describe the steps you would take when you witness four different sports injuries taking place. **P5**

Grading tips

Grading Tip **P5**

Choose four contrasting types of sports injury to demonstrate your knowledge of a range of treatment methods. Try to include injuries at different severity levels to show your understanding of a range of treatment methods.

Describe how you would approach the injury, and what you would expect to see using the SALTAPS procedure. Indicate at what point you would stop the SALTAPS procedure.

Consider the first-aid methods that are most appropriate for each specific injury.

17.4 Be able to plan and construct treatment and rehabilitation programmes for two common sports injuries

Treatment

Rehabilitation is concerned with restoring a sportsperson's functionality to a normal state, or as near as is physically possible. The rehabilitation protocols used are concerned with the body's physiological responses to the injury, and the healing process of the body's tissue. The healing process for many sports injuries can take time. With an appropriate and systematic rehabilitation programme, a sportsperson can return to training and performance more quickly. Without rehabilitation, the injured body area may remain weak, and the injury will be more likely to reoccur.

Ideally the rehabilitation process will involve a team of people providing specific support for the injured athlete.

These can be athletic trainer and assistants, an athletic physician, coaches, strength and conditioning specialists, family support and, crucially, the athlete him/or herself. The specialist advice that each group of individuals can give is important in the long-term success of the programme. This applies particularly to serious injuries where rehabilitation can be a long, time-consuming, and often painful and frustrating process. A strong support network can be vital in assisting athletes with their programmes – research has shown that severely injured athletes receiving strong social support from certified trainers are more likely to believe in their rehabilitation programme.

If rehabilitation is not done effectively, and/or the person returns to activity too quickly, the injured body part is far more susceptible to a reoccurrence of the injury. There is pressure on athletes, from both themselves and others, to return to competition – and also pressure on those involved in the rehabilitation. Particularly with high-level performers, sports injury rehabilitation can be more aggressive and game-related than for other individuals. It is vitally important that rehabilitation does not cross the potentially thin line between a well implemented programme and one that pushes an athlete too far. Sports-specific demands must be incorporated into the rehabilitation programme.

Decreased functioning due to injury

Restoring the injured person's functioning back to its optimum state must take into consideration different aspects of the negative effects of the injury. The body's reactions to an injury will mean that various anatomical changes have occurred, and these must all be addressed during rehabilitation. Negative anatomical changes that may have occurred include:

- ROM will have decreased at the site of injury, and possibly in other areas of the body
- connective fibres (e.g. muscles and tendons) may have shortened
- general and specific muscle strength and endurance will have decreased
- attachment points (ligaments and tendons) around the site of the injury may be weakened.

Development of all these elements must be considered, in a strategic and systematic manner, through a rehabilitation programme.

Rehabilitation

■ Functions of rehabilitation

There are a number of different aspects to a rehabilitation programme, all of which address the negative anatomical changes that have occurred in the body. Some important functions of a programme are to:

- reduce pain and swelling
- ensure correct immediate first aid is provided, resulting in sufficient reduction in pain and swelling

- minimise pain in subsequent hours, days and weeks
- re-establish neuromuscular control of the injured area of the body
- restore ROM of the affected joints
- restore lost muscular strength, power and endurance
- develop core stability, posture and balance
- maintain cardiovascular fitness to an attainable level.

■ The rehabilitation process

The five stages of the rehabilitation process are:

- acute stage
- re-establishing functional activity
- strengthening exercises
- ongoing treatments
- gradual increase in activity.

Key Terms

Rehabilitation Restoring a person's functionality to a normal state, or as near as physically possible.

■ The healing process

Many of the physiological responses to injury follow a clear sequence and time scale. The signs and symptoms of an injury can be a clear indicator of the progression of the healing process.

- Inflammatory response phase (see page 93) – occurs as soon as an injury takes place, and is the start of the healing process. Inflammation ensures that healing properties in the blood can access the injured part of the body while simultaneously disposing of injury by-products.
- Repair phase – occurs after a few hours of injury, and can last as long as six weeks. Some of the signs and symptoms are similar to the inflammatory response phase. Involves rebuilding the damaged structure and healing the damaged areas. Scar tissue will develop during this phase.
- Remodelling phase – scar tissue development will imitate the original structures prior to the injury. If appropriate care is given to the injury, long-term scarring will decrease, and strength and ROM will improve at the site of the injury.

Remember!

Each phase of the healing process can be prolonged by inappropriate management techniques. It is important to encourage movement exercises, as developing scar tissue can shrink over time and can limit ROM.

■ Specific rehabilitation principles

The various techniques used during rehabilitation of sports-related and other injuries aim to restore the individual's functioning to as near normal as reasonably possible. The following outlines some of the specific techniques used during injury rehabilitation. Consider which methods should be used for different types of injury, and at which phase of the healing and rehabilitation process.

Constant evaluation of the injury is important to determine the efficiency of the healing process and how well rehabilitation is progressing. Functional testing of aspects such as strength, power, ROM and general fitness can be incorporated into a programme in a systematic manner. It is also important to ensure a programme is flexible, to allow for setbacks or developments in functionality. Medication can be used alongside the physical aspects of therapy.

Pain

Pain serves a useful purpose, indicating damage to the body. Controlling pain is particularly important in the initial stages of injury, and can be an ongoing issue with more serious tissue damage. Medication is the most common method of pain control. People experience and cope with pain in different ways, some better than others. The psychology of pain is a complex subject, and different techniques can be used to help with pain management. A positive mental state can reduce pain and distract from the specific pain. Biofeedback (information given on physical functions such as heart rate and blood pressure, and the development of strategies to decrease pain), hypnosis, relaxation techniques and behavioural therapy are examples of psychological methods of controlling pain.

Bracing

Preventing excessive and damaging movements can be very important for some types of injury. For example, fractures will normally need a cast to allow the injury to heal and prevent potential worsening of the break. Braces may be used for a variety of injuries – braces for the knee, elbow and ankle are common, and often allow adjustable movement degrees. Many types of brace can be used immediately following an injury (e.g. a sprain), and also during rehabilitation and gradual return to training.

Taping

Another method of protecting or preventing worsening of an injury is taping. This can also be used to protect body parts (e.g. the ankle) when no injury is present. The aim is to provide stability to a joint without significantly inhibiting its function. Taping acute injuries can be problematic, as it will reduce blood flow to the affected area and inhibit healing. Taping is often most beneficial during rehabilitation.

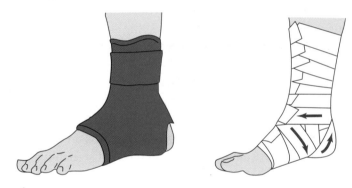

▲ An ankle brace (left) and ankle taping (right)

Proprioception and coordination

Proprioception is the mechanism by which the body can sense the stretch, pressure, tension and position of body parts. Retraining of a person's proprioception is important to restore normal functioning following injury. Located in muscles, tendons, joints and ligaments are proprioceptors (sensors) that detect changes in our body position and give constant feedback. Proprioception is critical to many sports, as it allows us to perform movements efficiently. It is related to coordination (which is more specifically skill-related). As a rehabilitation programme progresses, more specific sports-related exercises, and increased resistance and impact, should be incorporated. Some examples of proprioceptive rehabiliation exercises and equipment include:

- simple balance exercises becoming progressively harder (e.g. with eyes closed)
- balance board
- wobble-board exercises
- gym ball
- throwing and catching
- mini-trampoline (bouncing on different legs, etc.).

Stretching

Restoring the ROM is vital to limit the chances of an injury reoccurring. With the majority of injuries, inflammation and general damage will have dramatically reduced the movement possible at the joints near or at the site of injury. Potentially, ROM at other joints of the body will also have decreased, because exercise levels will have dropped.

Stretching of muscles is an important ingredient of any warm-up and cool-down and will minimise the risk of injury (see pages 52 and 55). Stretching should also be incorporated into a rehabilitation programme to regain ROM.

Advice on the best stretching methods has changed over the years, with some methods being replaced (some can cause damage to different parts of the body – e.g. bouncing while touching your toes puts stress on your lower back). Distinctly different methods of stretching are used in ROM exercises:

- dynamic stretching – controlled movements towards the limits of ROM (e.g. swinging arms and legs)
- static stretching – holding a stretch at the furthest ROM
- passive stretching – similar to static stretching, but involves stretching using either a piece of apparatus or another person
- active stretching – similar to static stretching, but involves holding a position with only the assistance of the surrounding muscle groups
- proprioceptive neuromuscular facilitation (PNF) stretching – combines stretching with muscular contraction.

PNF is fast-developing and is used in a number of sports (e.g. gymnastics and dance) as well as for rehabilitation.

Think it over

The different methods of stretching are all useful in developing ROM. Working in groups, decide at which stage of the rehabilitation process you would use the different methods identified.

A stretch is performed by moving the limb or joint toward the limits of ROM, then force is applied by the person stretching against a resistance (either a partner or apparatus) (see Unit 14, page 57).

General fitness

During rehabilitation, it is important to ensure the different components of fitness are not overlooked. It can be easy to become preoccupied with the specific injury, and forget about keeping up your general fitness levels and functioning of different parts of the body. For example, a person rehabilitating a leg injury will need to consider upper-body ROM as well as the knees, hips and ankles. Cardiovascular endurance levels will be negatively affected as a result of injury, and endurance exercise should be encouraged as soon as possible, in conjunction with other specific rehabilitation exercises.

Cryotherapy

Cryotherapy is the use of cold temperatures to treat both acute and chronic injuries. General benefits of this process involve reducing swelling, pain and muscle spasm. Cryotherapy causes vasoconstriction (narrowing of the blood vessels). In addition to the treatment of injuries, cold can be used for general sporting purposes. Ice baths are often used by athletes, following intense training sessions, to help speed the recovery process.

Thermotherapy

Following the first 48 hours of acute injury, heat treatments (thermotherapy) can be used to help with the healing process. An increase in blood flow to the affected area of the body will mean the blood's healing properties and nutrients can access the injury, speeding up the process. It is important not to use such treatments too soon (due to the risk of haemorrhage) as this can inhibit or worsen the healing of the injury. As well as acute traumas, heat treatments can also be used for overuse injuries.

Some specific methods of heat treatment involve:

- contrast baths (hot and cold treatments)
- ultrasound
- whirlpools
- hydrocollator packs (moist superficial heat).

Strength training

Strengthening exercises are very important throughout rehabilitation, as this aspect of fitness will have deteriorated as a result of an injury. Developing muscular strength, endurance and power is an essential element of rehabilitation. Muscle atrophy is a decrease in muscle size that will take place due to injury and reduced physical training. Static and dynamic strength-training methods can be used to address the problem, with increased resistance and impact later in a programme. Resistance machines, free weights and some endurance machines (e.g. exercise bike) can be used for this aspect of rehabilitation. Exercises should be specific to the injured area, but the whole body should also be considered to prevent muscular imbalances.

Massage

Sports massage is useful to athletes without injury (see Unit 20). Various massage techniques can reduce muscular tension, identify muscular imbalances, and restore balance to the musculoskeletal system. Massage can be beneficial as part of a rehabilitation programme, but is not advisable in the initial stages of acute injury, as it could worsen the problem – it is very important that massage is not used until at least 48 hours after an acute injury.

Electrical stimulation

The contraction of skeletal muscles is initiated by electrical impulses from the nervous system. For this reason, providing small electrical impulses can help with muscle strengthening following surgery. This type of treatment can also be used to assist with the healing process and prevent pain. A method of electrical stimulation involves a transcutaneous electrical nerve stimulation (TENS) machine. This provides small electrical impulses transmitted through pads placed on the skin, the user controlling the impulse strength.

Acupuncture can be effective in pain management

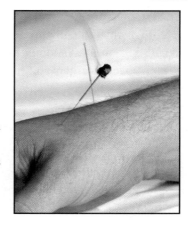

Acupuncture

An alternative type of treatment, which has been practised in China and other far eastern countries for thousands of years, is acupuncture. The use of acupuncture has grown in recent years, particularly with respect to pain management. According to the philosophy behind acupuncture, the body has many specific points that can be accessed to deal with a certain problem. The process involves inserting very fine needles into the relevant acupuncture sites just underneath the skin and assisting with the body's 'energy flow'.

Think it over

At which stage of the healing and rehabilitation process would it be best to use the different methods for different injuries? Working in groups, make a table like the one below.

Method	Inflammatory response	Repair	Remodelling phase
Flexibility stretching			
Taping			
Cryotherapy			
Strengthening exercises			
Coordination exercises			
Electrotherapy			
Massage			
Thermotherapy			
Acupuncture			

▲ Table 17.8 At which stage should each method be used?

The establishment of short- and long-term goals is a key feature of any rehabilitation programme. Goal-setting can also act as a psychological device, giving the injured person specific targets and time scales to aim for.

Key Terms

Acupuncture A treatment that involves inserting needles to different acupuncture points in the body. The technique is common in the treatment of pain.

Atrophy Decrease or wasting away of a body part (often muscle).

Cryotherapy Local or general use of low temperature, often to prevent bleeding, provide pain relief and reduce swelling.

Hydrotherapy Aquatic training that takes place in water. Can have both physical and psychological benefits.

PNF Proprioceptive neuromuscular facilitation – a method of flexibility training.

Proprioception Mechanism by which the body can sense the stretch, pressure, tension and position of body parts.

Thermotherapy Heat treatment that can assist the healing process for an injury after the acute stage.

Factors hindering the healing process

Recovery from injury can be a long process, and is often physically and mentally demanding. Complications can often occur due to specific problems with the extent of the injury; but other issues can hinder the healing and rehabilitation process. More serious injuries will inevitably take longer, and be more complicated to heal and rehabilitate. Also, the complexity of an injury can inhibit how well an individual can heal and train.

A history of a particular injury, or reoccurrence of an existing injury, can be a factor negatively affecting the healing process. The time scale, and also the effectiveness of healing, can be affected. Psychological factors can also influence the athlete, as fear of repeating an injury can affect their capabilities during rehabilitation. A negative outlook regarding an injury and rehabilitation can also be detrimental.

Many people have specific allergies or medical conditions, which can be hugely varied in nature. If someone has an allergy to a specific medication or treatment method, this could affect rehabilitation. Many alternative options are available for treatments, but some treatments may far outweigh others in effectiveness in particular circumstances. Different medical conditions, particularly near or at the site of an injury, will inhibit the type and quality of rehabilitation that can be used.

■ Haemorrhage

Haemorrhage is the medical term for bleeding. If haemorrhaging occurs during the healing of an injury, this hinder the process. With serious medical conditions, haemorrhaging can be a major problem, potentially requiring repeat or further surgery. If bleeding does occur, this will result in more tissue around the injury, increasing the size of the injury site.

■ Poor blood supply

The supply of blood to all areas of the body is critical in the distribution of healing products. Most muscles in the body will have a good blood supply to enable the oxygen delivery required for exercise. Some areas of the body have a better blood supply than others (e.g. large muscle groups). Generally, the more efficient the blood supply, the more efficient the healing process. If the vasculature (blood vessels) is damaged as a result of an injury, this can also hinder the body's ability to heal.

■ Muscle spasms

Like cramps, muscle spasms are involuntary contractions. These can be particularly prevalent in torn muscles and can inhibit healing of an injury. Spasms can occur through the body and can inhibit sporting activity without other injury.

■ Infection

Illnesses can complicate treatment of an injury, and if an injured part of the body becomes infected, this can result in further problems. The scarring resulting from an infection can be widespread and larger than for a regular injury.

Age and health

Fitter individuals will often heal more quickly than less physically able individuals. Similarly, the healthier we are, the more efficient the healing process. As we get older, many body systems deteriorate in efficiency. Older individuals can become more prone to injury and will not heal as well as younger sportspeople.

Remember!

A rehabilitation programme must be designed specifically considering individual abilities and characteristics. Depending on the speed of recovery, and any problems that arise, modifications may be needed on a regular basis.

Advances in prevention, treatment and rehabilitation

As we have seen, there are numerous methods of treating and rehabilitating people with different types of injury to different areas of the body. Due to our continuously developing knowledge and understanding of sports science, medicine and coaching methods, we are seeing many advances in prevention, treatment and rehabilitation methods.

Manufacturers, governing bodies and medical experts all aim to ensure sport provides activities that are as safe as reasonably possible, while not detracting from enjoyment of the activity by both participants and spectators. Rugby union has recently come under the spotlight with regard to the risk of spinal injury associated with scrummaging, with a view to potentially changing the rules. It is down to governing bodies, in negotiation with those providing medical advice, to consider the intricacies of the sport and what is best to protect the players without detracting from the game. In rugby, there is a need for more data to assess the number of spinal injuries worldwide – this will shed more light on the trends in, and causes of, spinal injuries, and if any appropriate action is needed to protect rugby players.

In addition to the various research into specific causes of injuries, and how to minimise the risks through modifications to training methods and rules, there have been major developments in the surgical techniques used to treat many sports injuries. Historically, a cruciate ligament injury may often mean the end of a career for a sports player (such as a footballer). With modern surgery, sports players can often return to play in four to nine months.

The increasing profile of sport and exercise, both as recreation and as a career opportunity, means that more individuals are involved in all aspects, including injury management and rehabilitation. It is important that those suffering from an injury seek professional advice from professionals at each stage of the rehabilitation process, as doing the wrong thing can jeopardise the chances of fully recovering from the injury.

People react differently, so knowledge of individual differences is essential – in the way we perceive an injury, heal and recover, and perform following rehabilitation. Factors including fitness levels, chosen sports discipline, personality profile, gender, age and motivation, among others, may also influence how well we respond to and recover from injury.

Psychology

The psychological aspect of how well an athlete deals with rehabilitation and the often slow return to competition is often neglected. Athletes, and any individual who suffers an injury, can experience a very wide range of emotions. Individual differences dictate that athletes will vary dramatically both in the physical aspects of the programme (including pain threshold and speed of recovery) and also in how well they deal with the mental aspects of an injury.

Many of the psychological techniques used to enhance performance and other coping strategies can be useful in dealing with the problems associated with sporting injuries. These techniques are covered in detail in Sport Book 1 Chapter 16, 'Psychology for sports performance'. Such psychological intervention techniques can be implemented alongside a rehabilitation programme to complement the processes.

Case study

You are working as an assistant psychologist in a professional football club. A first-team player has suffered from a cruciate ligament injury and is at the initial stages of the rehabilitation process. Highlight the potential psychological issues that could arise due to the injury and treatments, and the action you would take to combat the negative psychological complaints.

Psychological issue	Action to be taken
e.g. Anxiety about reoccurrence of injury	

Goal-setting

There are distinct phases in the healing and rehabilitation processes (pages 109–111), and injuries can be a major source of stress to sports players. One of the most important aspects of a rehabilitation programme for an athlete is that they can see improvements in the injury and that they are progressing towards competition fitness. It is of key importance to set appropriate goals for the athlete to strive towards in the administration of rehabilitation. Goal-setting can incorporate both long- and short-term goals. These should be designed in a progressive manner – a number of very specific short-term goals (week by week) are assembled to construct a more generalised set of long-term goals. Goal-setting can be a vital tool enabling a progressive rehabilitation programme, and well planned goals can act as a powerful psychological tool, helping the athlete to see significant progression and to remain focused on returning to fitness.

An appropriate method of implementing a goal-setting plan is to incorporate the SMARTER target principle.

- Specific – goals must be specific to the injury and sporting discipline of the athlete.
- Measurable – the goals set should be measurable, to gauge improvements.
- Adjustable – goals are written on paper, not cast in stone – changes in fitness or circumstances can cause a goal to be adjusted.
- Realistic – all goals should be difficult enough to push the athlete, without being too difficult to attain.
- Time-constrained – a specific time scale should be given for all the goals, to record progress.
- Exciting and challenging – goals should be interesting and different, to keep up motivation and interest.
- Recorded – keeping a record of the programme is very important for both the trainer and the athlete to refer to – see below.

■ Recording

It is important that the people involved in developing a rehabilitation programme are proficient in both the practical aspects and the accurate recording of the entire process. The records kept should detail accurately all the factors of the rehabilitation, from the initial injury evaluation to the end of the programme. This documentation is particularly relevant due to the increase in number of malpractice lawsuits surrounding the healthcare profession.

Things to consider when documenting a rehabilitation programme include:

- background information about the client (e.g. medical issues, injury history, specific requirements of rehabilitation)
- the activities undertaken
- the levels and development of the client
- problems or issues arising from the session
- complications (e.g. allergies or illness) that affect the quality of the client's progress during the session
- relevant consent forms for some activities

- parental involvement for younger sports players
- anything the coach has outlined for the athlete to achieve
- dates for review/functional testing (aims, objectives, etc.)
- any other information that may be relevant (highlighted by either trainer or client).

Activity

Describe the potential complications that could arise during the rehabilitation of injury for the following scenarios.

1   A nine-year-old football player experiencing a hairline fracture to the fibula and an ankle sprain.

2   A 55-year-old, physically healthy man who has developed knee cartilage problems.

3   A 17-year-old student representative hockey player who has developed lower back muscular spasms.

4   A formerly inactive 32-year-old individual who has developed achilles tendonitis 2 weeks after starting at a gym with the intention of losing weight.

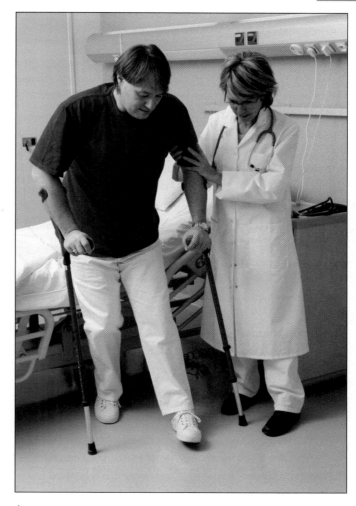

▲ Physiotherapy plays a major part in rehabilitation after injury

 ## Theory into practice

A range of different methods are available to help with the treatment and rehabilitation of sports injuries. These all have different specific roles, including reducing pain, preventing swelling, and reducing the risk of reoccurrence of the injury. Carry out research into the different types of treatment outlined in Table 17.9, and consider when and for which type of injury it may be used.

Table 17.9 Strategies to reduce the risk of sports injuries ▶

Treatment	Function and purpose of treatment	Time of application (time after injury/ point in healing process)	Example(s) of injury it may be used for
Bracing			
Cryotherapy			
Thermotherapy			
Massage			
Medication			
Electrical stimulation			
Acupuncture			

Drugs alleviating the negative effects of injuries

It is often said that 'sport hurts'. Hopefully this isn't always the case, as preventing sports injuries is far pleasanter than the cure. However, injuries in sport are sometimes inevitable as players strive for success by putting their body on the line. From this Unit, you should have developed a clear appreciation of some important first-aid methods, various rehabilitation techniques, and the psychology relating to how different people cope.

Sometimes, to help with pain management and to assist the healing process, certain drugs may be needed. It is fundamentally important that drugs are taken only on the specific advice of medical professionals. Nearly all pharmacological agents (drugs) have some side-effects, and can be potentially dangerous when not taken in the correct manner. There are thousands of different types of drugs, updated regularly with advances in medical science. Although detailed knowledge of all categories of drugs and their use is not vital (unless you intend to pursue a career in sports medicine or a related field), some knowledge of the subject can help in your understanding of the nature of certain sports injuries and the associated healing processes. Some of the main drugs that may be used for sports injuries can be classified as:

- drugs to combat infection
- drugs that inhibit pain
- drugs to reduce inflammation (swelling)
- drugs that produce skeletal muscle relaxation.

Activity

A large proportion of sporting injuries will require some form of medical intervention. Consult general sports medicine and sports injuries books, and conduct internet searches, to help you carry out the following tasks.

1   Investigate the purpose of the different types of medication in Table 17.10, and highlight the types of injury they would be appropriate for.

Medication	Role of medication	Type of injury for which used
e.g. Narcotic analgesics	Inhibit pain	Severe fracture (e.g. open fracture)
Penicillin		
Halogens		
Paracetamol		
Cortisone		
Aspirin		

Table 17.10 Types of medication and their uses

2   Investigate the different methods of administering different drugs used for sporting injuries, and complete Table 17.11 with additional methods of administration and the medication for which they are used.

Method of administration	Medication
e.g. Intravenous	e.g. Morphine
e.g. Inhalation	
etc.	

Table 17.11 Methods of administering medication

Assessment practice

The appropriate application of rehabilitation processes following injury is vital to restore an athlete's functioning and return to his or her specialist sport. In your role as a first-aider on work experience alongside the sports therapist, suggest a rehabilitation programme for a selected athlete who has suffered a sports injury. Include the following information in your programme:

- immediate and long-term plan
- identification of stages of rehabilitation with appropriate exercises
- methods to re-establish functional activity
- strengthening exercises
- gradual increase in activity
- ROM exercises (stretching – passive, active, PNF)
- coordination exercises
- psychological issues (e.g. goal-setting)
- examples of recording documentation – medical conditions and allergies, injury history, up-to-date and accurate information, appropriate forms, time scales and review dates, measurable objectives. **P6 M3 D1 D2**

Grading tips

Grading Tip P6

To gain this criterion you should acquire assistance from your subject tutor.

Ensure you provide appropriate time scales for a rehabilitation programme for two different injuries. Make reference to the psychological issues that could arise during the programmes.

Grading Tip M3

Select a suitably severe injury that requires a range of rehabilitation methods. This will demonstrate your research skills and knowledge of a range of rehabiliation protocols.

Make sure appropriate time scales are given that demonstrate progression in the intensity of the programme.

Grading Tip D1

Produce a well thought-out, clear, detailed selection of strengths and weaknesses that reflect on your rehabilitation programme. Justify your selection of rehabilitation methods and, where appropriate, provide alternative methods.

Explain how unforeseen circumstances may require changes and modifications to a rehabilitation programme.

Grading Tip D2

Consideration is needed of how the rehabilitation process will change in response to each specific phase of the healing process.

Link the type of activity to the injury and the duration/phase of healing process.

Provide explanations from the point of injury through to the end of a rehabilitation programme.

Give some examples of different types of injury to demonstrate your detailed understanding of the treatment and rehabilitation processes.

Consider the following areas of discussion:

BL	individual differences
ROM	region of the body
contraindications	previous injury
specific sport.	

Knowledge check

1 A football player experiences a fractured tarsal bone in a tackle during a match. How would you categorise this injury?

2 While training, a distance runner suffers a reoccurrence of a hamstring tear. How would you categorise this injury?

3 Give three examples of soft tissue injuries.

4 In relation to sports injuries, how would you define the following?

(a) Signs (b) Symptoms

5 What are the symptoms of the following degrees of sprain?

(a) First degree (b) Second degree

(c) Third degree

6 Define the following:

(a) Strain (b) Sprain

7 Identify four potential psychological responses to injury that an athlete may experience.

8 Explain why inflammation occurs at the site of an injured part of the body.

9 In relation to the initial treatment of various sports injuries, what does PRICED stand for?

10 Identify three different types of stretching that are used to regenerate lost range of motion after a sports injury.

11 Explain three different psychological issues that are important for a coach to be aware of during the rehabilitation of an injured athlete.

12 Explain the different reasons why it is important to record the progress of an athlete's rehabilitation programme after an injury.

Web links

www.medicdirectsport.com/ sportsinjuries/default.asp	Fitness and health information online	General information on sports injuries, and injuries categorised by specific sports
www.sportsinjuryclinic.net/	Virtual sports injuries clinic	Identifies sports injuries by body region and explains different treatment methods
www.brianmac.demon.co.uk/	A–Z database on a range of sport and exercise topics	Provides information on a range of topics to help athletes and coaches
www.nlm.nih.gov/medlineplus/ sportsinjuries.html	Medlineplus website	Offers up-to-date information regarding health and injuries (including treatment and rehabilitation)
www.niams.nih.gov/	National Institute of Arthritis and Musculoskeletal and Skin Diseases	Health information on a range of topics including range of injuries and treatments
http://bjsm.bmjjournals.com/	British Journal of Sports Medicine online	Journal database with various sports-related articles
www.humankinetics.com/products/ journals	Human Kinetics online	Journal database with various sports-related articles
www.pponline.co.uk	Peak Performance online	Coaching and sports science web site

End of Unit assessment

Preparation for assessment

1   Working as a trainee physiotherapist for a professional Rugby Union club, you are asked to provide a report outlining the various causes, preventive measures, treatment procedures, and the body's responses to a range of sports-related injuries. In your report you must refer to the following types of injury:

- sprains
- strains
- fractures
- haematomas
- tendonitis
- concussion.

(a)   The introduction to your report will describe the intrinsic and extrinsic risk factors associated with sports injuries, and explain how various preventive methods can minimise likelihood of an injury taking place. The risk factors that you might consider describing could include the following.

Extrinsic risk factors:

- coaching (e.g. poor coaching/leadership)
- environmental factors
- clothing and footwear
- misuse of equipment.

Intrinsic risk factors:

- muscle imbalance
- poor preparation
- fitness levels
- over-use
- postural defects.   **P1 P2 M1**

(b)   From the time of injury, the body responds in a number of ways. For the different types of sports injury you have listed, provide a description and explanation of *both* the physiological and psychological responses of the body. **P3 P4 M2**

(c)   The nature of competitive sports means that sports injuries do occur from time to time. Provide a description of the first-aid procedures and common treatments used for four contrasting sporting injuries.   **P5**

2   You have been allocated two clients who have each suffered a different sports injury. Produce an appropriate treatment and rehabilitation programme, paying attention to the different stages of the healing process and relevant phases of rehabilitation.   **P6 M3 D2**

3   You have the opportunity to apply for promotion within your organisation. To apply for the post of full-time sports physiotherapist, you are asked to provide a detailed evaluation of the two programmes you developed in question 2.   **D1**

To achieve a pass grade the evidence must show that the learner is able to:	To achieve a merit grade the evidence must show that, in addition to the pass criteria, the learner is able to:	To achieve a distinction grade the evidence must show that, in addition to the pass and merit criteria, the learner is able to:
P1 describe extrinsic and intrinsic risk factors in relation to sports injuries **Assessment practice page 92**	**M1** explain how risk factors can be minimised by utilisation of preventive measures **Assessment practice page 92**	
P2 describe preventive measures that can be taken in order to prevent sports injuries occurring **Assessment practice page 92**		
P3 describe the physiological responses common to most sports injuries **Assessment practice page 96**	**M2** explain the physiological and psychological effects common to most sports injuries **Assessment practice page 96**	
P4 describe the psychological responses common to sports injuries **Assessment practice page 96**		
P5 describe first aid and common treatments used for four different types of sports injury **Assessment practice page 109**		
P6 plan, with support, a safe and appropriate treatment and rehabilitation programme for two common sports injuries **Assessment practice page 119**	**M3** design a safe appropriate treatment and rehabilitation programme for two common sports injuries which includes provision for related psychological symptoms **Assessment practice page 119**	**D1** evaluate the treatment and rehabilitation programme designed, justifying the choices and suggesting alternatives where appropriate **Assessment practice page 119**
		D2 explain the relationship between the differing stages of injury and appropriate treatments and rehabilitation phases **Assessment practice page 119**

Analysis of Sports Performance

Introduction

This unit introduces the need to analyse sporting performance. During his or her career, every high-level or world-class athlete will suffer from a loss of form or a significant setback. By analysing their performance, athletes can address the issues that are affecting them and make the changes necessary to gain success. If no evaluation takes place after a poor or unsuccessful performance, athletes may continue to perform badly and miss out on medals or other measures of success. Coaches should understand the importance of this area, and how they can influence and support the athlete, both in training and in competition.

Coaches and athletes need to know how movement and physiology affect performance. There is also increasing awareness of sports psychology, and how the mind can affect performance – factors such as stress and motivation can make the difference between winning and losing. Also, performance may depend on a technical or tactical aspect. All sports depend on a multitude of factors for success.

After completing this unit you should be able to achieve the following outcomes:

- Understand the performance profile of a sporting activity
- Be able to analyse sporting performance
- Be able to provide feedback to athletes regarding performance
- Understand the analysis required for different levels of sporting performance.

Think it over

Imagine that you have just taken part in a race and performed much less well than you expected. Make a list of the factors that may have contributed to this result. You should consider the physiological, psychological, technical and tactical factors, and highlight how you feel you can address each of these in the future.

Performance profiling is a way of providing information to the athlete about what actually happened in their sport – rather than what they think happened. It involves both analysing the athlete's performance through observation, and also understanding the athlete's state of mind. There may be occasions when the athlete has underperformed due to nerves or lack of concentration. Therefore the purpose of performance profiling is to:

- assist the athlete with both their physical and their psychological needs
- assess scope for technical and tactical improvement
- thus improving the athlete's motivation and performance.

The coach should assess the athlete before and after the event, discussing physical, technical and tactical issues, and the following important psychological factors:

- confidence
- concentration
- commitment
- control
- refocusing of effort.

Understanding each of these will allow you to prepare a strategy to address the issues highlighted by the profiling.

Types of activity

Different sports have very different requirements, and the athlete and coach should be aware of the specific physical and psychological demands needed in order to achieve success. For example, a midfield player in football will need different physical and mental skills from a goalkeeper.

Individual-based sport

An example of an individual-based sport is snooker. This is an unusual sport in that the opposing player has no effect on the player at the table. Snooker players are required to concentrate for long periods, and the skills they use are described as 'closed'. A closed skill is one that takes place in a stable, predictable environment – the performer knows exactly what to do, and when. Skills are not affected by the environment, and tend to be habitual. Movements follow set patterns and have a clear beginning and end. The skills tend to be self-paced. A snooker player may have to wait for long periods before performing at the table. It is vital that the player can concentrate and remain focused, both throughout the waiting time and also at the table.

▲ Snooker players have to be completely self-reliant, and maintain focus both away from and at the table

Position in a team

Different sports make different demands on athletes – and different positions within the same sport also make very different demands. An example is a goalkeeper (in any sport), who will need to concentrate for long periods without being directly or physically involved in the action.

Performance profiling should take into account the individual and specific demands of both the sport, and the position within that sport. Performance profiling and analysis can be used to document, assess and predict the ability of a goalkeeper to meet the demands of performance, covering various aspects of physical capacity, psychological factors, technical skill and tactical awareness. These may include:

- physical tests of speed, strength, power and flexibility, core stability and endurance
- psychological assessment of personality, anxiety and confidence
- biomechanical analysis of movement technique
- notational analysis of performance.

While some of these factors may be relevant to other positions within the team, any profiling or analysis must identify requirements specific to goalkeeping.

Remember!

The four key areas of performance assessment are physical, psychological, technical and tactical.

Once the individual physical, psychological, technical (biomechanical) and tactical strengths and weaknesses have been identified in relation to the unique demands of goalkeeping, the next step is to use this information to set short-term and long-term goals for training. Setting goals gives purpose and direction to the training programme (see page 65), and promotes the intrinsic motivation, self-confidence and sense of responsibility that will strengthen the goalkeeper's adherence to the training programme. The profiling process should be repeated at regular intervals to monitor the effectiveness of the specific training programme, and highlight any areas of good or poor progress.

Research shows that, on average, a soccer goalkeeper spends 86 per cent of a match walking or standing still, and the remaining 14 per cent performing activities at moderate to high intensity. This equates to approximately 12 minutes' pressure on the goal over the duration of the match, with the rest of the time spent walking forwards, backwards or standing still in response to the play.

The goalkeeper must also be prepared mentally throughout the match. From a psychological perspective, the goalkeeper must be constantly alive to potential dangers, remaining focused and concentrating on the

The goalkeeper must maintain concentration and focus throughout the match – not just for the short periods when the goal is under attack

build-up of play, which will be linked to his or her physiological ability to recover quickly after each exertion in preparation for the next attack.

Specific action

Many sports require the analysis of a specific action. Complex actions, such as a tennis serve, should be broken down into smaller stages so that a clear analysis can be made.

Using a whole–part–whole method of analysis, it is possible for the coach and player to investigate key parts of a technique. This means that the whole skill can be analysed and practised, while more detailed or complex elements are learned and practised specifically and separately, in order to make up the whole skill. For example, the initial throw may be too far in front of the tennis player, so that he or she keeps serving into the net.

The performance profile

The purpose of analysing a sporting performance is to provide detailed feedback to the athlete or team in order for them to improve their game. When analysing the performance of an individual or team, you should consider a variety of questions, which might include:

- how well are specific skills executed?
- how focused and motivated are the athletes?
- are the athletes using the correct techniques?
- are the correct tactics adopted at the right time?

Although analysis can be performed during training, it should also be conducted during competitive situations and over a defined period. This will ensure the coach has a true picture of what is happening, rather than just a one-off 'snapshot', which may not be a realistic indication of the true performance. For example, an athlete may be able to perform a variety of skills during training, but may be affected by pressure during competition.

There are four key stages to an analysis of performance: observation, analysis, evaluation, and planning/performing.

■ Observation

This is the collection of data – such as the number of shots on target in hockey, or the number of fouls committed in football, by a team or an individual. Because of the fast-moving nature of many sports, it is often useful to video-record a performance and collect the data from the recording. This ensures that the information is accurate.

■ Analysis

Using the observed data that have been collected, the coach can analyse the performance. This allows a picture to be built up, and future training programmes and performance tactics can be created to address any key areas highlighted by the analysis.

The coach may also use observation and analysis of opponents' performance in order to discover any area of weakness that can be exploited.

■ Evaluation

It is important that both the coach and the athlete or team allow time to evaluate the data in order to improve performance. And when evaluating performance, the coach must be able to communicate his or her recommendations openly and clearly. Some athletes prefer detailed descriptions of performance, while others prefer simple, jargon-free feedback. It is important that, as part of the evaluation process, the athlete or team can express their views so that specific training or tactical goals can be devised.

■ Planning and performing

This is the end product of performance analysis, when the coach and the athlete or team plan a specific training or performance goal, and work towards achieving that target.

Theory into practice

The English Institute of Sport (www.eis2win.co.uk) provides elite athletes with the opportunity to undertake performance analysis in order to prepare for competition. The Institute describes performance analysis as the provision of objective feedback to performers trying to achieve a positive change in performance. In simple terms, this means providing the athlete with information on what they actually did, as opposed to what they think they did.

For a sport of your choice, use the English Institute of Sport's website to investigate how your sporting performance can be enhanced through performance analysis.

■ Physical assessment

Sport requires participants to have a high level of fitness in order to perform. It is also important to be physically fit simply for health reasons. There are five main components of fitness.

- Strength – the ability of a muscle or group of muscles to exert a maximal force, or overcome a maximal resistance, in a single contraction.
- Aerobic endurance – the ability of the heart, lungs, blood vessels and skeletal muscle to take in, transport and utilise oxygen efficiently and over a prolonged period.
- Muscular endurance – the ability of a muscle or group of muscles to make repeated contractions against light to moderate resistance and over a prolonged period.
- Flexibility – a measure of ability to move a joint through a complete and natural range of motion

without discomfort or pain.

- Body composition – the body's physical make-up in terms of fat and lean or non-fat body tissue, measured as a percentage.

Being able to measure these will help the coach and athlete develop a training plan that will meet the specific requirements of the sport and the chosen area of fitness. Fitness tests can be conducted to measure each area, and the results analysed in order to develop a training programme. Fitness tests can then be repeated after a period of training, and improvements can be monitored.

Activity

The measurement of heart rate is a good indicator of cardiovascular fitness. Using a simple test, you can measure your resting heart rate (RHR) by taking your pulse, with lower readings indicating a healthy cardiovascular system. An RHR between 60 and 70 beats per minute (bpm) is considered normal. Maximum heart rate (MHR) can be calculated as 220 – age (see Unit 14, page 63).

1 What is your RHR?

2 What is your MHR?

3 How can you use knowledge of heart rate as part of your training? Calculate your maximum heart rate, and the work-out training zones of 60, 70 and 80% of your maximum heart rate.

Heart rate can be measured during exercise with a heart-rate monitor. Athletes can train within target zones of their maximum heart rate, at a controlled intensity (see page 63).

Warm-up

To perform at the highest level, physical preparation before training and competition is paramount. A warm-up generally consists of a gradual increase in intensity in physical activity. For example, before running or playing an intense sport, you might jog slowly to warm your muscles and increase your heart rate. It is important that a warm-up should be specific to the exercise that will follow, preparing the muscles to be used and

activating the energy systems that are required for that particular activity. Stretching the active muscles is also recommended after doing a warm-up.

There are three main functions of a warm-up:
- to increase heart rate
- to raise body temperature
- to prepare the major joints of the body.

The warm-up should increase the heart rate in order to pump more blood around the body to the working muscle, in preparation for exercise. This in turn allows more energy to be produced using oxygen, and increases the body and muscle temperature. Increasing muscle temperature will improve the elasticity of the working muscles, making them less likely to become injured. The warm-up should involve a wide range of movements specific to the exercise or sport to be undertaken.

For a warm-up to be most effective, it should be tailored to the individual client.

Cool-down

The purpose of a cool-down is to return the body back to its pre-exercise state. A cool-down has three main objectives:
- to return the heart rate back to normal
- to remove any waste products that may have built up during exercise
- to return the muscles to their original state (or length, if stretched).

A cool-down will keep the metabolic rate high and the capillaries dilated to enable oxygen to flush through the muscle tissue, which helps to remove lactic acid waste created by the exercise. This should stop the blood from staying in the veins, which can cause dizziness if exercise is stopped too quickly. A cool-down can also reduce the effect of delayed-onset muscle soreness, which often follows strenuous exercise that the body is not used to. The final part of the cool-down should include stretching designed to facilitate and improve flexibility, as the muscles will be very warm at this stage.

Lung function

Being able to analyse lung function allows athletes to determine not only the size of their lungs, and therefore how much air they can inhale, but also the strength and efficiency of their lungs. Being able to inspire oxygen and deliver it to working muscle is essential to athletes of all abilities. Likewise, being able to expire waste products such as carbon dioxide is also vital to sporting performance.

Recently there has been much scientific research into lung function and aerobic sports such as cycling, long-distance running and rowing. Results indicate that the larger and stronger the lungs, the more able they are to deliver oxygen to the working muscle, especially during intense exercise. For example, an elite rower may be able to deliver up to 240 litres of air per minute in and out of the lungs. To put this in perspective, a typical value for an untrained male would be between 100 and 150 litres per minute during maximal exercise.

A spirometer is used to measure lung function. The athlete takes the deepest breath he or she can, then exhales into the spirometer as hard as possible, for as long as possible. The spirometer is then able to determine the following measurements:

- forced vital capacity (FVC) – the total amount of air that you can forcibly blow out after full inspiration, measured in litres
- forced expired volume 1 (FEV 1) – the amount of air that you can forcibly blow out in 1 second, measured in litres per second (along with forced vital capacity, considered one of the primary indicators of lung function)
- peak expiratory flow (PEF) – the speed of the air moving out of your lungs at the beginning of the expiration, also measured in litres per second.

■ Psychological assessment

Motivation

Understanding what motivates athletes to train and compete will help the coach devise varied and enjoyable training sessions. Motivation is the desire or need to perform a certain task; it is why we choose to do something. Motivation has been defined as 'the direction and intensity of effort' – meaning what we choose to do, and the amount of effort we put in. There are many theories on motivation (see Sport Book 1, Unit 16), but in general it can be regarded as intrinsic (internal) or extrinsic (external).

- Intrinsic motivation is the desire from within the athlete to perform – for example, performing for the pleasure of taking part, playing a sport simply for enjoyment.
- Extrinsic motivation is the desire to take part for external rewards, which may be praise or recognition, trophies, or even payment for taking part – here success is needed to ensure maximum results.

Activity

Many sportspeople will have a combination of both intrinsic and extrinsic motivation. It is common for high-level, professional sportspeople to focus on extrinsic rewards. For example, you may currently play cricket because you enjoy playing the sport, and gain pleasure from participating and achieving personal success (intrinsic). But as you progress, you may be offered money to play (extrinsic). If you have received extrinsic rewards, you may lose focus on why you are playing, and in the future play only for money or other financial rewards rather than simply for enjoyment.

Using the Table 18.1 below, identify intrinsic and extrinsic motivational factors found in sport.

Factor	Intrinsic or extrinsic?
Pride	
Money	
Certificates	
Praise from parents or coaches	
Medals	
Sponsorship	
Fitness	
Enjoy winning	
Being part of a team	
Fun and enjoyment	

▲ Table 18.1 Motivational factors

Anxiety

A certain level of stress is needed for optimum performance. If you are under too little stress, then you will find it difficult to motivate yourself to give a good performance. Too little stress expresses itself in feelings of boredom and not being stretched.

But too much stress and anxiety can seriously affect your ability to focus on your skills and performance. Both coach and athlete should recognise the symptoms of stress and anxiety to ensure performance is not affected.

Excessive levels of stress damage performance and damage your enjoyment of your sport, and may occur in the following circumstances:

- when you think what is being asked of you is beyond your perceived abilities
- when too much is asked of you in too short a time
- when unnecessary obstacles are put in the way of achieving goals.

An optimum level of stress will give the benefits of alertness and activation that improve performance.

Anxiety is different from stress. Anxiety comes from concern about a lack of control over circumstances. In some cases, being anxious and worrying over a problem may generate a solution. But normally it will just result in negative thinking, and have a detrimental effect on performance. An example would be an athlete worrying about what the spectators think about their performance and fearing making a mistake.

Arousal

Arousal is how interested we are in performing a specific sport or action. Every sport will develop a sense of excitement, but if this becomes too great then the athlete may feel anxious, with a negative effect on performance. It is important that the levels of arousal are suitable to the skills that are being performed.

Attention

A sportsperson will be presented with a wide variety of information when they are training and competing. Some of this information will be important and relevant, such as instructions from the coach and other players, while some will be of no use, such as negative comments from the crowd. It is essential that the athlete is able to focus on the relevant information that will lead to a successful performance. By selectively attending to only the important information, we are able to ignore negative factors that could affect performance. The demand for concentration varies with the sport:

- sustained concentration – distance running, cycling, tennis, squash
- short bursts of concentration – cricket, golf, athletic field events
- intense concentration – sprinting events, skiing.

Common distractions include anxiety, mistakes, fatigue, weather, public announcements, coach, manager, opponent, negative thoughts, etc.

Confidence

Confidence describes the feeling that we are going to succeed in a given situation: you will have self-confidence if you believe that you can achieve your goal. The more confident you are, the more likely you are to achieve your goals, which in turn is likely to result in sporting success. A confident athlete is likely to persevere even when things are not going to plan, show enthusiasm, be positive in their approach, and take their share of the responsibility for both success and failure.

Aggression

Sports such as rugby require the players to show aggression, and in this context can be considered a good thing. A player may make a hard tackle and win possession of the ball. But in most sports, and beyond a certain level, aggression is seen as bad. A player throwing a punch is seen as negative, and is normally punished by the laws of the game.

▼ Aggression on the sports pitch sets a bad example and will be punished according to the laws of the game

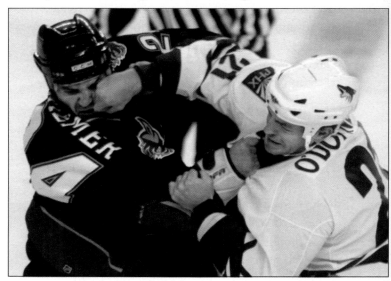

Key Terms

Aggression is defined as any behaviour directed toward intentionally harming or injuring another living being.

It is important that athletes are able to control their emotions and only use aggression in a controlled an appropriate way. Becoming frustrated by their own or others' performance may lead to feelings of anger, resulting in a lack of concentration on the task, deteriorating performance and a loss of confidence in their ability, which fuels the anger – a slippery slope to failure.

A coach must teach players that while aggression can be positive in trying to win, winning should only be achieved by playing within the rules of the game.

Think it over

Consider a recent example of aggression getting out of hand, from a sport of your choice. How did the incident start? How did the referee deal with it, and was their response fair? What were the reactions of the sportsperson involved, and their coach?

Relaxation

Relaxation is a technique that can be used to reduce anxiety and therefore enhance performance. There are a many ways in which the coach can assist athletes to relax, including mental imagery, progressive muscular relaxation and meditation.

Mental imagery

This is a technique used by athletes to imagine themselves in a variety of situations – perhaps performing a certain skill at a specific place, or in a relaxing situation such as lying on a beach. Research indicates that the more detailed the imagery, the more likely the athlete is to feel prepared for a specific situation. Imagery is useful in:

- developing self-confidence
- developing strategies to teach athletes to cope with new situations before they encounter them

- helping athletes focus their attention or concentrate on a particular skill they are trying to learn or develop.

Progressive muscular relaxation

This involves the purposeful contracting and relaxing of specific muscles. Each muscle is contracted for between four and six seconds and then consciously relaxed, with the athlete making a mental note of how they feel. This process allows the muscles to return to a more relaxed state.

Meditation

Meditation is used to reduce stress before an event, and with experience athletes can learn to relax different muscle groups and appreciate subtle differences in muscle tension. By making a note of their breathing and muscle tension, the athlete is able to relax and focus on the competition ahead.

Concentration

The ability to focus and concentrate on a given sporting task will aid performance and success. Concentration can be described as the ability to focus on a specific task. Due to the nature of sport, many factors may cause an athlete or team to become distracted – the crowd, the weather, or negative thoughts. Therefore an athlete should learn how to concentrate, especially under pressure.

Theory into practice

During the successful Rugby World Cup in 2003, England Coach Clive Woodward devised the strategy of T-CUP or Think Correctly Under Pressure. This meant that when players were beginning to lose concentration, they could take a moment to re-evaluate and focus on the specific tasks and ignore outside, negative influences.

Working in pairs, identify how you can adapt the T-CUP idea for a sport of your choice. You should consider when pressure occurs in your sport, and what you may focus on. Consider whether you focus on positive or negative factors, and discuss how these may affect your performance.

Different sports, and roles within sports, have different concentration levels. As noted above, a goalkeeper will spend much of his or her time away from the action, but must remain focused so as to be ready for action when needed. A batsman in cricket needs short, intense bursts of concentration when facing the opposition's bowlers.

■ Technical assessment

Sport involves many complex skills and techniques. As we learn and practise these skills, they become more 'natural' and we are able to refine and perfect them. For example, a cricketer will practise specific shots as part of his or her training programme, to the standard needed to execute them as part of a competitive match. All sports require athletes to have good techniques in order to achieve success. Therefore it is essential that the athlete and coach focus on how individual skills are performed. This may involve observational analysis and feedback, and examining complex skills broken down into simpler parts. Skills can be divided into three categories, as follows:

- discrete skills – have a very clear beginning and end, e.g. a serve in tennis
- continuous skills – have no obvious beginning or end, but tend to merge and flow into one another as the skill or sport progresses, e.g. cycling or swimming (the diagram shows how discrete and continuous skills can be classified as part of a continuum)
- serial skills – composed of both discrete and continuous skills, e.g. a tennis player playing a shot on the run.

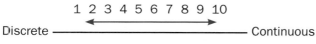

1 2 3 4 5 6 7 8 9 10

Discrete ——————————— Continuous

▲ **A skill continuum**

Think it over

Think of five sports and write down five skills from each. Using these, identify which skills are discrete, continuous or serial.

Biomechanics

Biomechanics is the science that examines forces acting on the human body in sport, and explains how performance can be affected by these forces. At the highest levels of sport, in which techniques play a major role, biomechanics provides an opportunity to investigate and analyse specific movements in order for improvements to be made. A knowledge of biomechanics is thus essential for coaches.

▲ **A researcher analysing a swimmer's stroke at an Olympic training centre in Colorado Springs, USA**

Quantitative analysis

Quantitative analysis involves a detailed, scientific approach to observation analysis. It uses direct measurement of a technique or performance, and is often very time-consuming due to the need for detailed data collection. The data produced are often very accurate and can produce very reliable results. One method of collecting information to watch a game and write down the action as it occurs – this is known as real-time analysis. However, sport is fast-moving and it is often necessary to video-record a performance – this is known as lapsed-time analysis. For example, in a basketball match it would be very difficult to collect statistical data such as successful shots as the action occurred.

As technology has advanced, suitable equipment such as video cameras and laptop computers has become affordable. This means that a coach will be able to collect data at training and competition and analyse it afterwards.

Examples of quantitative analysis may include:

- recording patterns of play
- recording successful passes in basketball
- examining the techniques used by a bowler in cricket
- the number of successful tackles in football
- the number of turnovers in a basketball match.

It is also important to use quantitative analysis to evaluate the opposition's previous performances so that suitable tactics can be devised in advance.

Qualitative analysis

This form of analysis is much simpler than quantitative analysis, as it simply requires general observation of a performance to be carried out. This can be done by a coach, spectators or even other players. Because this method is largely subjective (or open to interpretation), the information gathered may be biased. Therefore the more experience and knowledge an observer has, the more accurate the analysis is likely to be.

Key Terms

Quantitative analysis uses numerical data or statistics to describe sporting performance.

Qualitative analysis uses descriptions and words to describe sporting performance.

Linear displacement

An example of biomechanics being used as part of a performance analysis is the study of linear displacement. This describes how far and how quickly a person moves in a straight line. The information can then be used to determine the velocity and the acceleration of the object. Such information (quantitative data) may be useful for a 100-metre sprinter, for example. A coach will be able to determine if the runner is slow out of the blocks, or if they get slower (or decelerate) during the race.

Velocity of release

Sports such as the javelin or shot-put involve the athlete throwing the object the furthest distance. By using both qualitative and quantitative analyses, the performer and coach can determine technique and velocity of release. Qualitative analysis can aid the athlete by observing and

analysing the technique during the throw. A coach can then highlight key aspects of the technique and give descriptive feedback, with demonstrations if necessary. Collecting numerical data through video observation (quantitative analysis), the coach can work out if the velocity of release is too low. This would result in the javelin or shot-put being thrown shorter distances. Biomechanics and analysis will also allow the coach to investigate the optimum angle of release so that maximum distances can be reached.

■ Tactical assessment

All sports require tactics or strategies in order to achieve success. Sport contains many examples of tactics that a coach, athlete or team may adopt in order to win. These may include playing the offside trap in football, batting defensively in cricket, or using zone marking in basketball. When devising and using tactics, it is important that all the players understand the tactic and when to employ it. Failing to do this may lead to confusion and disrupt performance.

Key Terms

Tactics are a plan or procedure designed for gaining advantage or success.

Activity

For the following tactics, give a detailed description and explain when they may be adopted in a game:

- offside trap in football
- 'pinch' hitting in cricket
- long ball game in hockey
- icing in ice hockey.

Present your findings to the rest of your group.

Shooting

Sports such as football, netball, basketball and hockey all require players to hit a target in order to achieve points or goals. Therefore an important performance analysis is measuring how many shots either an individual player or team make, how many of these are on- or off-target, and how many are successful. Using notational analysis (see page 145) and evaluation of this data will allow the coach to recognise whether specific training and coaching is needed, or to devise specific tactics.

Crossing

Further analysis will allow the coach and athletes to determine the number of crosses that were successful in reaching a team mate, or in a shot on or off target. For example, if a player makes ten crosses in a game but only three of them reach a team mate, then further coaching is likely to be needed.

Catching

Many sports, such as rugby, cricket and basketball, require players to catch a ball either to defeat an opponent or to continue a pattern of play. Again, analysis will determine the number of catches that were successfully caught or dropped – if an area of weakness is discovered, further analysis can be carried out and training focused on this area.

Passing

A key component of most sports is passing a ball between players in order to reach a goal. Sports such as rugby, football or hockey all require players to pass to each other successfully. Analysis could include the number of successful passes made, number of passes that fail to reach their target, and whether short or long passes were more successful. It is important that both coach and players are clear about what is being observed, and clear definitions are made of 'success', and 'short' and 'long' passes. Tactics often use either long or short passes depending on previous analysis of individuals or opponents.

Tackling

Gaining possession through tackling is an important tactic in sports such as rugby and football. The coach and players should conduct an analysis that counts the number of successful tackles made, or the number of fouls committed (resulting in free or penalty kicks) through poor tackling.

Heading

Football requires players to head the ball. This may be required to pass the ball between players or to shoot at the goal. Notational analysis will count the number of successful headers, while a qualitative analysis will allow more detailed and descriptive feedback to be given, correcting poor technique.

Dribbling

The skill of dribbling can be analysed both quantitatively and qualitatively (see pages 133–134). The time, distance and individual player dribbles with the ball can be observed and analysed, or the coach may prefer to observe dribbling technique, ensuring that the correct skills are used.

Striking

Similarly to shooting, the way a soccer player strikes a ball will have a direct effect on where it goes (either successfully or unsuccessfully). Players such as Cristiano Ronaldo will use video analysis to observe their striking technique, and practise to perfect this skill. This quantitative analysis allows the player to observe a perfect model.

▲ Striking is a specific skill requiring both technique and tactics

Positional play

Modern technology allows coaches, players and even spectators to observe the movements of players throughout a match. Television pundits use this information to offer their expert opinion on why a team is either successful or unsuccessful. Being able to observe the position of individual players can help a coach identify why, for example, a goal was scored or conceded. The information can be used to develop patterns of play and tactics such as attacking or defensive play. This is particularly important in sports such as basketball, where a coach may prefer to use man-marking in preference to zone-marking.

Style of play

Performance profiling will allow a coach to devise tactics suited to both his or her team, and the opposition's style of play. A team may prefer to focus on attacking rather than defensive play, and their tactics may be to play long balls forward. Or a team may play defensively and try and score goals on the counter-attack. Various formations have been developed by coaches that will suit their players, tactics and strategies.

Key Terms

Performance profiling – providing feedback to the athlete about what actually happened – can be used for team sports such as basketball, individual sports such as snooker, or specific positions in sport such as a goalkeeper.

Key Terms

Performance analysis can be broken down into four stages: observation, analysis, evaluation, and planning and performing.

Performance assessment has four key areas: physical, psychological, technical and tactical.

Assessment practice

1. Your local sports acadamy coash has asked you (as a sports science student) how his or her students could improve through detailed analysis. Using your underpinning knowledge, help provide the coach with player profiles for a sport of your choice. Consider specific positions within this sport, as there may be different requirements. **P1**

2. Having described what is required in order to perform, discuss these factors with the performers for your chosen sport, making sure you explain them fully. To help you and the performers, prepare a short report that fully explains the profile you have outlined. **M1**

3. The performers are keen to understand how the profile you have outlined will help them improve in their sport. Analyse each aspect of the profile fully, and as part of your report explain the effect this may have on successful performance. **D1**

18.2 Be able to analyse sporting performance

Being able to analyse sporting performance clearly is vital if weaknesses are to be identified and remedied. An athlete should always evaluate his or her performance both during and after training or competition. They should also seek the advice of others, such as a coach or teacher. It is important that when performance is analysed, an honest, clear approach is adopted. This will enable the athlete to make decisions affecting future performance. It is also important to recognise the many factors that can affect performance. These may be unavoidable (such as age or the weather) or may include factors that can be controlled by the athlete (such as diet and training).

Science has proved an important asset in improving and enhancing performance. Scientific principles are often applied to help record sporting performance, and the use of data can be analysed by the athlete, the coach or a sports scientist, with the aim of improving future performances.

A modern coach will no longer simply try and improve an athlete or team by instructing them to 'try harder'. To be an effective coach, you should be able to analyse and correct specific techniques as part of a training programme. Being able to break down complex movements into simple tasks allows the athlete to identify and correct specific aspects of his or her technique. A coach may identify movements that are ineffective or unnecessary, and these can be altered or removed from a performance.

Activity

Think of a recent sporting performance, and consider how you may have performed better. Write a list of the parts of your performance you are happy with, and the aspects you would change. This is a simple performance analysis, and should be used after every time you play sport. Consider how else you could analyse your performance.

Factors influencing performance

Many factors can affect an athlete's performance in competition and training. It is important that the athlete and coach recognise and understand each of these, and adapt their training and competition accordingly. These factors can be divided into two broad categories: intrinsic and extrinsic.

Key Terms

Intrinsic factors are within the control of the athlete (such as diet and training).

Extrinsic factors are external to the athlete (such as age or the weather).

Intrinsic factors

■ Age

Age constantly affects a person's level of fitness. For all forms of competitive sport there are age divisions, usually junior, youth and senior.

Your body changes as you get older. This can be seen broadly as:

birth → infancy → early childhood → childhood → adolescence → adulthood → middle age → old age

Some activities are regarded as young people's sports and some as older people's sports. If an activity requires a great deal of physical exertion, it is more difficult to compete at a high level as we get older and our fitness levels begin to deteriorate. For example, an athlete's flexibility will decrease over time and will affect performance, especially in sports such as judo or gymnastics.

It is important that the athlete and coach realise how the following key components can affect sporting performance:

- practising and learning – very young people can't cope with too much information and are unlikely to be able to learn complex skills
- strength – a young person will not achieve their maximum strength until they reach full adulthood
- skill – this can improve due to growth (high jumpers may appear more skilful as they get taller)
- flexibility – this decreases with age, with a negative effect on sports that require a wide range of movement, such as gymnastics
- diet – the body's metabolism slows down as we get older, so weight is likely to be gained
- reaction time – this decreases with age and, as many sports require quick reactions, can have a negative effect on performance
- injury and disease – older people are more likely to suffer from injury and disease, and take longer to recover.

It is also worth remembering that experience comes with age – and will generally have a positive effect on sporting performance and success.

▼ Older players will have less flexibility and slower reaction time, but may have more experience and skill

■ Health

Health is defined by the World Health Organization as 'a state of complete physical, mental and social wellbeing, and not merely the absence of disease or infirmity.' Recently there has been a massive growth in the number of health clubs opening offering both exercise classes, and complementary and relaxation therapies. For an athlete to perform at an optimum level of performance, they must be in excellent health and free from injury or illness.

But sport and overtraining can have a detrimental effect on an athlete's health. Recent studies suggest that some athletes may be exposing themselves to a range of health problems associated with inadequate dietary intake. Such behaviour is thought to stem from an obsessive desire to win, coupled with pressure from coaches and society's overwhelming obsession with body image. It may also be caused by western society, where there is a powerful underlying belief that thinness leads to success, power, beauty and happiness.

■ Diet

A suitable and balanced diet is the key to both health and the foundation of high sporting performance. An athlete's diet should contain food for energy, food for growth and repair, and food for general physical and mental health.

As athletes are more likely to need higher levels of energy than an average person, it is important that they eat suitable amounts of carbohydrates. Research indicates that the following nutrient intakes are optimum for most sports:

- 60–70 per cent of calories in the diet from carbohydrates
- 12 per cent from protein
- 18–28 per cent from fat.

What an athlete eats on a day-to-day basis is extremely important for training. Diet affects how fast and how well they progress, and how soon they reach their personal goals.

A common question that is often asked is 'When is the best time to eat?' Many athletes will feel nervous before a competition and may not have an appetite. However, not eating should be avoided as the body's glycogen stores are likely to be low and will be needed when activity starts. The athlete should ideally have a high-complex-carbohydrate meal at least three hours before activity.

This will allow the body to digest and absorb the food and to 'top up' the glycogen stores. It is also important that the athlete considers rehydration both during and after performance.

■ Previous training

When analysing sporting performance, it is useful for the coach to have a picture of what the athlete has achieved previously. This may be through observation and working on a regular basis with an athlete or team, or it may be through asking questions, either in person or via questionnaires. Likewise, a coach can examine previous training sessions and determine what was successful and what was less successful. Using this knowledge, future sessions can be designed to meet the specific needs of the athlete or team.

■ Motivation

Motivation, the 'direction and intensity of effort', is important for any athlete who wishes to succeed in training or competition. Motivation can be viewed as either intrinsic or extrinsic (see page 130).

Think it over

Make a list of *intrinsic* factors that motivate you to take part in sport.

■ Confidence

Self-confidence – the belief that they can succeed in their sport – is important to athletes. When an athlete has self-confidence they will tend to:

- persevere even when things are not going to plan, both in training and competition
- show enthusiasm and a desire to win
- be positive in their approach to their sport and to others involved in the sport, such as coaches
- take their share of the responsibility for both success and failure.

Self-confidence will also allow the athlete to remain calm under pressure, be assertive when required, and set challenging and realistic personal or team goals. A confident athlete will take risks in their sport because they are playing to win, and will never give up even if defeat seems likely.

To improve their self-confidence, athletes can use a variety of techniques. Naturally, success will tend to lead to an increase in self-confidence, and praise and recognition of achievements can improve confidence. Confidence can also be improved by using mental imagery (see page 132). The athlete visualises previous good performances to remind them of the feelings of success, or imagines various scenarios they are likely to encounter, and how they will cope with them if they were to occur during training or competition.

It is important to recognise that a lack of confidence may lead to poor performance. An athlete suffering from a lack of confidence is likely to suffer from stress under pressure from outside factors, such as spectators or mistakes, avoid taking risks and making mistakes, and lose concentration because they are worrying about failing.

Equally, overconfidence or false confidence can be dangerous because it can lead to inadequate preparation, low motivation and low arousal.

■ Role of the coach

The coach's role is vital in supporting and developing the athlete. A coach should fully understand the need for confidence and how they can help the athlete to develop a positive approach. A coach should adopt an approach that will develop self-confidence through successful achievement. They should help the athlete to develop and select goals and levels of competition. Unrealistic goals or expectations are likely to result in a decrease in confidence and performance. The athlete and coach should focus on successful personal performance, not on winning – a successful personal performance is likely to result in a win.

▲ The elements of confidence

■ Ability level

One of the main factors affecting performance is the ability level of the performer. Much research has been conducted to determine whether a person has a fixed level of ability, or whether anyone can be coached into a world-class athlete. What is certain is that clear and professional coaching will allow an individual to maximise their natural ability in their chosen sport.

Taking it further

There are two very distinct viewpoints when it comes to sporting talent and ability. One view is that everybody is born with a natural level of ability (nature), and those with the greatest natural ability will become high-level athletes. The other point of view is that everybody can achieve sporting success through high-quality coaching, practice and analysis. This nurturing of talent allows anyone to develop into a skilled performer.

Working in groups, discuss the 'nature versus nurture' argument using examples to highlight the points you make. Remember that you must listen to both sides of the argument and try to draw your own conclusions.

■ The team

Group dynamics

The success of a sports team will be affected by the dynamics within the team or group. It is important that athletes and coaches understand the importance of group dynamics and how this can affect performance and success. A group can be defined as 'two or more persons who are interacting with one another in such a manner that each person influences and is influenced by each other person'. A group should have a collective identity and a sense of shared purpose. Successful groups will have:

- opportunities for members to socialise
- members who share goals and ambitions
- members who are able to communicate effectively
- strong cohesion
- members who value relationships within the group
- a successful coach or leader who ensures that all members' contributions to the group are valued.

The development of a group normally goes through the following stages:

- forming – the group gets together; a level of formality is common
- storming – heightened tension associated with competition for status and influence
- norming – rules and standards of behaviour are agreed
- performing – the group matures to a point where it is able to work together as a team.

Within a group or team there will be different forms of interaction, including social interaction (formation of friendships) and task interaction (the way the members cooperate to achieve goals).

Group cohesion

Group cohesion describes the desire of a group of players to focus on a common goal and strive towards achieving that goal together. Group cohesion also describes the identity of a team. Social cohesion, where team members socialise with one another, is important for successful

▲ A successful team must develop cooperation and cohesion

team cohesion. Research indicates that groups that get on with one another are likely to exhibit high levels of cohesion and ultimately team success. It is important to understand the factors that can affect team cohesion:

- stability – cohesion develops the longer a group is together with the same members, so a coach should attempt to keep the same players playing together
- similarity – cohesion develops where group members are similar in terms of age, skills, goals and attitudes
- size – cohesion develops more quickly in small groups
- support – cohesive teams tend to have managers and coaches who provide support to members and encourage them to support one another openly; this may include players sharing their thoughts and concerns in an open and honest forum
- satisfaction – cohesion is associated with the extent to which team members are pleased with each other's performance, behaviour, and conformity to the norms and values of the team.

Activity

Identify a successful team and explain how it shows examples of team cohesion.

Loafing

One of the major problems affecting team cohesion is loafing (or the Ringelmann effect), where individuals within a team will lessen their effort because they believe the team can still perform and gain success without them putting in maximum effort.

Causes of loafing may include:

- perceiving others to be working less hard than themselves, providing an excuse to put in less effort
- believing that their own efforts will have little effect on the outcome
- disliking hard work and assuming their lack of effort will not be noticed
- feeling 'off form' and believing team mates will cover for their lack of effort.

■ Temperature

Temperature can affect the athlete in terms of both physical and psychological performance.

The effects of extreme cold in sport are quite common. Through being cold, and a lack of appropriate warm-up, an athlete may suffer from torn muscles or tendons. Hypothermia (low body temperature) can also occur in extreme cases where the athlete is unable to maintain a suitable body temperature and loses heat. This can be very dangerous and can even result in death. However, it is more common for heat loss to simply affect sporting performance. To avoid hypothermia you should:

- try and stay dry, as moisture increases the speed at which body temperature drops
- wear suitable clothing for the conditions and the environment
- avoid direct wind exposure if possible.

High temperatures can cause the athlete to overheat, and fluid loss can cause performance to drop. Athletes must take on sufficient fluid before, during and after training or competition.

Temperature can also affect an athlete's motivation as the climate affects performance.

■ Time of day

The time of day when an athlete trains or competes may also affect performance. If an athlete performs at the end of the day, after work or education, they may be tired and unable to concentrate. Training very early in the day may also have a negative affect on performance, as the athlete will have a slower metabolism, making it harder to produce energy.

Some major sports events are now restricted by media coverage, and television companies may dictate at what time the match should take place. This has resulted in evening fixtures as well as fixtures at midday, where the sun will be at its strongest in terms of heat. Again, this is likely to impair performance.

Performance profile assessment

Physical assessment

■ Multi-stage fitness test

You are probably familiar with the multi-stage fitness test (commonly referred to as the 'bleep test') to measure VO_2 max. This is a predictive test that can be used by individuals or teams to estimate their current VO_2 max. Undertaking the test is relatively straightforward. Two cones are placed as markers 20 metres apart, and the participants have to run to each cone in time with the predetermined bleeps. These get progressively quicker, decreasing the time it takes to reach each marker cone and increasing the intensity of the exercise. The results are then recorded according to the stage you have reached, and can be converted to a predictive VO_2 max level. The multi-stage fitness test is a cheap and valid alternative to individual laboratory testing, which is expensive and requires specialist training to analyse performance.

The results can be used by the athlete or the coach as the foundation of an aerobic training programme. The athlete and coach can re-test at set intervals to gauge whether aerobic fitness has improved or decreased.

This test is very good for games players, as it is specific to the nature of the sport, but due to the short turns it is less suitable for rowers, runners or cyclists.

Calculating VO_2 max
There are a number of automatic VO_2 max calculators available on the web. One way to calculate VO_2 max is as follows.
Walk a flat one-mile course as quickly as you can without stopping or breaking into a run. At the finish, record your elapsed time and heart rate. Then fill out the following equation.
VO_2 max (ml/kg/min) – 132.853 – 0.1692(weight in kg) – 0.3877(age in years) + 6.315(gender*) – 3.2649(elapsed time in min) – 0.1565(heart rate at end of test)
*gender = 0 for female, 1 for male
Example: a 35-year-old male who weighs 71 kg and walked the mile in 10 min 30 s and finished with a heart rate of 170
132.853 – 0.1692(71) – 0.3877(35) + 6.315(1) – 3.2649(10.5) – 0.1565(170) – 52.7 ml/kg/min

▲ Table 18.2 Calculating VO_2 max

Key Term

VO_2 max is the maximum capacity to transport and utilise oxygen during incremental exercise.

Activity

What are the advantages of using a multi-stage fitness test?

What are the disadvantages of using a multi-stage fitness test?

What factors may affect a person's VO_2 max?

Why is measuring VO_2 max important to an athlete?

■ Repeated sprint test

A repeated sprint test allows the athlete and coach to analyse sprint performance. Using quantitative analysis the coach can determine the time it takes to complete a sprint, the speed or velocity of the sprinter, and areas of acceleration and deceleration. Using this information, areas that need further training can be identified and specific training programmes can be devised. By repeating the sprint test over a number of weeks or even sessions, the coach is able to see whether improvements have been made.

The repeated sprint test is also a good way to train the anaerobic systems of the body.

■ Heart-rate monitors

A heart-rate monitor is a convenient way of measuring heart rate before, during and after exercise. A strap attached round the athlete's chest sends an electrical impulse to a watch worn on the wrist. This allows the athlete to measure their heart rate and work within aerobic training zones (training zones are used to determine the level of intensity at which you are working; see below). Some heart-rate monitors allow the recorded data to be downloaded to a computer, and the coach and athlete can analyse their training performance further. The use of such data gives valuable information so that training programmes can be devised or amended to suit the individual.

Training zones

There are four main training zones (in percentage of maximum heart rate, MHR):

- **fitness zone** – 60–70 per cent MHR
- **aerobic zone** – 70–80 per cent MHR
- **anaerobic zone** – 80–90 per cent MHR
- **red line zone** – 90–100 per cent MHR

Training zones are used to determine the level of intensity at which you are working. This is particularly important for cardiovascular training or exercise. Heart-rate training zones are calculated by taking into consideration both your MHR and your RHR (see page 129): see Unit 14, page 63. Because it is difficult to exercise and measure heart rate manually at the same time, it is useful to use a heart-rate monitor.

Karvonen principle

The Karvonen formula allows you to determine how fast your heart should be beating when you are in one of the heart-rate training zones:

desired heart rate (HR) =
RHR + [(MHR – RHR) × percentage intensity].

The use of a heart-rate monitor to set exercise intensity is based on the principle that as the work increases, oxygen consumption and therefore heart rate increases in a linear relationship until near-maximal intensity.

There are a number of important factors that can affect heart rate, including:

- stress
- illness
- overtraining
- medication
- time of day
- food and drink (caffeine)
- altitude
- temperature
- hydration levels
- weather conditions.

Case study

Calculating the heart rate for a training zone

Erin wants to train for a period of time in the anaerobic zone (85% intensity). Her resting heart rate is 70, and her maximum heart rate is 180.

HR = RHR + [(MHR – RHR) × percentage intensity]

so in Erin's case

HR = 70 + [(180 – 70) × 0.85]

so the heart rate to aim for is **163 bpm**

Measure your own RHR and MHR, and work out the target heart rate for 50% intensity.

■ Peak flow

Strong, efficient lungs are essential to sporting performance. The ability to obtain and utilise oxygen will be affected if the lungs are unable to deliver oxygen (and remove carbon dioxide) in relation to exercise intensity.

Peak flow is a measure of how fast you can blow air out of your lungs, using a spirometer. This measures how wide the airways in your lungs are.

Factors that can cause the airways to become narrow include:

- swollen lining
- mucus in the airways
- tubes constricted by the special muscles surrounding the airways.

All these may happen if you have asthma. For people with asthma, this simple test shows how well their asthma is being controlled.

Psychological assessment

■ Interviews

One of the easiest methods of analysing sporting performance is to interview the performer after training or competition. This gives valuable feedback on how they felt their performance went, and what areas they feel they need to improve. Using information on the athlete's personal strengths and weaknesses will allow the coach to develop a strategy for future performances. Interviews can also be used to discuss tactics they may wish to use against a particular team or individual.

■ Questionnaires

Questionnaires can be designed to gain valuable information about performers. This information can be used to develop tactics and strategies as part of training preparation. The information gained as part of the questionnaire may include strengths and weaknesses, likes and dislikes in training, and concerns about past and future performances. Key areas can then be addressed by the coach and players. Some questions to ask might include:

- Why do you play sport?
- On a scale of 1–5 (1 = not at all; 5 = completely), how much do you enjoy training?
- What aspects of training do you find particularly enjoyable?
- What do you dislike about training?
- How do you feel before a competition?

Key Terms

Strengths – positive aspects of the athlete's game – what are they good at?

Weaknesses – what areas of performance need improving?

Opportunities – what external factors should aid performance (e.g. access to video analysis or training equipment)?

Threats – what factors may cause the athlete to fail?

- How do you cope with the pressure of competition?
- What are your strengths in terms of sporting performance?
- What areas do you feel you need to address in order to improve?

Technical assessment

When profiling sporting performance, it is often stated that good technical skills are required for success. These skills are often compared with a 'perfect model', and training and analysis should focus on developing skills that are technically correct to perform a range of motions or shots (see Sport Book 1, Unit 26).

Biomechanics applies the laws of mechanics and physics to human performance in order to gain a greater understanding of performance in athletic events through modelling, simulation and measurement. This may involve filming training or performance and then analysing technique. Using computer analysis, it is

Activity

Here is an example of a completed SWOT analysis for a golfer.

Select an athlete of your choice in a different sport and perform a SWOT analysis on them to identify their strengths, weaknesses, opportunities and threats.

Strengths	Weaknesses
Good swing when driving	Not accurate with short clubs
Good balance	Poor technique out of bunkers
Consistent drive of ball off tee	Inconsistent putting
	Poor accuracy in wind
Opportunities	**Threats**
Good course knowledge	Opponent is a better player
Practised short game in recent weeks	Easily frustrated by a poor shot
	Worries too much about club selection

possible to identify areas that can be altered in order to improve, and the computer may also produce a visual 'perfect' model.

Other areas of biomechanics that may be used are the study of projectiles such as javelins, balls or even the human body and examining how they move through air or water. This is of particular concern to sports equipment designers who wish to examine how natural forces such as air or gravity can affect performance.

Case study

The use of sports science is now very common in all levels of sport, and technical analysis is a fundamental method used to improve an individual's technique in order to improve their performance. For example, a professional cricketer will use video footage that can be replayed in slow motion and watch how they coordinate their body in order to produce a complex movement such as bowling. Such analysis not only identifies areas for improvement, but also can highlight where injury may occur if technique is not altered.

What techniques can you analyse in your sport in order to improve?

How can you analyse your techniques?

Activity

Working in pairs, and with the support of your teacher or coach, video a simple technique for a sport of your choice (e.g. a tennis serve or a golf swing). Now play back your recording and try to analyse the technique, looking at specific parts of the body. Repeat this process, and write a short technique analysis feedback report.

The use of tactics and strategy is a key aspect of all sports. Tactics can be described as a specific, predetermined plan that can be implemented during a sporting performance. For tactics to be effective, it is important that all players understand what is required and are able to execute it effectively.

Notational analysis

When studying sport it is possible to analyse performance through observation. This may be done either 'live', actually at the sports event, or by video after the event.

Notational analysis studies movement patterns in team sports, and is primarily concerned with strategy and tactics. Patterns of play that led and did not lead to scoring against specific opponents can be identified, and this information is then used as a tactic or strategy in subsequent matches to outperform opponents.

Being able to analyse past performances and the performances of upcoming opponents is an essential tool used by modern football managers, and it is now common to see a laptop on the training ground, or a television and video recorder in the changing room. Most managers now have their team's matches filmed, so they can be reviewed afterwards to highlight the strengths and weaknesses of players as well as patterns of play. This enables the manager to give players feedback as part of the coaching process, highlighting specific areas to address.

Key Term

Notation is the collection of data, either using a computer or by hand. This process normally involves counting the frequency of an event, such as a shot on-target.

Tally charts

A tally chart is a useful tool when observing sporting performance. The tally chart may include simply counting performance factors such as:

- shots on-target in football
- number of fouls committed in basketball
- wide balls bowled in cricket
- number of double serves in badminton
- number of shots played to the forehand and backhand in tennis.

This information can then be analysed by the coach and the player or team, so that areas or strength and, importantly, weakness can be identified and altered as part of training.

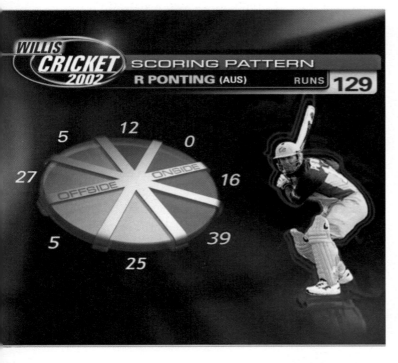

▲ A wagon wheel – a batsman's scorechart in cricket, each line on the outfield signifying the direction and value of a scoring shot, revealing the batsman's strengths and favourite scoring avenues

Activity

In groups of two or three, watch a game of tennis and record simple information. You should collect information such as:

- shots to forehand
- shots to backhand
- number of serves
- number of successful serves
- points won on serve
- number of successful backhand shots
- number of successful forehand shots.

Now analyse the data. What does the collected information show? Discuss with your group members:

- what was good about your data collection system?
- what were the problems with this method?
- how could your group ensure the collected data were accurate?

Assessment practice

1 An amateur athlete has approached you and asked you to help them prepare for an upcoming competition. They are particularly keen to understand how different factors can affect their performance. Write a report describing at least five factors that can have an effect on performance. **P2**

2 Having outlined various factors that may affect performance, produce a performance profile for the athlete to help them recognise what is required to improve. **P3**

3 To gain the merit grading criterion, you should perform this profile without teacher support. **M2**

4 To assist the athlete, prepare a report that analyses fully three of the factors outlined in their performance profile. This analysis is designed to help the athlete improve, and should give clear feedback as well as making recommendations on areas that need to be addressed. **D2**

The nature of feedback

Strengths

When providing feedback, it is important that the coach highlights the strengths of an athlete's performance. Being able to understand what went well and to develop this area further will enhance future performances both within training and in competition. It is important that the coach highlights the positive aspects of the performance, rather than concentrating on the negative parts. This will enhance the performer's confidence, as opposed to focusing on what is being performed incorrectly or badly.

Target-setting

Target-setting is a vital aspect of sporting performance and analysis. Being able to set clear, well defined targets is a valuable tool when giving feedback to the athlete. Target-setting is a powerful technique that appears to work by providing a direction for our efforts, focusing our attention, promoting persistence and increasing our confidence (provided we achieve the targets we set ourselves). When setting targets, there are a number of aspects to consider, generally defined as the SMART principle:

- Specific
- Measurable
- Achievable
- Realistic
- Time-based.

(This is sometimes expanded to SMARTER – see page 65.)

■ Specific

Targets should be specific or definitive. For example, instead of saying that a player is a 'poor batsman' in cricket, a coach may identify specific aspects of batting that need to be improved, such as defensive play or a cover drive.

■ Measurable

Goals or targets should be capable of being measured. For example, if you are trying to improve your possession of the ball in football, you may wish to count successful passes, long passes, short passes or successful crosses. This can be done before, during and after a training programme, and any improvements can be recognised. It is important that, when measuring targets, clear criteria are used and that any data collected are analysed correctly.

■ Achievable

Any target or goal that you set out to achieve must be possible to achieve in a fairly short period of time. It is pointless to set targets that are impossible, too difficult or too far off. It is also important that set targets are not too easy, as this will have a demotivating effect on the athlete. An example of poor target-setting would be for a novice runner to complete a marathon in under two hours. Failure in meeting goals is useful in improving technique and long-term success, as long as you draw useful lessons from it and feed these back into your training programme. ('A' is sometimes taken to stand for 'adjustable' – meaning that the achievability must be monitored and the goal can be changed to suit the circumstances if necessary.)

■ Realistic

If targets are too difficult or impossible, it is likely the athlete will become demotivated and may even give up training or competition. Targets should be challenging and realistic, pushing the athlete in their desire and ability.

■ Time-based

Set targets must have defined time limits so that a coach or athlete can review progress. Open-ended targets tend to be less successful than those that have a set period in which to achieve the target. For example, an athlete may be set a six-week training programme to improve their muscular strength. After (and even during) this six-week period, a review can be carried out to see whether the specific targets have been achieved. If not, the programme can be amended to take into account any personal changes.

Goals

When setting goals, it is important to understand that to achieve the 'dream' goal there should be a number of short- or medium-term targets to achieve on the way. The athlete who dreams of winning an Olympic gold medal will need to set short-term 'day-to-day' goals in order to focus their effort. Goals can be classified into short-, medium- and long-term.

■ Short-term goals

Short-term or daily goals are most important because they provide a focus for training in each session. Past research on Olympic athletes found that setting clear daily training goals was one factor that distinguished successful performers from their less successful counterparts.

■ Medium-term goals

Medium-term or intermediate goals are markers of where you want to be at a specific time in your training

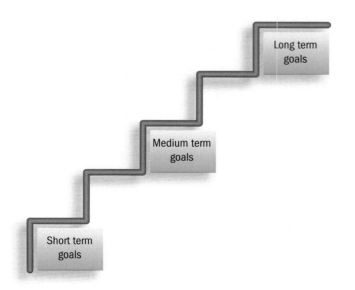

programme. For example, if your long-term goal was to lower your 1500m personal best time by one second over 10 months, a medium-term goal could be a half-second improvement after five months.

■ Long-term goals

Long-term or 'dream' goals are those that seem a long way off and difficult to achieve. In time terms, they may be anything from six months to several years away. These goals should be comprised of short- and medium-term goals.

Recommendations

The purpose of any performance analysis is to provide feedback to the athlete so that improvements can be made. Identifying specific areas of weakness is essential if changes are to be made.

■ Training for specific components of fitness

Having observed and evaluated performance, the results may indicate that the athlete needs to address a specific component of fitness. The key components of fitness are:

- strength
- aerobic endurance
- muscular endurance
- flexibility
- body composition.

By identifying the specific area, the coach can design new training programme or adapt existing ones so that improvements can be made.

■ Psychological training

It is now recognised that an athlete's performance can be affected by their mind and it is important that the coach understands the psychological requirements. Therefore a coach may use interviews or questionnaires to find out how the athlete feels both during and after performance. This information can be used to design specific psychological training methods such as imagery or meditation.

Case study

Imagery is a form of mental practice that is designed to improve concentration, control and confidence in sport. The process involves the performer imagining their performance as part of their preparation, and visualising the experience in their mind. Former World Cup ski champion Steve Podborski used imagery as part of his training. He describes his use of imagery in skiing as the ability to visualise not only the way it looks when you are going downhill, but how it feels '... the muscle tension that you actually go through when you make the turns, and to experience what attitude your body is in ... I feel what things will feel like and see everything run through my head. I have a moving picture with feelings and sensations. I run through the entire course like that.'

For your chosen sport, write a short account of how you visualise the experience of taking part.

■ Skills training

Feedback may provide information to address a specific skill that has been identified by observation. A coach may have identified that a golfer has poor balance when addressing a ball on the tee. The feedback would be very specific to the balance skill component. Using effective feedback will enable the coach to observe, demonstrate and correct the poor skill, and as part of the training a specific drill can be used to address this problem.

■ Technique coaching specific to movement

A typical training programme will contain an element that addresses an athlete's technique. Coaches will regularly observe, demonstrate and correct poor technique. This feedback can be through discussion, observation, or watching a video of the performance so that the athlete can see their own actions. A training programme should give the athlete an opportunity to practise a specific technique so that the 'perfect' model can be achieved. For example, a coach may observe a cricketer's bowling action and decide that, by videoing the action, clearer feedback can be given. Through

discussion, the bowler can address poor technique and correct it as part of their training or practice.

■ Tactical recommendations

Being able to analyse and understand specific tactics is an important part of the feedback process. Both the tactics adopted by your team, and those used previousy by an opposing team or player, will help improve future performance. The coach and players must have a clear understanding of the different tactics that can be used, as well as their effectiveness during competition. If a certain tactic has not been successful, then the coach must change it. Likewise, an understanding of the opposition's tactics will help both coach and team understand how they must play in order to achieve success.

Activity

Looking at the list of technical weaknesses below, decide how you would design practices that could improve them. Try and identify at least three practices for each sport. You may need to talk to a coach or a teacher, or carry out research to design a specific drill.

- Goalkeeper – poor kicking of back passes.
- Golfer – hits the ball left when driving.
- Netball – misses too many goals.
- Tennis – backhand return always too long.

Assessment practice

Having completed a performance assessment for the amateur athlete, it is important that you give clear feedback. This may be in the form of a short presentation, and should allow the athlete to ask questions. This may be done with the support of a tutor. **P4**

To gain the merit grading criteria **M3** you should give your feedback independently without the help of a tutor.

Levels of performance

There are many different levels of performance, depending on ability. This is best illustrated in what is commonly known as the sports development continuum.

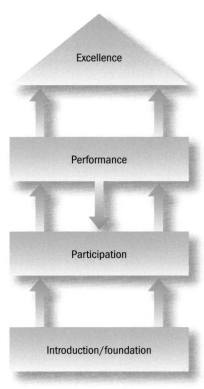

▲ The sports development continuum

Each level of the 'pyramid' represents the stage you are at in your chosen sport. The terms can be described as follows.

- Foundation – the early development of sporting skills (throwing, catching, hand–eye coordination), on which most later sports development is based. These are normally the skills taught as part of PE lessons in schools. Without a sound foundation, young people are unlikely to become long-term sports participants.
- Participation – sport undertaken primarily for fun and enjoyment, often at basic levels of competence.

This includes people who play sport on a regular basis, such as a Sunday league football player.

- Performance – a move from basic competence to a more structured form of competitive sport at club or county level. This includes performers who have been identified as having potential in their sport and may be selected to represent district or county teams.
- Excellence – about reaching the top, applies to performers at the highest national and international levels. Players such as Olympians or professionals are considered to be in the excellence category.

Foundation

■ School

Very often, school is where children will have their first taste of organised and varied sport. This is part of the National Curriculum, which states that children must be taught at least two hours of high-quality PE and sport at school. In addition, the government aim is that by 2010, children will be offered two or more hours beyond the school day, delivered by a range of school, community and club providers. The government's overall objective is to enhance the take-up of sporting opportunities by 5–16-year-olds. The ambitious target is to increase the percentage of schoolchildren who spend a minimum of two hours a week on high-quality PE and school sport.

It is important that as many children as possible are actively involved in foundation sport. Not only does this provide fun, enjoyable and healthy activities, it will also mean that more children are likely to excel in sport and progress further in their sporting abilities.

■ Beginners

Foundation level also includes sport for all beginners, regardless of age. Many organisations offer beginners lessons in their chosen sports, and these taster sessions often lead on to regular participation.

At this level, it is important that the fundamental skills are taught correctly and that participants are given an opportunity to practise these in an enjoyable environment. Learning and developing such skills will aid future performances, and a coach should ensure that skills are taught well and practised correctly and regularly.

Activity

As part of a research project, identify the key organisations involved in delivery of sport to beginners. Give an example of a specific campaign or initiative designed to get people involved in sport.

Participation

■ Saturday league player

Participation sports are undertaken mainly for fun and enjoyment. Other reasons may include health and fitness, and participants will also enjoy other aspects associated with physical activity, such as social aspects and a sense of purpose and achievement. An example may be a Saturday league player who enjoys being part of a team, and has progressed from foundation level. The player will have a range of basic skills that have been practised and developed so that they are competent in their sport. A coach will aim to analyse these skills through observation and discussion, and areas such as tactics can be introduced to improve performance and success. There are many highly skilled and talented players who choose to play at the participation level simply because they enjoy the sport, or for general health and fitness.

■ Out-of-school clubs

A key area that the government is keen to develop is the number of out-of-school sports clubs that offer a range of sports. The purpose of these is to ensure children are able to take part in sport after their school day or at weekends. Strategies have been devised to link local schools together, as well as linking to local sports clubs. This

is to ensure that if children wish to continue in sport, they have a local opportunity to do so. The government has promised to invest over £1.5 billion between 2003 and 2008. To aid the development of this strategy, the government has enlisted the help of 22 National governing Bodies in:

- athletics
- badminton
- basketball
- canoeing
- cricket
- cycling
- football
- golf
- gymnastics
- hockey
- judo
- netball
- orienteering
- rowing
- rugby league
- rugby union
- sailing
- squash
- swimming
- table tennis
- tennis
- volleyball.

Performance

■ County or National Standard

When a player has consistently participated at a good standard, they may have their sporting talents recognised by local, regional or county organisations. These will provide the player with further opportunities to develop and enhance their skills using high-quality coaching and equipment. Players at this level will compete at county or even national standard.

Many local sports development units will have strategies in place to ensure talented athletes are offered opportunities for competition and training, and to support talented performers.

Through high-quality coaching and analysis, the performer may have an opportunity to further their sporting career and develop to the excellence level of the continuum.

Excellence

■ Olympic or world-class athlete

An Olympic or world-class athlete will need a high level of analysis as part of their training and performance in order to maximise their potential. Using the latest analytical techniques, combined with advanced technology and coaching, the high-level athlete will be able to develop their skills and aim for the 'perfect' model. The use of sports science is now common, and an athlete is just as likely to find him- or herself in a laboratory as on a training field.

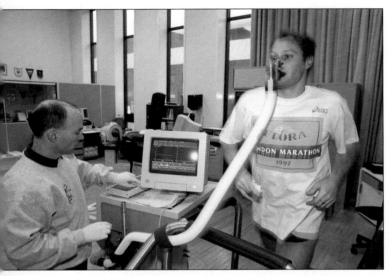

▲ Performance and excellence-level athletes need a high level of analysis to maximise their potential

Purpose and resources

Reasons for analysis

There are a number of reasons why analysis is required in sport, at all levels. These may range from identifying talent in children, through to assessing specific techniques in high-level performers. The resources used to perform an evaluation will also differ. An analysis may involve simple observation by a coach using a clipboard to record results, through to advanced video and computer technologies to analyse physiological behaviour during exercise. Either way, the methods used will be designed to enhance the understanding of performance and lead to improvement over a given time period.

■ Talent identification

Observation is used to identify talented athletes or produce a report on an opposing team. This is commonly referred to as scouting, and involves an experienced coach observing a performance and evaluating their findings (see Unit 19). Reasons for doing this may include identifying new players, or preparing for a match where information about the opposition will allow you to devise a specific tactic. For example, if you observe a cricketer who struggles to play the ball off their legs, then a tactic would be to bowl in this region, hoping to get their wicket or limit their run-scoring.

■ Monitoring current fitness levels

Another purpose of analysis is to gain data about an individual's current fitness level. Using a variety of fitness tests, we are able to measure the various components of fitness, and this information can be used as a starting point of any training programme. Throughout training programmes, regular fitness tests can be conducted to ensure that the benefits are being gained. If results indicate that targets are not being met, training can be adjusted to take into account any changes.

Think it over

Analysis is an important aspect of modern sport at all levels. Regardless of whether sport is being played at foundation or excellence level, analysis can be used for a number of different reasons.

Consider the four stages of sport (foundation, participation, performance, excellence) and identify the reasons for analysis for each. How may an analysis be performed, and what equipment or specialist training is needed?

■ Identification of strengths and areas for improvement

A key reason for undertaking a performance analysis is to identify areas of strength and of weakness. This is of particular importance when investigating technique.

Once you have identified areas that need to be improved, it is possible to develop a training programme to address these issues. For example, analysis may show that a goalkeeper is poor at gathering crosses. A training programme will incorporate specific training to improve this key area.

Feedback on performance

By assessing a team or an individual in a competition situation, you are able to see whether players are affected by outside factors such as the crowd or the opposition. This type of analysis will allow you to develop specific tactics that can be used under game conditions. Using defined conditions during training will allow a team to develop both their techniques and their tactics. An example of this would be if a team struggles to defend using man-marking in basketball. A practice may include using specific drills to highlight marking, and every time this happens the coach can stop the practice and demonstrate if it has been effective or not.

Performance assessment may also use tally charts or notational analysis to record what is happening during a specific performance. The data gathered can be evaluated and feedback used to inform players about areas that can be improved.

Recovery from injury

If an athlete has been sidelined due to either short-term or long-term injury, it is useful to perform a number of assessments before they recommence training or performance (see Unit 17). This ensures that the athlete has recovered sufficiently so that injury does not reoccur. Simple fitness tests can be conducted both on the injured area, and also generally to identify a base level from which to start training again. It is important that the athlete does not over-train, as this can result in continued injury and will prevent them from performing.

The coach may also wish to talk to the athlete about their injury in case there are problems or concerns about a reoccurrence. A player may have been hurt by a tackle, and may have developed a fear of tackling. Using this information, the coach will be able to support and encourage the athlete to overcome any psychological factors.

Assessment of health status

It is common to use fitness testing and health screening to analyse whether a person is able to participate in exercise programmes. This may be specific to an individual who has not taken part in sport for a long time, or to a high-level athlete recovering from illness or injury. Either way, assessment of health will provide the coach with information regarding whether or not they are able to perform specific exercises, or to gauge the level at which a training programme should be set.

Squad selection

Analysis can be used to monitor player performance both in training and in competition. Sports such as rugby and football now use large squads of players, and through performance analysis a coach will be able to select the players most likely to achieve success. If a player has been underperforming, this can be addressed and additional support given. A coach can analyse the opposition team in preparation for a match, so that tactics involving certain players can be developed and used. For example, an opposing team may have a tall centre-forward and so a tall defender may be required to deal with him or her during a match.

Goal-setting

By using detailed analysis and evaluation of performance, it is important that clear and well defined targets or goals are set by the coach and athlete. These goals can be seen as a target that the performer wishes to achieve, and may be either short or long-term goals. Goals should be set using the SMART principle (page 147) and should be discussed openly with the coach and the athlete. By including the athlete in the decision-making, it is likely that they will remain more motivated to train as they feel they are in control of their training.

Resources

Fiscal resources

Equipment for analysis costs money. As noted above, the ways in which performance can be analysed vary greatly. An effective evaluation can be performed by a coach simply watching a performance and feeding back their findings or thoughts to the athlete or team. Alternatively, technologically advanced equipment can be used to video techniques and use computer software to analyse specific movements. The benefit of this equipment is that it can slow techniques down to tiny movements, and measurements can be made, such as velocity of movements or joint angles. But this can be both expensive and time-consuming.

■ Equipment

The equipment a coach can use to perform an analysis varies greatly. A clipboard can be used to record observations during a match, and a simple stopwatch can be used to record times. But more elite performers will require highly detailed analysis with more advanced equipment, such as movement-analysis software, force platforms and respiratory analysers. Such performance equipment is commonly found in sports science laboratories that are designed specifically to record human performance.

Key Terms

Movement analysis software is used to identify and compare specific sporting techniques in slow motion using video footage and a computer. Software such as Dartfish© can fully analyse complex techniques, and allows performers to watch themselves in action and measure techniques such as the angle of joints in a tennis serve or the speed of a bowler in cricket.

Force platforms are used to measure the size and direction of a force during sport. For example, a runner may wish to analyse their running technique – a force platform can analyse what part of their foot hits the ground and how hard the impact is. They can use this information to ensure that the correct footwear is used.

Respiratory analysers are used by athletes to examine the efficiency of the lungs when inspiring and expiring during sport. This information can be used to identify respiratory condition and fitness.

Activity

For the list below, identify how equipment has changed in recent years and the effect this has had on the sport:

· tennis
· golf
· football
· cricket.

■ Time

Performance analysis can be a very time-consuming process. If a video analysis is conducted, the coach will have to review the performance, interpret the data that have been collected, fully evaluate the data, and develop the results into training programmes or tactics. For an analysis to be effective, it is important that the coach and players allocate sufficient time to evaluate findings as part of the coaching process. If evaluation is hurried, errors are likely to occur and the findings may be inaccurate.

■ Facilities

It is common for high-level athletes to find themselves in a sports science laboratory as part of a performance assessment. Such laboratories will contain up-to-date scientific equipment, and the use of this allows highly accurate and detailed physical performance information to be collected and analysed. Unfortunately, this equipment can be very expensive, and coaches may need specialist assistance in gathering information. But it is still possible to collect relevant information using common equipment such as stopwatches and simple notational analysis.

It is also important to remember that performance can be affected by where the athlete is performing. This must be taken into account when undertaking any form of assessment.

■ Human

The best asset in developing sporting performance is people who are enthusiastic about the goal. These may be coaches, players, parents or spectators, and each plays a valuable role in improving an athlete's or a team's performance. Gaining feedback from people will aid training and performance, and using such advice should be part of the coaching process. Sharing the experiences of other players will also aid performance, and a young or inexperienced athlete should seek advice from others.

Assessment practice

1   Your work experience at the local sports college involves you working with a range of performers of different abilities. It is important that you are able to identify the different forms of analysis that can be used for the four different levels of sport. To help the athletes, prepare a presentation that outlines and describes the purpose of analysis for a sport at two different levels (e.g. foundation and excellence) and the resources you require. **P**5

2   Having done this, you have been asked to highlight fully the differences in analysis and resources between the different levels in a selected sport. **M**4

Knowledge check

1   Giving examples, explain what is meant by discrete skills, serial skills and continuous skills.

2   For a sport of your choice, explain the specific skills that are required to perform at excellence level.

3   Discuss how an understanding of sports psychology can aid performance.

4   Using a sporting example, explain how training programmes can be developed to include the principal components of fitness.

5   Name two methods of psychological training that can be used to enhance performance, and discuss why these methods may work.

6   Outline the psychological factors that can affect a performance, and explain how a coach can address these as part of a training programme.

7   What is notational analysis and how is it used in sport?

8   What is meant by goal-setting? Use examples from a chosen sport to explain this.

9   List and explain the four levels of sporting performance.

10 How may a coach use performance analysis for a group of beginners?

11 How may a coach use performance analysis for a high-level athlete?

12 What are the advantages and disadvantages of performance analysis?

13 What is meant by the terms qualitative and quantitative data collection?

14 How can technology improve sporting performance?

15 For a sport of your choice, explain how you might perform a quantitative analysis.

End of Unit assessment

Preparation for assessment

1 You are assistant to the coach of a leading cricket team, and you have been asked to analyse the performance of the emerging young players. Write an initial plan of what methods of analysis you intend to use. Remember to incorporate the four main types of assessment: physical, psychological, technical and tactical. **P1 M1 D1**

Grading tips

Grading Tip M1

Explain the analysis you have performed, highlighting any differences between the roles of the players in the team.

Grading Tip D1

Fully analyse the performance profile for each of the players. Consider the specific role of the players, and any differences there may be.

2 You have agreed your plan with your coach and team, and have carried out an initial analysis by observing the players during a competitive match. But the players didn't perform nearly as well as you both expected. Describe five or more factors that may have affected the players' performance. Again, remember to incorporate the four main areas of assessment. Consider both intrinsic and extrinsic factors. **P2 M2 D2**

3 Bearing in mind the factors affecting performance, discuss with your tutor which are the three key areas to concentrate on. These could be physical, psychological, technical or tactical – or a mixture.

Decide how you would assess performance for each of the three key areas. Remember to consider other factors – time, money, equipment available. **P3 M3**

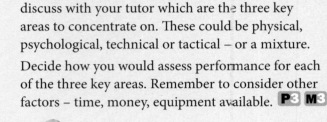

Grading tips

Grading Tip M2

Complete a detailed performance assessment independently and without tutor support. Remember to identify clearly what you are assessing as part of the performance.

Grading Tip D2

You should prepare a short report that highlights the players' strengths and areas for improvements, and make specific suggestions on how you feel players can improve in future. Remember to consider fully the specific types of assessment, and explain any strategies you feel would aid the players.

4 Based on the assessment of the three key factors you selected, discuss with your tutor how best to provide feedback to your athlete/team. It may be useful to write a list of strengths and areas for improvement that you can give to the players.

Allocate sufficient time to give feedback – and make sure that you are honest in your evaluation. **P4 M4**

Grading tips

Grading tips

Grading Tip **M3**

Give clear and specific feedback from your performance analysis to the players, without tutor support.

Grading Tip **M4**

Explain fully the differences between the two outlined levels. You should consider any similarities, as well as the different types of resources that may be available between the foundation and excellence levels of performance.

5   Your assessment was carried out for a bowler, at the performance level. What would you do differently if your athlete was at:

- the foundation level?
- the excellence level?

Take into account the requirements of the particular level and the resources that would be available to you.   **P5**

To achieve a pass grade the evidence must show that the learner is able to:	To achieve a merit grade the evidence must show that, in addition to the pass criteria, the learner is able to:	To achieve a distinction grade the evidence must show that, in addition to the pass and merit criteria, the learner is able to:
P1 describe the performance profile of a selected sporting activity **Assessment practice page 136**	**M1** explain the performance profile of a selected sporting activity **Assessment practice page 136**	**D1** analyse the performance profile of a selected sporting activity **Assessment practice page 136**
P2 describe five factors that may influence performance of an athlete **Assessment practice page 146**		
P3 perform an assessment of a selected athlete undertaking sporting activity using three components of your performance profile with tutor support **Assessment practice page 146**	**M2** perform an assessment of a selected athlete undertaking sporting activity using three components of your performance profile **Assessment practice page 146**	**D2** analyse the performance of a selected athlete using three components of your performance profile providing comprehensive feedback and recommendations for improvement **Assessment practice page 146**
P4 provide feedback to the athlete based on the assessment of their performance with tutor support **Assessment practice page 149**	**M3** provide feedback to the athlete based on the assessment of their performance **Assessment practice page 149**	
P5 describe the purpose of, and the resources required for, analysis at two different levels of sports performance **Assessment practice page 155**	**M3** compare the purpose of, and resources required for, analysis at two different levels of performance **Assessment practice page 155**	

Talent identification and development in sport

Introduction

Professional sports clubs and governing bodies of sport are constantly looking for stars of the future, and have established academies and talent identification programmes to help them in this process.

It is important to realise that this is a far from straightforward process – there are several examples of athletes who show early promise but then 'fall by the wayside', as well as athletes who prove to be late developers.

It is generally agreed, though, that potentially talented athletes can be identified in all sports, and this talent can be developed by appropriate training. Early identification is no guarantee of future success, but is believed to improve the athlete's chances of fulfilling their potential not just at the highest levels, but at all levels of sport.

This unit is designed to help you to understand the predictors of talent and ways of developing talent in individuals at all levels of performance, and to devise programmes to identify and develop talent in different sports.

As you work your way through this unit you will come across case studies and examples that will help you to appreciate the various aspects of talent identification in sport.

After completing this unit you should be able to achieve the following outcomes:

- Understand key predictors of talent for individuals in sport.

- Be able to design a talent identification programme for a chosen sport.

- Understand talent development in sport.

- Be able to design a talent development programme for a chosen sport.

Types of talent

Before we can begin to identify talent, it is first important to understand what we mean by it. Coaches have identified four main types of talent in sport, as follows.

Unidimensional talent

Unidimensional talent is talent in one activity or aspect of performance only. A good example of this would be a 100-metre sprinter who cannot compete at 200 metres or any other distance. This type of athlete is obviously limited in potential, in the sense that they have few sports skills that are transferable to other events.

Multidimensional talent

Sports talent may also be broad, as in the ability to play in midfield in football, or to be a world-class tennis player such as Andy Murray or Roger Federer. These athletes have to combine physical, emotional and intangible skills every minute they are in the game. They rarely run fast in a straight line, but instead have to make decisions, call plays, handle a ball or racquet, run, change direction, avoid defenders, and react to team-mates and opponents. Their sports talent is multidimensional.

Unisport talent

Most professional athletes, and virtually all world-class athletes, are proficient in only one sport; for example Tiger Woods is a professional golfer, not an all-round athlete. This might be the result of early specialisation, competition (particularly at an early age), and the huge amounts of money paid to professional athletes.

The unisport athlete is not so prevalent at the primary, middle and secondary school levels, but with the establishment of academies for children as young as six, the trend is certainly going in that direction. Although most coaches and sports officials agree that the trend towards unisport athletes is a fact, they also think this trend is a mistake.

Multisport talent

Case study

Born in 1872, C. B. Fry was perhaps the greatest sportsman ever in the UK. He played cricket for Surrey and was captain of England, scoring 94 first-class centuries as well as six consecutive centuries; a record that still stands. As England captain he never lost a test match and his career batting average was 50.

Not only that, he also took part in the first-ever international athletics match between Yale and Oxford, where he won both the long jump and the 100-yard dash, and in 1893 he equalled the then world record of 23 feet 6½ inches (7.17 metres).

In 1900 he signed as a professional footballer for Southampton FC, and he reached the FA cup final with them in 1901/02. In that season he was also capped for England in a match against Ireland.

As if this wasn't enough, he also played rugby for Oxford University, Blackheath and the Barbarians.

▲ C.B. Fry – not just a cricketer

Case study

An American candidate for the title of 'most talented all-around athlete ever' was Jim Thorpe, who won the 1912 Olympic decathlon and pentathlon, and was a two-time All-American running back at the Carlisle Indian School. As well as playing professional football and baseball, he was a standout in basketball, lacrosse, tennis, handball, bowling, golf, swimming, billiards, gymnastics, rowing, hockey, boxing and figure skating. He was able to play just about any sport. When he was in his 50s, he was still talented enough to drop-kick field goals from the 50-yard line during exhibitions at high-school football games.

Thorpe and Fry represent the upper end of multisport talent. They could play just about any sport at the highest level. Unfortunately, multisport athletes are becoming an endangered species, for the reasons mentioned above. Many coaches believe such athletes should be encouraged to play as many sports as they can before they finally decide to specialise in one sport.

Predictors of talent

How can we identify such talented individuals and help them develop their potential? The Australian Institute of Sport has identified the following areas to consider when assessing a potential athlete's talent. This model has been copied by other countries; in particular the UK, when developing their own programmes.

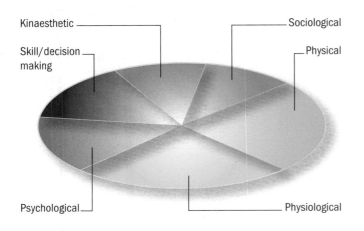

The easier it is to measure an attribute such as physical or physiological characteristics, the easier (relatively) it is to predict future talent, and these predictors are considered in turn in the following section. Some coaches consider that the difference between world-class performers and others is mainly psychological, in that if an athlete 'throws in the towel' often and easily, it is unlikely that they will become successful. The most successful athletes will continue with unfamiliar, sometimes difficult tasks until they have mastered them.

Here are some subjective tests that have been used by coaches to test this natural fight or spirit.

A coach of budding young tennis stars asked them to hit the tennis ball into the ground to make it go as high as possible. The tennis stars couldn't use their own equipment – instead, he gave them an old racquet and an old tennis ball with a hole in it, and left them on their own for 30 minutes. The coach observed them closely from a secluded position. Those who gave up hitting the ball during that time were asked not to come back.

In a similar strategy, a successful Romanian rowing coach would watch potential rowing prospects during a 'dog-and-bone' wrestle. A thick baton or stick (bone) was gripped tightly by two combatants. Like a dog wrestling with a bone, combatants tried to force one another outside a circle to win the game, and therefore the bone. Often the rowers were purposefully mismatched in size to observe their level of persistence in an unwinnable situation. The rowing coach was not interested in who won, but in how the athletes persisted in their struggles.

Another common test in talent identification involves cycling or running for approximately 10–15 minutes at a steadily increasing level of effort. These tests culminate in voluntary exhaustion, and can cause great temporary discomfort for the athlete. Coaches who observe such testing sessions are assessing the 'mongrel factor' – which athletes show the doggedness to continue when the test becomes hard. Many athletes have been overlooked for selection based on the subjective impression that they gave only 95 per cent effort, not the full 100 per cent. For some coaches (and athletes), an athlete's ability to extract the final 5 per cent is vital:

◀ Assessing a potential athlete's talent (Source: www.ais.org.au)

'There's no easy way'

Allan Wells (1980 Olympic 100-m champion)

'You have to go into the jungle, find the lion, and spit in his face ... then shoot him. You guys are not good enough to win on talent alone ... you have to want it.'

Herbie Brooks (coach of 1980 US Olympic hockey team)

Physical predictors of talent

Coaches have identified the following physical characteristics that can be measured and used as a predictor of future talent:

- height
- body mass (weight)
- somatotype
- muscle girth.

Other physical predictors are:

- arm span
- basketball throw
- vertical jump.

These tests are easy to administer and interpret, so can be used by almost any school or sports club. Normal values for each can be found in Table 19.2 on pages 167–168.

■ Height

Standing height is the height from the floor to the top of the head, measured with the athlete standing barefoot. It is measured with a tape measure to the nearest 0.1cm (see figure).

■ Body mass (weight)

Body mass is the athlete's weight in kilograms, and is easily measured with a set of (accurate) bathroom scales or a set of balance scales to the nearest 0.5kg.

■ Somatotype

People can be divided into three body shapes or somatotypes: endomorphs, mesomorphs and ectomorphs. These somatotypes were first described in the 1940s by Dr William Sheldon, who also stated that they were associated with certain personality traits (Table 19.1). The majority of scientists today generally consider these theories from the 1930s and 1940s outdated, but the words endomorphic, mesomorphic and ectomorphic are still a useful way of defining body types, especially in association with weight training aimed at gaining muscle.

(a)

(b)

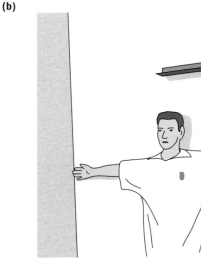

▲ Measuring (a) height; (b) arm span

Body type	Associated 'personality traits'
Endomorphic • soft body • underdeveloped muscles • round shape • overdeveloped digestive system	• love of food • tolerant • evenness of emotions • love of comfort • sociable • good-humoured • relaxed • need for affection
Mesomorphic • hard, muscular body • overly mature appearance • rectangular shape • thick skin • upright posture	• adventurous • desire for power and dominance • courageous • indifference to what others think or want • assertive, bold • zest for physical activity • competitive • love of risk and chance
Ectomorphic • thin • flat chest • delicate build • young appearance • tall • lightly muscled • stoop-shouldered • large brain	• self-conscious • preference for privacy • introverted • inhibited • socially anxious • artistic • mentally intense • emotionally restrained

▲ Table 19.1 Somatotypes and personality (source: www.kheper.net/topics/typology/somatotypes.html)

As we have noted, the idea of linking personality traits to somatotype is somewhat outdated. Although it is true that many endomorphs seem reluctant to exercise (the 'couch potato' scenario), is this a result of their body shape, or is their body shape a result of their reluctance to exercise? In fact there are some endomorphs who are successful athletes (shot-putters, Sumo wrestlers), so many observers are reluctant to link personality and body shape in the way Sheldon did back in the 1940s.

■ Muscle girth

Low body fat and high muscle girth can also be used as predictors of talent in young athletes. Generally speaking, the greater the muscle girth, the greater the muscle mass and so the stronger the athlete.

It is important to ensure the *muscle* girth is measured, not simply the girth of the limb, to try and eliminate the effect of body fat on the measurements. This is best done by measuring the muscle not in its relaxed state, but when it is fully contracted. This measure indicates the true muscle girth. Areas measured include neck, chest, upper arms and forearms, waist and hips.

■ Arm span

Arm span is the horizontal distance between the tips of the middle fingers with the arms extended laterally and at shoulder level (see figure on page 164). It includes the width of the shoulders and length of both the upper limbs.

■ Basketball throw

The basketball throw task is designed to measure upper body strength, and is performed with the athlete sitting against the wall and throwing a size 7 basketball as far as possible using a two-handed chest pass.

Distance is measured to the nearest 5cm and the throw is repeated twice, with the longest distance being recorded.

The basketball throw is used as a baseline measure for each individual athlete, rather than a comparative measure between athletes.

▲ **Basketball throw**

■ Vertical jump

The vertical jump task measures the ability to spring in a vertical direction. The athlete dips his or her fingers in chalk and reaches up as high as possible to touch a wallboard. He/she then jumps as high as they can to touch the board again. The standing measure is then

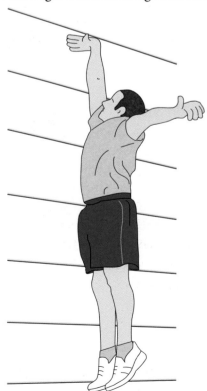

◀ **Vertical jump**

deducted from the jumping measurement to give the vertical jump height.

There are two main physiological predictors of talent: anaerobic and aerobic capacity.

■ Anaerobic capacity

The athlete's anaerobic capacity is determined using the 40-metre sprint test, as follows. The athlete runs 40m in a straight line, as fast as possible, twice. The time is taken to the nearest 0.1s, and the better of the two times is recorded by the tester.

This is a measure of the individual's anaerobic capacity – their ability to work without oxygen – as the exercise is completed using the energy stored in the muscles only.

■ Aerobic capacity

Aerobic endurance is measured using a 20-metre shuttle run (more accurately known as the multi-stage fitness test or 'bleep test'), as the level achieved by the athlete is a direct measure of their ability to use oxygen while exercising.

- The student runs to the opposite end of a 20m marked distance on a surface that is flat, even and slip-resistant, and places one foot behind the line by the time the next beep sounds. If they arrive before the beep, they should turn (pivot) and wait for the signal, then run to the opposite line to reach this in time for the next signal.
- At the end of each minute, the time interval between beeps is decreased, so running speed becomes progressively faster.
- Ensure the student reaches the end line each time and does not turn short. Emphasise to students to pivot and turn, rather than running an arc (this takes more time).
- Each student continues running for as long as possible until he/she can no longer keep up with the beeps. The criterion for eliminating a student is two lengths in a row where he/she is more than two steps from the end.

■ Normal values

In Table 19.2 the data are presented in percentiles – for example, in the first group (12-year-old girls), 95 per cent will weigh less than 64.8kg, have an arm span of less than 170cm, and be shorter than 167.8cm. It is important to realise that a talented child does not need to be in the top percentile (the best 5 per cent) in all areas, but the various attributes may be tailored to the individual sport. For example, height is a positive attribute for basketball players, so a child with height in the top category may be a good player even if their vertical jump, etc. is not so good.

▼ Table 19.2 Normal values for physical and physiological predictors

Females age 12 / Males age 12

Percentile	Height	Mass (weight)	Arm span	Vertical jump	Anaerobic capacity (40m sprint)	Aerobic endurance (shuttle run)	Height	Mass (weight)	Arm span	Vertical jump	Anaerobic capacity (40m sprint)	Aerobic endurance (shuttle run)
95	167.8	64.8	170	36	6.50	8.7	166.9	59.8	171.2	45	6.00	10.5
90	165.6	59.0	168.0	35	6.65	7.9	163.0	55.0	167.0	40	6.20	9.8
80	162.0	53	164.4	32	7.00	6.4	159.4	49.0	163.0	36	6.54	8.9
70	159.0	50.0	160.0	30	7.15	5.8	157.0	46.0	160.8	35	6.80	8.1
60	157.00	47.0	158.7	29	7.36	5.3	155.0	45.0	157.0	33	6.96	7.4
50	155.6	45.0	156.0	28	7.50	5.1	153.0	43.0	155.0	31	7.07	7.0
40	153.2	43.0	153.0	26	7.66	4.5	151.0	41.0	152.0	29	7.24	6.2
30	151.0	41.0	150.0	25	7.84	4.0	148.9	39.0	149.6	27	7.41	5.5
20	148.8	38.6	148.0	23	8.09	3.4	146.0	37.0	147.0	25	7.61	4.9
10	145	35.0	143.6	20	8.50	3.1	144.0	35.0	143.0	22	7.96	3.8
5	143.5	32.5	140.0	19	9.00	2.7	141.0	34.0	139.4	19	8.28	2.8

Females age 15 / Males age 15

Percentile	Height	Mass (weight)	Arm span	Vertical jump	Anaerobic capacity (40m sprint)	Aerobic endurance (shuttle run)	Height	Mass (weight)	Arm span	Vertical jump	Anaerobic capacity (40m sprint)	Aerobic endurance (shuttle run)
95	175.0	72.0	177.0	43	6.01	8.9	185.0	81.0	190.6	57	5.38	11.9
90	173.0	68.0	174.9	40	6.30	8.0	183.0	76.0	187.0	55	5.50	11.1
80	169.8	63.0	172.0	36	6.50	7.2	180.5	70.5	184.0	50	5.78	10.3
70	168.0	59.0	168.0	34	6.79	6.4	179.0	68.0	181.0	46	5.98	9.9
60	166.0	56.0	166.0	32	6.94	5.4	177.0	65.0	179.0	44	6.10	9.1
50	164.0	55.0	164.0	30	7.10	4.9	175.0	63.0	176.0	42	6.20	8.5
40	162.0	53.2	161.0	28	7.20	4.4	173.0	60.0	174.0	40	6.40	7.6
30	161.0	51.0	160.0	27	7.40	4.1	170.0	57.0	172.0	38	6.60	6.8
20	158.0	50.0	156.7	25	7.60	3.7	168.0	55.0	169.0	34	6.95	6.1
10	155.4	46.8	154.0	23	8.00	3.2	164.0	50.0	164.0	30	7.35	5.2
5	153.0	45.4	151.2	20	8.52	2.5	160.0	47.1	160.0	28	7.77	4.0

| Percentile | Females age 17 | | | | | | Males age 17 | | | | | |
	Height	Mass (weight)	Arm span	Vertical jump	Anaerobic capacity (40m sprint)	Aerobic endurance (shuttle run)	Height	Mass (weight)	Armspan	Vertical jump	Anaerobic capacity (40m sprint)	Aerobic endurance (shuttle run)
95	175.00	75.0	175.7	44	6.00	9.9	189.5	87.4	192.0	55	5.30	12.2
90	173.0	68.0	174.0	41	6.20	8.9	187.0	80.0	191.0	56	5.20	11.7
80	171.0	63	170	38	6.50	8.1	184.0	75.0	186.3	52	5.50	10.7
70	169.0	61.0	168.0	35	6.70	7.1	181.8	73.0	184.0	50	5.78	9.8
60	167.0	59.5	166.0	34	6.81	6.2	179.2	70.0	181.0	48	5.94	9.2
50	165.0	58.0	164.0	32	6.97	5.7	177.0	67.0	179.0	46	6.10	8.6
40	164.0	55.0	163.0	31	7.20	5.0	175.0	65.0	176.0	43	6.20	8.1
30	162.0	54.0	160.0	30	7.44	4.4	173.0	63.0	175.0	40	6.42	7.5
20	160.0	52.0	158.0	28	8.00	4.1	170.9	61.0	172.0	36	6.60	6.9
10	156.1	49.2	153.0	26	8.64	3.4	168.5	57.4	170.0	33	7.00	6.4
5	153.9	48.1	150.0	25	9.00	3.1	167.0	55.0	167.0	29	7.40	5.9

Physical/physiological measurements are not the only predictors of talent – other factors, including sociological, psychological, technical and tactical skills, may be equally as important.

Sociological factors in talent identification

There are many outside influences on young athletes that will have a direct effect on their potential to become high-level performers. Some authors have talked about the 'circle of influence' on young athletes, as represented in the diagram below.

The most important individuals in this circle of influence are the athlete, the coach, and the parents.

■ Parental support

Research has shown that parental involvement affects both general and sport-specific aspects of young athletes'

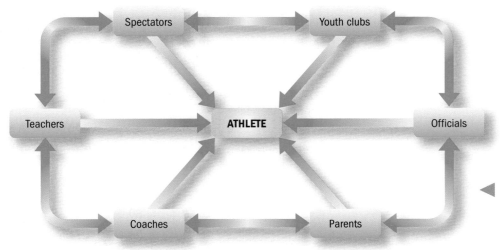

The 'circle of influence' on young athletes (adapted from Hellstadt, J.C. 1987. The coach/parent/athlete relationship. *Sport Psychologist* 1: 151–160.)

participation in and performance of sport, both positively and negatively. For instance, the less parental pressure felt by young male and female basketball players, the greater their enjoyment of the sport. In one study, young male wrestlers who reported enjoying their sport also reported more positive adult interactions, particularly with their mother.

Parental support is associated with higher levels of self-esteem, while parental pressure is associated with negative self-evaluation. This suggests that the right balance of parental involvement in youth sport activities has implications for both immediate and long-term attitudes to participation in sport.

■ Practice opportunities

Another sociological factor deemed important by young athletes, and their coaches and parents, is the opportunity to practise. The fewer opportunities there are for athletes to practise and train, the slower their development.

For example, France has 103 professional tennis players compared with Britain's 45, although their populations are of a similar size. This may be because France has 160,000 people playing competitive tennis, while Britain has just 20,000. Maybe this results from the fact that France has 9200 tennis clubs compared with Britain's 2598, and four times as many courts as Britain. Also, government spending on all sports in France is £5 per person per year, compared with Britain's £1.30.

If we compare Britain with other countries, the situation is even worse (see Table 19.3), and many coaches and others have related this to lack of facilities and access to good quality coaching.

▼ Table 19.3 Men in top 200 world tennis rankings, by country

Country	Population (million)	Men in top 200
Britain	60	2
Belgium	10.2	6
Croatia	4.4	4
Russia	145	7
Spain	40	23

■ Education

In some countries, the education system is used as a first step in identifying talent. In the UK there is a programme to appoint Gifted and Talented Co-ordinators in schools in order to identify talented individuals in both sport and the arts and refer them to the appropriate governing body.

Psychological factors in talent identification

Psychological factors include confidence, concentration, anticipation, decision-making and game intelligence.

■ Confidence

Competitive events cause both arousal, which prepares the athlete for increased performance; and anxiety, which can have a negative effect on performance. Generally speaking, an athlete with a higher level of confidence in their ability will have a lower level of anxiety during competition.

■ Concentration

Concentration is the mental ability to focus on the task in hand. The greater the athlete's power of concentration, the greater is their ability to perform the task effectively and efficiently. Research has identified the following types of concentration:

- broad–narrow continuum – the athlete focuses on a large number of stimuli (e.g. position of players on both sides) or a small number of stimuli (e.g. position of goalkeeper when shooting)
- internal–external continuum – the athlete focuses on internal stimuli (feelings) or external stimuli (ball).

Also, the level and duration of concentration required vary with the sport:

- sustained concentration – distance running, cycling, tennis, squash
- short bursts of concentration – cricket, golf, shooting, athletic field events
- intense concentration – sprinting events, bobsleigh, skiing.

Common distractions for athletes include anxiety, mistakes, fatigue, weather, public announcements, coach, manager, opponent, negative thoughts, etc.

Strategies to improve concentration are very personal. One way to maintain focus is to set short-term goals for each training session or competition. The athlete will have an overall long-term goal, for which they will identify a number of short-term goals that help focus on specific aspects of the task. For each of these goals the athlete can use a trigger word (a word that instantly refocuses the athlete's concentration on the goal), for example, sprinting technique requires the athlete to focus on being tall, relaxed, smooth and to drive with the elbows – a trigger word could be 'technique'.

Individuals with athletic potential will tend to show higher levels of concentration than others, right from the beginning of their athletic career. They will be the ones who are prepared to practise over and over again, and who remain 'on task' throughout a session. For example, if you ask a group of athletes to repeat an action 100 times, the talented individuals will try to do 100 perfect actions, whereas others will either give up or rush through the activity without considering proper technique.

Kinaesthetic and skill/decision-making

■ Anticipation

Sometimes called the speed of anticipation, this is the ability of athletes to 'read the game'. For example, in cricket a fast bowler may bowl at 80–90mph. This means the ball takes only about 0.5s to reach the batsman after it leaves the bowler's hand, which is the time it takes for the body to see the action and begin to initiate movement – in other words, the batsman cannot even begin the stroke physiologically. So how can he play the shot? Actually, the batsman begins to play the shot before the bowler completes his action, and he does this by reading the bowler's body position, hand position, etc. – he anticipates what the bowler is going to do.

In 2002 this theory was tested when a group of researchers looked at novice and high-level karate competitors. When shown either a video or a still photograph of an opponent, the high-level competitors could anticipate where the attack was to be (head, body or legs) both more quickly and more accurately than the novices. Talented novices will also have this ability. In the karate study, some individuals within the novice group were as accurate as the high-level performers. These individuals should be tagged as promising.

■ Decision-making

High-level athletes tend to make the right decisions more often than those of lower ability. That is to say they will make fewer errors in either technique, tactics or strategy than less skilled competitors. Roger Federer, for example, is renowned for making very few unforced errors during a tennis match, and it is this consistency that makes him one of the best tennis players of all time. Perhaps a better example is someone like Nick Faldo, the most successful European golfer ever who 'made the cut' (was in the top half of the field) in 229 of his 298 tournaments (winning 42), and was ranked world number one for 81 consecutive weeks in the early 1990s. This ability can be spotted even in raw novices, as they will often read the game better than their peers, although they may not have the same technical ability. For example, they will spot a player in space during a football game, even though they may not be able to make the 'killer' pass.

■ Game intelligence

Athletes are very careful about how they use their energy; they know when to put on pressure and when to take it easy so as to conserve energy. They sense the important moments and time their efforts accordingly. We often hear the comment that an individual seemed to perform 'effortlessly'. It is important to realise that the performance was not really effortless – it appeared so because of many hours, days, weeks, and sometimes years of careful, dedicated preparation. It is an illusion to think that high level athlete has achieved excellence by taking short cuts. High levels of performance require intelligent application of mind and body. Even when setting out on their athletic career, people with the potential to become high-level athletes can state their aspirations and give a timescale for them. Many of the promising juniors in British athletics have already determined that 2012 will be their year, and some will have set a plan to achieve that.

As 1980 US Olympic track-and-field athlete Mary Osborne Andrews stated:

'what we know about peak performers and high achievers is that these are individuals who are able to imagine what they want before they ever get it, and can balance the priorities in their life in the process of reaching it.'

■ Skills

One other extremely important factor is skill, which can be subdivided into two areas – general motor skills and technical/tactical skills.

General motor skills

General motor skills make up what is often called coordination, and include attributes such as balance, hand–eye coordination (catching skills), and body awareness. High-level athletes tend to have better motor skills than either the general population or recreational athletes.

Technical and tactical skills

Technical and tactical skills are skills learned by game play. Many coaches believe that the difference between athletes who are among the best in their country and world class athletes is their tactical awareness (often called vision) or ability to read the game.

Taking it further

Another test often used by athletes is the so-called POMS test. Find out what POMS stands for. After you have completed the test, compare your findings with those from the SCAT test. Which do you think is the most accurate, and why?

Assessment practice

For work experience, you are shadowing the talent scout for your local athletics club. Together you are visiting local schools to give a talk about the different types and predictors of talent in your specific event. Devise a short presentation for the talent scout to deliver, using PowerPoint or another presentation program, or flipcharts and display posters, stating what you look for in prospective athletes. **P1 P2**

Grading tips

Grading Tip **P1 P2**

In your presentation you need to include, height, weight, somatotype and determination as traits identified with successful athletes, along with some indication of how these may differ for different sports.

Activity

Find from the internet or elsewhere a Sport Competition Anxiety Test (SCAT) and complete it. Repeat this with several colleagues and/or friends, and discuss your results. Do you think the results match how people see you as a person, and if not why not?

Current talent identification programmes

Many clubs and governing bodies have talent identification programmes that are unique to their sport, but they all share some important features.

Following the lead taken by the Australian Institute of Sport, UK Athletics and others have plans to set up a three-phase programme to help to identify potentially talented athletes.

Phase one: adolescents aged 14–16 are screened within their school via a series of eight physical and physiological assessments, the results of which are correlated against a national database. If the youngsters' scores show a favourable correlation against the national standards, then they progress on to phase two. Phase one serves as the identification stage of development.

Phase two: the testing or screening process continues in this phase, but becomes more sport-specific. The testing protocol serves to hone the results in phase one. If increased potential for a specific sport is indicated, then more advanced laboratory assessments will probably be conducted; this is the 'selection' phase.

Phase three: young athletes who have been identified as talented, and selected for a particular sport via testing, will be invited to participate in a talented athlete programme – the 'development' phase.

The Australian Talent Search Programme was developed in the late 1980s and fully implemented by 1994. Guided by the Australian Sports Commission, plans and programmes were created for particular sports, including athletics (track and field), canoeing, rowing, swimming, triathlon, water polo and weightlifting. The programme was created in order to develop talent over the six-year interval leading up to the 2000 Sydney Olympic Games.

Many professional clubs, particularly football clubs, depend on the subjective assessment of their experienced scouts and coaches, employing a list of key criteria. These are often set out as acronyms; for example:

- TIPS – technique, intelligence, personality, speed (the key phrase incorporated in the scouting process of Ajax Amsterdam)
- TABS – technique, attitude, balance, speed
- SUPS – speed, understanding, personality, skill
- PAS – pace, attitude, skill.

The problem with these assessment methods is that they are subjective – they depend on someone's opinion. This makes comparison between athletes difficult, as well as creating difficulties in measuring their progress objectively.

Talent identification checklists

In the UK, the Department for Children, Schools and Families (formerly the Department for Education) has devised the following checklist to help identify gifted and talented schoolchildren in the areas of physical education, sport and dance.

Generic skills checklist

- Balance
- Coordination
- Timing
- Anticipation
- Speed of movement
- Efficiency of movement
- Spatial awareness
- Control

Physical performance

- Use advanced skills/techniques in chosen sport
- Execute movements with precision and fluency
- Execute movements with accuracy and appropriately
- Select appropriate movements for a given situation

Cognitive development

- Thorough understanding of appropriate skills/ strategy/tactics or composition (SSTC)
- Can apply range of SSTC
- Demonstrate originality, proficiency and flair in the application of SSTC

Observation and evaluative skills

- Understanding of how SSTC can affect the quality and originality of a performance
- Recognise quality performance and make evaluative judgements of that performance
- Can offer suggestions/modifications on how to improve own and others' performance
- Able to make judgements independently and prioritise aspects for further development

Health and fitness

- Consistently apply appropriate knowledge and understanding of health and fitness in all aspects of their work
- Can actively use appropriate knowledge to improve fitness for their chosen sport.

Pupils are marked as average, above average, well above average or exceptional in each of the areas, and are then enrolled in the National Academy for Gifted and Talented Youth (www.nagty.ac.uk), based at Warwick University, which monitors their progress.

Athlete profiling

Athlete profiling (sometimes called performance profiling) is a way of planning an athlete's development by looking their strengths and weaknesses. Performance profiling comprises four steps:

1. coach outlines the performance profiling process
2. athlete identifies the characteristics of a high-level athlete for his/her sport/event
3. athlete rates each in terms of level of importance and self-assessment
4. athlete and coach analyse the results and agree a way forward.

Performance profiling can help coaches develop a better understanding of their athletes by:

- highlighting perceived strengths and weaknesses
- clarifying the athlete's and coach's vision of the key characteristics of performance, and highlighting any differences
- highlighting discrepancies between the athlete's and coach's assessment of performance
- providing a means of monitoring progress.

The detection and selection of talented youths for sport participation has several advantages for both the sport and the athlete.

1. The time taken by the athlete to reach a high performance is reduced.
2. The amount of work required for the athlete to achieve a high level of performance is reduced.
3. The coach's time is used more effectively by training mainly athletes of superior ability.
4. The number of athletes competing at the higher levels of the sport is increased.
5. The national team will work together better.
6. The athlete's self-confidence increases because he/she knows that he/she is among an elite group of athletes.
7. The application of the sports sciences to training programmes is improved by involving sport scientists in the selection process.
8. Selecting those sports qualities, in advance, that are less amenable to training may ultimately enhance performance.
9. The athlete can be channelled to a sport where he/she has the highest probability of success.
10. Potential individual limiting factors to performance can be identified early and steps taken to reduce and/or eliminate them.
11. In sports with a stature component, such as gymnastics, the athlete can be spared from spending years training for a sport that he/she will ultimately outgrow or never develop the physique necessary to participate at a high level.
12. By identifying talent early, the athlete can begin the training process with enough time to prepare for the age at which he/she will reach a physical peak without having to rush through the developmental process. This usually results in a more thorough and well designed approach to training, ultimately resulting in a safer and sounder approach for the athlete.

(Source: Bompa, T.O. 1990. Theory and Methodology of Training: The Key to Athletic Performance. Kendall/Hunt, Dubuque, IA, USA.)

The World Class Potential Plan is based on the World Class Talent programme, which supports athletes from seven to ten years away from the podium. At this level, each athlete is tested to see if they have the necessary skills to realise their potential. This level serves as the entry point to the World Class Pathway for the vast majority of athletes. It provides UK Athletics with a way to identify those who have genuine capacity to reach the top, and the athlete with a personalised programme to address weaknesses and build on strengths.

'The identification of talent is difficult, time consuming, and ongoing. Because of the specificity of the effects of training on performance, in the final analysis, the only way to precisely determine if the athlete is suitable for gymnastic training and performance is actually doing it!'

(Dietrich Harre, author of Principles of Sports Training, 1982.)

Structure of talent identification programmes

Phases of the programme

Each talent identification (ID) programme must have a clear set of aims, a purpose, structure and format, and these are discussed in more detail below.

■ Aims

Talent ID is a fairly complex blend of scientific knowledge and assessment, alongside the more subjective art of coaching. It aims actively to seek out those individuals who possess the raw material for world class success, and will respond positively to an intense training and competition environment.

■ Purpose

The purpose of any talent ID programme is twofold: it gives athletes the opportunity to develop their full potential via a programme (such as the World Class

Pathway programme); and gives the sponsoring governing body (and Sport UK) international success.

■ Structure and format

Every talent ID programme has to have a recognised structure and format. One possible structure has been described on pages 167–168, where the predictors of talent are measured in schoolchildren and then compared with normal values. Another type of structure is that followed by the Lawn Tennis Association in the Case study below.

Case study

The Lawn Tennis Association (LTA) has 10 national coaches based across Britain, including Scotland and Wales. Their main role is to drive the Junior Talent ID and Development Programme for players under 16, and they work closely with LTA tennis managers and club development officers based at the county offices, as well as clubs and coaches, to create the Talent ID Programme.

Juniors aged between eight and 12 are recommended by LTA county officers and coaches, and then attend their area's Talent ID day, which brings them to the attention of the National Training Team. From here, players are selected to attend the National Assessment Roadshow.

At the roadshow, LTA coaches have a target of assessing approximately 500 players through a series of tennis sessions, coordination drills and physical testing. Players also provide national coaches with an outline of the goals they are working on, and the coaches complete a report on each player.

Promising players are also spotted through a number of other routes, from tournaments to special County Talent Days and National Performance Roadshows.

Once potential world-class performers have been identified by the above process, they are monitored by national coaches, and special training camps are organised for them at the National Tennis Centre as well as UK regional centres of excellence.

1   **Is the LTA's programme enough to get the UK back on the world tennis stage? How does it compare with the system in France, for example?**

■ Timescales

As noted above for the Disability World Class Potential Plan, it takes about seven to ten years for an athlete to become world class. This is also true of able-bodied athletes, so almost all development programmes work on this timescale.

Use of test batteries

A battery of physical fitness tests is a group of tests that closely represents the various physiological demands of a particular sport or event.

The first step is to break down the sport into its different fitness components. For an event such as a sprint or marathon, this is fairly straightforward. Games such as basketball, rugby and volleyball are a little more complex.

One of the more complex examples is soccer, which is an intricate blend of aerobic and anaerobic endurance, strength, power, speed and agility. The test battery should include physical fitness tests that measure each of these components. Each test aims to replicate the energy demands and movement patterns within the sport. For example, for soccer, walking one mile as quickly as possible is less sport-specific than running in 20m bursts backwards and forwards (multistage shuttle run).

Once the precise energy and movement demands of the sport are understood, the most appropriate physical fitness tests can be chosen.

Activity

Compile your own test battery for two different sports, such as rugby and cricket. You need to consider the physical demands of both sports and apply tests accordingly. Can you find any similarities between the two? What are their main differences?

Resources needed to run a talent ID programme

Talent ID programmes need resources.

■ Human resources

These include coaches, sports scientists, administrators, etc. There must be enough of each to run the programme efficiently, as well as other professionals such as sports medicine professionals, who ideally should be available to athletes on a daily basis during their development. They will also be used in the identification process to measure potential athletes against normal values and to interpret the results.

■ Physical resources

These include training facilities, transportation to and from events, medical facilities, assessment facilities and equipment, etc.

■ Fiscal resources

This is the money required to provide all the other resources. In 2005, UK Sport committed to spending £75 million to identify and develop talent leading up to the Beijing Olympics in 2008.

▲ The coach is one of the most important human resources in identifying talent

■ Talent is not always apparent by observation alone

To be talented in sports usually requires a blend of favourable characteristics. While strength is an important component of weightlifting, so too is the ability to apply strength quickly (power), as well as possessing short arms and short legs. Also, while it is true that 'big legs' are helpful to the sprint events in track cycling, leg girth must be almost entirely due to muscle, not fat. However, muscular lean legs are not enough – the existing muscle fibres must also be of the type that has the ability to contract very quickly. The point is that there are often several key characteristics associated with a sport that must be taken into account to optimise or predict performance in that sport. Often you cannot see these characteristics, but you need to measure them objectively or scientifically.

■ Be a big fish in a big pond – not in a small pond

A child shows real talent when they outperform all comers. Comparing a child's talent with local groups, friends and family members can lead to an inflated idea of their real talent. They must be compared with the performances or attributes of the entire population, and this is done by evaluating the child's performance on a series of standard tests or measures, as described above. Comparing the child's performance against normative data (norms), or a sporting organisation's own historical data, is usually the best indicator of talent.

■ Don't specialise in just one sport – try several

With the exception of a small minority of sports, such as gymnastics and swimming, a broad sporting focus is preferable to a narrow one for attaining sporting excellence. Before the teenage years, parents can help maximise the their children's chances of succeeding in a range of sports by allowing them to participate in activities that have:

- an aerobic or endurance component (such as running, swimming, hiking, cycling, rowing, dancing)

- a motor-skill or coordination component (such as hitting, kicking, throwing and catching sports, gymnastics)
- a social or interactive component (such as team-based sports).

Activity

Imagine you are a chief scout or national coach for a sports club or association. It is your job to identify up-and-coming talent from local schools, youth clubs, etc. Design a screening programme for teachers and volunteers, which is quick and simple to use, and will enable coaches and volunteers to identify children with athletic potential so that they can then be referred to you for further assessment.

Taking it further

Try to design a secondary assessment that will enable you to identify, from the group above, children who are talented in your particular sport. In order to do this, you must identify the special characteristics required for that sport, as well as any mental attributes the athlete may require.

Assessment practice

1 To add to your presentation in section 1, describe the current talent identification programme in the club's athletics programme, explaining clearly to the audience (schoolchildren and their parents) how and why the programme works. **P3 M1**

2 The talent scout has identified a talented young person for your athletics club. Design a talent ID programme for them, justifying the choice of activities and stating why these will be of benefit. **P4 M2 D1**

Grading tips

Grading Tip P3 P4

You may want to include here some of the tests from the test battery you devised for the last unit, for example a 20m run test, vertical jump, and so on.

Grading Tip M1 M2 D1

In order to achieve a higher grade, you need to explain why these are relevant and how the information they give relates to your chosen sport.

19.3 Understand key factors in talent development in sport

As we have seen, there are physical and mental attributes that help us to identify potentially gifted athletes – but this does not guarantee that these athletes will fulfil their potential. So what are the factors involved in developing this talent, and therefore the athlete's potential – and what obstacles might they meet on the way?

Physical factors

There are certain physical characteristics that almost all talented athletes share (see section 19.1), but if they are to fulfil their promise in a particular sport, their physical attributes need to match the activity. For example, weightlifters need short limbs in relation to their height, as this helps them to develop both strength and power during both training and competition. They should also have a stocky build, which gives them a rather squat appearance in contrast to, say, sprinters or basketball players.

Height

Tall athletes will need to be developed in sports that take advantage of this physical characteristic. An obvious example is that the average height for male basketball players in Europe is around 6 feet 4 inches (1.95m) compared with the average male height of 5 feet 10 inches (1.75m). Rugby also shows a similar trend, in that

players in all positions are becoming taller. The difference between the two sports is mainly that of somatotype (see page 165), with basketball players tending to show ectomorphic traits (lean build), while rugby players tend to be mesomorphs with endomorphic traits (stocky build).

▼ Physical factors such as height need to be matched to activity

Weight (body mass)

One other factor in talent development, again a function of somatotype, is the athlete's body mass. Athletes should be encouraged to play sports that are suitable for their body size. If we look at two athletes of the same height, the heavier athlete will be more suited to power sports such as rowing, whereas the lighter athlete may be more suited to sports such as running or jumping. A good comparison is between two of the greatest-ever Olympic athletes, who between them won a total of 14 gold medals over five Olympics. Sir Steve Redgrave is the only athlete to win gold medals at five consecutive games in the sport of rowing (1984–2000); Carl Lewis won nine track and field golds between 1984 and 1996. Both athletes were born in 1961 and are roughly the same height (Redgrave 6 feet 5 inches; Lewis 6 feet 3 inches), but Redgrave weighed in at around 100kg while Lewis was only 88kg. Body mass was a factor in both athletes' development – the lighter Lewis developed more speed than the heavier Redgrave, who in turn developed more muscular strength than Lewis.

Muscle girth

Muscle girth is a measure of the muscle's size and therefore its potential strength. Athletes who have a greater muscle girth will, on average, do better in strength/power-based events, while those with smaller muscles do better in skill/agility-type events. A recent study showed that when runners and basketball players (who are both generally ectomorphs) were compared, the basketball players had a higher average muscle girth and greater strength. This indicates that athletes of equal stature and somatotype should be encouraged towards a particular sport based on their muscle girth, which indicates their ability to develop strength.

Somatotypes

As we saw earlier (page 165), people may be divided into three basic body shapes or somatotypes: endomorphs, mesomorphs and ectomorphs. These body types can be related to sporting activities. For example, weightlifters tend to be stocky (endomorphs); sprinters tend to be muscular and athletic (mesomorphs); while marathon runners tend to be tall and thin (ectomorphs).

Activity

Look at the three body types on page 165 and compare them with famous athletes. Can you associate a sport with a body type?

Taking it further

Try to think of people you know in each body type. Do you think Sheldon's description of personality traits (page 165) is correct? If not, why not?

Physiological factors

Another factor in athletic development is the athlete's physiological make-up. For example, muscles are made up of a mix of slow-twitch and fast-twitch fibres. As the names suggest, slow-twitch fibres contract more slowly than fast-twitch, but they also take longer to tire. Sprinters will have a high proportion of fast-twitch fibres, whereas marathon runners will have more slow-twitch fibres, and this is determined genetically. That is why sprinters struggle to run marathons, and *vice versa*.

Aerobic endurance and anaerobic power

Another aspect of talent development is an athlete's aerobic and anaerobic endurance or capacity. If we continue the comparison above, sprinters will have a well developed anaerobic capacity, while marathon runners will have a greater aerobic capacity.

These physiological differences mean that their athletic talents can be developed in different ways. To continue comparing sprinters and marathon runners, even if both individuals followed the same training regime, the sprinter would never develop into a high-level marathon runner and *vice versa*, simply because their physiology would not allow it. Therefore training needs to be tailored to the athletes' physiological make-up in order for their true potential to develop.

Theory into practice

A recent study of elite Gaelic football, hurling and soccer players in Ireland showed that players in all three sports were of a similar size (height and weight), and could run at roughly the same speed. However, soccer players had the best aerobic capacity, Gaelic footballers the best endurance, and hurlers were the strongest, reflecting the needs and demands of the three games.

It follows that, to develop the best talent in these three sports, those individuals who show good aerobic capacity when young should be encouraged to play soccer; those with the best endurance, Gaelic football, and the strongest, hurling.

1   How could you identify the characteristics needed for each sport?

2   What training/development programme would you use for individuals in each sport?

3   Would you encourage players to play each sport (cross-train), and if not, why not?

(Source: McIntyre, M.C. A comparison of the physiological profiles of elite Gaelic footballers, hurlers, and soccer players. British Journal of Sports Medicine 39, 437–439.)

Think it over

Think of some sports and the physiological profile of the players/competitors. Can you predict the type of sport someone might be suited to physiologically? For example, would a more naturally aggressive person be drawn to a combat sport such as boxing, or perhaps a contact sport like rugby, whereas a less aggressive person might be attracted to running or gymnastics?

Sociological factors

Some people think this is the most important part of talent development. This is not to talk about a person's class or place in society (although that can have a bearing), but how they are perceived and supported by their friends, coaches, fellow athletes and family. Of all these, family is probably the most important – and the most important family members for a young athlete are his or her parents.

Parental support

Research shows that parental support is associated with greater enjoyment of sport, more positive assessment of performance ('I played my best although we lost' rather than 'I was rubbish, that's why we lost'), and greater self-esteem.

Parental pressure, on the other hand, is associated with a lack of enjoyment; stress associated with performance, and lower levels of self-esteem.

Parents can provide tangible support for their child as he/she develops in their athletic career by providing funds for training, transport to and from training, accommodation etc., as well as intangible support in the form of encouragement, emotional support (a shoulder to cry on) and so on.

Education

Developing a junior performance athlete should not be at the expense of a child's education. The goal is to produce a top-level competitor who is also well rounded and well educated. At the same time, training of talented athletes should not be neglected in order to fulfil educational needs.

Young athletes should combine an intensive sports-specific strength and conditioning training schedule with a reduced academic timetable. Along the way, they should also learn self-study skills and how to manage their time more effectively, which is also important in their development as performers.

Athletes may enrol at a state or independent school near their training centre, which works in partnership with their performance programme, and may study for a range of GCSEs. The school should give athletes the flexibility to attend competitive events and to receive support with their work when they return. Extra tutoring can also be arranged.

Another option is for athletes to study for the same range of GCSEs through a distance-learning programme. These players benefit from a dedicated study environment at the training centre. Study sessions are carefully structured into the athletes' weekly schedule, and an academic mentor or manager oversees the programme and coordinates the work of tutors, who also come to the centre for regular face-to-face tuition.

In both cases, players are able to attend all their scheduled training sessions, while the academic programme means they can move through the education system without disadvantage. There is always regular communication between schools, tutors, parents and coaches in order to assess progress.

Support from the school or college can play a vital role in an athlete's development. Some schools may have their own professional coaching staff. Eton College, for example, has its own professional rowing coach, which is probably why a number of their boys have been selected to row for Great Britain at all levels, including Sir Matthew Pinsent, Ed Coode and Andrew Lindsay, who were gold medallists at both the Athens and Sydney Olympics.

Opportunities for deliberate practice

These two key factors of both parental and educational support mean that the young athlete will have more opportunities for deliberate, structured practice. The greater the opportunities to practise, the more quickly the athlete will develop. They will also, with greater exposure to coaches, develop better game intelligence, tactical awareness and strategic skills.

So what factors can we say are important in the development of talented athletes? In order to give athletes the best chance to fulfil their potential they should have:

- the appropriate physical traits for their sport (body type, aerobic capacity, etc.)

- psychological strength
- parental support
- educational support
- the opportunity to practice
- access to facilities and coaches.

Role of the coach

Access to good quality coaching is very important. The coach's primary role is to speed up and facilitate the process of individual development through achievement of an individual's athletic potential. This means that the coach accepts the athletes' long-term interests as of greater importance than short-term athletic considerations. To fulfil this role, the coach must behave in an ethical manner, bearing in mind the following main points.

- Coaches must respect the equal rights of each athlete, with no discrimination on the grounds of gender, race, colour, language, religion, political or other opinion, national or social origin, association with a national minority, birth or other status.
- Coaches must ensure that practical environments are safe and appropriate, taking into consideration the age, maturity and skill level of the athlete. This is particularly important in the case of younger or less developed athletes.
- Coaches have a responsibility to influence the performance and conduct of the athletes they coach, while at the same time encouraging the independence and self-determination of each athlete by their acceptance of responsibility for their own decisions, conduct and performance.
- Coaches must assert a positive and active leadership role to prevent any use of prohibited drugs or other disallowed performance-enhancing substances or practices. This includes educating athletes on the harmful effects of prohibited substances and practices.
- The coach must acknowledge and recognise that all athletes have a right to pursue their athletic potential, including when an athlete's development would benefit from a change of coaching situation. The coach must ensure that, in these cases, any formation of a coaching partnership or transfer to another coach is actively explored with the athlete, whose decision is supported.
- Coaches must hold recognised coaching qualifications. Coaches must respect that gaining

coaching qualifications is an ongoing commitment, achieved through upgrading their knowledge by attending accredited courses and through practical coaching experience. Coaches also have a responsibility to share the knowledge and practical experience they gain.

- Coaches must enter into full cooperation with all individuals and agencies that could play a role in the development of the athletes they coach. This includes working openly with other coaches, using the expertise of sports scientists and sports physicians, and displaying active support of their national and international governing bodies.

■ Skills of coaches

Trainer

The coach needs to develop the athlete's physical capacity in all areas so that they can compete more effectively.

Motivator

A good coach will motivate each athlete individually, as well as the team/squad as a whole.

Planner

The coach needs to plan sessions, not only in isolation, but as an ongoing process throughout the athlete's career.

Demonstrator

The coach needs to be able to demonstrate what he/she wants from their athlete.

Role model

The coach acts as a role model for their athletes. If a coach is always late for sessions, argues with officials, etc., then the athletes may consider such behaviour not only acceptable, but desirable. If a coach is always on time, works hard during sessions, and accepts decisions gracefully, then athletes should also follow this example.

■ Techniques

There are several techniques that successful coaches use during their sessions. These include:

- use of praise – athletes are praised for good work, rather than just being criticised for mistakes
- creating an atmosphere of expectancy – athletes turn up to the session knowing they are going to work and learn

- use of feedback – athletes are given feedback, both individually and as a group
- giving the athlete choices – alternatives are presented by the coach to suit athletes' needs
- maintaining on-task behaviour – athletes are not left hanging around, but are active or preparing to be active throughout the session.

Psychological factors

Earlier (page 169) we discussed psychological factors to be identified in talented athletes, and these traits need to be developed if the athlete is to fulfil their potential.

■ Confidence

In order to develop confidence, athletes must set realistic yet challenging goals, both in training and during competition. These goals should drive the action of both training and competition plans. Accomplishing goals in practice through repetition in settings similar to the competition environment will instil confidence. Confidence helps to make participation fun, and is critical to the athlete's motivation.

Athletes may be more motivated by accomplishing short-term than long-term goals, but successful athletes will always have a long-term goal underpinning their training programme.

■ Concentration

Concentration is an essential mental skill for optimal performance in all sports, including team sports. Like other skills, it can be learned. Concentration means being fully in the present, not analysing or focusing on what happened one second ago, or what will happen one second from now. This is sometimes known as the focus of attention. The more complete the focus of attention, the greater the level of concentration.

Skills involved in concentration fall into two major categories:

- focus of attention on targeted, relevant information
- dissociation from (ignoring) non-targeted, irrelevant and potentially distracting information.

Concentration involves both focus of attention and dissociation from potential distractions, at the same time.

Anticipation

As we saw earlier, athletes will anticipate the actions of the opposition in order to take appropriate action as soon as possible. This skill is developed by repetitious practice and by competition against various opponents.

Decision-making

High-level athletes tend to make the right decisions more often than those of lower ability. That is to say, they will make fewer errors in technique, tactics or strategy than less-skilled competitors. Coaches can help develop this decision-making ability – this may be done by reviewing performances (perhaps on video), and analysing decisions made by successful athletes during the game (see Unit 18).

Game intelligence

Successful athletes are very careful about how they use their energy; they know when to put on the pressure and when to take it easy so as to conserve energy. They sense the important moments and time their efforts accordingly. This is a result of constant practice and analysis throughout their development, where athlete and coach together consider the most efficient way to perform during both practice and competition.

Even if all these things are in place, however, some very gifted athletes in all sports will fail to make the grade – this is one of the biggest dilemmas facing all sports. Some of the possible obstacles to success are discussed below.

Obstacles

Injuries

The first potential obstacle for athletes is injury, during either training or competition. Injury is an inherent risk in all sports. Among 10–15-year-old boys in 1998 the injury risk was one in 22 (for every 22 boys playing sport, one was injured). For girls the injury risk was one in 55. These figures might reflect the difference in the most popular sports for boys and girls – more boys than girls play games such as rugby and football and compete in combat sports such as boxing, judo, karate, etc.

Injury is almost always a serious concern in that even a slight injury will affect the training/competition schedule, and a serious injury may well be career-threatening. A study in 2005 suggested that as many as 16 per cent of talented young athletes will have their career ended by injury sustained in their teenage years.

Peer pressure

A more prevalent reason for athletes giving up sport is peer pressure. The same study showed that the majority of young athletes (46.7 per cent) said that pressures related to school, university or work had caused them to drop out of their sport, and this shows the importance of sociological factors, such as parental support, mentioned earlier.

Athlete role ambiguity

One reason why athletes may not progress is role ambiguity – a condition where the athlete is unsure of his or her role in the team or in the sport. For example, an athlete who has excelled at school may find that, when they join the county or national squad, they are in fact just an average player. Another example is the football player who is played out of position, or in a lot of different positions throughout a season, and is therefore unsure of his role within the team. This ambiguity (or uncertainty) usually has a detrimental effect on performance and development.

Gender differences

Research has shown that most boys become involved in sport, while most girls do not. This is not due to biological differences, but rather to subtle social learning – sport is often considered a masculine activity, and success in sport leads to enhanced male status (athleticism = virility, machismo, male heterosexuality). As children, boys are often given trucks, guns, tractors and manipulative toys, while girls are given dolls, toy kitchens and clothes such as nurses' uniforms; it is said that boys and girls may therefore develop a preference for these toys, which will determine their attitude to sports. By the time children reach school age they often

▲ Gender differences may still be an obstacle to girls progressing in sport

have determined for themselves that active sports are masculine, not feminine.

This reinforcement of gender differences often continues through school, with boys' play tending to be outdoors, complex and in large groups, whereas girls' play tends to be indoors, in small groups, repetitive, taking turns, and less challenging. Therefore boys tend to learn goal-setting, interdependent roles, advanced techniques of performance, and how to adjust rules of the game, settle disputes and abide by compromise; while girls tend to learn to cooperate and avoid competition.

Age considerations

Another factor is age – an athlete who is apparently extremely talented at the age of 11, for example, may not stand out as an adult. This may be because the athlete was more physically or mentally mature than his or her peers at age 11, started playing earlier, or had better coaching during their primary school years. This may also be related to the onset of puberty, which, particularly in female athletes, produces profound body changes that often have a detrimental effect on athletic performance.

Sport-specific factors in development

Technical and tactical skills

All athletes need to develop tactical and technical skills in order to develop their potential. These will obviously vary from sport to sport, but generally all athletes need to develop hand–eye coordination and strategic skills (be able to 'read the game').

Deliberate practice

All developing athletes need periods of what is termed 'deliberate practice'. That is, a fixed period (one or more sessions) where they work on a specific aspect of their sport. This helps to address weaknesses and develop strengths in the athlete so that their all-round skills improve.

Assessment practice

To add to your presentations in sections 1 and 2, describe how your club would contribute to developing the talents of any promising athletes the talent scout identifies. List the five key factors in talent development, and who is primarily responsible for each. **P5**

Grading tips

Grading Tip **P5**

In order to achieve this you need to identify the roles of the coach, support staff (therapists, etc.), family, other team/squad members, and so on; these need to be linked to each of the five aspects of talent development discussed previously.

Current talent development programmes

Before you can develop your own programme, it will be useful to look at a variety of other development programmes run by the government and by various sporting bodies.

World Class Performance Programme

There are a variety of programmes used in the UK to develop world class athletes, such as the World Class Performance Programme, World Class Performance Pathway and World Class Podium Programme. Each sport calls their programme one of the above. This can be rather confusing, so only one – the World Class Podium Plan – is discussed here in detail, as they all follow very similar principles.

■ World Class Podium

One sport where the UK has been successful because of a well planned and executed development plan, called the World Class Podium Plan, has been modern pentathlon – in 2006 Mhairi Spence won two silver team medals at the Senior World Championships; individual silver medal and two gold team medals at the Junior World Championships; individual bronze medal and team gold and team relay silver at the European Senior Championships; and individual silver medal and team silver at the European Championships.

Sport England, Sport Scotland and Elite Cymru currently fund (until March 2009) 11 athletes operating at talented athlete level, in their training and preparation to win medals at junior and youth levels. The key aim for the development programme is to develop young athletes to become capable of winning medals at senior level, and develop competition programmes with the aim of winning medals in significant international competitions now and within the next four years, particularly at the Olympic Games in Beijing 2008.

The World Class Podium Programme employs three full-time staff and has a high-tech headquarters based at the High Performance Centre at Bath University.

All talent development programmes follow a similar pattern, and each one has a set of criteria for athletes on their programme. The World Class Podium programme uses the following pattern.

Level D

- Athlete must be in full-time training at the Bath National Training Centre.
- Meets individual performance targets set.
- Complies in full with contract/charter.

Level E

- Athlete must be within a maximum of 18 months of the year of reporting for full-time training at the Bath National Training Centre and commit in writing to do so.
- Meets individual performance targets set.
- Complies in full with contract/charter.

Level F

- Athlete must have agreed in principle in writing that they will report for training at the Bath National Training Centre when eligible by age or stage of education to do so.
- Meets all Organisational Development Plan (ODP) performance targets.
- Complies in full with contract/charter.

Only athletes who meet these criteria will be considered for international selection at youth, junior and senior levels.

■ World Class Development Programme

In addition, UK Sport has a talent development programme called the World Class Development Programme (WCDP). This programme supports the stage of the pathway immediately beneath the Podium Programme. For most sports it will contain athletes who are typically six years away from the Podium but, due to the length of development time for a modern pentathlete, this is thought to be unrealistic and is extended.

World Class Programmes

The World Class Programmes are made up of Start, Potential and Performance, and offer exceptional opportunities for Great Britain's most talented athletes, including expert training from coaches, sports science and medicine support, and funding towards international competitions. Their mission is to optimise GB podium success on the world stage through the identification and development of potential world class athletes, and they are linked with the World Class Podium and Development programmes outlined above.

Other current programmes

Besides the programmes outlined above, there are several other development programmes within the UK, some of which are outlined below:

Talented Athlete Scholarship Scheme

In England, the government has created the Talented Athlete Scholarship Scheme (www.tass.gov.uk) in order to help talented athletes to develop their potential. TASS athletes are awarded either a scholarship to enable them to receive sporting services (currently to the value of £3000), or a bursary to receive sporting services (currently £1000). National governing bodies of sport (see page 14) design a customised package of core sporting services for their TASS athletes comprising, for example, coaching, sports medicine, sports science, strength and conditioning, and lifestyle management.

TASS athletes also have access to good quality training facilities within educational institutions, and operate across England through nine regional consortia. Each consortium is made up of several higher and further education institutions that work together to provide a package of sporting services to TASS scholars and bursars in their region. There are currently over 90 educational establishments across England delivering sporting services on this programme.

Currently, TASS scholarships are for 18–25-year-olds who are undertaking higher or further education, while TASS bursaries are for 16–19-year-olds who are undertaking further education or have left education

to follow a career. Both schemes have an extended upper age limit of 35 for athletes with a disability, and at the moment there are 47 sports that are eligible to be supported by TASS, of which 15 are disability sports.

The performance of TASS athletes is regularly monitored and assessed by the relevant national governing body to ensure they make full use of the services and facilities provided for them; awards are reviewed yearly.

Gifted and Talented Athlete Register

Gifted and talented athletes are identified and put onto a register (www.talentladder.org), and are then eligible to enrol onto the Junior Athlete Education Programme. This is a talent support programme for school sport partnerships to help their talented young sports people manage and balance both school and sport demands.

Key features are:

- support workshops for talented young athletes
- a workshop for their parents
- mentor support from identified staff in school.

Junior Athlete Education workshops cover aspects of lifestyle management, target-setting and planning, to give young people skills to balance their schedules of school and sport.

English Colleges Football Association

The English Colleges Football Association was formed in 2002, and developed the English Colleges Football League. This league is sanctioned by the Football Association to provide a competitive context for young, talented footballers recruited into College Football Development Centres around the country. Once selected, players have an alternative route into the football business, other than the traditional apprenticeship at league clubs.

Football Development Centres

These centres have been put into place at 70 colleges throughout the UK for players who are of above-average ability, to work with players of a similar standard. Players work in an environment that aids their progression and helps them to achieve their highest possible level of performance. Once players have reached a certain level, they can be recommended to a School of Excellence or Academy.

Players attend the Development Centre by invitation only, and will normally have taken part in a local Football Development Scheme activity in the past.

■ Long-term athlete development models

The UK has adopted the long-term athlete development (LTAD) model, devised mainly by Istvan Balyi in 1990 following his work with the Canadian Alpine Ski team in the 1980s. The LTAD approach was designed to help prepare players to reach the higher levels, but is equally valid for a healthy lifelong participation in sport.

▲ The long-term athlete development model was developed with skiers but is now used more widely

It takes around 10 years of sports training to develop a high-level athlete. This does not mean the athlete needs to spend 10 years training in just one sport. LTAD suggests that playing other sports is part of the 10-year development programme, and the programme has six phases to achieve high-level performance and enable people to continue their participation after retirement. These phases are split into three areas:

- objective: what the athlete should be able to do at the end of the phase
- content: the activities contained within the phase
- frequency: how often the athlete should train during the phase.

Phase 1 – FUNdamentals (FUN)

Objective: to learn fundamental movement skills.

Content: overall development, focusing on ABCS (agility, balance, coordination, speed) to underpin the generic skills used in many sports (running, jumping and throwing).

Frequency: perform physical activity five to six times per week.

Phase 2 – Learning to Train (L2T)

Objective: to learn fundamental sports skills.

Content:

- concentration on the range of FUNdamental sports skills, such as throwing, catching, jumping and running
- introduction to readiness – being mentally and physically prepared
- basic FUNdamental tactics, e.g. if fielding, net/wall, invasion games can be introduced
- cognitive and emotional development are central
- skills are practised in challenging formats.

Frequency: as phase 1. If there is a favoured sport, it is suggested that at least 50 per cent of the time is allocated to other sports/activities that develop a range of skills.

Phase 3 – Training to Train (T2T)

Objective: to build fitness and specific sports skills.

Content: this phase ideally occurs post-puberty; attention switches to:

- fitness training
- detailed mental preparation
- a focus on sport-specific skill development, including perceptual skills (reading the game/tactical understanding)
- decision-making
- detailed and extensive evaluation.

Frequency: for the aspiring performer, sport-specific practice will now be six to nine times per week.

Phase 4 – Training to Compete (T2C)

Objective: to refine skills for a specific event or position.

Content:

- event and position-specific training
- physical conditioning
- technical and tactical preparation

- advanced mental practice
- all of the above come together and are developed under competition conditions.

Frequency: Training could be up to 12 times per week.

Phase 5 – Training to Win (T2W)

Objective: to maximise performance in competition.

Content: development and refinement of the aspects above, but with more use in competition modelling, and more attention to rest periods and prevention of injury due to heavier load.

Frequency: training could be up to 15 times per week.

(Some sports stop at this phase as this is the highest competitive level.)

Phase 6 – Retainment

For athletes/players retiring from competitive sport, many sports are developing Master's programmes. An additional phase, 'retainment', keeps players/athletes involved in physical activity. Experience gained as a competitor can be invaluable, should they move into administration, coaching or officiating.

A move to another sport, perhaps at a more recreational level, may suit some athletes better.

Some coaches, and indeed athletes, question this model as there is little (if any) research to back up the claims made by Balyi that LATD really works. Also, there are differences between what are called early specialisation sports; such as gymnastics, and late specialisation sports, such as football and other team sports. The LATD programmes differ as follows:

Early specialisation model	Late specialisation model
• Training to train • Training to compete • Training to win • Retirement and retainment	• FUNdamental • Learning to train • Training to train • Training to compete • Training to win • Retirement and retainment

Each phase of the programme has its own restrictions and requirements. The box shows a sample six-day training camp programme for the Australian New South Wales Talented Athlete Programme for swimmers.

Day 1 - Sunday

Time	Activity	Facility	Staff
4–5pm	Arrival 3.45–4pm Pool session	Dining room Pool (× 6 lanes)	Coaching staff
5.15–5.45pm	Introductory talk/course overview/expectations	Lecture 4	Coaching staff
Dinner: 6pm	Dinner	Dining room	
7pm – 8pm	Lecture - Sports psychology	Lecture 4	Sports psychologist
8pm – 9.15pm	Sports specific skills session	Pool (× 6 lanes)	Coaching staff
Supper: 9.30pm			

Day 2 – Monday

Time	Activity	Facility	Staff
7am – 8am	Walk / run	Surrounds	Coaching staff
Breakfast: 8am			
9am – 10am	Sports testing	Gymnasium	SAS staff
10am – 11am	Sports testing	Gymnasium	SAS staff
11am – 12.30pm	Sports testing	Gymnasium	SAS staff
Lunch: 12.30pm			
1pm – 2pm	Pool session	Pool ($\times$ 6 lanes)	Coaching staff
2pm – 3.15pm	Pool session	Pool ($\times$ 6 lanes)	Coaching staff
3.30pm – 4pm	Study session	Lecture 4	
4pm – 5pm	Study session	Lecture 4	
5pm – 5.30pm	Study session	Lecture 4	
Dinner: 6pm			
7pm – 8pm	Basketball	Basketball Courts ($\times$ 2)	Coaching staff
8pm – 9.30pm	8--9.15 swim session	Pool ($\times$ 6 lanes)	
	with coaches		
Supper: 9.30pm			

Day 3 – Tuesday

Time	Activity	Facility	Staff
7am – 8am	Walk/run	Surrounds	Coaching staff
Breakfast: 8am			
9.30am – 10.30am	Speed/agility session (Group 1)	Oval 3	South Australian Swimming (SAS) staff
10.30am – 11.30am	Speed/agility session (Group 2)	Oval 3	SAS staff
11.30am – 12.30pm	Drugs in Sport lecture	Lecture 4	SAS staff
Lunch: 12.30pm			
1pm – 3pm	Beach session	Big Beach Bus	Coaching staff
3pm – 4pm	Beach session		Coaching staff
4pm – 5pm	Beach session		Coaching staff
5pm – 5.30pm	Beach session	' '	Coaching staff
Dinner: 6pm			
7pm – 8.30pm	Study session	Lecture 4	
Supper: 8.30pm			

Day 4 – Wednesday

Time	Activity	Facility	Staff
7am – 8am	Walk/run	Surrounds	Coaching staff
Breakfast: 8am			
8.30am – 10am	Study session	Dining room	
10am – 11am	10.30am – 12 Pool session	Pool ($\times$ 6 lanes)	Coaching staff
11am – 12pm	10.30am – 12pm	Pool ($\times$ 6 lanes)	Coaching staff
Lunch: 12.30pm			
1pm – 3pm	Beach session	Big Beach Bus	Coaching staff
3pm – 4pm	Beach session		' '
4pm – 5pm	Beach session		' '
5pm – 5.45pm	Beach session	' '	' '
Dinner: 6pm			
7pm – 8pm	Video	Lecture room 4	
8pm – 9.30pm	Video	Lecture room 4	

Day 5 – Thursday

Time	Activity	Facility	Staff
7am – 8am	Walk/run	Surrounds	Coaching Staff
Breakfast: 8am			
8.30am – 10am	Study session	Lecture 4	
10am – 11am	Pool session	Pool ($\times$ 6 lanes)	Coaching staff
11am – 12pm	Pool session	Pool ($\times$ 6 lanes)	Coaching staff
Lunch: 12.30pm			
1pm – 2pm	Ropes/Leap of faith	Ropes – lake	SAS staff
2pm – 3pm	Ropes/Leap of faith	Ropes – lake	SAS staff
3pm – 4pm	Ropes/Leap of faith	Ropes – lake	SAS staff
4pm – 5pm	Ropes/Leap of faith	Ropes – lake	SAS staff
5pm – 5.45pm	Ball games	Oval 1	Coaching staff
Dinner: 6pm			
7pm – 8pm	Program evaluation/ debrief	Lecture 4	Coaching staff
8.30pm – 9.30pm	Pool session	Pool ($\times$ 6 lanes)	Coaching staff
Supper: 9.30pm			

Day 6 – Friday: Debrief and wrap-up sessions

This type of intensive training camp would be used in phases 3–5 in order to prepare the athlete (in this case a swimmer) for high-level competition. It would be linked to a less intensive weekly programme, which would vary in intensity and duration depending on whether it was out of season, pre-season or in season. One suggested regime is that you should train at around 30 per cent of competition intensity in the off-season, building up to about 80 per cent in the pre-season period and 100 per cent during competition.

The training intensity mentioned above can be calculated in two ways: using maximum heart rate (MHR; see page 63) or using last season's personal best (PB).

So if we take a 20-year-old 200-metre sprinter with a PB of 22s and an MHR of 200 (MHR is 220 minus age = 200), his off-season training intensity would be a speed of around 28–29s with a heart rate of between 60 and 100 beats per minute. This would build up to a time of around 24–25s and a heart rate of 160. So competition/in-season training intensity should be at last year's PB, or a heart rate of 160–200.

Activity

Design a training programme for a 22-year-old footballer, using the guidelines above, taking her from off-season through to the first match of the season.

Taking it further

As well as the programme above, design a programme for a forward and a midfield soccer player using the same guidelines. These programmes must include some skills training appropriate to the positional demands of the players.

Structure of talent development programmes

Each talent development programme must have a clear set of aims, a purpose, structure and format. These are discussed in more detail below, using UK Sport's World Class Development Programme as an example. Other programmes will follow a different structure.

Aims

The World Class Development Programme caters for athletes who are within three to six years of reaching a World or Olympic podium, as well as already proven individuals currently recovering from injury, and previously successful athletes who show the potential to regain world class levels of performance.

Purpose

The purpose of the programme is twofold:

- it gives athletes the opportunity to develop their full potential and to achieve a podium finish at world or Olympic level
- it gives their sponsoring governing body (and Sport UK) international success.

Structure and format

The structure of any talent development programme should mirror the long-term athlete development model (page 186). The timescale for each phase varies according to the athlete and the sport, but in general the 1st and 2nd phases last until age 13 or so, between 14 and 18 athletes develop strength and technical skill (phases 3 and 4), and after 18 phase 5 (training to win) becomes the main focus. It is worth bearing in mind that around 80 per cent of world-class athletes are world-class by the age of 22, and that only 20 per cent of athletes who show talent at an early age will develop into higher or world-class athletes.

Therefore any development programme has to provide a balance between multi-sport training and specialisation. One factor in non-development is early specialisation, which limits the athlete's eventual options.

Establishing norm values

The norm values are those used as a yardstick against which to measure talented athletes. These norm values are given in Table 19.2 (pages 167–168).

Use of test batteries

At first generic test batteries (see page 175) will be used to identify potential talent, but later more sport-specific tests will be used to place athletes appropriately and focus their training, as well as to screen them for potential weaknesses in their abilities.

Phases of the programme

Athletes should pass progressively through the phases of the programme outlined above, from FUNdamentals to training to win (page 186), without taking shortcuts or attempting to skip phases.

Timescales

Remember that this development programme will, as mentioned earlier, take between seven and ten years, so this programme requires a major commitment by the athlete, coach and governing body.

Resources required to run a talent development programme

■ Human resources

These include all the elements described on page 175. They will also be used in the developmental process to measure athletes' progress against normal values and their previous results, and to interpret those figures.

■ Physical resources

These include all the elements described on page 175, including facilities, coaches, medical support, etc.

■ Fiscal resources

This means the money required to provide all the other resources. UK Sport has committed £75 million pounds to identifying and developing talent leading up to the Beijing Olympics in 2008. There are six levels of funding for development (A–F, with F being the lowest), and the developing athlete moves through these levels according to their performance while on the programme.

■ Communication

Coaches, administrators, teachers and governing bodies must develop good feedback and communication skills so that they can guide athletes through their development, and give them a clear programme to follow throughout the process.

■ Goal setting

Development of the athlete must be measured against a set of both long-term and short-term goals. These goals will change according to the stage of the athlete's development, and should be set collaboratively by both athlete and coach.

■ Definitions of success

Not all athletes identified at a young age will develop into high-level performers, so it is important that they are not solely driven by winning at an early age. The most important factor is that athletes continue to participate up to and including adolescence, so that they maximise their chance of fulfilling their promise. And that they continue to enjoy their sport.

■ Deliberate practice

As mentioned above (page 183), athletes need a period of deliberate practice in order to develop new skills or refine existing ones. For example, Johnny Wilkinson still practises taking place kicks for several hours a day, as this way he retains and develops his skill.

Other considerations in athletic development

■ The value of sport to different groups

Different ethnic and social groups have different attitudes to sport, and this will affect participation and potential development. For example, 65 per cent of parents would not allow their children to box, whereas only five per cent would stop their child from playing cricket. So a child wishing to become a boxer may well have less parental support than a young cricketer (or may even face parental opposition).

Reasons for participation in sport

Reasons given for encouraging participation in sport may include to:

- encourage a healthy lifestyle
- promote self-esteem
- learn goal-setting
- learn and experience teamwork
- learn about dealing with adversity
- have fun!

But for many competitive athletes, sport is all about winning, or at least competing at a high level, and it is these individuals who respond best to an athletic development programme.

Impact on children and adolescents

Giftedness (being talented) can affect different people in different ways. Sports participation generally increases self-esteem in adolescents and children, as well as developing traits such as confidence and independence (see Unit 23). Another point of view, however, is that the gifted are more sensitive to interpersonal conflicts and experience greater degrees of alienation and stress than do their peers, so gifted children are at greater risk of emotional and social problems, particularly during adolescence and adulthood. Currently there appears to be no firm evidence one way or the other, but many talented athletes do focus on their sport/performance very strongly, ignoring social interaction.

Self-perception

A study comparing the self-perception of female athletes with non-athletes of the same age found that athletes derived a large component of their self-worth from their perceived athletic competence – the better they were at sport, the better they felt about themselves. However, this is contradicted by other research findings that children with 'fragile' egos are at special risk when winning is emphasised, combined with extremely high expectations regarding personal performance.

The creation of a learning environment

The coach should create an environment where people feel comfortable voicing their opinions about what is working or not working – at the right time. The coach needs to create an environment where questions can be safely asked without retribution, honest feedback is given, confidentiality is maintained where necessary, and people are taught how to give constructive positive and negative feedback effectively.

Role of the coach

As we have seen (page 180), the coach acts as a trainer, motivator, planner, demonstrator, technician and role model, and these roles continue throughout the development of the athlete's career. The relationship will change, however, in that the coach will become more of a mentor, allowing the athlete to take a greater collaborative role with time. The skills and techniques discussed on page 181 will also be used by the coach in development, although again the coach may modify them from time to time.

Goal-setting

Types of goals with different ages/genders

Development of the athlete must be measured against a set of both long-term and short-term goals. These goals will change according to the age of the athlete, and may well be different according to gender. For example, a swimmer's goals may be set according to times achieved by other swimmers in the relevant age group and of the relevant gender.

Feedback and communication

Coaches must also develop good feedback and communication skills so that they can guide athletes through their development, as well as communicating their ideas to the athlete, their parents, teachers, etc.

Case study

Here are some comments about the use of video feedback as a communication tool by coaches in rowing.

We were interested in measuring the sequencing of events (catch, finish, etc.) for members of a rowing squad during on-water rowing. To achieve this we travelled in a coach's boat and videoed rowers individually and as a team from the side using a digital camera fixed on a tripod on a travelling barge. The distance between the coach's barge and rowers was approximately 3m.

We were able to set the clock and advance the video frame-by-frame to identify the timing of the various phases of the rowing stroke.

We were also able to measure knee angles, and using this analysis could provide rapid feedback to our rowers. The video feedback helped to identify which rowers were ahead or behind other team members in various phases of the rowing stroke and allowed them to improve their synchronisation as a team.

1 Suggest another sport for which this type of tool could be very valuable.

Assessment practice

The athletics club where you are shadowing the talent scout has identified three promising young athletes in different events. To encourage them to go forward, describe an example of a currently existing development programme that they might become a part of, and evaluate how useful this could be to them at their current stage. **P6 M3**

For one of the young athletes, design a detailed talent development programme in their event. Explain and justify the activities you have chosen, and analyse how these activities will lead to improvement and development. **P7 M4 D2**

Grading tips

Grading Tip **P6 P7**

Write up a case study tracing your chosen athlete's development through the talent identification programme phases as outlined in this unit. Remember that this athlete will be on the programme for several years, so you have plenty of time to consider each phase.

Grading Tip **M3 M4 D2**

Think about how the athlete is going to progress between phases and therefore fulfil their potential.

Knowledge check

1 List five factors that are important in an athlete's development.

2 What are the phases of a long-term development plan?

3 What are the roles and responsibilities of the coach?

4 What social factors may prevent long-term development in an athlete?

5 What forms of communication can a coach use to help an athlete's development?

6 Name three important physical factors that may help you to identify talented athletes.

7 What does TASS stand for, and how does it help developing athletes?

8 Who is eligible for help under the World Class Podium Plan?

Preparation for assessment

You have been employed by your local hockey team as a talent scout. As part of your job, you have to write a general scheme for the club coaches and others to identify potential players from local schools, as well as a development plan for the existing youth academy. Your plan should contain:

1 a series of simple tests for coaches and teachers to determine their students' physical capabilities

2 a description of the physical factors that are considered important in high-level hockey players

3 an outline development programme for potential players from ages 10–18

4 a test to assess the athletes' mental toughness and determination.

Grading tips

Grading Tip   P3 M2 D1

Tasks 1, 2 and 4 relate to these grading criteria.

Grading Tip    P4 P6 M4 D2

Task 3 relates to these grading criteria.

To achieve a pass grade the evidence must show that the learner is able to:	To achieve a merit grade the evidence must show that, in addition to the pass criteria, the learner is able to:	To achieve a distinction grade the evidence must show that, in addition to the pass and merit criteria, the learner is able to:
P1 define the different types and predictors of talent **Assessment practice page 171**		
P2 describe five different predictors of talent for individuals in sport **Assessment practice page 171**		
P3 describe one current talent identification programme in a selected sport **Assessment practice page 176**	**M1** evaluate one current talent identification programme in a selected sport **Assessment practice page 176**	
P4 using a standard structure, design a talent identification programme for a selected sport **Assessment practice page 176**	**M2** justify the choice of activities for a talent identification programme for a selected sport **Assessment practice page 176**	**D1** analyse the choice of activities for a talent identification programme for a selected sport **Assessment practice page 176**
P5 describe, using examples, five different key factors in talent development in sport. **Assessment practice page 183**		
P6 describe one current talent development programme in a selected sport **Assessment practice page 193**	**M3** evaluate one current talent development programme in a selected sport **Assessment practice page 193**	
P7 using a standard structure, design a talent development programme for a selected sport **Assessment practice page 193**	**M4** justify the choice of activities for a talent development programme for a selected sport **Assessment practice page 193**	**D2** analyse the choice of activities for a talent development programme for a selected sport **Assessment practice page 193**

Sports massage and therapy

Introduction

Massage is a natural therapy. It can be practised anywhere, and can be used for general relaxation of the musculoskeletal system, as well as being directed at local problem areas to improve recovery of the muscular system.

Using massage, the therapist can remove the accumulation of general aches and pains that some sports people may seem to accept as normal, due to their gradual build-up of exercise, or perhaps try to suppress with drugs. These aches and pains can lead to more serious problems, so the benefits of massage for injury prevention are great. When dealing with specific injuries, massage can explore the soft tissues more intimately than any other therapy, and the problem areas can be diagnosed and treated very accurately.

After completing this unit you should be able to achieve the following outcomes:

- Understand the effects and benefits of sports massage.
- Understand the role of sports massage professionals.
- Be able to identify the sports massage requirements of sports performers.
- Be able to demonstrate different sports massage techniques.

Think it over

In groups, discuss what you think the benefits of massage are likely to be. In your discussion you might also want to think about why so many sports people see massage as an important part of their training regime.

If you can find someone who has had a massage treatment, ask what they think its benefits are.

Massage as a form of soft tissue treatment has been around for thousands of years. It was first documented in Chinese literature over 3000 years ago. It is also described in the histories of the ancient worlds of Egypt, Greece, India and Rome. The gladiatorial arenas of ancient Greece and Rome often had massage therapists working on the combatants. Perhaps the most famous of these was Galen, who was a trainer to Roman gladiators and is considered by some people as the first sports massage therapist.

Today, sports people utilise the advanced scientific application of massage to enhance performance and recovery from demanding training programmes as well as treatment of injury. It is used in both prevention and cure, and has become a vital part of many athletes' training programmes.

The basic aim of massage therapy is to maintain or restore normal function. The aim of the sports and exercise massage professional is to assist in improving technique/performance as well as reducing the risk of injury. It should be an integral part of training, especially at the highest levels of performance. Many injuries in sport are caused by overuse, and while the root cause should be identified and preventive measures taken, massage can reduce the likelihood of these types of injury.

Effects of massage

Soft tissue therapy can be used for:

* relieving stress and tension
* aiding recovery
* treating minor soft tissue injuries
* providing pre- and post-event massage
* maintaining optimal condition of muscle tissue
* increasing flexibility
* referring people to relevantly qualified professionals.

Physical and mechanical effects

■ Blood and lymphatic circulation

Massage helps the circulation in two ways:

* the pressure of the therapist's hands supplements the pumping action of the muscles and soft tissues on the blood vessels
* the increased heat caused by the massage leads to an increase in circulation to the area being massaged, as well as within the body as a whole.

The increased circulation means that extra oxygen and nutrients are carried to the area within the blood vessels. As well as the blood vessels being stimulated by massage, the lymph vessels are also stimulated. Massage aids lymphatic drainage, which helps to reduce swelling and promote the removal of waste products from the body.

■ Tissue permeability

Massage improves the absorption of substances within the body tissues. It also affects cell permeability, allowing nutrients and other substances to enter the cell more readily, and again aids the outflowing of waste products from the cell.

Key Terms

Cell permeability Allowing or activating the passage of a substance into, out of, or through cells, or from one cell to another.

■ Stretching

Massage can also achieve stretching in muscles, tendons and fascia. It can stretch tissues, which cannot be stretched effectively by any other means. Normal stretching usually stretches the muscle group as a whole.

With massage, fibres can be stretched in all directions. The stretch can be applied locally and worked through the area systematically, so that tight areas can be worked on specifically.

Stretching a particularly tight area may produce discomfort. This indicates a neuromuscular reaction may also be taking place, which adds to the mechanical effect of the stretch.

Key Terms

Adhesions – pieces of scar tissue that attach structures within the body that should be separate from each other, limiting movement and sometimes causing pain.

■ Reducing and remodelling scar tissue

Muscles are made of lots of tiny fibres. These contract individually, and this is what causes movement. If they are put under pressure, perhaps from a fall, a kick or a strain of some sort, these fibres break. Like any break of

the body's fibres, as they heal they lose their elasticity and become rigid and brittle. This is what causes scar tissue.

Movement within that fibre will be limited, which in turn affects the strength and flexibility of the muscle and, if left untreated, may cause a permanent weakness in that area.

Massage produces friction within the tissues, and this deep friction helps to loosen scar tissue and adhesions within the muscles and other soft tissues.

■ Opening microcirculation

Massage opens (dilates) the blood vessels and capillaries by stretching them, enabling nutrients to pass through more easily.

Physiological effects

■ Autonomic nervous system

The autonomic nervous system functions in an involuntary, reflexive manner. For example, we do not notice when blood vessels change size, or when our heart beats faster.

Sympathetic and parasympathetic nervous systems

Massage soothes the sensory nerve endings and helps relaxation. It also stimulates the sympathetic and parasympathetic nervous systems, which helps to remove tension from both the local area and the body as a whole. This helps clients feel as though their aches and pains have been relieved.

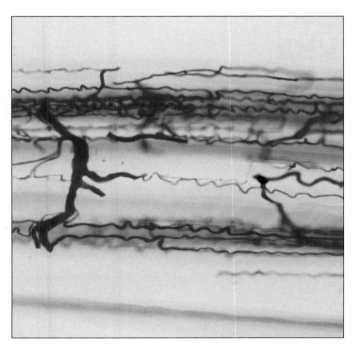

▲ The capillary blood supply in muscle (microcirculation) is improved by massage

Key Terms

The **autonomic nervous system** is divided into three parts:

sympathetic nervous system – .....

parasympathetic nervous system –......

enteric nervous system – ....

Benefits

General effects of massage on the client include stress reduction, an enhanced feeling of wellbeing, improved body awareness, pain reduction and a feeling of relaxation.

Benefits of different techniques

The different techniques used in massage offer different benefits. The effects of each type of massage are summarised below, and more details about each technique are given on pages 219–220.

■ Effleurage

A stroking movement using the hand so as to cover a large surface area. Its main effect is in pumping the circulation, and it is usually used to finish off the massage to leave a good feeling of warmth and relaxation.

Effleurage:

- improves general circulation
- increases the supply of oxygen and nutrients to skin and muscles
- aids lymphatic drainage, removing waste products more effectively
- soothes sensory nerve endings, which helps relaxation
- produces warmth
- enables the patient to become familiar with the therapist's touch
- aids desquamation (the removal of loose skin cells)
- is used to start and finish a massage
- joins other movements together.

■ Petrissage

A variety of techniques that lift, compress and stretch the tissues. They also mechanically pump the circulation system and warm the tissues.

Petrissage:

- improves local circulation
- increases flow of lymph
- improves absorption of substances within tissues
- brings nutrients to the area
- loosens adhered or scar tissues
- moves tissues over the bone
- removes tension from the area, which helps relieve aches and pains
- produces warmth.

■ Tapotement

Also known as percussion movements, stimulating percussive techniques using both hands alternately, working quickly and rhythmically – include clapping, hacking and beating.

Tapotement:

- is extremely stimulating
- causes erythema (reddening of the skin)
- produces localised heat
- stimulates muscle fibres
- increases in cellular activity.

Case study

'At the Tykes we believe sports massage is essential to recovery and performance, **and** high quality sports massage for our first team squad has been vital in preparing them to perform at their peak throughout the season, particularly in the build-up to our 2005 Powergen Cup Success.'

Dave Stringer BSc (Hons) MCSP SRP, Assistant Physiotherapist (Leeds Tykes RUFC)

1 How do you think sports massage has helped prepare the team to perform during the season?

Assessment practice

You are working as an assistant at your local amateur rugby club, which has recently taken on a new sports massage therapist. To encourage athletes to use the therapist's services, design a short leaflet (two sides of A4) setting out the effects and benefits of sports massage. **P1**

Grading tips

Grading Tip **P1**

List the effects and benefits of massage as stated in this unit.

Grading Tip **M1**

Explain how the above effects are achieved; for example, circulation improves because the kneading action on the muscles acts as a pump on the veins.

20.2 Understand the role of sports massage professionals

Types of work

Sports and exercise massage professionals work in a wide range of settings, including private practice, sports injury clinics, sports clubs, health farms, health and fitness clubs, the hotel and leisure sector, and teaching and training.

It must be remembered that sports and exercise massage professionals are primarily (but not exclusively) involved in treating sportsmen and women, and so must always bear in mind the effects of massage and related therapies on the athlete's performance.

It is also essential to remember that sports masseurs are not trained to diagnose medical conditions or other problems. If the practitioner feels a client may have a medical problem, then they should be referred to a health professional such as a doctor, sports therapist or physiotherapist.

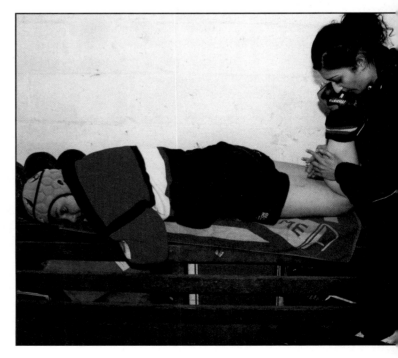

▲ Massage is helpful both pre- and post-performance

Case study

David – full-time sports therapist for a professional football club

David was keen to become a professional footballer while at school, but a stress fracture in his spine meant that this was not an option. On leaving school he trained as an engineer, but spent his weekends coaching and providing first aid for a local amateur football team. David continued to study and took a part-time degree in sports therapy at London Metropolitan University, graduating in 2002. David currently earns £30,000 a year with benefits (car provided, free sports kit and medical insurance) and the club is organising a testimonial year for him.

David thoroughly enjoys his role, which is varied and at times unexpected. Working for a small club means that he has a very wide brief and is not just responsible for treating and rehabilitating players' injuries but also gets involved in advising on nutrition and fitness training.

He feels that interpersonal skills are very important as he has to liaise with players, club directors, coaches and the medical professions. He also feels that an awareness of the psychological needs of an injured player is a very important part of their treatment and rehabilitation. A flexible approach is needed as he may not have access to a treatment room at away matches and will need to make do in a dressing room. Good organisational skills are important as David has to ensure that all the equipment he needs is packed and available at away matches.

David feels that his job is most stressful if one of the club's star performers is injured, as he will be under a lot of pressure from directors and coaches to get the player back to full fitness quickly, which is not always possible. It is also important to be self-confident on match days and not be upset by abuse from the opponents' fans – or from his own club's fans if he decides a star player cannot continue playing.

During the football season, David needs to be available seven days a week and will have to travel to away matches at weekends, which can disrupt family life.

(Source: www.prospects.ac.uk)

1   Why does David need to be available seven days a week?

2   What does David see as the most important aspect of his job?

3   Besides therapy, what other services does David provide to his players?

Remember!

If a client has a medical problem they should be referred to an appropriate health professional.

Types of activity

The types of activity that a sports and exercise massage professional can expect to undertake are diverse, and range from administration duties (maintaining patients' records, making appointments, etc.), through assessing clients' suitability for various massage therapies, to applying treatments. Remember! if a client has a medical problem they should be referred to an appropriate health professional.

Case study

Below is a description of a typical day for Jo, a self-employed massage therapist.

8.00	Arrive at clinic and check messages on answer machine
8.30	First client arrives – full body massage given (1 hour)
9.45	Telephone clients who have left answer machine messages. Open post.
10.00	Second client
11.15	Third client
12.30	Lunch break; answer post and write up treatment notes while eating sandwich
13.45	Fourth client – sports massage to legs, plus strapping of lateral ankle sprain
15.00	Fifth client – full body massage
16.15	Tidy towels etc., ensure clinic is clean and tidy, vacuum clinic and entrance hall
17.00	Leave clinic – domiciliary visit to client
18.45(ish)	Arrive home.

1 **What extra tasks does a self-employed therapist have to do in addition to providing massage?**

2 **Are there any additional requirements for people who are self-employed in order for them to comply with, for example, tax regulations?**

3 **If this a typical day, how many hours per week would you expect this therapist to work?**

Treatments applied

Massage therapists can apply several different types of treatment according to their training and level of experience. The main ones are as follows.

■ Massage

Massage is the manipulation of soft tissue such as muscle, ligament and tendon using various techniques (see page 200).

Inferential therapy for a knee injury ▶

■ Relaxation

Many massage therapists are trained in relaxation techniques, although gentle massage in itself is relaxing for many patients. Relaxation techniques may be particularly helpful for athletes as they can be used to reduce performance anxiety before competition or to help the athlete to unwind following competition.

■ Strapping and taping

Strapping and taping techniques are often used by massage therapists to support injured joints (such as sprained ankles) or to help with postural correction, for example.

■ Manipulation

Soft tissue manipulation can be defined as the stretching or lifting of tissues without lubrication, or the physical manipulation of joints to aid movement. Manipulation (after the appropriate training) is used by some therapists in order to help with realignment of tissues and/or joint surfaces that may have been misaligned due to injury, etc.

■ Electrotherapy treatments

Massage therapists may also be trained in the use of electrotherapy such as ultrasound and interferential therapy, although this is not part of a massage therapist's standard training.

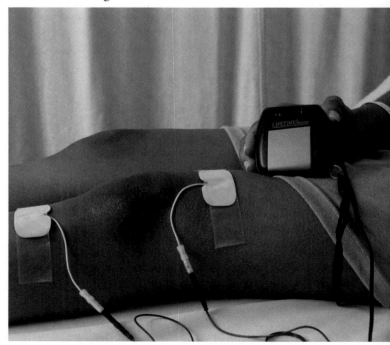

Ultrasound therapy is the application of high-frequency sound waves to soft tissue and helps to promote healing and reduce inflammation.

Interferential therapy is the application of an electrical current to the skin and soft tissues, which helps to reduce pain, swelling and muscle spasm.

Knowledge and resources

Sports massage is not currently regulated by law in the UK. The recognised professional body is the Sports Massage Association (SMA, www.sportsmassageassociation.org), which represents the profession as a whole. The SMA was launched at the Commonwealth Games in Manchester in 2002 to be an independent body regulating sports massage practitioners in the UK. By 2007 it represented over 1000 members and was recognised as the lead body for sports massage by the major employers in the UK.

The SMA aims to:

- establish and maintain minimum standards for sports massage training organisations
- give confidence to the general and sporting public, the medical profession and government agencies that sports massage practitioners are suitably trained to provide a quality service
- hold the National Register for Sports Massage Practitioners
- establish and maintain the ethical, professional and educational standards for sports massage practitioners
- support and promote its members and the profession as a whole
- ensure the best possible sports massage care is available to sports participants at all levels
- lead the sports massage profession towards state regulation.

■ Training

The SMA provides a list of accredited courses for people interested in becoming a sports massage practitioner. Entry level for the SMA's professional standard is aligned to Level 4 of the National Qualifications Framework (specialist learning and the application of that learning in a professional environment with a substantial degree of autonomy). This equates to a certificate of higher education.

In addition, many courses in sports massage are available at Level 3 of the National Qualifications Framework through further education colleges and private training providers. Graduates of these courses cannot work independently, but need to work under the supervision of a qualified medical practitioner (e.g. physiotherapist).

The SMA's standards of full membership are now recognised and supported by a number of key employers in the UK, including the British Olympic Association, UK Sport, home country sports institutes and many sporting national governing bodies. Those taking a Level 3 course can join the SMA as an affiliate member and can progress to become a full member through the professional examination process.

Once qualified, the sports and exercise massage professional must follow a process known as continued professional development (CPD), which is the process of systematic maintenance, improvement and broadening of knowledge and skills, and develop the personal qualities necessary for the execution of professional and clinical practice. The SMA stipulates that all full members must complete an average of 40 hours' CPD per year in order to renew their membership, although other bodies may have different CPD requirements.

■ Career opportunities

At present most massage therapists in the UK are self-employed, but there are increasing employment opportunities in areas such as professional sports teams, fitness centres, spas, hotels and so on. The English Institute of Sport, for example, employs sports masseurs at all its sites to treat its athletes, while Mark Warner holidays also employs massage therapists at both its summer and winter resorts. For graduates, the website www.prospects.ac.uk contains details of job vacancies. Some NHS trusts have recently employed massage therapists in either hospitals or community clinics.

Case study

Kate – clinic-based sports therapist

Kate knew she wanted to be a sports therapist from the age of 11 after she went to a football match for the first time and saw the physiotherapist run onto the pitch. After doing work experience at a hospital while at school, she realised that she did not want to work for the National Health Service and enrolled on a sports therapy degree course at London Metropolitan University, graduating in 1999.

Kate is employed part-time as a sports therapist in a sports injury clinic and also lectures in sports therapy and sports science at a local further education college. In the clinic, Kate works with a range of clients including professional and amateur athletes, people who keep fit for fun, children and adolescents, as well as people who have been injured in accidents. In addition to her private practice, she works with the England under-16 ice-hockey team, two county rugby squads, and has worked for the Great Britain women's ice-hockey squad. She started working in a clinic after graduating and gradually built up her sports team work through contacts and personal recommendations.

The aspects of the work that Kate finds particularly rewarding are meeting clients after she has discharged them, and hearing about what they are able to do now and how she has improved their lives. She also enjoys working with international athletes and likes the opportunities to travel that this brings. She likes the teaching side of her work, particularly enabling her students to learn new things. Drawbacks are the unsocial hours and sometimes being away from home on New Year's Eve or over Christmas. During the season the job can involve working up to seven days a week.

(Source: www.prospects.ac.uk)

Compare Kate's pattern of working with those of David and Jo.

1 What are the differences between them?

2 How are their working patterns similar?

■ Application to sport

Sports massage is a vital part of the athlete's training regime – it is used to enhance performance and recovery from demanding training programmes, as well as treatment of injury. It is used in both prevention and cure of athletic injuries, as its basic aim is to maintain or restore normal function.

Massage should be an integral part of training, especially at the highest levels of performance. Many injuries in sport are caused by overuse, and while the root cause should be identified and preventive measures taken, massage can reduce the likelihood of these types of injury.

The aim of the sports and exercise massage professional is to assist in improving technique/performance as well as reducing the risk of injury, and such professionals form a vital part of the athlete's support team.

Assessment practice

A local league football club is seeking a sports massage practitioner for the forthcoming football season. The worker would be required to attend matches on Saturday afternoons. The position is voluntary, which would ideally suit a student who needs the experience. Write a job description setting out the tasks and skills required. **P2**

Grading tip

Grading Tip P2

In order to pass this unit you should include the role of pre- and post-exercise massage; the role of massage in treatment and prevention of injury; application of strapping and taping.

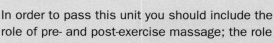

Assessment

Initial consultation

No treatment should ever be commenced without taking a thorough case history. The purpose is to make important decisions about the suitability of the patient for therapy, as well as more specific decisions relating to their individual treatment plan.

The information on a patient's file should consist of basic information including name, address, contact details, occupation, date of birth, etc. Other information, which forms a concise patient file, includes sports and hobbies, who the patient was referred by, GP details, X-rays and any related medical reports.

For the sports massage therapist, it is essential the initial consultation form asks for presenting symptoms, past history, medication and allergies. A subjective assessment is very important in the assessment process as this tells you how the patient feels about their injury as well as their hopes and expectations for recovery. It may also

help to decide which is the most appropriate form of treatment for this client, and whether or not they need to be referred to another professional such as a physiotherapist or sports therapist (see page 202).

On page 207 is an example of a completed patient questionnaire.

Posture

It is rare to find a good posture. This is mainly due to the lifestyle we lead and the bad habits we get into. Good posture avoids unnecessary strain on the body, which then allows it to work to its fullest capacity.

For good posture:
- head and shoulders should be level
- scapulae should be an even distance from the spine
- vertebral column should be straight down the back and not curved in either direction
- abdomen should be flat and buttocks not protruding
- waist should be evenly curved, with hips level
- arms should be in a relaxed position at the side and hang evenly
- legs and knees should be straight, with the feet together or just slightly apart and facing forwards.

▲ A preliminary patient consultation is vital

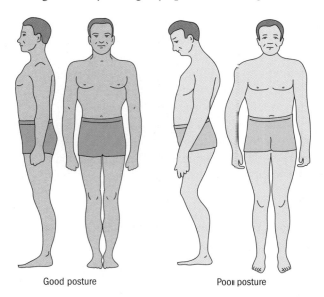

Good posture   Poor posture

▲ Good and poor posture

CONSULTATION QUESTIONNAIRE

PERSONAL DETAILS

Name _____

Address _____

Telephone number _____

Date of birth _____

GP's name and telephone number _____

_____

_____

PATIENT'S PROBLEM

Problem	LBP (lower back pain)
Exact location?	right or left side?
How was it done?	Accident? Sport?
When was it done?	Recently?
What is the pain like?	Sharp, ache, constant, intermittent
What makes it worse?	F/B (forward bending)
	B/B (backward bending)
	Rotation
	am (after just getting up)
	Exercise (better or worse?)
	Sitting (better or worse?)
	Getting up from sitting?
	Driving?
What makes it better?	Rest?
	Activity?
	Heat? Ice?
Does it radiate into other area of body?	Leg? Arm? _____

Exact location?   Posterior? Anterior? Medial?

Is it sore to touch?   _____

History of problem?   _____

First time area has been injured? _____

If not, obtain history   _____

Severity of injury at the time treatment given? _____

_____

What type?   _____

Results of treatment?   _____

GENERAL INFORMATION

Check for contra-indications

Some of the following may not contra-indicate the treatment but need to be known as treatment may be affected.

- ☐ Pacemaker
- ☐ Metal pins or plates
- ☐ Heart condition (type)
- ☐ Diabetes
- ☐ Epilepsy
- ☐ Fainting/dizziness
- ☐ Contagious or infectious diseases
- ☐ Any major illnesses
  - – Asthma
  - – Pneumonia
  - – TB
  - – Cancer
  - – Urinary or kidney symptoms
  - – Gynaecological problems
  - – Car accidents
  - – Any falls
  - – Any fracture (bone may shorten by 1/2")

■ Postural analysis

To assess clients' posture, ensure that the client:

- is relaxed
- wears light clothing or underwear
- is standing in bare feet or socks.

Posterior (behind)

Look at the levels and heights of the following:

- ears
- shoulders
- spine of scapulae (shoulder blades)
- angles (bases) of scapulae
- spine – lateral curve? (scoliosis; see page 88)
- waist crease line
- iliac crests
- posterior, superior, iliac spine (dimples)
- gluteal creases
- popliteal lines (knee creases)
- medial malleoli (ankles)
- feet pointing either outwards or inwards.

Lateral (sideways)

Look for the following:

- head tilted forward
- body tilted forwards/backward
- scapulae projected (sticking out)
- thoracic curve increased (kyphosis; see page 88)
- lumbar curve increased (lordosis; see page 88)
- abdomen protruding
- knees hyper-extended
- longitudinal arch of foot low (flat-footed).

Range of movement

- Forward bending (legs straight)
  - Note ease with which this was done.
  - Are the vertebrae stiff or mobile?
  - Are the hamstrings tight?
- Side bending
  - Note any restriction.
  - Compare with other side.
- Backward bending
  - Again, check restriction and ease with which this is done.

- Turn head left and right
  - Is the chin in line with the shoulder?
  - Compare with other side.
  - Tilt head forwards and backwards.
  - Can chin touch chest?
  - Can back of head touch cervical/ thoracic junction of spine?
- Gait
  - How does the subject walk?

■ Flexibility

This is how much you stretch. Can you touch your toes? Can your heel touch your buttocks?

By testing how much a muscle or muscle group can stretch, the therapist can tell how elastic it is. Generally, the more flexible the muscle, the less likely it is to be damaged. The only exception to this is if a muscle is too flexible, this can make the joint unstable, which may allow too much movement to take place. This can cause damage to joints or even cause a joint to become dislocated.

It is important that stretching exercises should always be included in any exercise scheme. They should be included after a warm-up so that performance is enhanced and the risk of injury is reduced, and they should also be included in the cool-down, as it will reduce any stiffness or muscle soreness (see pages 54 and 57).

Dermatomes and myotomes

The skin over the whole body is supplied by somatic sensory neurones that carry impulses from the skin into the spinal cord and brain stem. Likewise, the underlying skeletal muscles receive signals from the somatic motor neurones that carry impulses out of the spinal cord. Every spinal nerve contains both sensory and motor neurones, and supplies a specific segment of the body.

The area of skin that provides sensory input to one pair or spinal nerves is called a dermatome. Skeletal muscles receive their innervation from motor neurones within spinal nerves. All muscles innervated by the motor neurones in a single spinal segment constitute the myotome. Myotomes roughly underlie the corresponding dermatomes.

It is possible to locate damaged regions of the spinal cord, because we know which spinal cord segment supplies each dermatome and myotome. If the skin in a particular region is stimulated and the sensation is not perceived (the patient may say they feel numb, or feel pins and needles), the nerve supplying that dermatome is probably affected. If the muscles in a particular myotome are paralysed or partially paralysed (the patient may complain of weakness, or you may test for muscle strength), the motor neurone in that spinal segment may be affected.

Table 20.1 highlights the relationship between a particular spinal level and the organs it supplies.

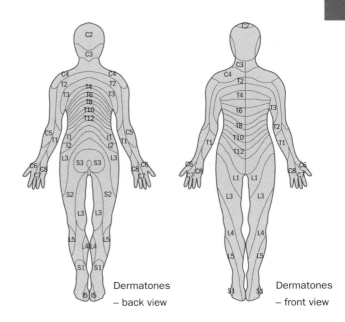

Dermatones
– back view

Dermatones
– front view

▲ Distribution of dermatomes

▼ Table 20.1 Organ–spinal segment relationships

Segment	Area supplied	Possible effect
C1	Blood supply to head, pituitary, scalp, bones of face, inner and middle ear, sympathetic nervous system	Headaches, nervousness, insomnia, head colds, high blood pressure, nervous breakdown, chronic fatigue, dizziness
C2	Eyes, sinuses, mastoid bone, tongue, forehead	Sinusitis, allergies, deafness, eye trouble, earache, fainting
C3	Cheeks, outer ear, facial bones, teeth	Neuralgia, neuritis, acne, eczema
C4	Nose, lips, mouth	Hay fever, catarrh, hearing difficulties,
C5	Vocal cords, glands of the neck, pharynx	Laryngitis, throat conditions e.g. sore throat
C6	Neck muscles, shoulders, tonsils	Stiff neck, pain in upper arm, tonsillitis
C7	Thyroid gland, shoulders, elbows	Bursitis in the shoulder, colds, thyroid conditions
T1	Forearms, hands, oesophagus, trachea	Asthma, cough, difficult breathing, shortness of breath, pain in lower arm and hands
T2	Coronary arteries, heart	Functional heart conditions and chest pain
T3	Lungs, bronchial tube, pleura, chest, breast	Bronchitis, pleurisy, congestion, influenza
T4	Gall bladder and common bile duct	Gall bladder conditions, jaundice, shingles
T5	Liver, solar plexus, blood	Liver conditions, fevers, low blood pressure, poor circulation
T6	Stomach	Stomach troubles including nervous conditions, indigestion, heartburn
T7	Pancreas, duodenum	Diabetes, ulcers, gastritis
T8	Spleen, diaphragm	Hiccoughs, lowered resistance
T9	Adrenal glands	Allergies
T10	Kidneys	Kidney troubles, chronic tiredness

Segment	Area supplied	Possible effect
T11	Kidneys, ureters	Skin conditions (acne, eczema)
T12	Small intestines, fallopian tube	Rheumatism, certain types of sterility
L1	Large intestines, inguinal rings	Constipation, colitis, diarrhoea, hernias
L2	Appendix, abdomen, upper leg	Abdominal cramping, difficulty breathing, acidoses, varicose veins
L3	Sex organs, bladder, knee	Bladder problems, mental problems, bed wetting, impotence, menopausal symptoms, knee pain
L4	Prostate gland, muscles of the lower back, sciatic nerve	Sciatica, problems with urination
L5	Legs	Poor circulation in the legs, swollen ankles, weak ankles and aches, leg cramps
Sacrum	Hips, buttocks	Sacroiliac conditions, spinal curvatures
Coccyx	Rectum, anus	Haemorrhoids, pain in coccyx on sitting

Palpation

Palpation is an important part of the assessment procedure. Throughout the examination the patient will sit, stand or lie successively supine and prone on the table, in whichever order is most efficient and useful.

Key Terms

Supine position – lying down with the face up

Prone position – lying face down

The palpatory examination has two parts:
- general assessment of the tissues in each area
- precise palpation for taut bands in the muscles, tender or trigger points.

Both parts are continuous and contiguous with therapy: as you treat, you examine.

Activity – palpation

Look at the area you are about palpate. Notice its colour and compare it with other parts of the body. Is it pale or pasty, is there any swelling, redness or any contrast in coloration?

Begin with a broad, gentle, general touch. Lay your hand on the area and let it rest there for a moment. Feel for any temperature of the area. Is it cold? Cool? Hot? Warm? Does it feel damp, or sticky, or unpleasantly dry?

Allow your hand to press a bit deeper, and move the skin over the underlying layers. Check the underlying layers for feeling stuck, loose or mobile – do the layers feel connected or sticky? Pliable? Differences in temperature and moisture can be signs of sympathetic nervous system activity in response to problems in the underlying tissue.

Move your hands, palpating different parts of the muscle, to feel for taut bands and knots in the tissue. Ask the client to let you know what areas are tender, ticklish and numb, or feel in any way strange. Be aware of the patient's non-verbal responses that may signify something significant – such as facial wincing, holding their breath, muscle spasms or body wriggling.

You can palpate for trigger points or other sensitive areas, not pressing too firmly. As you gain experience, you will know which areas of the body are more sensitive to trigger points. Also, your awareness of the client's complaint and history will guide the clinical choices made regarding the areas to palpate.

Remember, when palpating always examine the antagonists. If there is a particular problem in a muscle or group of muscles, then it is likely there is a problem with its antagonists. Record the information you gain from palpation in an easily referenced manner.

Key Terms

Agonist is the kind of muscle that causes movement to occur.

Antagonist is the kind of muscle that acts in opposition to the movement generated by the agonist, and is responsible for returning a limb to its initial position.

Referral to practitioners

There are some occasions where clients need help from other health professionals, such as a physiotherapist, sports therapist, doctor or surgeon.

This can be where there is no clear diagnosis, a significant injury such as a fracture, or complete tear of a tendon or ligament. Also, there are certain signs called 'red flag signs', which mean that the client should be referred immediately for medical attention as they may indicate the presence of serious disease such as cancer.

■ Red flag signs

The main red flag signs are listed below – the presence of more than three in a client indicates a serious medical problem.

- Medical history (current or past) of
  - cancer
  - TB
  - HIV/AIDS or injection drug abuse
  - osteoporosis.
- Weight loss 10% body weight (3–6 months).
- Incontinence of urine or faeces and/or altered sensation around the genitals and/or anus.
- Severe night pain.
- Weakness and/or lack of coordination of the lower limbs.
- Altered reflexes.

Treatment area

■ Anatomical position

This is the position used as a reference when describing parts of the body in relation to each other. Used in conjunction with terms of relationship, terms of comparison and terms of movement, the anatomical position allows a standard way of documenting where one part of the body is in relation to another, regardless of whether the body is standing, lying down, or in any other position.

A person in the anatomical position is standing erect with the head, eyes and toes pointing forward, feet together with arms by the side. The palms of the hands also point forward.

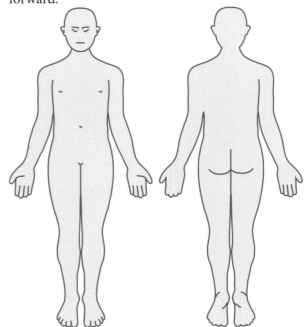

▲ Anatomical position

■ Anatomical planes

Four imaginary planes pass through the body in the anatomical position, which help to describe movements and body positions. These are the median, sagittal, coronal and horizontal planes.

The median plane is an imaginary vertical plane that passes through the middle of the body, dividing it into left and right halves. The sagittal plane is a vertical plane that runs parallel to the median plane, but does not necessarily pass through the body's midline. In effect, the median plane is a specific type of sagittal plane. The coronal plane is a vertical plane perpendicular to the median and sagittal planes, and is sometimes also referred to as the frontal plane. The horizontal or transverse plane splits the body or body part in question into upper and lower parts.

▼ Anatomical planes

■ Terms of movement

The terms of movement are used to describe movements of body parts, which occur at the joints (see Table 20.2, opposite).

■ Anterior

The client should be observed while facing you, so that you can see the front or anterior surface of the body, looking for any distinguishing features such as difference in shoulder height, whether the client leans to one side, etc.

■ Posterior

The client should be observed while facing away from you so that you can see the back or posterior surface of the body, looking for any distinguishing features such as difference in height of the shoulder blades, whether the client has one hip higher than the other, etc.

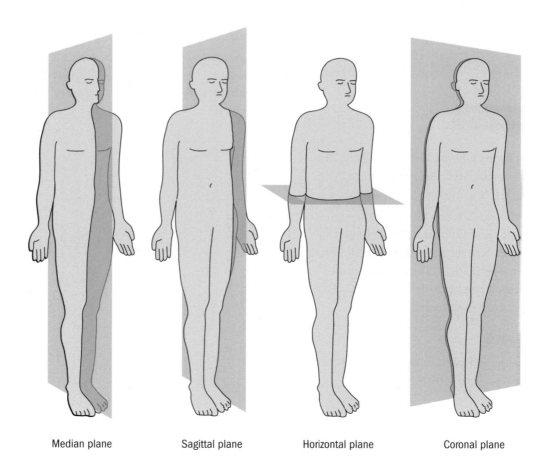

Median plane   Sagittal plane   Horizontal plane   Coronal plane

▼ Table 20.2 Terms of movement

Term	Meaning	Example
Flexion	Bending the joint to make the angle between the two bones smaller. Occurs in the sagittal plane.	When you touch your right shoulder with your right hand, your elbow is in flexion (flexed).
Extension	Straightening a joint to make the angle larger. Occurs in the sagittal plane.	If you straighten your legs, the knees have undergone extension (extended).
Abduction	Moving away from the median plane. Movement occurs in the coronal plane.	When you stand with your feet apart, your legs are in abduction (abducted).
Adduction	The opposite of abduction.	If you sqeeze your knees together, you are adducting your legs.
Lateral flexion	A movement in the coronal plane used to describe a movement of the spine.	If you tilt your head to touch your ear to your shoulder, you have laterally flexed your neck.
Internal rotation	Rotation of a limb where the anterior surface of the limb moves medially.	You internally rotate your shoulder when you scratch your back.
External rotation	The opposite of internal rotation.	You externally rotate your hip when you point your feet out to the side.
Circumduction	A circular motion combining flexion, extension, abduction and adduction.	Making circles in the air with your arms.
Supination	A movement of the forearm in which the palm faces posteriorly.	When screwing in a screw with a screwdriver using your right hand, you have to supinate your forearm.
Pronation	A movement of the forearm in which the palm faces anteriorly.	When unscrewing a screw with your right hand, you must pronate your forearm.
Protraction	Moving anteriorly.	Sticking your chin out.
Retraction	Moving posteriorly.	Pushing your shoulders back to squeeze your shoulder blades together.
Opposition	Movement of the hand where the thumb touches the fifth finger.	
Dorsiflexion	Movement of the ankle in the sagittal plane which decreases the angle between the foot and the lower leg.	When you point your foot towards your head.
Plantar flexion	Movement of the ankle in the sagittal plane which increases the angle between the foot and the lower leg.	When you stand on 'tip-toes' your ankles are in plantar flexion.
Elevation	Upward movement.	When shrugging your shoulders you elevate them.
Depression	Opposite to elevation.	

■ Legs

Legs should be checked to see whether they are of the same length, hips, knees and ankles move freely and equally, and muscle bulk is the same on both sides.

■ Upper back

Is there any kyphosis/scoliosis or restricted movement? (see page 88). Also look for muscle spasm or any differences in muscle bulk on one side compared with the other.

Lower back

Is the lordosis normal (see page 88) or is the back flat? Can the client move freely without pain?

Shoulders

Is one shoulder higher than the other? Are the contours (shape) of the shoulders equal, and are collar bones level?

Neck

Can the neck move freely, and does it sit on the spine correctly or is it held forward?

Simple injuries

Haematoma

This is a contusion or bruise. There are two varieties of haematoma (see pages 102–103).

- Intermuscular haematoma – may produce bruising along the whole length of the limb, as it follows the blood tracks between the muscle and the bruising may reach the surface at any point. It is due to a tear in the connective tissue, not the muscle. Although joints may be sore, movement of them remains full or, if not, rapidly returns to normal.
- Intramuscular haematoma – bleeding is contained within the muscle sheath, and is generally more serious. This can cause high pressure. This sort of injury can cause stiffness and pain, which may heal slowly. Treat with rest and ice. Remember – rest refers to the joint, not the patient.

Muscle tear

Strains or tears are the most common type of muscle injury (see page 102). Most are fairly minor, but without good treatment even minor strains may heal poorly, which can lead to permanent scarring and adhesions, which will affect the function of the muscle.

Tendon injuries

Tendons attach muscles to all other structures. They are often painfully overstrained in sport. The typical acutely painful swelling of the tendon (tendonitis) is caused by inflammation of the tendon, and requires rest or immobilisation.

Inflammation

Inflammation is the process by which healthy tissue responds to an injury. It helps to destroy and remove substances recognised as being foreign to the body; to prevent minor infections from becoming overwhelming; and to prepare any damaged tissue for repair.

The so-called 'cardinal signs' of inflammation are heat, redness, swelling, pain and loss of function.

Ligament injuries

Ligaments attach bone to bone and give stability to joints. Ligaments of major joints are relatively weak, and depend heavily on the muscles to help give muscle stability. Ligaments are also subject to sprains (see pages 101–102).

Documentation

Record cards

It is important that all consultations and treatments are recorded, and that these records are kept safe and confidential.

It is generally recommended that all client records be retained by the therapist for a period of around six years following the last consultation or treatment session.

Many therapists now like to store records on computer, and it is important to realise that all such records are subject to regulations such as the Data Protection Act, and should be totally confidential between client and therapist. They may only be passed to other health professionals, and then only with the permission of the client.

Effect of treatments

The record card should contain a brief description of the treatment given as well as the effect of the treatment on the client.

For example, an entry might read:

'General massage given to back and upper limbs. Patient felt more relaxed and had greater range of movement in shoulders and neck.'

These entries should always be dated and signed by the therapist.

■ After care

The patient should be given the following advice immediately after their massage treatment:

- rest – the muscles have just been worked and they may feel tired or bruised
- drink plenty of water – the circulation has been improved so the body's systems are working more efficiently, oxygen and nutrients are being carried more effectively through the body, and carbon dioxide and toxins are being removed thoroughly from the body – drinking more water is an extension of this, helping to flush out the body's systems.

■ Home care

The therapist should also advise clients on self-care at home, as they will have to manage the condition themselves between treatments.

Eliminate cause

The root cause of the condition should have been discussed and identified during the consultation. Suggest ways in which this problem may be eliminated – for example, for lower back pain a support such as a girdle may be needed, or a lumbar support while driving.

Reduce inflammation

Ice the area if needed. The patient may need to take anti-inflammatory medication, although any medication should ideally be supervised by the patient's GP if the condition is long-lasting or severe.

Reduce tension in area

Stretching exercises will ease tightness in muscles (see pages 198–199). Give advice on correct posture to help to ease the strain on the area if this is contributing to the problem.

Prevent re-occurrence of problem

Give advice on strengthening exercises for the affected muscles and for the surrounding muscles, which will give added support.

Health and safety

Massage therapists are regulated, like all businesses, by acts such as the Health and Safety at Work Act (1974) and the Disability Discrimination Act (2005). This means there should be, for example, clearly signed fire exits and procedures in place for spillages, and premises should be accessible to people with disabilities.

Other acts, such as COSHH (Care of Substances Hazardous to Health), may also apply, as well as professional bodies' health and safety regulations.

Proposed treatment

Pre-event massage treatment

This is treatment performed in the run-up to a sport or activity. The athlete or performer should stretch as normal, and use massage to complement his or her warm-up routine. The aim of the massage is the same as the warm-up – to increase circulation, bringing oxygen and nutrients to the muscles, and to stretch muscle fibres to prevent injury. The specific benefit of pre-event massage is that it can stretch muscle fibres in all directions. If there has been a tear or a strain to the muscle, this is often the last place to loosen, making the area susceptible to repeated injury.

Requirement:	Pre-event massage
Rate/speed:	Fast
Pressure:	Firm
Range of techniques:	Mostly petrissage and tapotement

Maintenance/preventive massage

This is performed in between events or activities, to sort out any aches or pains the athlete may be experiencing. It is used both to treat injuries and to prevent them from occurring. It can and should be used on a regular basis, although five days should be left between treatments for the muscles to heal.

There are a variety of reasons you may wish to adapt your massage. You may want your treatment to be more relaxing, or perhaps more stimulating. You can change the outcome of the treatment by asking yourself the following questions:

- what outcome/effect does the patient require?
- what rate or speed should I use?
- what pressure should I use?
- what range of techniques can I use?

By varying any or all of these, you will get different results. First, you must find out what your patient wants.

Requirement:	Maintenance/preventive massage
Rate/speed:	Varied, to suit area being treated
Pressure:	Varied, to suit area being treated
Range of: techniques:	All may be used, but generally deep effleurage and petrissage

Post-massage treatment

This is performed directly after the sport or activity has taken place. It is used to complement the athlete's cool-down routine – but should not be used instead of it. When exercising, it is natural that muscle fibres get torn. Massage helps to realign these fibres and helps them to heal as quickly as possible with as little loss of flexibility or strength as possible. Post-event massage also works on the blood and lymphatic circulation to help bring oxygen and nutrients back to the tissues, and remove carbon dioxide and lactic acid from the muscles to prevent stiffness.

Requirement:	Post-event massage
Rate/speed:	Slow
Pressure:	Lighter, patient comfort
Range of techniques:	Mostly effleurage, some petrissage

Massage procedure

All movements of massage should be rhythmical, and should begin and end gently. Generally, a slower rate is useful for relaxation, and a faster rate for stimulation. The therapist can adjust the pressure to the contours of the body. Massage therapists should take care over bony and delicate areas, such as the back of the knee or the sides of the neck.

All massage should begin lightly, increase in depth, and finally finish lightly. Always be aware of individual differences – the pressure one patient considers too light will be far too heavy for another. Make sure the pressure is not greater than the patient can comfortably tolerate. Always let your patient know that they can and should tell you if the pressure is too heavy or too light. Never take your hands off the patient until the treatment ends. If changing sides, maintain contact with one hand and walk around the table.

Contra-indications

Client history

There are certain instances where the application of massage is not applicable. These are known as contra-indications, and can be:

- local – a particular area must not be massaged
- general – it may not be advisable for the person to be massaged at all.

Some of the main contra-indications for sports massage are:

- acute trauma – open wounds, burns, broken bones, contusions, soft tissue ruptures, joint dislocation
- acute inflammatory conditions – arthritis, phlebitis, bursitis, gout, etc.
- infections – bacterial, fungal or viral.

Other instances where massage would not be appropriate include bleeding disorders, thrombosis, any unidentified lumps or tumours, and pregnancy. Wherever there appear to be major signs of inflammation (heat, redness, swelling, pain and joint dysfunction) massage is not to be encouraged, as with any medical condition that needs to be assessed and diagnosed by a qualified medical practitioner.

Remember!

If in doubt – do not massage.

The following sections give more information on some specific contra-indications for massage therapy.

Type of injury

Massage is not appropriate for the following types of injury as it may increase inflammation in the affected areas:

- fractures
- swollen, hot or painful joints
- recent sprains.

Location of injury

Massage can be applied to any area of the body, although care may be needed around the injury site itself. Also, massage should not be applied directly to the eyes.

Skin conditions

The following skin conditions should never be massaged directly as the skin is too fragile and may be damaged by even gentle pressure:

- cuts and abrasions
- recent extensive bruising
- recent haemorrhage
- new scar tissue
- recent operation
- sunburn or windburn
- spastic muscles.

Circulatory conditions

Massage should never be used in the following circulatory conditions as it may increase the risk of blood clots circulating around the body:

- thrombosis
- phlebitis
- history of embolism
- varicose veins.

This, in turn, may increase the risk of stroke or heart attack.

Multiple sclerosis

Although these patients can benefit from massage, care needs to be taken as, in some patients, it can increase their muscle spasm and therefore pain. Generally speaking, patients with MS may benefit from gentle stretching, but percussion techniques should never be used.

Cancer

Patients with cancer should not receive massage therapy as the pressure may cause the tumour to break up and spread throughout the body, accelerating the course of the disease.

Case study

The World Tennis Association (WTA) Tour has a massage therapy team of nine internationally based therapists. These massage therapists provide high-quality massage therapy services for players at tournaments throughout the world, and consider sports massage as 'an important component of any tennis player's routine to maximise performance, prevent injuries and enhance recovery from injury and tough competition environments.'

(Source: www.sonyericssonwtatour.com)

1 **Why do you think the WTA employs massage therapists?**

2 **What benefits might the players get from such a service?**

20.4 Be able to demonstrate different sports massage techniques

Preparing the client

Following your initial consultation, the client will need to undress and lie on the massage table.

It is vital that the therapist makes the client feel comfortable during this part of the session, and this is best done by allowing the client to undress in private and cover themselves with towels before the therapist re-enters the room. During the treatment the therapist must also ensure that any areas not being treated remain covered to avoid embarrassment.

Demonstrating different techniques

Safe and effective massage

The following points are essential for good technique in all massage:
- maintain evenness of rhythm and establish correct speed of movement
- keep hands flexible to enable contouring of body part
- maintain correct posture and stance, and positioning of client
- regulate pressure of technique in relation to tissues being treated and purpose of treatment

- maintain correct direction of movement
- sufficient knowledge of anatomy and physiology.

Massage techniques

■ Effleurage

This is a stroking movement using the hand so as to cover a large surface area. You should apply long strokes to cover a whole part. Maintain contact with the skin at all times, so apply the main stroke in the direction of venous and lymphatic flow and then return by just sliding the hands back with little pressure. Effleurage is the first basic technique and should start the treatment. Its main effect is in pumping the circulation. Also use it to finish off the massage to leave a good feeling of warmth and relaxation.

Deeper effleurage can be applied using smaller surfaces of the hand to concentrate the pressure, or on larger areas by using a more considerable force. Deep effleurage should be applied in both longitudinal and transverse directions, using the pad of the thumb, pads of fingers, the heel of the palm or the ulnar border of the forearm.

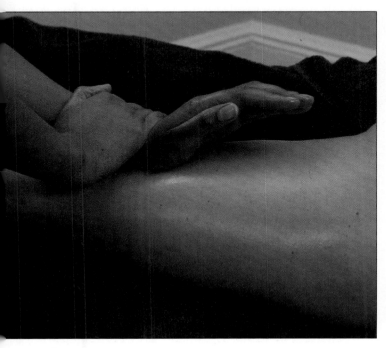

▲ Effleurage

■ Petrissage

This includes a variety of techniques that lift, compress and stretch the tissues. They also mechanically pump the circulation system and warm the tissues. Wringing and kneading is the most common, whereby the tissues are alternately grasped, lifted and released.

- These are compression (pressure) movements.
- They include kneading, wringing, rolling, friction.
- It can involve the whole hand or just part of the hand.
- The movement consists of lifting, rolling or pressing.

▼ Petrissage

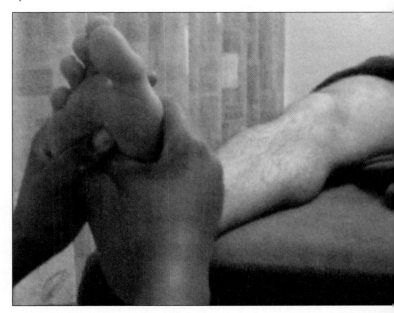

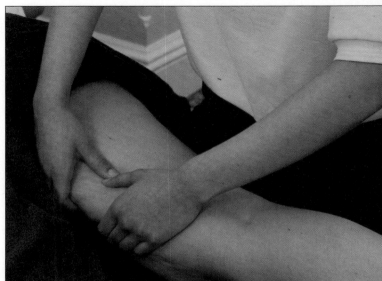

Frictions

Frictions are a specific form of petrissage used on specific localised problem areas to loosen and mobilise adhesions and realign scar tissue.

Massage over the skin creates frictional heat. Friction also occurs between the deeper tissues as they are moved against each other, generating more heat. This is beneficial as relaxation is encouraged and tissues become more pliable.

The circulatory system can be mechanically pumped, as can the lymphatic system. As massage is applied there is increased pressure in the blood vessels, and this pressure change assists the venous and lymphatic flow. This increased circulation will improve the interchange of nutrients and waste products, including gases.

Muscles can be stretched transversely and longitudinally. This will improve intramuscular circulation, increasing the ease of movement and possibly the range of movement.

Adhesions can be mobilised and therefore assist in restoring optimum function. Scar tissue can be realigned after soft tissue injury. Frictions can help restore contractile properties and enhance movement.

Tapotements

These are stimulating percussive techniques using both hands alternately, working quickly and rhythmically.
- Also known as percussion movements
- They include hacking, clapping or cupping, beating, pounding, tapping.

▼ Tapotement – hacking

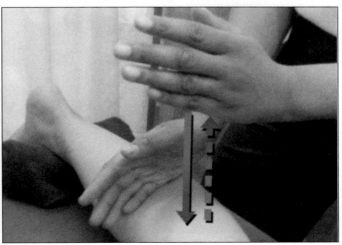

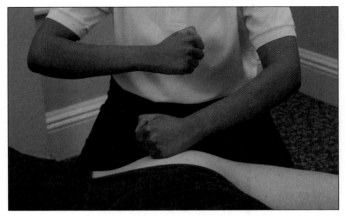
▲ Tapotement – beating/pounding

Application of techniques

Correct techniques

It is important for the sports and exercise massage professional to remain in a good posture throughout the massage treatment. A good posture is achieved when the body's weight is evenly distributed throughout the body (the spine and the major muscle groups). This will reduce strain on the bones, tendons, ligaments, tissues and organs, allowing the body to work most efficiently and reducing fatigue and muscular aches and pains for the practitioner.

Remember!

Maximum efficiency = minimum effort.

Stand with your feet comfortably apart to maintain good balance, and with your back straight. Stand close to the couch. It is necessary to use body weight rather than arm strength.

Walk standing is the position assumed when the therapist is working longitudinally down the length of the muscle. Stride standing is the position assumed when the therapist is working transversely across the muscle.

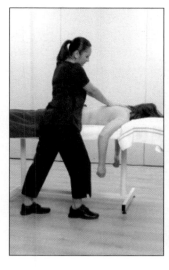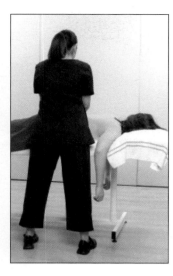

▲ **Stride standing (left) and walk standing (right) positions**

Use just the necessary amount of massage oil – too much, and grip and control are lost; too little, and skin soreness and inflammation of the hair follicles is possible.

Massage strokes should be directed centripetally towards the heart when working on the arms and legs to assist lymphatic and venous flow. If you apply pressure in the opposite direction, you can damage the valves of lymphatic vessels and superficial veins. Massage should not be performed in just a longitudinal direction along the soft tissues, nor should it only be in a transverse direction. The most effective way to apply massage is with a combination of techniques in different directions.

■ Follow a set routine

It is always best to follow a set massage routine, and each therapist will develop their own. One example is given below.

- Relaxing scalp massage begins the routine.
- Relaxing warm-up and stretching of back muscles.
- Thorough massage of upper back / shoulders / neck.
- Thorough lower back massage.
- Deep (not painful) compression of gluteal muscles.
- Therapeutic and relaxing bottom-of-foot massage including some percussion.

- Extensive posterior leg massage including massage of calf.
- Continued massage on bottom-of-feet and Achilles heel.
- Half-way point reached – client carefully turns over onto back.
- Tops of feet are massaged including some gentile passive ankle joint range-of-motion manipulations and leg stretches.
- Extensive anterior leg massage (lower and upper).
- Hands are massaged thoroughly including gentle wrist range-of-motion manipulations.
- Arms (upper and lower, anterior and posterior) and shoulders are massaged thoroughly and extensive back-of-neck massage performed.
- Optional chest and stomach massage if desired.
- Soothing neck and additional shoulder massage.
- Conclusion with lengthy relaxing scalp and facial massage and light effleurage of body to conclude.

■ Appropriate duration

A full body massage will usually take around 45 minutes to an hour, although it may be shorter if only one particular area is being worked on.

■ Client/therapist rapport

As a massage therapist, you should always strive to maintain a high level of professionalism in order to put your clients at ease. It is also worth, perhaps during the consultation, establishing a list of the client's work activities and hobbies in order to establish a rapport between client and therapist.

■ Mediums

For use as massage lubricants, most practitioners prefer a choice of oil, cream, talc or gel. Oil is generally used for most if not all massage treatments, but cream may be the choice of medium if a client is extremely hairy. It is important to be aware that some massage oils may contain traces of nut oils, for example arachis oil, which is peanut-based, so patients should always be checked for allergy to nuts.

Activity – massage of the lower limb

A Patient prone

1 Effleurage
   - Entire limb, firmly up and lightly down, including foot

2 Foot
   - Effleurage whole foot
   - Knuckle-knead sole of foot gently
   - Thumb frictions to dorsum, circular frictions around malleoli
   - Separation of metatarsals
   - Tapotement to sole of foot (nerve stimulation)

3 Passive movements of the ankle (bend to 90°)
   - Dorsiflexion, plantarflexion, rotation

4 Achilles tendon
   - Firm frictions and S-movements

5 Effleurage
   - Entire lower limb

6 Calf
   - Effleurage
   - Kneading:
     Palmer kneading
     squeeze calf from ankle to knee
     rolling
   - Circular frictions and sliding frictions to calf, separating heads of gastrocnemius, gentle frictions to popliteal fossa and medial and lateral aspects of the knee
   - Vibrations to calf
   - Effleurage

7 Passive movements of knee
   - Flexion, medial and lateral rotation with knee flexed at 90°

8 Effleurage
   - Entire lower limb

9 Thigh
   - Effleurage
   - Kneading:
     Palmer kneading, rolling
   - Firm frictions from knee to ischial tuberosity, across to greater trochanter, then down iliotibial band – use heel of hand, knuckles, fingers and thumbs
   - Vibrations to thigh
   - Effleurage

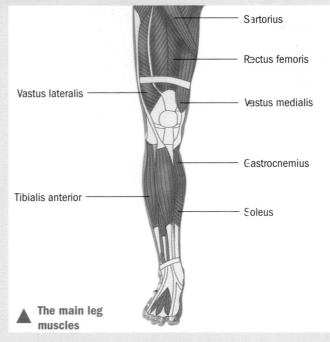

▲ **The main leg muscles**

Labels: Sartorius, Rectus femoris, Vastus lateralis, Vastus medialis, Gastrocnemius, Tibialis anterior, Soleus

10 Effleurage
    - Entire lower limb

11 Cover with a towel and repeat on other leg

B Patient supine

1 Effleurage
   - Entire lower limb, firmly up and lightly down, including the foot and avoiding pressure on the patella

2 Foot
   - Effleurage both sides of the foot and toes
   - Kneading: sandwich foot between palms, circular kneading; wringing foot
   - Frictions: to dorsum, sole and circular frictions around the malleoli

   Toes
   - Effleurage and knead
   - Passive movements – flexion, extension, rotation and traction

   Metatarsals
   - Passive movements – separation of the metatarsals and pressing on metatarsal heads

   Sole
   - Knuckle kneading

3 Ankle
- Passive movements – rotation, figure 8, dorsiflexion, plantarflexion, inversion, eversion
- Stretch achilles tendon (dorsiflexion)

4 Effleurage entire lower limb

5 Leg
- Effleurage
- Kneading: Palmer and rolling
- Friction over muscle attachments

6 Effleurage entire limb

7 Thigh
- Effleurage
- Kneading; Palmer kneading, rolling

- Friction with thumbs or heels of hands, knuckles, fingers or thumbs round patella and all muscle attachments, including greater trochanter
- Tapotement

8 Hip
- Passive movements – Flexion, rotation, figure 8 movement

9 Effleurage entire limb

10 Vibration
- To entire limb

11 Effleurage and stroking

12 Cover with a towel and repeat on other leg

Activity – massage of the back

1 Stroking
- To apply oil

2 Effleurage
- From sacrum to shoulders, covering as large an area as possible up the paraspinal muscles and down the lateral aspects of the back. Repeat six times, getting progressively heavier

3 Kneading
- Paraspinal muscles. Stand facing across patient's back and work on the opposite side of the body from where you are standing. Begin at the base of the spine, making large circular movements using palms of the hands, working from the spine and moving laterally; cover the area from the gluteal to the shoulders and back again several times
- palmer kneading buttocks to shoulders
- repeat on other side
- rolling from one side of the body to the other

4 Gluteals
- Effleurage, kneading using heels of hands, frictions using thumbs, fingers or knuckles

5 Effleurage
- The entire back

6 Frictions
- Small circular frictions close to the spine, including the sacrum and iliac crest
- Sliding frictions along the paraspinal muscles
- Repeat on other side

7 Scapula area
- Circular effleurage

- Frictions along the medial border of the scapular and over the scapular muscles
- Repeat on other side

8 Trapezius
- Knead trapezius muscle with alternating pulling movements using fingers of both hands
- Kneading from tips of shoulders to base of neck, thumb posteriorly, fingers anteriorly
- Using thumbs in a rolling movement to release tension in the upper trapezius area at the top of the shoulders and the base of the neck

9 Neck
- Effleurage, Palmer kneading, circular and sliding friction along paraspinal muscles and the base of skull

10 Effleurage
- From shoulders to gluteals including the neck. Stand at the head of the table

11 Scalp
- Circular frictions to scalp

12 Effleurage
- From shoulders to gluteals including the neck. Stand at the head of the table

13 General back movements
- Sliding friction rapidly all over back
- Tapotement
- Cross over effleurage

14 Effleurage
- Entire back and stroking

Activity – massage of the upper limb

Patient supine

1 Stroking and effleurage
   – Entire limb including the hand and shoulder

2 Hand
   – kneading palm – sandwich hand between your palms squeezing
   – frictions to palm and dorsum of hand
   – separations of metacarpals

3 Fingers
   – Effleurage and knead each finger and thumb
   – Passive movement – flexion, extension, rotation and traction

4 Efflurage hand

5 Wrist
   – Frictions around the carpal bones
   – Passive movements – rotation, flexion, extension, traction

6 Forearm
   – Effleurage both sides of forearm

   – Kneading: Palmer kneading and rolling
   – Frictions: deep thumb sliding friction from wrist to elbow, circular frictions around muscle attachments at wrist and elbow
   – Effleurage

7 Upper arm
   – Effleurage
   – Kneading: palmer kneading and rolling
   – Frictions: sliding from elbow to shoulder and circular frictions around muscle attachments
   – Effleurage

8 Shoulder
   – Passive movements – rotations, tractions
   – Effleurage entire limb
   – Tapotement entire limb
   – Relaxation movement
   – Shake arm
   – Vibration and shaking
   – Stroking
   – Cover with towel

Activity – massage of the neck

1 Effleurage
   – Stand at head of table. Effleurage the neck from T1 (top of spine) to occiput using alternate hands

2 Frictions
   – To neck muscles working from T1 to occiput. Frictions from centre to mastoid process with finger frictions

3 Frictions
   – To trapezius muscles from occiput to acromium, using thumbs, fingertips or knuckles

4 Effleurage
   – From acromium along trapezius up to occiput. Work with deep finger pressure along base of skull

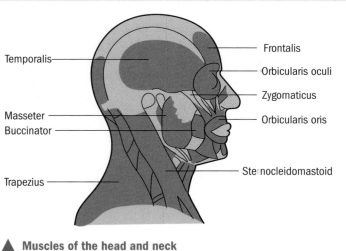

▲ Muscles of the head and neck

- Support patient's head in your right hand and turn client's right ear towards table (side bend/lateral flexion). Effleurage and friction left trapezius from occiput to acromium. Repeat on other side

5 Traction
- One hand under chin, the other under occiput
- Traction with towel
- Relaxation movement with towel

6 Effleurage sternocleidomastoids (SCM)
- Support patients head in your right hand and gently laterally flex patient's neck towards their right shoulder. Effleurage left side of neck along SCM. Avoid pressure on anterior neck

7 Effleurage
- as in 1.

Activity – abdominal massage

1 Stroking
Apply oil to abdomen

2 Effleurage
Facing client's head, hands travel up midline, then laterally taking in the lower aspects of the rib cage, down the oblique muscles then lifting upwards to finish

3 Palmer kneading
- lightly

4 Colon
Circular frictions
- Small searching movements working up the ascending colon, across the transverse and down the descending colon, using fingertips
Effleurage
- Ascending colon with the heels of hands, facing client's feet
Deep, sliding movements
- Left hand up ascending colon, across transverse colon, hold and fingers of right hand strip down descending colon

Kneading
- Left hand makes small circles over small intestine while right hand traces only small arc

5 Abdominal muscles
Lift oblique muscles
- From sides of client towards navel

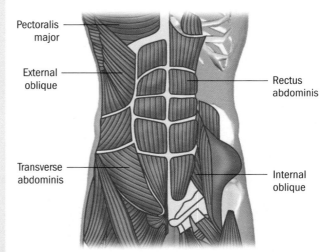

Pectoralis major

External oblique

Rectus abdominis

Transverse abdominis

Internal oblique

▲ Muscles of the trunk

Rectus abdominus
- Push away with heel of hand while pulling toward you with fingers of other hand, forming an 'S' in the rectus abdominus
- Grip rectus abdominus over a towel, and shake

6 Palmer kneading
- as in 3.

7 Vibrations
- From inferior to superior from lateral aspect to midline

8 Effleurage as in 2

Activity – chest massage

Stand at patient's head

1. Stroking
   apply oil, figure 8 movement

2. Effleurage
   Lightly across front of neck and across pectorals
   (in male, figure 8 movement to chest)

3. Kneading
   – to pectoral muscles

4. Frictions
   – Either side of sternum and between ribs

5. Assisted breathing movements

6. Kneading
   Stand at client's side, facing towards their feet.
   Using alternate hands, effleurage lower ribs, from
   lateral to medial

7. Tapotement

8. Effleurage as in 2

Assessment practice

1. Return to the requirements and suggested
   treatments you produced for the two players on
   page 210. Working in pairs, practise carrying out
   the massage treatments. Between you, should try
   to cover all major treatments and all major muscle
   groups within the body. **P5 M3**

2. For one of the players, write up the treatments
   you have given, with reasons and notes on what
   aftercare to suggest to the client in order to help
   rehabilitation. **D2**

3. With your partner's help, identify your strengths
   and areas for improvement. **P6**

Knowledge check

1. Can you name three different types of massage
   that can be used to treat an athlete?

2. What are the main benefits and effects of
   massage?

3. Why is it important to keep good patient records?

4. Name three different types of massage medium.

5. How is pre-event massage different from post-
   event massage?

6. List three massage techniques that may be used
   to treat an athlete.

7. What effect will tapotement have on the body?

8. List three dos and don'ts of personal
   presentation and how they might affect the image
   of the workplace.

9. Name two laws which the massage therapist
   must adhere to.

Preparation for assessment

1 Present two case studies of different patients showing how they have benefited from a course of massage therapy. This could be in the form of a treatment diary or patient record. As part of the record you should also explain how the effects and benefits are achieved, either on the record card or in the form of a handout which can be given to the patient. **P1 P2 P3 P4 P5 P6**

2 In addition you should include a reflective diary for each patient outlining alternatives to the treatment given and analysing your performance while delivering the massage itself. **M1 M2 M3 D1 D2**

To achieve a pass grade the evidence must show that the learner is able to:	To achieve a merit grade the evidence must show that, in addition to the pass criteria, the learner is able to:	To achieve a distinction grade the evidence must show that, in addition to the pass and merit criteria, the learner is able to:
P1 describe the effects and benefits of sports massage **Assessment practice page 201**	**M1** explain the effects and benefits of sports massage **Assessment practice page 201**	
P2 describe the role of sports massage professionals **Assessment practice page205**		
P3 conduct an assessment on two different sports performers, identifying areas that require massage **Assessment practice page 218**	**M2** explain the sports massage requirements of two different sports performers **Assessment practice page 218**	**D1** compare and contrast the sports massage requirements of two sports performers **Assessment practice page 218**
P4 describe six contra-indications to massage treatment. **Assessment practice page 218**		
P5 demonstrate appropriate sports massage treatment, for a selected sports performer, with support. **Assessment practice page 226**	**M3** demonstrate appropriate sports massage treatment, for a selected sports performer **Assessment practice page 226**	**D2** analyse the appropriate sports massage treatment, for a selected sports performer **Assessment practice page 226**
P6 review their performance in demonstrating sports massage treatment, identifying strengths and areas for improvement **Assessment practice page 226**		

Rules, regulations and officiating in sport

Introduction

The rules and regulations of sport are continuously changing and evolving. This may be to improve the safety of the sport, or to improve the experience for participants, spectators and officials. Sport governing bodies are realising that the more exciting their sport is, the more marketable it is.

Officials are essential to the success of all sports at all levels, whether on the international stage or at a local Sunday league game. Officials will apply pre-set rules and maintain health and safety, and will need to have self-management skills, empathy, communication skills – and, importantly, a passion and enthusiasm for the sport.

In the past, officials have tended to be former players or people with experience of the sport. As sport has developed, with changing rules, it has become faster and people with experience are not always as fit or mobile as the game demands. So governing bodies are now looking to younger generations to start officiating as early as possible and build up their experience as match officials.

This unit examines the rules and regulations of a number of selected sports and explains the roles and responsibilities of the officials who participate in them. The performance of officials in selected sports is analysed, and you are given an understanding of how to officiate in your chosen area.

This unit will prepare you for the skills and knowledge required to undertake a practical officiating role within your chosen sport.

After completing this unit you should be able to achieve the following outcomes:

- Understand the rules and regulations of a selected sport.
- Understand the roles and responsibilities of officials involved in a selected sport.
- Be able to analyse the performance of officials in a selected sport.
- Be able to officiate effectively in a selected sport.

Think it over

For your chosen sport, in which you intend to demonstrate that you can officiate, write a list of what you think are the most important functions of the referee, umpire or other chief official. When you reach the end of this unit, compile a second list and compare it with the first. What three elements of officiating had you not considered at the start?

Rules of some major sports

Football

The object is to score by manoeuvring the ball into the opposing goal. Only the goalkeepers may use their hands or arms to propel the ball in general play; the rest of the team use their feet to kick the ball, and occasionally use their torso or head to intercept a ball in mid-air. The team that scores the most goals by the end of the match wins. If the score is tied at the end of the game, either a draw is declared or the game goes into extra time and/or a penalty shoot-out, depending on the format of the competition.

The Football Association (FA) is responsible for ensuring that the international Laws of the Game are applied on the field, and that the rules and regulations concerned with running football in England are observed by officials, clubs and players off the pitch as well as on it. These rules are updated regularly, and it is the responsibility of everybody involved in football to have a thorough knowledge of them.

The Laws of the Game are determined by the International Football Association Board (IFAB), and the Rules and Regulations of the Football Association are aimed at establishing an efficient and fair structure. These rules and regulations cover matters ranging from the affiliation of clubs within a league (both grassroots and higher levels), dealing with misconduct of players and coaches, amending on-field match rules, and defining specific competition regulations. The FA also has a responsibility to ensure the health and safety of both players and spectators is maintained during play.

The rules are regularly updated and published as part of the FA Handbook. Further information can be found on the FA website (www.thefa.com).

Rugby Union

The aim of the game is very simple – a team has to score more points than the other team. Points can be gained from a try, conversion, drop goal or penalty in the opponent's goal area. If both teams score the same amount, or no points are scored, the match is a draw.

■ Try

A try is scored when a player puts the ball on the ground with downward pressure (which is very important) inside the opposition's in-goal area between the try line and the deadball line, and is worth five points.

■ Ruck

If a tackled player goes to ground, they must release the ball immediately. The opposition will want to get their hands on the ball, while the team in possession will not want to give it away. So a ruck is formed when the ball is on the ground, with at least one player in physical contact with a member of the opposition. To get hold of the ball, both sides will drive over to make it available for their nearest team-mate. Only players on their feet can handle the ball in a ruck. If a player joins a ruck, they can only do so from behind the line of the ball. This means they can't come in from the sides of the ruck otherwise the referee will award a penalty to the opposing team. Also, every player must be 'bound' in the ruck. This means they must have at least one arm round a team mate who is involved in the ruck. If the ball does not come out of the ruck quickly enough, the referee will award the team moving forward at the ruck the feed at the scrum.

There are very strict rules for a ruck, which every player must follow, otherwise they will give away needless penalties. These rules are designed to ensure all the players remain safe.

■ Scrum

A scrum is a way of restarting the play after:

- the ball has been knocked on
- the ball has gone forward
- an accidental offside
- the ball has not come out from a ruck or maul.

Not everyone can join a scrum – only eight players from each team can take part. The scrum is formed at the place where the infringement happened, and all scrums must take place at least 5m from the touch or try lines.

■ Ball not released

When a ball carrier has been tackled to the ground, they have to let go of the ball – there are no exceptions to this law. It is common for players to purposely hold onto the ball when they have gone down in a tackle, to stop the other team getting hold of the ball and starting a quick attack. If the referee sees a player holding onto the ball on the ground, he (or she) will immediately award a penalty to the opposing team.

A comprehensive review of the regulations was undertaken during season 2005/06, and a new Handbook published in 2007. The regulations can be obtained from the Rugby Football Union (www.rfu.com).

Cricket

Cricket is a team sport for two teams of 11 players each. A formal game of cricket can last anything from an afternoon to up to five days. Although the game play and rules are very different, the basic concept of cricket is similar to that of baseball. Each team will bat in successive innings and attempt to score as many runs as possible within the over or time limits allocated. The opposing team then fields and attempts to bring an end to the batting team's innings by getting each of the opposition batsmen out. The ways in which a batsman can be given out are:

- caught
- bowled
- stumped
- run out

- handle ball
- leg before wicket
- timed out.

After each team has batted for an equal number of innings (either one or two depending on the rules of the competition), the team with the most runs wins. If scores are equal at the end of the match, then the game is often called a tie. If the game runs out with a team still batting, then it is considered a draw.

For further information about cricket and its laws, contact the English Cricket Board (www.ecb.co.uk).

Badminton

The aim of badminton is to hit the shuttlecock back and forth over a net without permitting it to hit the floor in bounds on your side of the net.

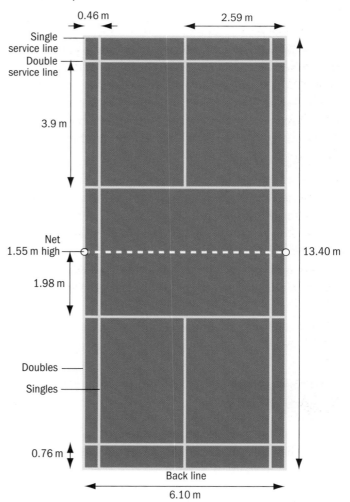

The layout of a badminton court ▶

Like tennis, badminton can be played by singles and doubles, mixed or same-sex players. Matches are played to the best of three sets.

Recently the sport's governing body, the International Badminton Federation, has introduced a series of rule changes to make the game faster and more entertaining. Under the old system, the first player (or team) to reach 15 points won the set, except in women's singles when the target was 11 points.

Both men and women now play up to 21 points. If the score reaches 20–20, the winner is the player (or team) with a two-point advantage. If the score goes up to 29–29, the winner is the first to reach 30 points.

In badminton, the serve is of huge importance. Points used to be won only on serve; under the new rules a player or team can win the point without holding serve. A team now has only one serve in doubles, rather than two under the old rules.

■ Serving

In singles, players serve diagonally from one service box to another, alternating between the left and right side of the court as points are won. The server always serves from the right-hand box at the start of a game and when they have an even number of points. They serve from the left-hand court when they have an odd number of points.

In doubles, the player on the right always starts the serve and, when a point is won, the players switch sides and the server then serves from the left, continuing to alternate until a serve is lost.

■ Service action

The shuttlecock must be hit below the server's waist and the racket head must stay below the server's wrist, which means the shot must be played underarm.

The official laws of badminton can be obtained from Badminton England (www.badmintonengland.co.uk).

Rugby League

The aim of the game is simple – you must score more points than the other team. Each team is given six tackles or chances to score. If, after six tackles, they have not scored, the ball is handed over to the other team, who then get the chance to score with their six tackles.

A game consists of two halves of 40 minutes, with injury time added at the end of each half. In between the two halves there is a 10-minute break, after which both teams change ends and attack the half they were defending.

A hooter or whistle will indicate the start and finish of the half. Play is allowed to continue only after the whistle or hooter sounds if the ball is still in play.

The half will end immediately once a tackle is made, or the ball goes out of touch. Time can be extended for a penalty kick or a kick at goal. In that case, the half will end when the next ball goes out of play or a tackle has been made.

Rugby league is played on a pitch no more than 100m long and 68m wide. The pitch has several markings to indicate the different lines in the game. The three most important lines are the goal lines, deadlines and the half-way line. There are also several 10m markings from the touchline on the pitch to show where scrums and restarts should be taken.

The Rugby Football League publishes the Laws of the Game (www.therfl.co.uk).

Basketball

Basketball is played by two teams, who score points by throwing a ball into the opposing team's basket. The team that scores the most points wins. Each team has a squad of 12 players to choose from. Five of those players are allowed on the court at any one time, with unlimited substitutions. Players can move the ball around the court by passing, tapping, throwing, rolling or dribbling.

The game consists of four quarters of 10 minutes each, with a 15-minute break at half time. There are also two-minute intervals between the first and second periods, and the third and fourth periods. If the game is tied after the fourth period, it continues with an extra period of five minutes, then as many five-minute periods as necessary to break the tie.

The main officials include one referee and one umpire. The court is divided between them, and they swap places after each foul involving a free throw penalty, as well as after each jump ball decision. They use whistles and hand signals to make and explain their decisions.

Points are scored for shooting the basketball through the hoop. Two points for a goal outside the three-point semicircle, and three points for goals scored from outside. Free throws, taken from the free-throw line and awarded after a foul, are worth one point.

The four independent national basketball associations of Scotland, Wales, England and Ireland are each separately affiliated to the International Basketball Federation (FIBA, www.fiba.com).

Netball

Netball is a non-contact sport, and players cannot make physical contact with one another on the court. A good thing about this rule is that it stops taller and larger players using their size to unfair advantage.

Defenders have to stand 0.9m (3 feet) away from the player with the ball. From this distance, a player can try and win the ball back, but only when it has been thrown into the air. Players can defend a member of the other team who does not have the ball, but they cannot touch them or snatch the ball from under their nose.

If a player makes physical contact and disrupts play, then a penalty pass is awarded.

The rules can be found on the England Netball website (www.england-netball.co.uk).

Volleyball

The aim of volleyball is to get the ball into the opposing team's court area while preventing them getting the ball into your area. There are six players on a court in each team, with these divided into three at the front (nearest the net) and three at the back. The team that reaches 25 points first wins.

The game starts with a serve from the backline of the court and, after serving, the server moves back onto the court to help their team. Once the ball has been served, any player can move anywhere on court, and even chase the ball out of court if needed.

■ Hitting the ball

The ball can be hit with any part of the body (hand, head, chest, even the foot). The exception to this rule is the serve, which must be hit with the hand. The hit has to be clean – no scoops, catch-and-rethrows, dunks etc. are allowed.

Your team has up to three touches to return the ball over the net – although it can be returned by the first or second touch. A player cannot have two consecutive hits – but hitting it first and third is permitted.

During the rally, players cannot touch the net. The ball can touch the net on the way over provided it doesn't touch the supporting posts. Your team can win points if:

- the ball touches the court floor on the opposite side
- the ball touches one of the opposition players and then the floor/wall
- the other team hits the ball more than three times.

■ Blocking

This describes jumping at the net with the arms up to stop the ball coming over the net. Players must not touch the net, and they are not allowed to block a serve. Blocking doesn't count as a regular hit – so your team still has three more hits. If you block then you are allowed to make the first hit.

Rotation is an important part of volleyball. This means that every time your team wins the serve, all your players rotate their position on court clockwise. The team that loses the serve doesn't rotate, and if you keep the serve your team doesn't rotate.

■ Winning

The winner is the first to reach 25 points by two clear points. If you serve and get the point, you keep the serve. If you don't get the point, the other team gets the serve and also a point. In other words, the score changes every time there is a serve.

The latest edition of the Official Volleyball Rules can be viewed on the website of the Fédération Internationale de Volleyball (FIVB, www.fivb.org).

The aim of the game is simple – to hit the ball into the opponent's goal. The team scoring the most points wins. To score a goal, the ball must pass between the goalposts and beneath the crossbar. If both teams score the same number of goals, or no goals are scored, the match is a draw.

The game is started with a pushback from the centre spot. (A bully-off, where two players line up opposite each other and tap their stick on the ground and then against each other's stick before competing for the ball, is no longer used.)

A game is split into two halves of 35 minutes each. At the beginning of each half, play begins with a pass from the centre of the halfway line. After a goal, the match is restarted in the same way. There is a five-minute half-time interval, or longer if previously agreed.

Each goal is worth one point. Goals can be scored only from inside the shooting circle – a semi-circular area in front of the opponents' goal. Goals scored from outside this area are disallowed.

There are 11 players in a hockey team and up to five substitutes. Every team must have a goalkeeper. The other 10 are field players. The field players can be attackers, defenders or midfielders. The exact line-up will depend on the team strategy, so the exact number of forwards, midfielders and backs will vary.

Hockey is played with a hard ball, and the emphasis is placed on safety. Players must not play the ball dangerously or in a way that leads to dangerous play. It is the responsibility of officials to ensure the laws are always followed. A ball is considered dangerous when it causes legitimate evasive action by players.

One of the basic rules of hockey is that you can only use the flat side of the stick to hit or control the ball. The rules state that players must 'hold their stick and not use it in a dangerous way'. Players must not play the ball with any part of the stick when the ball is above shoulder height, except that defenders are permitted to use the stick to stop or deflect a shot at goal at any height.

The Rules of Hockey are published by the International Hockey Federation (www.fihockey.org).

Tennis is played on a rectangular court by two players (singles) or four players (doubles). Players stand on opposite sides of the net and use a stringed racket to hit the ball to one another.

Each player has a maximum of one bounce after the ball has been hit by their opponent to return the ball over the net and within the boundaries of the court; if they fail, they lose the point. The running score of each game is described in a manner peculiar to tennis: scores of zero to three points are described as 'love' (or zero), 15, 30 and 40, respectively. When at least three points have been scored by each side and the players have the same number of points, the score is 'deuce'. The aim is to win enough points to win a game, enough games to win a set, and enough sets to win a match. A set consists of a sequence of games played with service alternating between games, ending when the count of games won meets certain criteria. Typically, a player wins a set when he or she wins at least six games, and at least two games more than his opponent. When each player has won six games, a tiebreaker is usually played that allows one player to win one more game and thus the set, to give a final set score of 7–6. Matches consist of an odd number of sets, the match winner being the player who wins more than half of the sets.

The Rules of Tennis are available from the International Tennis Federation (www.itftennis.com).

Rules and regulations

The rules and regulations of any sport are usually written, enforced and amended by its national governing body. Rules and regulations can also be set by an international sports federation. The purpose of rules is to ensure participants are safe and that the sport is played fairly. Rules also define how a team or player can win.

It is quite common for national governing bodies or international sports federations to amend or change the rules as they look to improve their sport. For example, the Fédération Internationale de Football Association (FIFA), the world governing body for football, amended the back-pass rule to prevent teams from wasting time and to make the game more enjoyable. The UK's national governing body, the FA, ensured that all the players and officials were aware of this important rule change.

Remember!

National governing bodies are responsible for establishing and maintaining the rules or laws of a sport.

It is also the role of the national governing bodies and the international sports federations to define common, standardised rules so that anybody can play their sport, regardless of where it is being played and their level of participation. For example, a governing body will define the size and dimensions of a pitch, the number of players allowed per team, and the length of time a match will last.

Activity

For the following sports, identify both the national governing body and the international sports federation:

basketball   volleyball
rugby union   hockey.

Court or pitch layout

One of the key regulations of any sport is to define the area in which the sport can be played. Sport can take place on a pitch, court, swimming pool, table or rink, and most sports will define the size of the playing area in order for a standard competitive game to take place. The dimensions of the playing surface are clearly stated by the governing body, and a breach of these can invalidate the competition. For example, an Olympic-size pool is defined as 50m in length, and all international competitions will use this as a standard. Some sports are more flexible in their rules concerning playing dimensions. For example, football can be played on slightly different-sized pitches as long as they are between 90 and 120m long and 45 and 90m wide. However, the dimensions of the markings on the pitch will be of a standard size, as will the size of the goals.

Playing surface

Sports are played on many different surfaces, inside and outside, and will require a range of different equipment and clothing. The type of surface can affect the performance or the tactics used by athletes. It can also affect the equipment, such as footwear, that can be used. A good example is tennis, where the surface of the court can be grass, clay or a hard surface, and the game can be played both outside and inside. It is important that officials and players are aware of any existing rules that take into account the different surfaces.

▼ Table 21.1 Examples of national governing bodies and international sports federations

Sport	National governing body	International sports federation
Badminton	Badminton England www.badmintonengland.co.uk	Badminton World Federation www.internationalbadminton.org
Tennis	Lawn Tennis Association www.lta.org.uk	International Tennis Federation www.itftennis.com
Football	Football Association www.thefa.com	Federation Internationale de Football www.fifa.com
Cricket	England and Wales Cricket Board www.ecb.co.uk	International Cricket Council www.icc-cricket.com
Netball	England Netball www.england-netball.co.uk	International Federation of Netball Associations www.netball.org

The standard dimensions of a football pitch

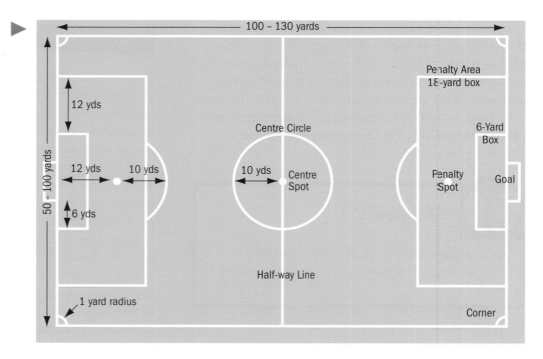

100 – 130 yards

50 – 100 yards

Penalty Area
18-yard box

Centre Circle

6-Yard Box

12 yds

12 yds   10 yds

10 yds   Centre Spot

Penalty Spot   Goal

6 yds

Half-way Line

1 yard radius

Corner

Another example of a sport where the surface is critical is hockey. Historically, hockey has been played on grass pitches, but with the development of technology and the creation of synthetic pitches, hockey is now played on artificial water-based surfaces. The advantage of this is that the pitch is even and the ball will not bobble. This has made the game faster, as players no longer have to worry about pitch conditions. Artificial pitches also reduce the need for maintenance and can be used in all weathers.

Officials must also ensure the surface of the pitch is suitable for sport before a competition begins. An official will check that the surface is safe and free from dangers such as broken glass, damaged drinks cans and divots. Indoor courts must be free from water or dirt, which may cause players to slip or injure themselves. Outdoor pitches may become waterlogged or frozen, and an official must decide whether the pitch is safe to play on.

Fouls and sanctions

It is the responsibility of the officials to ensure the rules or laws of the sport are applied correctly. If the rules are broken, it is normal for the official to recognise foul play and punish the offending team or player. This punishment may include:

- awarding points to the opposition
- awarding possession to the opposition
- cautioning a player or team
- awarding a free kick or free throw
- removing a player from the field of play.

Remember!

Rules are designed to ensure the sport is played fairly and safely, and it is the responsibility of the officials to make impartial and objective decisions that prevent the rules from being broken.

Hockey benefits from a synthetic pitch

Number of players

Different sports will have different numbers of players. Some sports, such as golf and tennis, are usually considered individual sports, while others, such as basketball or cricket, are team sports. Some sports can be played as both – for example, badminton and tennis can be played either individually or as part of a doubles team.

Substitution

The officials must always check that the correct number of players are on each team before a competition starts. Most sports now allow for substitutions during a match, and officials must always know when a player leaves or enters the field of play, to ensure the correct number are always participating. A team may substitute a player because they are injured or underperforming, or for tactical reasons, such as to replace a defender with a striker when seeking to score a goal.

▼ **Many sports allow substitutions, either for tactical reasons or to replace an injured player**

Activity

Complete the following table.

Sport	Number of players
Football	11
Netball	
Hockey	
Rugby union	
Rugby league	
Volleyball	

Time

Most team sports have time constraints and can be divided into different periods of play. For example, football is played for two periods (or halves) of 45 minutes, while netball is played for four quarters of 15 minutes. The team with the most points or goals at the end of this time is declared the winner, while if the scores are tied the game is normally declared a draw. Some sports will have a stop/start clock where the game is stopped every time the ball leaves the field of play, or if the official stops play for infringements. This means that a 60-minute game, for example, can often last much longer. An example of this is basketball, and tactics can be developed by the coach to use a 'time out' to reorganise his or her team.

In many sports, if the scores are even at the end of the normal period of play, then extra time is used to declare a winner. This is common for cup competitions, where a clear winner is needed to progress to the next stage of the tournament. Where extra time is not used, a replay between the teams is sometimes organised, or even a penalty shoot-out.

In some sports, a winner can be declared before the allocated time has elapsed. Cricket will often last for four or five days, and the team that has scored the highest amount of runs in this time, while bowling out the opposition, will be declared the winner. A cricket test match is scheduled to last five days, but often can finish before this time.

Officials and players should also recognise the effect of time on performance. The longer the game lasts, the more tired players will become. This can lead to impaired performance and an increased risk of injury. Most elite players will train specifically to perform to the normal time constraints of the game.

▼ **The time is often displayed prominently so players and spectators know how much longer the game will last**

Remember!

Sports differ in terms of the time they take; whether time is a factor; and whether game time is stopped and restarted or is simply allowed to lapse.

Facilities and equipment

It is the responsibility of officials to ensure the facilities are suitable for competition before the sport or event starts. This is to make sure that both players and spectators are safe before, during and after a game.

The equipment used by the players must be suitable and must pose no risk of injury to players or officials. For example, players' footwear must be appropriate to the surface on which the sport is being played and where studs are used these must not be sharp or damaged. It is common to see officials checking the footwear of players before they enter the field of play.

Many sports require players to wear the correct protective equipment to reduce the risk of injury. In football, for example, players must wear protective shin pads while they are playing; and in cricket players wear protective padding and helmets.

Safety

It is the responsibility of the officials to ensure all participants are safe at all times before, during and after a game. This will mean that officials check the facilities, and also the playing surface to ensure it is suitable and free from dangers such as broken glass. The officials should also check the equipment used by the players to make sure it is not damaged or unsuitable. Before a match, officials should check that players have removed all jewellery and that long hair is tied back. Players who are wearing any form of jewellery or lack the necessary protective equipment should not be allowed to enter the field of play under any circumstances.

It is also the responsibility of the officials to ensure the laws of the game are applied correctly and impartially. Many rules are designed to protect players from injury, and if foul play is witnessed, this should be dealt with according to the laws of the game. An example of this is a spear tackle in rugby union and rugby league. This is where a player is picked up by a tackler on the opponent's side, and turned so that they are upside down. The tackler then drops the player on the ground, often head or neck first. It is highly dangerous and can cause serious injury or even death.

Scoring

Every sport has a different scoring system designed to identify the winning team or player. It is normal that the team with the highest number of points or goals is declared the winner. The exception to this is golf, where the winner is the player who has the lowest score – or in other words has played the fewest number of shots.

Scoring may involve placing or kicking a ball into the opponent's goal, or shooting the ball through an object such as a hoop (e.g. basketball or netball). Some sports will give different amounts of points depending on where the ball goes, or where the player took the shot from. For example, in cricket it is possible for a player to score between one and six runs per ball; and in basketball an extra point will be awarded if a player successfully scores a basket from outside the three-point arc.

Some sports require players to place or hit an object into the opponent's court, for example badminton or tennis.

Methods of victory

Victory in sport is normally awarded to the team or player with the highest score at the end of the match, and can be measured in points or goals. However, extra time may be used if the scores are identical at the end of normal time, or a penalty shoot-out may be used to find a clear winner. Some sports, such as marathon running, are time-based rather than a direct race, with the athlete completing the course in the fastest time being the winner.

Situations

Player in illegal position

Many sports require players to remain in specific areas of the pitch or court. It is normal for pitch or court markings to define clearly where boundaries exist, to aid both players and officials. Leaving these designated areas is an infringement, and a free kick or throw can be awarded to the opposing team. Examples of this include netball, where players can play only in certain sections of the court depending on their given position in the team. For example, a goal shooter cannot leave the final third of the court. Likewise, in football a player can be considered offside if he or she is the last remaining player between the goalkeeper and the goal when the ball is played to them. It is the role of the officials to recognise if a player either enters or leaves an area they are not supposed to. Many sports will require more than one official to oversee such infringements, with assistant referees used to help match officials.

Player injured

By the nature of sport, it is likely that players will become injured at some point during competition. Injuries may be caused by collision with other players, or pulling muscles. The officials should try and help players avoid injury if possible. This can be done by ensuring that the rules of the game are followed to prevent fouls or dangerous tackles; that protective equipment (such as shin pads) is worn; and that the facilities or pitch are suitable and free from hazards.

If injury does occur during play, it is normal for the official to stop the game so that the player can receive treatment. When this happens, the official will stop the clock so that time is not wasted. If possible, the injury should be treated off the pitch so that play can resume as quickly as possible. In more serious cases, a player may have to be substituted if they can't continue, and the official should allow this within the rules of the game.

A recent development in both rugby league and rugby union is the creation of the 'blood' substitution rule. This means that a player has to leave the field of play if they have received a visible bleeding injury. While treatment is being received, the team may temporarily replace the player with a substitute until the injured player is fit to return to the game.

Ball out of play

Most sports have defined boundaries that outline to players and officials whether the ball has left the field of play or court. These lines are important, as they influence who has possession of the ball when play resumes, which can have a direct effect on scoring. For example, in tennis if a ball is considered out of play, then a point will be awarded to the opposing player. It is essential that officials can see whether a ball is out of play or not.

▼ Line judges are used to determine whether a ball is in play or not

A fairly recent development in sport is the use of technology to aid officials to determine whether a ball is in or out of play. This video technology has recently been implemented in tennis to see whether an umpire has made the correct decision, and is used in rugby to see whether a ball has crossed the line for a try. The use of Hawk-Eye is becoming more popular in a range of sports, and is an example of how technology can help to ensure officials have made the correct decision.

Case study

Wimbledon 2007

'Just two days in, it seems fair to say that Hawk-Eye, operating for the first time at the most traditional of the four Grand Slams, has been a great success. It is not infallible, and controversies will arise because of it. But provided any serious miscalculations are kept to a minimum, it seems certain to be accepted with open arms by the championship committee.

The crowd here have done exactly that, enjoying the dramatic wait for the big-screen verdict as the chair umpire first explains that a player has made a challenge. Spectators have responded to the theatrical element of the system by uttering anticipatory 'Ooohs' as the virtual ball is shown travelling down the virtual court and landing up one side or the other of the chalked white line.

The introduction of Hawk-Eye has also forced the players to accept it as a factor in their psychological and tactical planning. They have three incorrect challenges per set – they can challenge any number of times provided they keep getting it right – and so far they have husbanded those options carefully. As is often the case with time-outs in basketball, we have been coming pretty close to the end of sets before players start exercising their right to challenge.

There are sure to be occasions where Hawk-Eye's video reconstruction of a serve does not tally with the evidence of a viewer's own eye – or at least, those occasions are sure to persist for a while yet. For the system is still in its infancy, and it is reasonable to expect it to become more and more sophisticated as the technology improves and its operators accumulate experience. After all, less than two years have passed since the International Tennis Federation tested the system in New York and decided it was worthy to be used at a professional tournament. The Nasdaq-100 Open last March was the first time Hawk-Eye was used at a tour event, then later that year the US Open became the first of the four Slams to adopt it.

(Source: www.sport.scotsman.com)

1 **Within your group, discuss the positive and negative aspects of using technology in sport. How can such use aid officials? Give examples.**

Illegal challenge

It is the role of officials to ensure players conduct themselves appropriately and follow the rules or laws of the game. A player who is challenging another player outside these rules will be penalised, and a free kick or other advantage is normally awarded to the opposing team. In more serious cases, a player can be sent from the field of play as a punishment for their actions. It is essential that officials deal with illegal challenges in accordance with the rules, as allowing these to occur can result in serious injury to the players.

Grading Tip

Grading Tip **M1**

Explain the basis for your decision and application of the rules in each of the three scenarios.

Assessment practice

1 In pairs, choose one sport and explain the rules, laws and regulations, including any recent changes to the rules. Consider why these changes were made, and any problems the new rules may have caused. **P1**

2 For this sport, invent three scenarios or events within a match or other contest to present to your partner. For each situation you are presented with, state how you would apply the rules/ regulations of your selected sport. **P2 M1**

21.2 Understand the roles and responsibilities of officials involved in a selected sport

Officials

Different sports will have many different types of official, each with their own roles and responsibilities. For example, sports may use umpires, referees, line judges, third umpires, timekeepers, scorers or judges. Each of these will play a specific part in the management of play and competition, and will ensure the teams and players follow the rules and laws of the game in question. These officials can be categorised in two ways, as performance controllers or performance managers.

Umpire

An example of a sport that uses umpires is cricket. The umpire (or official) is responsible for all on-field activity during a match. They will ensure that the laws

Key Terms

Performance controllers – officials who regulate the sport within or close to the action (e.g. cricket, football, tennis).

Performance managers – officials who reassure and remind players against standards (e.g. gymnasts, sprinters or snooker players).

of the game are followed and that the spirit of the game is maintained (sportsmanship). The umpire will also make key decisions such as whether a batsman is out, or whether a bowler has bowled a wide ball. To ensure that spectators, players and scorers understand the decisions that have been made, a series of hand signals are used. These clearly demonstrate each decision.

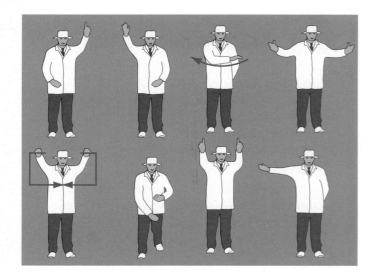

▲ The umpire's signals in cricket (from left to right): out, bye, four runs, wide, TV replay, leg bye, six runs, no-ball

Activity

Complete the following table, identifying the sports where indicated.

Official	Sport
Umpire	
Line judge	
Timekeeper	
Linesman	
Scorer	
Referee	
Fourth official	

Line judges

Line judges are required to indicate whether a ball is in play or has travelled outside the court markings. These are used primarily in tennis, and their signals will be used by the umpire to make a decision. A line judge will use a clear and easily recognised signal to indicate their decision. Recent developments have led to the use of automated computer systems that can judge whether a ball is in or out (see page 240). The advantage of this technology is that it is not affected by human error, and therefore the decisions made should be more accurate than those made by human line judges.

Timekeepers

Many sports will use official timekeepers to keep a record of how long play has continued. The timekeeper is responsible for ensuring that the clock starts and stops during play, and their contribution allows the on-field match official to concentrate solely on making the correct decisions. One example of a sport that uses timekeepers is basketball.

Scorers

The most important aspect of any sport is keeping a record of the score. This must be accurate at all times, and many sports will use specific scorers. These will record not only the points or goals scored, but also information such as the time of goals, number of balls bowled, and number of conversions.

Linesmen

The role of the linesmen in sport is to assist the referee. To this end, they are now often referred to as assistant referees. They may provide information on foul play, or whether or not the ball has left the field of play. Linesmen will also determine whether a play is offside in football, for example, and are a valuable part of the game.

Referees

The role of the referee is to ensure that all the rules or laws of the game are followed. Normally the referee will be a part of the on-field competition and has the authority to make decisions about play. However, some sports use match referees, who are not an active part of the play. For example, cricket uses match referees to support the umpires, make judgements concerning the correct conduct of the game, and hand out penalties for breaches of the laws of the game. Another example of a sport that uses an off-field referee is tennis.

Fourth officials

It is now common in football to see a fourth official. The role of this official is to support the other officials, such as the on-field referee, and linesmen (assistant referees). In the event of an injury to an on-field official, the fourth official may be called on to replace him or her. Other duties of the fourth official include:

- assisting the referee in pre-match preparations, such as collecting team sheets from each manager and ensuring the pitch is fit for play
- inspecting players' equipment, such as condition of their boots, including studs; this may include ensuring that protective equipment is worn
- organising substitutions during play and notifying the referee and spectators of the substitutions
- indicating the amount of time to be played at the end of each period of play (injury time) – this is done using a large electronic display board that is visible to players and spectators alike
- developing and maintaining relationships with managers, coaches and substitute players and intervening if these people become frustrated or aggressive
- ensuring that all non-participants, such as managers and coaches, remain in their technical area.

The fourth official is a key member of the officiating team, even though they are not on the field of play. This official can be considered a performance manager, as they will regularly have to remind non-playing staff of their conduct. The fourth official is also useful in providing the on-field officials with an extra pair of eyes, and can advise on situations that arise away from the field of play.

The fourth official will also keep an extra set of records, such as the scorers, and players who have been booked for foul play. This is to ensure that the on-field referee does not make any mistakes, such as cautioning the wrong player.

▲ The fourth official is responsible for organising substitutions during play

Video referees

More and more sports are now using video referees to support on-field officials. The role of the video referee is to use television footage to adjudicate or make key decisions on a sporting event that the on-field officials may feel they are uncertain of. Video referees are used in many sports, including cricket (third umpire), rugby union, rugby league and ice hockey. However, because of the cost of the specialist equipment, the use of video referees is normally limited to professional or high-level sport.

Judges

Sports such as boxing and athletics use judges to officiate. The role of the judge is to ensure that the rules and laws have been correctly followed, and to make a judgement on performance. It is often the judge's decision that will determine whether a person has won or not.

Roles

An official will play many roles as part of their duties. These roles have to be learned, understood and implemented for an official to be successful.

Presentation

A good official should act as a role model for those taking part in the sport. The way officials present themselves to players and spectators is very important. An official must be professional in terms of their conduct and their appearance. The conduct of an official must display confidence and authority, so that decisions are understood and respected. This respect will be gained if a professional appearance and manner are established and maintained, and rules are correctly interpreted and implemented.

▼ The roles of an official

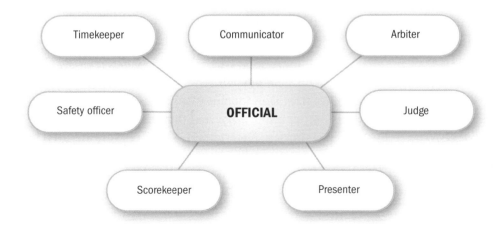

Communication

It is the role of the officials to ensure that their decisions are communicated clearly and unambiguously. An official will have to communicate with a wide variety of people, including other officials, players or participants, coaches or managers, spectators and the media. New or inexperienced officials will need to develop their communication skills as part of their officiating practice and training. Being able to communicate openly and effectively will ensure that difficult and potentially confrontational situations can be dealt with effectively.

Knowledge and use of rules and regulations

■ Arbiter

An arbiter is a person who has the authority to make decisions and to decide on matters during sport. Their decision should be viewed as final and should not be questioned by the players. It is vital that officials are completely neutral and do not display any bias towards a team or individual player. The laws of the game must be enforced completely objectively, and personal opinion or emotion must not be used to make a decision. The role of the official is to ensure that fair play is upheld at all times.

■ Judge

In many situations, it is necessary for officials to make judgements according to the rules/laws of the game, and within the nature and spirit of the activity. Officials should also do their best to communicate their decisions to all concerned. This communication may be through discussion with players and other officials on the field of play, or it may involve using recognised signals so that spectators know what decision was made. Such communication of decisions is just as important to the players as it is to the spectators. The judgement process must be fair and objective, and must only judge the specific situation in accordance with governing body rules.

Activity

In pairs, discuss how an official should communicate with the following:

- players
- co-officials
- spectators
- media.

Report your findings back to the rest of your class.

Activity

For the following sports, identify specific rules designed to protect the participants from injury.

Sport	Law/rule
Football	No tackles from behind
Cricket	
Netball	
Rugby union	
Hockey	

■ Scorekeeper

Many sports, such as football and netball, require the on-field officials to keep a record of the score during play (in addition to their other on-field duties). Therefore it is essential that such records are accurate and up-to-date, so that scores can be quickly relayed to others at any point during or after the game. It is useful to keep a written record of scores rather than trying to remember them – this will prevent confusion and inaccuracy.

■ Timekeeper

As noted on page 237, it is important to keep accurate track of the exact duration of play, and many sports use official timekeepers to keep a record of how long play has continued.

■ Safety officer

There can be a risk of injury in most sports. Any sport that involves teams contesting the possession of an object will have a high risk of injury through collision with other players or the opposition. An official must therefore take all possible steps to ensure that all participants are safe at all times. This will involve the correct interpretation of the rules, and making clear and confident judgements. Players who deliberately break the laws should be subject to predefined (by the governing body) sanctions. An official must always have complete control of the game.

Responsibilities

Application of the rules

To be a successful official, you must have both an up-to-date and thorough knowledge of the rules, and a clear understanding of how these rules should be applied during a game. It is the responsibility of the official to ensure that the rules are correctly implemented and that the decisions made are clear and without confusion. However, an official will need a degree of common sense when implementing the rules. Officials should allow a game to flow, and only intervene when necessary.

Think it over

Consider a football match where you have just been fouled. The referee has recognised that a foul has been committed, but as you have managed to retain possession you have an advantage as you are still attacking.

Would it have been better for the referee to stop the attack to award you a free kick, or to let play continue?

It is often suggested that a referee or official should enhance a game rather than interfere with over-exuberant use of the whistle. Most officials are happy if the players and spectators are unaware they are there, as this means the game is flowing well and the decisions made are correct.

Scoring

One of the key responsibilities of the officials in sports such as hockey, football and netball is to keep a track of the score during the game. It is essential that any records are accurate and that all officials involved in a competition also keep track of the scores, and that they are accurate and consistent.

Communicating information

It is the responsibility of officials to communicate with a wide variety of people involved in their sport. These may be players, co-officials, managers and spectators. However, because of the nature of sport it is important to communicate with a number of people simply by using verbal communications. Most sports will use clear non-verbal signals to indicate their decisions. These signals are important to both players and spectators, and must convey the correct information. Officials will also have to speak to the media, and this must be performed in a professional and proper way.

Establishing and maintaining relationships

To be a successful official it is important that you are able to establish and maintain a positive relationship with players, other officials, managers and coaches. Being able to deal with people in a variety of situations will aid the sport, as conflict and aggression can be dealt with effectively. An official should use clear communication to explain decisions, and must be confident in their judgements. This will develop with experience where an official will be subjected to a wide variety of situations. Using these experiences and self-analysis means that should it occur again, the official will be able to recount

how they dealt with it on a previous occasion. Likewise, an official should remain polite and thank players and other officials. Most officials will say that they are happy with their performance if they are unnoticed. This means that they have not become the centre of attention and have allowed the game to be played normally.

▲ Chelsea captain John Terry argues with the referee after a penalty is awarded to Sheffield United

Health and safety

All sports officials have a duty of care to the participants. This means they are expected to exercise a reasonable amount of care in ensuring that all participants remain safe and free from harm during sport. Therefore an official must ensure that health and safety is at the forefront of their mind when making decisions. Many sports, such as netball and basketball, specifically state that contact between participants is not allowed. The official should correctly penalise the offender and award a free throw. Other sports, such as football and rugby, allow contact but within clear guidelines. This means that an official will have to judge whether contact is within the rules, or whether such contact is unfair or even dangerous. Again, sanctions can be applied if the official feels that unfair contact has been made.

Sports such as boxing or martial arts actually require the participants to make contact with one another. This will obviously have a high risk of injury, and officials must ensure that all rules are correctly and effectively implemented.

The role of the official not only includes contact with players. The official must ensure that facilities and equipment are checked for health and safety risks prior to participation. For example, indoor courts must be free from water (including sweat) that may pose a risk of slipping to the competitors, and outside pitches must be checked for divots, broken glass or other unsafe objects. The weather should also be considered, especially if pitches have become frozen or waterlogged.

Anybody involved in sport will have a desire to improve.

Remember!

If you feel the safety of participants is in question, you are within your rights to postpone a game.

Assessment practice

In pairs, identify and explain the roles and responsibilities of the offiicials in a spport of your choice. Why are these responsibilities so important, and what do you think would be the consequences if an official was to ignore these? **P3**

21.3 Be able to analyse the performance of officials in a selected sport

This is true of both players and officials, and there are a number of ways in which improvements can be made. Recent research indicates that to improve in sport, you must be able to analyse your performance objectively. This can be done as part of a self-evaluation, or it can be performed using other people to give advice and guidance.

Officials

There are a number of considerations that an official must take into account when undertaking their duties.

- Consistency – making sure that the correct decision is made regardless of pressure from others, such as players or spectators. Being consistent will bring respect from players and build your own confidence.
- Enjoyment – an important and often forgotten part of officiating is ensuring that you enjoy the experience. Often too much pressure is put on officials by people such as players, media and spectators, and this can have a negative effect on performance. In some sports, such as football, there is now a shortage of

officials due to the unnecessary stress put on officials to perform.

Theory into practice

The FA has recognised that there is a need for qualified and experienced officials. It is no longer a case of recruiting ex-players who wish to 'give something back to the game'. The FA is now looking to train and recruit 10,000 referees annually in order to officiate at games at all levels. They estimate that, at present, in some parts of the country up to 20 per cent of all games take place without officials. Without these officials the FA recognises that competitive football cannot take place. The FA is keen to recruit referees, both male and female, aged between 16 and 25 so that they have time to reach the top of the game.

Use the internet to try and find out how the FA is going about reaching people and encouraging them to train as officials. What else could they do?

- Self-control – sport can be very emotive, and players are often seen surrounding an official to contest a decision. Being able to deal with such confrontation will help you become a leading official.
- Knowledge of rules – key to any decision is having a thorough knowledge of the rules. Without this, confusion can ensue and incorrect decisions can be made, which may cause further problems with players lacking respect for the officials.
- Control of players or individuals – there will be occasions in sport where some players may become confrontational or difficult. It is the responsibility of the official to remain calm and professional and to deal with the player as necessary, and in accordance with the laws of the game.

Self-evaluation

In order to improve in officiating, it is important to evaluate your own performance, or have your performance measured. After every game you may wish to consider the following questions and evaluate your own performance. These questions can also be used when evaluating other officials. Did you demonstrate:

- up-to-date knowledge of the rules or laws of the game?
- ability to remain calm under pressure?
- understanding of how the game should be played (spirit of the game)?
- ability to recognise performance and play from a player's point of view?
- ability to remain controlled and considered when making decisions?
- ability to work well and communicate clearly with co-officials?
- ability to remain focused throughout performance and competition?
- ability to communicate with players during performance?
- ability to be organised when officiating?
- professional manner and appearance?

Activity

Officiate in a sport of your choice, and then rate yourself out of 10 for each category (1 = poor, 10 = excellent). Remember to be honest in your evaluation.

1 Knowledge of rules
2 Communication with players
3 Mistakes made/incorrect decisions
4 Focus and concentration during performance
5 Dealing with conflicts
6 Dealing with discipline issues

How well did you do? What did you find difficult, and how can you improve in future performances?

An analysis of performance must consider the following process:

analyse current behaviour

compare current actions with desired performance

identify how to change and develop your behaviour

write action plan to change current behaviour into desired behaviour

implement action plan so that desired behaviour can be achieved

Remember!

Officials could be assessed for decisiveness, dealing with conflict, consistency, self-control, judgement, communication, fitness, application of the rules/laws, health and safety, relationship with players, and allowing the game to flow.

Analysis

Method

There are many ways in which an official can analyse their skills in order to improve. The purpose of these is to recognise both strengths and weaknesses, and to develop their officiating skills further.

■ Observation and video

An easy way in which to improve and develop officiating skills is to observe others. This is best done by watching a high-level or experienced official and noting their strengths and weaknesses. You should be able to identify the key techniques required to improve. Another way of analysing performance is simply having your performance filmed. This will provide you with an objective record of what happened, with the advantage of being able to analyse in slow motion or real time. You will see yourself as others see you, and there is no need to try and remember everything that happened during your performance.

■ Notational analysis

When studying performance, it is possible to analyse how effective the officiating skills were through observation. This may be done either live, where you are actually at the sports event, or by video after the event. Because sport can be so fast-moving, it is often useful when observing to video the performance so that it can be reviewed afterwards and in slow motion.

One method is notational analysis, which studies movement patterns in team sports, and is primarily concerned with strategy and tactics. It can also be a useful method for officials to analyse their movement during a match, as well as the number of decisions made. Patterns of play can then be identified and strengths and weaknesses highlighted, and this information can be used as a strategy in subsequent matches to improve performance.

Performance profiling

Performance profiling and analysis can be used to document, assess and predict the ability of the official to meet the demands of performance, covering various aspects of technical skill, tactical awareness, physical capacity and psychological factors.

Performance profiling is a way of providing information to the official on what actually happened in their sport, rather than what they think happened. This will involve not just analysis of performance through observation, but also understanding the official's state of mind. For example, there may be occasions when the official has underperformed due to nerves or lack of concentration. The purpose of performance profiling is to:

- assist the official with their psychological needs
- improve the official's motivation and performance.

Performance profiling assesses the official both before and after the match, and should address the following important psychological factors:

- confidence
- concentration
- commitment
- control
- refocusing of effort.

Understanding each of these will allow you to prepare a strategy that can address any issues that have been highlighted as part of the profiling.

▲ Videoing an event

Strengths

It is important that, when analysing performance, the official does not concentrate solely on his or her weaknesses. Through observation and discussion, the strengths of performance should also be highlighted. To aid this further, it is useful for the coach to observe an experienced official, so that their strengths and skills can be identified.

Areas for improvement

The purpose of any performance analysis is to identify any strengths and weaknesses. Having identified these, the official can develop strategies to improve certain areas. Regular evaluation is needed to ensure skills are up-to-date and suitable for a variety of match situations. Having identified areas for improvement, the official should investigate how to alter these. This may involve enrolling on recognised courses, or taking refresher sessions.

Taking it further

Most sports governing bodies offer a range of courses designed to train officials or to update existing skills. Contact the governing body of your chosen sport for further information, and compile a list of what you would need to do to qualify as an official.

Development

Practice

One of the easiest ways in which an official can improve is to practise in a variety of situations. By practising and evaluating performance, an official will be able to understand their strengths and weaknesses and devise ways in which to develop further. For example, a football referee may wish to officiate in junior boys' football and gain valuable experience and confidence before they progress to men's football. Likewise, it is common to become an assistant referee before undertaking the role of referee. This allows the official to lean new skills as well as developing existing ones.

Training

Any successful official will train regularly. This means they will update their skills regularly and practise using them in a variety of situations. The official will also undertake regular physical training similar to the players. Many sports will require the official to have a high level of fitness, and they will need to be able to keep up with play during a competition. This is of particular importance in sports such as football, rugby and basketball, which can be very fast-moving. Being physically fit will also allow the official to make the correct decision even if they are feeling the signs of fatigue.

Theory into practice

In football, the FA sets very clear guidelines for fitness levels for new referees. To qualify as a referee, a standard fitness test must be passed:

- eyesight test (car number plate at 25m)
- two runs of 50m each in less than 7.5 seconds
- two runs of 200m each in less than 32 seconds
- a minimum distance run of at least 2700m in 12 minutes' continuous running.

For another sport of your choice, research what are the fitness requirements.

Qualifications

Most officials will have gained a recognised qualification at some point in their career. It is generally accepted that to improve, you should at some stage become qualified. For some sports, this may be the only way of receiving any kind of training prior to gaining experience. Most national governing bodies will offer up-to-date qualifications that will not only train you, but also keep you up-to-date with relevant rule changes and different scenarios. Gaining a recognised qualification will also allow you to achieve a certificate, as well as introducing you to other officials so that you can share ideas and skills.

After gaining a qualification, an official may wish to join an official association and/or governing body. These can help provide the official with points of contact for assistance and further development, which can be extremely useful for a novice or inexperienced official.

Remember!

One of the best ways of learning and developing your officiating skills is to talk to experienced officials and discuss how they deal with a variety of situations.

Methods of analysis

There are a number of ways in which it is possible to analyse your officiating. Each of the methods can be used in a variety of sports and at all levels, and you should try each one to see which you prefer. It is important to point out that there is no correct or necessarily more accurate method.

■ Self-reflection

One method that can be used, and is relatively easy to undertake, is self-reflection. This means that you consider your own performance after the event and carefully think about the strengths and weaknesses in order to suggest what you may do better in the future.

An example could be becoming angry at a particular player who continually questions your decisions during a game. You may have found yourself arguing or acting in an undesirable or unprofessional way, and this may have disappointed you. Having reflected, you may decide that it was not beneficial and set about deciding how to avoid that reaction being repeated in similar circumstances. Sometimes you may require outside help in order to devise an action plan. You should seek the help of a coach, experienced official or colleague.

Activity

Officiate in a competition in a sport of your choice. Having done this, complete the following performance evaluation.

Evaluate	Good						Bad
How well did I do?	1	2	3	4	5	6	7
Amount of mistakes made							
Communicating with participants							
Dealing with distractions							
Implementing the rules							
Dealing with disruptive players							
Resolving conflicts							

■ Checklist

A checklist is a simple and easy-to-use list that can be applied in real time by an observer, or used as part of a video analysis, and can be used to help provide you with feedback about your match performance. Checklists are also useful tools to assist you in self-analysis after a performance.

A suitable checklist may include:
- effective communication
- professional appearance and manner
- up-to-date knowledge of rules
- communication with co-officials
- fitness for the sport and level
- manner
- correct interpretation of the rules/laws
- health and safety considerations (duty of care)
- use of common sense
- dealing with pressure from players, spectators and coaches/managers
- dealing with conflict and confrontation.

■ Buddy systems

Another way in which officials can improve is to use a buddy system. This is where an experienced official will mentor a new or inexperienced official and help them develop their skills and techniques. This system allows the new official to observe and learn from their colleagues, and to ask questions and seek advice when needed. A buddy system can provide an official with invaluable information, such as how to deal with a wide variety of situations or how to deal with conflict within

the sport. Often, as a new official it is easier for peers to relate to the kind of situations you might be in, and offer you the benefit of their own experiences and ways in which they have dealt with challenging situations.

Assessment practice

1 For the sport of your choice, prepare a checklist that can be used by the match officials to analyse their performance. This checklist may include questions such as number of correct/ incorrect decisions made, or how well they dealt with conflict or aggressive behaviour. **P4**

2 For the sport of your choice, watch (live or on TV) two matches or competitions, and analyse the performance of the officials in each event, identifying strengths and areas for improvement. **P5**

Grading tips

Grading Tip M2

Explain why you identified these strengths and weaknesses and make your own suggestions relating to how the officials could improve their performance.

Grading Tip D1

Justify your recommendations, explaining why you have made these.

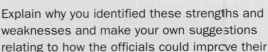

21.4 Be able to officiate effectively in a selected sport

Officiating

Application of rules or laws

For a sport to be developed and well managed, the application of the rules/laws is an essential part of the game. Even during childhood, games are bound by rules, and although an official is very rarely present in playgrounds or parks, children will devise their own rules and as a result judge the boundaries of their activities.

Unfortunately, this self-regulation doesn't continue to adult life, and an official is an essential part of structured games or competitions to ensure fair play and correct implementation of the rules. The official carries the authority to judge where indiscretions have occurred, and is required to administer punishment

for infringements, acts of over-aggression or persistent rule-breaking. In many sports the official will play a major role in keeping score, ensuring there is no bias towards one person or another, and will have the final say in all decisions. You must therefore ensure you are very familiar with the rules or laws of your sport.

Think it over

Working in pairs, one should take the role of the official and the other a player. The player is complaining to the referee and becoming angry about his or her decision. As the referee, you must calm the player down but maintain control of the game. Then switch roles. What did each of you do that defused the situation? Why did it work?

Control of the game

There are numerous ways in which an official can control the game to ensure the safety and smooth running of the sport. Invasion games, such as rugby league, rugby union, netball, football, basketball and hockey, are controlled primarily by a referee/umpire and their assistants, who will use a whistle to signify the beginning and stoppages in play that require intervention in the game. Sports such as golf, tennis, badminton and athletics, which are non-contact and rely more on technical development, still require an official, but the control of situations is more passive and will normally be directed by verbal instruction in the form of score updates and clarification of rules and decisions.

Using scoring systems effectively

Any official who is in charge must have an understanding of the scoring system to ensure the game is managed correctly. Not all sports carry the one-point scoring system that is seen in football, and in some areas there is no logical progression between scores. Tennis is an excellent example of this (see page 244), while basketball has a two-point score, but a three-point score when a basket is scored outside the arc.

Before taking charge of a game, it is essential that the official is aware of these scoring systems, and it is most helpful to have independent scorers watching the game to ensure accurate recordings are made.

Ensuring health and safety of all participants

There are many potential hazards when playing sports, and the official is responsible for minimising the risk to participants. For example, this can be achieved by checking the playing surface is:

- dry
- flat
- suitable for the sport
- marked out correctly
- free from debris

and ensuring participants have:

- removed jewellery
- are wearing correct footwear
- are wearing the required protective equipment.

▲ Long-distance runner

As an official, there is an ongoing responsibility to ensure everyone participating behaves in a manner that will not cause harm to other participants. If you feel there is cause to warn a player, this should be done, and in certain situations the player can be withdrawn from the game for a short period (at the official's discretion) or for the remaining time in the game.

In sports such as boxing, judo, karate and long-distance running, the official has the responsibility to gauge the physical wellbeing of the participants. If they are in distress and could not defend themselves or sustain normal physical activity, the event should be stopped or the individual withdrawn.

Relationships with others

A good official should possess the relevant skills to develop positive relationships with those people involved in the sport they are working in. Unfortunately, officials may become the focal point for blame for many coaches, spectators and performers because their team or individual has not performed as they could/should have done.

An official should remain impartial at all times, and should act in a manner appropriate to a person in authority – there should be no bias shown and players should not expect special treatment during the game. The official should try to display their natural personality, and develop a relaxed but authoritative stance where players feel free to talk to them about the game or the decision that has been made. In return, coaches and players need to understand that there are boundaries that must not be crossed – verbal abuse, in particular, is unacceptable, as is the questioning of an official's decision, which must be accepted regardless of personal opinion.

Professional football has seen the development of targeted abuse from spectators toward football referees, and it is a trend that has made its way into the grassroots of the game. Developing a positive relationship with spectators is possible – it is possibly the most difficult area of officiating but, if mastered, it can potentially be very rewarding.

Conflict management

Due to the competitive nature of sport, it is likely that there will be occasions when frustration or conflict will develop between opponents and/or coaching staff of the opposing teams. The official has to ensure these volatile situations are defused quickly and a balanced

Theory into practice

The 'ABC (Advanced Buffer Circle) of conflict' is a simple visual concept, which football referees can refer to when considering the best place to position themselves when dealing with major conflict on the field of play.

'When you need to deliver a public warning, or to issue a card, don't forget that your duties and responsibilities extend to all the other players, not just the one you happen to be dealing with. You can't do this by turning your back on them – unless you have eyes in the back of your head! ... Think of the 'ABC of conflict' as you (the referee) standing in the centre, surrounded by three wide circular rings (like sugary doughnuts with holes in) – each doughnut is progressively wider than the other, and they all surround the referee.'

(Source: http://footballreferee.org)

Visit the Referees' Association to learn more detail about this concept. What are the basic principles, and could the idea be expanded to apply to conflict resolution in other sports?

environment is restored as soon as possible. In situations where it is difficult to resolve the problems, the same control measures as are used with players can be applied, and coaches can be removed from the playing areas. This is a last resort, but is used frequently, especially in professional sport.

Successful officials will speak to players and coaches before the start of play to explain their style of officiating and what they expect from everyone involved in the activity.

Other considerations

■ Checking equipment

Before officiating in any event, it is vital to ensure that you are well prepared and have any equipment at your disposal to enable to you to perform to the best of your ability. This may include timekeeping instruments (normally two), pens, pencil, markers for run-ups, score sheets, cards to enforce discipline, whistle, counting instruments. This is not a complete list, and a good official will find different and personalised equipment to make them as efficient as possible.

As part of the responsibility for safety, a good official will check all equipment that is to be used by the players or athletes. This may mean that the tennis net is at the correct height, the football net is attached correctly, and the ball pressure is correct. Without these checks, the official is endangering the participants and ultimately is failing to do everything within their power to prevent injury. Injury caused by equipment malfunction while playing sport is rare, but regular checks are necessary and will prevent accidental injury from occurring.

■ Use of signals

An official will use signals or gestures in order to signify a decision or action. This is seen in cricket when the umpire raises his finger to give a batsman out after an appeal, or when a line judge in tennis raises their arm to the side to signal that the ball was out. Use of signals is a useful form of communication, especially when players are too far away to hear the official's instructions but near enough to see a signal or gesture (this is important in professional sport when crowd noise may affect the message being heard by the players).

■ Dealing with pressure

Like any performer, an official will be nervous before they take part, especially if the performance is in an important game/match or event. Coping with these nerves is difficult as, unlike many of the participants, the officials are on their own, with only the support of their assisting personnel. It is important to enjoy the performance, perform as well as you can, and ensure you provide a safe and enjoyable area for people to play in.

Remember!

Your overriding thought when officiating should be that you have faith in your own ability, and that you will officiate in a way that shows no bias and will allow the match/event or game to flow.

Review

Formative and summative

Your review of your performance should be first formative and then summative. These may be referred to as 'assessment for learning' and 'assessment of learning', respectively.

Key Terms

Formative assessment – generally carried out throughout a course or project, used to aid learning. This might be a teacher (or peer), or the learner, providing feedback on a student's work, and would not necessarily be used for grading purposes.

Summative assessment – generally carried out at the end of a course or project; typically used to assign students a course grade.

Feedback

It is important to make sure that with any performance there is a desire to improve. The key to this is finding out how you performed through the eyes of the players, coaches, observers, supervisors and spectators. To be worthwhile, the feedback needs to be honest and designed to assist performance, rather than just being over-critical or dictated by the result – in other words, if a player loses and blames the loss on the official, they will not provide worthwhile feedback.

Criticism is not a negative force, and should be delivered in a constructive form designed to help and not undermine the official. Players often provide a good interpretation of an official as they can see them close up and assess their methods of dealing with challenging or disruptive behaviour that coaches or spectators who are further away may not be able to pick up on.

Coaches and spectators can observe from a distance and look at the bigger picture, focusing on the way that the official looks, the image they project and their body language in specific areas and situations. This is often a good way to form a judgement as there is no spoken word to affect the visual appearance.

Strengths and areas for improvement

When an official receives feedback, it is good to take on board what has been said as it is potentially very useful to aid future performance, especially if a number of people have picked up on the same points. The purpose of feedback is to look naturally at what is successful and what participants have liked about the performance, and take positives away from this. Any negative comments then set up a situation where areas for improvement can be developed. It is important to accept that there will always be areas to work on, and if the weaknesses are identified and worked on in a fairly short space of time, they will begin to disappear from the official's performance.

It is important not to ignore this feedback, as it will quickly become a major part of an evaluation and analysis process. Being able to understand and accept feedback is an invaluable tool in the search for perfection.

Assessment practice

In order for you to fully understand the roles and skills required to be an effective official, you should undertake officiating in the sport of your choice, with support from your tutor. This will allow you to deal with a wide variety of situations, such as making decisions (enforcing the rules/laws), communicating with players, and dealing with confrontation. **P6**

Grading tips

Grading Tip **M3**

Undertake officiating in your chosen sport without support.

Grading Tip **P7**

Having been involved in a practical officiating scenario for a sport of your choice, it is essential that you stop and consider how well you performed. To do this you must spend some time reviewing and considering your personal performance. This may include identifying the areas that you felt went well, in addition to the areas you found difficult.

Grading Tip   **M4 D2**

What are your strengths, why do you think these are strengths, and what can you do to improve on any areas of weakness?

Knowledge check

1 For a sport of your choice, describe the roles and responsibilities of an official.

2 Who is responsible for devising and amending rules in sport?

3 Why is it important to analyse the performance of an official?

4 What can an official's performance be measured against?

5 Using examples, describe how an official may deal with a conflict or confrontation.

6 Why is confidence important in officiating?

7 For a sport of your choice, explain how you can communicate with players and spectators.

8 How can an official ensure that health and safety are maintained?

9 Using a sport of your choice, describe any recent rule changes and explain why these have been introduced.

10 What is meant by common sense, and how can this be applied to the rules of a game?

Preparation for assessment

1 The local sports development officer has approached you and asked you to prepare a presentation on the rules, laws and regulations of a number of sports to be shown to local primary school children. To make sure the children are interested and fully understand the chosen sport, the Sport Development Officer has asked you to make a large, colourful and eye-catching poster suitable for primary-age children, highlighting all the key rules, laws and regulations for your chosen sport.

   In addition to your poster you may wish to prepare a leaflet that can be given to the children as a summary of your presentation. **P1**

2 Having prepared your poster for the local children, it has been decided that the best way of describing your rules is to show how they can be applied in a game situation. You must apply your described rules, laws and regulations of your chosen sport in three different situations that are common to your sport. Ensure that the situations are likely to occur in your sport so the children can see how the rules and laws control the game. **P2**

3 Following your work with the local school, a teacher has approached you and asked you to talk to the children about the roles and responsibilities of officials in sport. The teacher is concerned that the children do not understand the purpose of officials in sport, and that there has been a recent rise in arguments involving the children questioning officials' decisions. Identify a chosen sport and prepare a short presentation that describes the roles and responsibilities of the officials. **P3**

4 Having outlined the roles and responsibilities of officials, you feel that it would be of use for the children to analyse the performance of a high-level official. Prepare for them an analysis checklist that can be used to observe an official in your chosen sport. (Ensure the checklist is relevant to your chosen sport.) You may wish to consider communication (verbal and non-verbal), application of the rules, relationships with the players, and health and safety. Try and be objective – only analyse what you see. **P4**

5 Having prepared a checklist that can be used to analyse performance, this should now be used to analyse the performance of two officials in your chosen sport. The analysis should identify the strengths of their performance as well as any weaknesses or areas for improvement. **P5**

6 Having worked closely with the school, helping them with the roles of officials in sport, you feel it would be beneficial if you were to officiate in a sport of your choice. Select a sport and, with support, undertake officiating within a game or match situation. **P6**

7 Having undertaken an officiating role, you must now review your performance. This review should be honest and identify what went well, and any areas that you feel you need to address to improve in future. For this you may wish to prepare a checklist prior to officiating, or ask somebody to video your performance so that you can review it objectively. **P7**

Grading tips

Grading Tip **P1**

Ensure you summarise the rules – do not simply copy a list of the rules.

Grading Tip **M1**

Explain the purpose of these rules, laws and regulations in your three chosen game or match situations.

Grading Tip **M2**

Explain the strengths and weaknesses you have recognised and make your own suggestions relating to performance.

Grading Tip **D1**

Now justify your recommendations, explaining why you have made these so that the official's future performance can be improved.

Grading tips

Grading Tip **M3**

Undertake the role of an official without support (independently).

Grading Tip **M4**

TUse the information you have compiled above to explain your performance and make recommendations on how you can improve.

Grading Tip **D2**

Ensure that you can justify your own performance and explain why you behaved in certain ways. What went well, and what areas of your performance were disappointing? If you have identified any areas for improvement, justify how you can address these in order to improve in future.

To achieve a pass grade the evidence must show that the learner is able to:	To achieve a merit grade the evidence must show that, in addition to the pass criteria, the learner is able to:	To achieve a distinction grade the evidence must show that, in addition to the pass and merit criteria, the learner is able to:
P1 describe the rules/regulations of a selected sport **Assessment practice page 241**		
P2 apply the rules/regulations of a selected sport in three different situations **Assessment practice page 241**	**M1** explain the application of the rules/regulations of a selected sport in three different situations **Assessment practice page 241**	
P3 describe the roles and responsibilities of officials in a selected sport **Assessment practice page 246**		
P4 devise suitable criteria to analyse the performance of officials in a selected sport. **Assessment practice page 252**		
P5 analyse the performance of two officials in a selected sport, identifying strengths and areas for improvement. **Assessment practice page 252**	**M2** explain the identified strengths and areas for improvement of two officials, and make suggestions relating to improvement **Assessment practice page 252**	**D1** justify suggestions made in relation to improving performance for two officials from a selected sport **Assessment practice page 252**
P6 officiate, with support, in a selected sport **Assessment practice page 240**	**M3** officiate in a selected sport **Assessment practice page 240**	
P7 review own performance in officiating in a selected sport, identifying strengths and areas for improvement **Assessment practice page 240**	**M4** explain the identified strengths and areas for improvement, and make suggestions relating to improvement **Assessment practice page 240**	**D2** analyse own performance and justify suggestions made in relation to improving own performance. **Assessment practice page 240**

Working with children in sport

Introduction

Many sports coaches deal with large numbers of children, either in schools or elsewhere, and this brings with it special responsibilities for the coach.

Sports coaches often have a very close relationship with children, and will spend a lot of time with them when their parents are not present, for example travelling to and from competitions or on overseas tours. Sometimes the coach might need to guide a part of the child's body, such as their leg or arm, especially in a sport such as gymnastics or dance. For this reason, certain laws and procedures have been introduced, which all coaches must follow in order to eliminate the risk of child abuse.

It is important to remember that children are not 'mini-adults' and that they have special status in law. Activities that might well be suitable for adults may not be suitable for children, particularly small children.

Coaches are also role models for children in their care, so it is important that children's coaches behave appropriately at all times.

When you have completed this unit you will have developed the knowledge, understanding and practical skills needed to lead sporting activities with a particular age range. You will be able to identify children's needs and to plan, prepare and lead children's activities.

After completing this unit you should be able to achieve the following outcomes:

1 Understand the needs and rights of children.

2 Understand the effects of sport in the development of children.

3 Know about good practice in the protection of children in sport.

4 Know about signs of potential child abuse and appropriate courses of action.

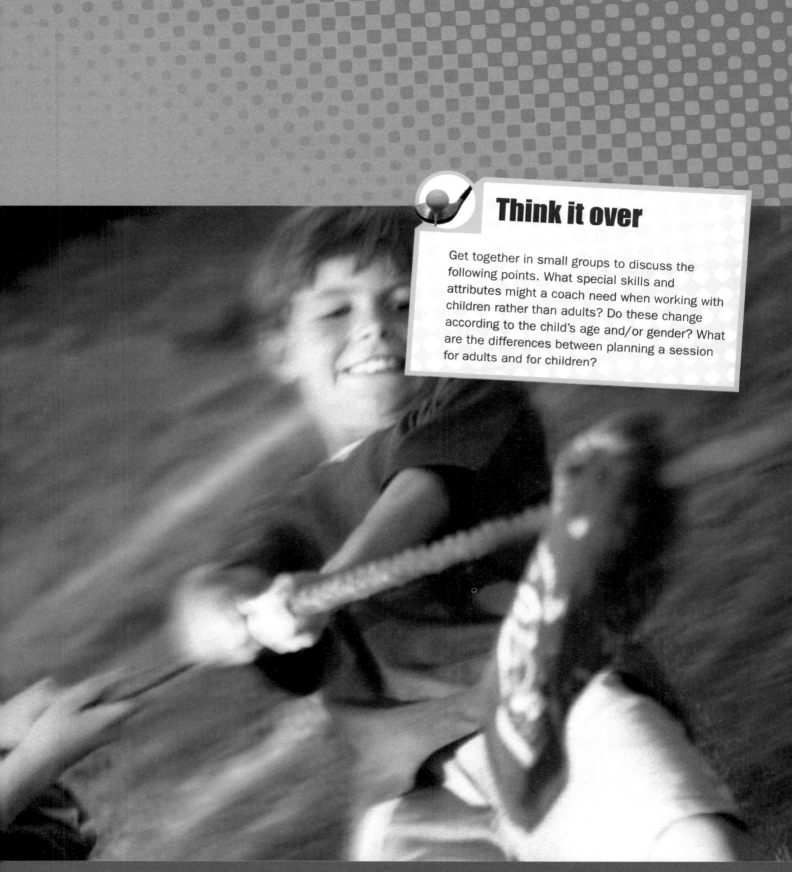

Children's needs

Children have certain physical, mental and social needs, which should be met if they are to develop into mature adults. These can be broadly divided into:

- educational
- psychological
- cultural
- social.

Sport can help to fulfil these needs in children of all ages.

Educational needs

Individuals need to develop certain physical skills during childhood and adolescence, including the development of activity-specific physical skills (either work-related or recreational skills); motor programming skills and spatial awareness.

■ Skills development

Work- and leisure-related skills are the physical motor skills needed in order to perform the task at hand. As sport helps to develop coordination, balance and motor skills, children who regularly play sports are advantaged in this regard. A study in 2003 showed that athletic training for as little as 12 weeks improved co-ordination and motor skills in adolescents.

■ Motor programming

These are skills involved in the execution of movements or tasks. As with work and leisure skills, sports players have greater motor programming skills than non-participants. For example, someone who plays sport will be able learn how to perform a given task more quickly, and to be more accurate when performing that task, than a non-athlete.

■ Spatial awareness

This is the ability to determine where you and others are, both in space and in relation to each other. When playing team sports such as football, skilled players know where their team mates and opponents are without having to stand still and look around the pitch. This skill is useful in everyday situations as it helps the individual to develop better balance and more efficient movement patterns.

Psychological needs

All athletes, whether adults or children, have the following basic psychological needs.

■ Motivation

Athletes need to be motivated, not only to perform and compete, but also to train so that they can compete to their full potential. This is not purely about winning – athletes are often motivated to compete with themselves, and many athletes strive to set a personal best in competition or in training as a way of measuring their improvement.

■ Communication

Athletes need to be able to communicate with their team mates, coaches, officials and others. The better their communication skills, often the better the performance, particularly in team games such as rugby and soccer. A good example of communication in sport is cricketers running between the wickets, where a bad call can lead to a run-out.

■ Confidence-building

Children need to have confidence in their abilities, as well as social confidence in order to form friendships. Sport helps to build self-esteem as well as a sense of belonging between team and/or club members. The team strip or track suit can be considered as a sort of uniform, helping to identify team members and distinguish them from other groups.

Cultural needs

Everyone has cultural needs according to their race, religion, gender and class, and sport can often help to address these needs.

Social inclusion

Membership of a sports team gives people of all ages – but especially children – a feeling of belonging to a special group. Children are proud to wear the team strip or colours to show that they belong to 'the best team in the world'.

Gender awareness

When very young (before puberty), all children play sports together, but as they get older almost all sports are divided into male and female events. As males tend to be around 10% stronger and faster than their female counterparts, mixed competition is generally not allowed in contact sports such as rugby or football, or in speed events such as sprinting or marathon running. This again helps children to develop a sense of self and awareness of their own gender identity.

Community identity

Many sports teams' names reflect the area where they are situated or were formed (Manchester United, Wolverhampton Wanderers, etc.). This means that many people support their local team, and perhaps dream of playing for them one day. In this way, a sense of community is developed between supporters of a team, and rivalries between teams can develop. Local derbies in football often bring out the strongest feeling between supporters.

Social needs

Sport can provide a route to meeting some particular social needs, including the following.

Anti-crime initiatives

Participation in sport has been shown to reduce participation in petty crime such as shoplifting and vandalism. In turn, this may prevent the growth of a young petty criminal into an adult career criminal. Some good examples of this can be found throughout all sports (see Unit 11, page 30), but particularly in boxing – the champions Muhammad Ali, Chris Eubank, Frank Bruno and George Foreman all learned to box while in reform schools for petty criminality.

Anti-social behaviour

An issue often mentioned in newspapers is that of anti-social behaviour. Participation in sports reduces anti-social behaviour, and several studies show that children (particularly adolescents) have better attendance and achievement at school and display less anti-social behaviour both in and out of school than those who do not play sports.

Health promotion

One of the biggest health problems facing the UK is that of obesity, with around 40 per cent of children being either overweight or obese. Regular sport and exercise can help reduce this problem, as well as reducing the incidence of diseases such as diabetes, high blood pressure and heart disease.

Children's rights

Legislation

In the UK, children have certain rights in law under the Children Act 2004 (see page 278), aimed at protecting the health and safety of all children under the age of 18.

Every child matters

The main aims of this legislation are outlined in the document *Every Child Matters*, which is concerned with the wellbeing of children and young people from birth to age 19, and intends to enable them, whatever their background or their circumstances, to have the support they need to:

- be healthy
- stay safe
- enjoy and achieve
- make a positive contribution
- achieve economic wellbeing.

This means that the organisations involved with providing services to children – from hospitals and schools to police and voluntary groups – should team up to share information and work together, in order to protect children and young people from harm and help them achieve what they want in life.

■ UN Convention on the Rights of the Child

Every Child Matters is based on the UN Convention on the Rights of the Child, which states that 'For the purposes of the present Convention, a child means every human being below the age of eighteen years unless under the law applicable to the child, majority is attained earlier.'

It goes on to say that, as far as the law and all public services are concerned, the best interests of the child must always be considered.

This includes the right of the child to:

- rest and leisure
- engage in play and recreational activities appropriate to the age of the child
- participate freely in cultural life and the arts
- be protected against all forms of discrimination or punishment on the basis of the status, activities, expressed opinions or beliefs of the child's parents, legal guardians or family members
- have such protection and care as is necessary for his or her wellbeing

- be protected from all forms of physical or mental violence, injury or abuse, neglect or negligent treatment, maltreatment or exploitation, including sexual abuse, while in the care of any other person
- if mentally or physically disabled, enjoy a full and decent life in conditions which ensure dignity, promote self-reliance and facilitate the child's active participation in the community.

The right to rest and leisure

This includes the right to have time off from work or full-time education, and to indulge in sports or other leisure activities such as games and socialising with others. This means that children should not be exploited by adults for commercial gain, for example by being used as child labour in factories or other places of employment, and that facilities should be made available for children to take part in organised sport.

The right to engage in play and recreational activities appropriate to the age of the child

This means that children should be able to play sport at the appropriate level, and that adult sports should be adapted to meet the needs of the child. A good example is rugby, where there are several rule changes according to age. For example, the length of matches varies by age (see Table 23.1). Specific techniques are also different for children, for example the 'squeeze ball' law for under-13s to under-18s, inclusive:

> 'No player involved in a match at any age level from under 18 downwards shall use in training or in a match the technique known or referred to as squeeze ball.
>
> Note: "Squeeze ball" is a technique where the ball carrier goes to ground, head forward (touching or close to the ground), irrespective of immediate contact with opponents) usually keeping parallel to the touchline, holding and protecting the ball close to the chest and, when on the ground, pushes the ball back between the legs.
>
> Penalty: Penalty Kick'
> Source: www.community-rugby.com

Table 23.1 Rugby rule changes according to age (source: www.community-rugby.com)

Age group	Playing time not to exceed:	Extra time	15-a-side festivals not to exceed:
Under-13 and -14	25 minutes each way with a size 4 ball	After 50 minutes' playing time, no extra time to be played in the case of a drawn match	Four matches of 10 minutes each way = 80 minutes
Under-15	30 minutes each way with a size 5 ball	After 60 minutes' playing time, no extra time to be played in the case of a drawn match	Five matches of 9 minutes each way = 90 minutes
Under-16 to -19 inclusive	35 minutes each way playing with a size 5 ball	After 70 minutes' playing time, no extra time to be played in the case of a drawn match	Five matches of 9 minutes each way = 90 minutes

The right to participate freely in cultural life and the arts

This is closely linked with the right to rest and leisure, and is really aimed at providing the child with a cultural context – an understanding and appreciation of the society in which they live. The state should provide opportunities for children to develop a sense of identity. In the UK this means access to buildings such as museums, art galleries and so on.

The right to be protected against all forms of discrimination or punishment on the basis of the status, activities, expressed opinions, or beliefs of the child's parents, legal guardians, or family members

Discrimination stems from a negative attitude or stereotyped beliefs people hold about those who they perceive to be different from themselves. In this context, it can mean someone who has a different religion, political opinion or social class from whoever is in authority. In essence, this article states that all children should be treated equally. This is particularly true in terms of sport, where they should be categorised only by talent.

The right to have such protection and care as is necessary for his or her wellbeing

This article states that children should be protected from the harmful actions of others, including both adults and other children. They should not be put in a position where there is a risk of physical harm. Where a risk is unavoidable, that risk should be reduced as much as possible. This does not mean that children should be 'wrapped in cotton wool' – but they should not face excessive physical risks or demands.

The right to be protected from all forms of physical or mental violence, injury or abuse, neglect or negligent treatment, maltreatment or exploitation, including sexual abuse, while in the care of any other person

This means that children (and their parents or legal guardians) should be confident that any adult supervising them is not going to cause them any harm, and is in fact going to protect them while under their care. This applies in all situations.

A good example of both this article and the previous one would be a sailing expedition. On such an expedition, the children would have to be supervised by an adult with the appropriate technical skills so that they are not at risk of either sinking or crashing the boat, or getting lost due to poor navigation. They would all have to wear appropriate equipment, such as warm, waterproof clothing and life jackets, in case they fell overboard; and their behaviour would have to be guided so that it is safe and fitting for the activity.

In the UK, partly as a result of this article, any adult supervising children has to have a Criminal Records Bureau check (see page 280) to ensure they are safe to work with children.

If mentally or physically disabled, the child has a right to enjoy a full and decent life in conditions which ensure dignity, promote self-reliance and facilitate the child's active participation in the community

This article of the UN Convention not only covers recreational aspects of a disabled child's life, but also means they have a right to education, access to public services, and so on. This obviously has implications for sports provision in that every coach and sports club now has to make provision for athletes with disabilities. In the UK this is regulated by the Disability Discrimination Act 2005, which states that it is unlawful for clubs with more than 25 members to refuse membership or to place special conditions on membership of a disabled person. Such organisations also have to ensure that people with disabilities have full access to club premises and facilities.

▲ **Disabled children have the right to active participation**

All coaches should also ensure that they are fair and equitable, and should remember that coaching children with disabilities is no different from coaching able-bodied children. The children need to be treated as individuals, and the coaches need to know the child's limits and their capabilities. The coach needs to emphasise these qualities so that the child will attain, and possibly exceed, the goals set for them.

Educational rights

■ Right to education

In the UK, every child has the right to an education between the ages of four and 16, and between these ages it is compulsory to attend school. Free education is also provided between the ages of 16 and 18, either in a sixth form at school, or at college.

■ Parental responsibility

Parents have certain responsibilities with regard to the children in their charge. In educational terms, this means ensuring the child is educated according to the national curriculum and attends school regularly.

Parental responsibility also means the adult has the right to make important decisions about a child's life in areas such as medical treatment and education. Adults with parental responsibilities also have a duty to care for and protect the child.

According to current law, a mother always has parental responsibility for her child. A father has this responsibility only if he is married to the mother, or has acquired legal responsibility for his child. Living with the mother, even for a long time, does not automatically give a father parental responsibility.

■ Accountability of officials

Sports coaches, officials and administrators also have a parental-type responsibility to the children in their charge, in that they must ensure that all training and competition must be run fairly and there must be no discrimination on grounds of age, gender, disability, race or religion. Coaches and administrators are accountable to both parents and children for their actions, both on and off the field of play.

Issues surrounding children's rights

In order to protect children's rights there are a number of issues that children, parents, coaches and administrators all need to consider when dealing with higher-level child athletes in particular. These include the minimum and maximum ages that mixed-sex competition can occur, the cost of winning, and the potential for economic exploitation.

Most sports are single-sex after the onset of puberty (men compete against men and women against women). The age at which this split occurs varies, with mixed football not allowed after age 11, while mixed-contact rugby is allowed only up to age 10.

Pressure on players to win can also be detrimental – if pressure is put on too young a player, it can become stressful to the child and may lead to them giving up the game. On the other hand, a child who wins easily all or most of the time may become complacent, and when faced with their first defeat may have their confidence destroyed and give up the sport altogether.

A further issue that can affect young elite athletes is that of economic exploitation. Where children are earning large sums of money (or have the prospect of being signed by, for example, a Premiership football club), coaches and parents could be tempted to push child athletes into playing too early and/or too often, which can lead to injury and psychological ill-health.

Case study

Of nearly 250 million children engaged in child labour around the world, the vast majority – 70 per cent, or some 170 million – are working in agriculture. Child agricultural workers frequently work for long hours in scorching heat, haul heavy loads of produce, are exposed to toxic pesticides, and suffer high rates of injury  from sharp knives and other dangerous tools. Their work is gruelling and harsh, and violates their rights to health, education, and protection from work that is hazardous or exploitative.

In Egypt, Human Rights Watch examined the cotton industry, Egypt's major cash crop, where over one million children work each year to manually remove pests from cotton plants.

In Ecuador, where nearly 600,000 children work in the rural sector, the organisation investigated conditions for children working in banana fields and packing plants. In the United States, Human Rights Watch examined conditions for the estimated 300,000 children who work as hired labourers in large-scale commercial agriculture, planting, weeding, and picking apples, cotton, cantaloupe, lettuce, asparagus, watermelons, chillies, and other crops.

In India, Human Rights Watch looked at bonded child labourers working in agriculture, as part of a larger study of bonded child labour. There are as many as 15 million bonded child labourers in India, most of whom are Dalits (untouchables) or lower caste. More than half, and possibly as many as 87 per cent, of these bonded child labourers work in agriculture, tending crops, herding cattle, and performing other tasks for their 'masters'.

(Source: Human Rights Watch, 2002)

1   **Look at the above report from Human Rights Watch and consider it against the list of children's rights in this unit. In groups debate which, if any, conventions are being broken, and how.**

Assessment practice

1   Make a poster outlining the needs and rights of children in sport. This should include a statement of the UN Convention on the Rights of the Child as they relate to sport, and a statement of the social, cultural, psychological and educational needs of children. **P1**

2   To accompany your poster, create a pamphlet of around 1000 words to explain why these needs and rights are important, and how sport helps to meet them. **M1**

Sports activities have three main types of effect on children:

- social – developing interactions between children, and between children and adults
- psychological – developing self-esteem and confidence
- physiological – changing the way the body develops.

Social effects

Children who play sport show several differences compared with those who do not. The main differences are discussed below.

Learning respect for others

Generally speaking, sports – especially team sports – develop players' respect not only for their team mates, but also for their opponents.

There are some differences between boys and girls throughout the school years – boys' play tends to be outdoors, complex and in large groups, whereas girls' play tends to be indoors, in small groups, repetitive, taking turns, and less challenging. Therefore Psychological research tells us that, in general, boys tend to learn goal-setting, interdependent roles, advanced techniques of performance, how to adjust rules of the game, settle disputes and abide by compromise; while girls tend to learn to cooperate and avoid competition – but do you think these differences apply to sportswomen you know?

Think it over

From your experience, do you think it is true that boys learn how to settle disputes and compromise, and girls tend to avoid competition? Can this sort of generalisation have any basis in fact?

Development of coping ability

Sport is also often said to be 'character-building', in that it promotes ideas of fair play, sportsmanship, teamwork, respect for opposing players and/or teams, and respect of and adherence to the rules of play. According to many writers, it also helps to promote determination in performers (the will to win) – and the ability to deal with disappointment (when you lose).

Development of self-concept

Self-esteem is the collection of beliefs or feelings we have about ourselves, or our self-perceptions. How we define ourselves influences our motivations, attitudes and behaviours, and affects our emotional adjustment. Several studies in the 1990s showed that children who play sport regularly have an improved 'self-concept' – in other words, a better body image and more confidence when dealing with others, or in unfamiliar situations.

Teenagers who play sport also show an improvement in their eating habits, are less likely to smoke or indulge in risky sexual behaviour, and display better sexual health than their non-sporting counterparts. They are also more likely to delay drinking alcohol and to drink in a more controlled manner than non-sporting peers.

Improved emotional wellbeing

An interesting finding is that both boys and girls who play team sports have lower levels of depression and a more positive body image than those who do not. Australian studies have also shown that children who play sport regularly have:

- greater ability to relax physically and therefore avoid the complications of chronic muscular tension (such as headache or backache)
- improved social skills
- improved personal skills, including cooperation and leadership.

Theory into practice

The finding that children who play team sports have lower levels of depression seems to contradict studies in individual sports, such as running or gymnastics, which suggest that participation, particularly at a high competitive level, can lead to eating disorders such as anorexia and/or bulimia, particularly in female athletes.

1 What factors might account for this difference in research results from different studies?

Improved communication and interpersonal skills

An important aspect of all sports is communication between players and team mates, as well as between players and coaches. This communication on the field carries over into other areas of the athlete's life, at school, at home, and in social situations with friends and others. Nearly half of active participants – and more than 40 per cent of volunteers and attendees – rate sport as very important in meeting new friends and acquaintances and providing venues for socialising beyond the immediate family.

Improved cooperation skills

Team work requires cooperation, and this carries over into daily life. Young athletes are more likely to cooperate with others than non-athletes, as well as being more ready to consider other people's point of view.

Increased social competence

A study of after-school sports clubs in 1997 showed increased social skills and decreased behavioural problems in children (particularly teenagers) when compared with non-attendees. This was supported by studies in 1999 which showed an improvement in work habits, school attendance and punctuality, better behaviour, better academic grades and social skills in these pupils. Not only that, but there was also a decrease in aggression, particularly in conflict or potential conflict situations.

Psychological effects

Sport also has important psychological effects on children and adults, including increased self-esteem, increased range of motor skills, development of a sense of success and failure, reduced anxiety, increased motivation, and the development of tactical awareness.

Greater confidence and self-esteem

As seen above, athletes tend to have greater self-esteem than non-athletes, will be more comfortable in social settings, and enjoy group activities as well as independent activities. When challenges arise, the athlete is able to work toward finding solutions and tends to be more positive when things go wrong. For example, rather than saying, 'I'm an idiot', a child with healthy self-esteem says 'I don't understand this'. He or she knows his or her strengths and weaknesses, and accepts them. He or she also tends to have a sense of optimism in all aspects of daily life. This seems to be especially true of adolescent girls, who show more benefits from sport than either adults or adolescent boys, especially in areas such as enhanced self-esteem, body image and confidence.

Increased range of motor skills

Young athletes tend to be reasonably good at a range of sports rather than just one or two. This is because regular participation in sports improves hand–eye coordination, neuromuscular coordination and balance. For this reason, many coaches resist early specialisation for athletes, encouraging them to play a range of sports before finally settling on their best event.

Developed sense of success and failure

All athletes face both success and failure during their career in sport. The most successful develop coping strategies to deal with both events. This prevents complacency when winning, and despair after a loss. To quote ex-Wimbledon champion Boris Becker: 'I love the winning, I can take the losing, but most of all I love to play.'

Reduced anxiety

Generally speaking, athletes are more able to relax, and have better sleep patterns, than non-athletes. Studies have shown that children who exercise regularly sleep for longer, show less disturbed sleep patterns, and have better quality sleep (awaking more rested) than those who do not play sports.

A study on tennis players showed that winning tennis players displayed significantly higher self-confidence, lower anxiety levels, and lower total mood disturbance scores than losing players.

Effects of family and parental involvement

Research has shown that children whose parents are involved in their education are more likely to attain higher academic achievement and better social skills than children whose parents do not get involved. This carries through to a child's athletic achievement as well. A child whose parents are actively involved in their development and support their progress will achieve more in less time. But some parents can put too much pressure on both their children and their coaches, and this may ultimately lead to the child athlete giving up the sport.

Increased motivation

Children play sport for a variety of reasons. These may include ego, pride, fear of failure, the challenge of competition, a desire and determination to succeed, the feeling of achievement from perfecting a skill, and acknowledgement/encouragement from peers, coaches and family.

Research has shown that intrinsic rewards are the most important motivating factor in sports participation – rewards such as the enjoyment gained from throwing a ball, learning a new skill, or merely being involved in sport with their friends, tend to mean more to young athletes than the extrinsic rewards of receiving trophies or prizes.

Development of technical and tactical awareness

Athletes need to develop game intelligence or a sense of tactical awareness. This involves skills such as the development of special awareness and working together as a team, an understanding of the principles of play (the fundamental requirements of the sport); a 'game sense' approach to playing of the sport, as well as generic skills such as decision-making and game analysis (see Unit 19).

These skills can all be transferred into non-sport situations and used to help the athlete's social interactions with schoolmates, family and others.

▲ Parental involvement is usually a benefit

Case study

Brazil Slum Outreach Project

Following a conference at the University of Chicago in October 2002, José Roberto Bueno returned to Brazil 'inspired to create a non-profit organisation to educate children of the slums through the practice [of the martial art] of aikido'. Soon after, in a *favela* (slum area) outside São Paulo, Bueno led students from his *dojo* to create Ação Harmonia Brasil (Harmony Action Brazil). Now some 30 volunteers work with Harmony Action Brazil to better the lives of impoverished children. Every week, teams of aikido black belts and senior students coach dozens of children between ages seven and 17. Volunteer Janaina Oliveira describes the program:

'Two years ago we had problems of aggressive behaviour among children. It was obvious that they lived in a violent environment, at home and in their community. Children and adolescents used to report what they had seen the day before, such as their uncle attacking his neighbour, their father hitting their mother, neighbours fighting over drug traffic. They described these events as something common and natural; this type of incident was part of the normal scene of their lives.

'Aikido came and showed a new way, a new posture, a new heart. Levels of physical and verbal aggression decreased significantly. We could observe more security, self-confidence and respect, not only among the children, but also for the staff, the family, and even at school.

'They learned to work together as a team and respect others because aikido promotes these qualities. Today we have a group of children who are making progress toward transformation of body care, mind, and good heart. They are making a difference in their families, at school and in the community.'

Bete Romanzini, a volunteer instructor with Mr Bueno for more than a year, also remarked on the substantial changes he sees taking place.

'Normally, our students cannot pay any attention, or even receive a hug. They exhibit serious difficulties in their relationships, lazy-mindedness, and any other troubles one can imagine. After one year of aikido classes, to my great delight, they look happy and disciplined. Their bodies are changing, energy is coming up. Personally, I feel that aikido helps them be happy. And in a happy mind, violence cannot enter.'

1 **Discuss what effect aikido has had on the children in Brazil.**

2 **Using the internet or other resources, find some similar projects (such as the Compton Cricket Club in Los Angeles, USA) and discuss what effects they are having on disadvantaged youth.**

Physiological effects

Young athletes are developing physically from early childhood to late adolescence. This means they have different capabilities for, and adaptations to, exercise, and for this reason young athlete training programmes should not be just scaled down versions of adult training programmes. The main benefits from athletic training for children are as follows.

Improved general health and weight management

Athletes tend to have lower body fat percentages than non-athletes, even if they weigh more. They also maintain this lower body fat level for longer. Athletes tend to have better general health than the population at large, and these benefits continue into old age. A Swedish study reported that ex-athletes had physical fitness levels comparable with non-athletes who were 20 years younger.

Fitness is usually defined as a combination of cardiovascular fitness (how well your heart and lungs work), strength and flexibility (suppleness). The importance of each element will differ according to the sport – this is known as sport-specific fitness.

Several training studies have been carried out on children to find out what effect a cardiovascular training programme will have on fitness levels. In general, the research shows that if children follow a three- to five-times-a-week routine of at least 20 minutes' continuous activity over 12 weeks, then an improvement in VO_2max (see page 142) of 7 to 26 per cent is possible. On average, though (and the results of some of the better-controlled experiments support this), a child can expect a 10 per cent improvement in VO_2max after following an 'adult-like' cardiovascular training programme.

Strength can also be developed by following a training programme, and the American College of Sports Medicine recommends the following guidelines for athletes to develop enough strength to compete at higher level.

Age 14–16 – the athlete begins by lifting 30–40 per cent of his or her body weight as a one-rep maximum (for example, an athlete weighing 50kg would lift 15–20kg and increase the weight lifted until they are lifting 60 per cent of their body weight as a maximum).

Age 16–17 – begin with 60 per cent of body weight as a one-rep maximum, building up to a maximum of 80 per cent.

Age 17–18 – begin with 80 per cent of body weight as a one-rep maximum, leading to 90 per cent as a maximum.

A further aspect of fitness is flexibility, which again is increased in athletes when compared with non-athletes. However, some studies suggest that too much flexibility (greater than 'normal' range) may lead to joints becoming unstable, with detrimental affects on both performance and injury rates. Flexibility of muscle helps to generate power, and it is advised that all athletes maintain full range of movement at all joints.

Training has benefits for children – but overtraining leads to problems.

■ Growth and puberty

The fastest rate of growth occurs in the first two years, the growth rate then slows until the adolescent spurt, when the growth rate increases again. The adolescent spurt lasts approximately two years and takes place, on average, at 10–12 years for girls and 12–14 for boys. Growth rate then decreases until full height is reached.

Muscle mass increases steadily until puberty, at which point boys show faster muscle growth, particularly in the shoulders and arms. This is associated with an increase in the hormone testosterone, which also causes the voice to break, the development of facial hair, and increased bone growth.

Muscle fibres do not reach adult size until around age 15 (in both boys and girls), so weight training is not usually recommended before that age.

The hormonal changes at puberty also affect body composition in terms of fat: at birth, both boys and girls have around 10–12 per cent body fat; pre-puberty, both girls and boys still have a similar 16–18 per cent body fat; but post-puberty, girls have around 25 per cent body fat due to high serum oestrogen, which causes the hips to widen and extra fat to be stored in the same area, while boys have 12–14 per cent body fat.

■ Overtraining

Overtraining in puberty can have negative effects on both male and female athletes.

In female athletes, such as gymnasts and dancers, excessive training can lead to the delayed onset of puberty, resulting in stunted growth and osteoporosis (thinning of the bones) and/or infertility in adulthood. Some female athletes who have reached puberty and begun menstruating may find that their periods become irregular or stop if they are training excessively.

Male athletes who overtrain have different problems, mainly related to excessive force on the sites where muscles attach to bone. Two common examples caused by excessive running are Osgood–Schlatters disease, where the quadriceps tendon of the knee pulls on its bony attachment causing a painful lump, which may be permanent; and Sever's disease, an inflammation of the Achilles tendon at the heel.

Injuries in young athletes

Some injuries in young athletes are common to both boys and girls, and the most common of these are described below.

■ Growth plate injuries

Growth plates are areas in the bones where growth occurs, and are found near the joints. Repetitive actions, such as throwing, can cause damage and inflammation to the growth plates of the bones in the arm, while repetitive sprinting and jumping can damage those in the leg. These injuries can also occur as a result of a fracture.

■ Joint surface injuries

These injuries are similar to growth plate injuries in that they are the result of either overuse or repetitive high-impact activities, but they affect the internal surfaces of the joints and are often hard to detect.

■ Stress fractures

Stress fractures are weak spots or small cracks in the bone caused by continuous overuse. Stress fractures often occur in the foot after training for basketball, running and other sports. There usually is no swelling, but pain and tenderness often increase during movement. They can also occur in the back, particularly among gymnasts and fast bowlers in cricket, as a result of excessive bending and stretching combined with high-impact landings on one or both feet.

■ Skeletal growth and development

The skeleton has various functions, including:

- support – of both the muscles and the organs of the body; the skeleton is what gives the body its shape
- movement – bones provide the attachment for muscles and work as levers to create actions such as walking, running, jumping, etc.
- protection – bones protect the vital organs of the body, for example the soft brain is protected because it is encased within a bony shell (the skull), which protects it from impact
- blood formation – long bones such as the femur (thighbone) contain marrow; blood cells are manufactured in the marrow before they are passed into the veins and arteries.

Babies are born with 300 bones, but adults have only 206 as some bones fuse together while we are growing. Long bones such as the femur (thighbone) grow from the ends of the shaft and lengthen until adulthood, but as we have seen, overtraining can damage these growth plates, affecting the child's height or leading to deformity within the bone.

It is important to realise that bones do not usually reach their optimum density and strength until the age of around 21 years, so care is needed until then to avoid overuse. With proper training, athletes will have higher bone density and therefore stronger bones than non-athletes, due to their increased levels of activity.

Other benefits of athletic training for children include:

- improved thermoregulation – athletes are better able than non-athletes to both control and maintain their body temperature
- improved immune system function – athletes have more highly developed immune systems than non-athletes, which means they are better at fighting off infections and diseases; but if athletes overtrain, their immune system can be damaged and make them more prone to infection
- improved coordination – as noted above, athletes have better hand–eye coordination and motor skills than non-athletes.

Assessment practice

1. Imagine you are a sports development officer for a local authority. As part of your role you have to 'sell' sport to the local community. In order to do this, you need to write a brochure of around 500 words outlining the benefits of regular sports participation to both parents and children. **P2**

2. In addition to your brochure, produce an essay for local teachers explaining how the benefits outlined in the above task are achieved. **M1** **M2**

3. Using examples, write a report about how sport has been shown to benefit children's development (social, physical and emotional) both in the UK and abroad. **D1** **D2**

23.3 Know about good practice in the protection of children in sport

Good practice

When coaching children, it is of paramount importance that they are safe and protected from abuse.

Nine principles

According to the Child Protection in Sport Unit, the following. nine underlying principles should be adhered to in order to protect children in sport:

- policy
- procedures and systems
- prevention
- codes of practice and behaviour
- equity
- communication
- education and training
- access to advice and support
- implementation and marketing.

There are several rules when coaching children

■ Prevention

The organisation will take measures to prevent the abuse of children by those in a position of trust, such as teachers, coaches, administrators or officials.

■ Codes of practice and behaviour

Codes of practice and behaviour should be developed in order to create a safe, encouraging and positive atmosphere for children in sport.

■ Equity

Organisations should combat discrimination in order to include children of all races, religions, political beliefs, sexual orientation, age and gender in the safeguards implemented by the organisation.

■ Communication

Information about safeguards implemented by the organisation should be available to all participants and their parents and/or guardians.

■ Education and training

Training and development opportunities should be made available to all coaches and other volunteers involved with the care and supervision of children.

■ Access to advice and support

Advice on where to find support when abuse is suspected should be made available to both children and their carers.

■ Implementation and marketing

Child protection procedures should be written and published, and reviewed every three years or sooner if there is a change in legislation.

Observation of behaviour

Children should be observed for possible signs of abuse (see pages 281–283), and the coach should be monitored in order to ensure that his or her behaviour is both professional and appropriate.

Empowering children

Children should also be encouraged to report any behaviour that makes them feel uncomfortable, whether from fellow athletes, coaches, or anyone else involved in their care and supervision.

Relationships with agencies

Ideally, sports coaches and organisations will have a contact number for bodies such as the National Society for the Prevention of Cruelty to Children (NSPCC, www.nspcc.org.uk) and the local authority social services department, and these should be made available to all children and parents. They should also liaise with such bodies in order to ensure that all procedures and practices are up to date.

■ ACAP

One example of a scheme related to child protection is East Lancashire Primary Care Trust's Accident Prevention Team (formerly the Action on Children's Accidents Project, ACAP), which provides free advice, demonstrations and safety equipment free of charge to members of the public, aiming to reduce accidents among children at home and elsewhere.

Good practice policy

All sports clubs should have a policy that allows them to implement good practice. This usually means the creation of various procedures and codes of conduct with regard to both participants and coaches.

Recruitment

The sports club and/or association should have a policy on recruitment of coaches and others. As a minimum, all coaches and volunteers must have a Criminal Records Bureau check (see page 280) and, in the case of coaches, special qualifications that allow them to coach children. This could be a special coaching qualification, a childcare qualification or a teaching qualification.

Identifying and managing problems

Each club should implement a system whereby problems with coaches and others can be identified, and a set of procedures that allow them to resolve such problems speedily. This may involve regular monitoring of coaches, meetings with parents, liaising with the local authority, etc. There should be a clear procedure to follow where there is cause for concern – if a coach or someone else is concerned for the wellbeing of a child, either in sport or elsewhere.

Whistle-blowing

'Whistle-blowing' is where a member of an organisation tells either a fellow member or an outsider about problems within that organisation. This should not result in disciplinary action for the individual concerned, provided the information is true and in the public interest.

Codes of conduct

Every sports club should have a code of conduct, not only for coaches but also for officials and volunteers. An example of a coaches' code of conduct is given in the box below and right, but all codes of conduct should aim to ensure equity and fairness for every member of the sports club.

All coaches should ensure they are fair and equitable, and remember that all children need to be treated as individuals. Coaches need to know the child's limits,and their capabilities, and to emphasise these qualities so that the child will obtain, and possibly exceed, the goals set for them.

Coaches' code of conduct

All coaches involved with children should also behave ethically. Guidelines for this behaviour cover the following areas.

Humanity
- Coaches must respect the rights, dignity, and worth of every human being and their ultimate right to self-determination.
- Coaches must not discriminate on any grounds other than ability.

Relationships
- Coaches are concerned with the safety and wellbeing of their performers.
- Performers should be encouraged to develop independence.
- There must be clear boundaries to relationships.
- Coaches must ensure that physical actions cannot be misconstrued.
- Performers must be allowed to consent to or decline any activity.

Commitment
- Coaches should clarify in advance the number of sessions, cost and method of payment, plus expectations.
- Coaches must declare any other coaching commitments and liaise with other coaches as appropriate.

- In the case of conflict between performers and national governing bodies, the coach must explain his or her obligations clearly to both parties.
- Coaches should expect a reciprocal commitment from their performers.
- Coaches should receive appropriate acknowledgement and/or reward for their contribution to the performer's achievement.

Cooperation
- Coaches should cooperate and communicate with other sports and allied professions in the best interests of their performers.
- Coaches must communicate and cooperate with registered medical and ancillary practitioners in the diagnosis, treatment and management of psychological problems.

Integrity
- Coaches must not encourage performers to violate the rules of their sport.
- They must not advocate measures that constitute an unfair advantage.
- They must ensure all activities are appropriate to the performer.
- They must treat, and encourage their performers to treat, opponents with respect.
- They should accept responsibility for their performers' conduct both in and out of the arena.

Advertising

- Sports coaches must advertise in a professional and restrained manner.
- They must provide evidence of current coaching qualifications on request.
- They must not claim affiliation with any organisation in a manner that falsely implies sponsorship or endorsement.

Confidentiality

Information given to the coach should be considered as confidential except:

- when the performer agrees it can be divulged
- for competition selection
- recommendations for employment
- in pursuit of disciplinary action
- where there are legal or medical requirements
- recommendations to parents/guardians
- when the performer's health and safety is at risk
- to protect children from abuse.

Abuse of privilege

Coaches:

- must not attempt to exert undue influence on performers
- must display high personal standards
- should never smoke whilst coaching
- should not be intoxicated whilst coaching

Safety

Coaches have a duty of care to their performers and should take all reasonable steps to ensure they are safe.

Competence

Coaches should:

- ensure they coach only those areas in which their competence has been confirmed by their national governing body
- undergo continuous professional development
- be accountable to performers, colleagues, employers and national governing bodies
- be able to recognise when to refer performers to other coaches or agencies.

These points have all been incorporated in the Coaches' Charter, available from Sports Coach UK (www. sportscoachuk.org), who also state that as a further safeguard for children involved in sport in the UK, anyone who coaches children must comply with the provisions of the Children Act (revised 2004) and guidelines issued by the Child Protection in Sport Unit (www.thecpsu.org. uk) which was set up in 2001 as a joint initiative of Sport England, Sport Scotland, Sport Northern Ireland, Sports Council Wales, Children 1st and the NSPCC.

The Coaches' Charter

1. Coaches must respect the rights, dignity and worth of every person and treat everyone equally within the context of their sport.
2. Coaches must place the wellbeing and safety of the performer above the development of performance. They should follow all guidelines laid down by their sport's governing body and hold appropriate insurance cover.
3. Coaches must develop an appropriate working relationship with performers, especially children, based on mutual trust and respect. Coaches must not exert undue influence to obtain personal benefit or reward.
4. Coaches must encourage and guide performers to accept responsibility for their own behaviour.
5. Coaches should hold up-to-date, nationally recognised governing body coaching qualifications.
6. Coaches must ensure the activities they direct or advocate are appropriate for the age, maturity, experience and ability of the individual.
7. Coaches should, at the outset, clarify with performers, and where appropriate their parents, exactly what is expected of them and what performers are entitled to expect from their coach.
8. Coaches should cooperate fully with other specialists (e.g. other coaches, officials, sport scientists, doctors, physiotherapists) in the best interest of the performer.
9. Coaches should always promote the positive aspects of their sport (e.g. fair play) and never condone rule violations or the use of prohibited substances.
10. Coaches must consistently display high standards of behaviour and appearance.

This Charter is reproduced by courtesy of Sports Coach UK.

Case study

Every other day, my ninth grade [year 9] gym class met in the small gymnasium crowded with two other classes. Mr Ruby, my teacher, was a traditional man; some might say he was sexist. He was nice, but he just couldn't see that the males and females were equals. Every class, he split the students into all-male and all-female teams. Female teams played female teams. Male teams played male teams. And every class, I protested and claimed he was being unfair. On many occasions I even claimed that Mr Ruby was a sexist pig. His response was always the same, 'You call it what you want. I call it fair.' Girls, he believed, couldn't play up to the level of guys. This infuriated me.

One day, when we were playing hockey, I saw my chance to prove Mr Ruby wrong. The guys were short of a player, so I asked if I could play with them. Mr Ruby agreed – more because he didn't want to listen to me than anything else. As I walked onto the gym floor, Mr Ruby reminded me that, if I got hurt, it would be my

own doing. As the 15 minutes passed by, I blew the teacher's beliefs to shreds. I scored six goals.

When the whistle blew, I walked off the floor with my head held high and said, 'Girls can't play to the "level", huh? Then what was that?' Mr Ruby didn't address my question, or even acknowledge that I had spoken to him. He simply dismissed the class and went into the locker room. The next time our class met, I played with the girls.

(Source: Jill Cunningham, Penn State University, www2.yk.psu.edu/~jmj3/s_anec.htm)

1 **What was wrong with the coach's behaviour?**

2 **If he had applied the Coaches' Code of Conduct, what action would he have taken?**

3 **How would you encourage him to improve his behaviour?**

Legislation regarding children in sport

■ Children Act 2004

Sport comes under the provisions of the Children Act 2004, which provides a legislative spine for the government's wider strategy for improving children's lives. The overall aim is to encourage integrated planning, commissioning and delivery of services, as well as to improve multidisciplinary working, remove duplication, increase accountability, and improve the coordination of individual and joint inspections in local authorities. The legislation provides local authorities with a considerable amount of flexibility in the way they implement its provisions.

The Children Act 2004 places a duty on local authorities to promote the educational achievement of looked-after children.

■ The Protection of Children Act 1999

This legislation is based on The Children Act 1999, which:
- reformed the law relating to children
- made provision for local authority services for children in need and others
- amended the law with respect to children's homes, community homes, voluntary homes and voluntary organisations
- made provision with respect to fostering, child-minding and day care for young children and adoption, and for connected purposes.

The government document *Every Child Matters* (see page 204) gives guidance on these Acts.

The legislation is based around the UN Convention on the Rights of the Child (see page xx).

■ Child Protection in Sport Unit

In the year 2000 several agencies joined forces to create a safer sporting environment for children, and created the CPSU. It aims to provide a safer sporting environment for children, as well as safety guidelines for their parents, sports coaches and others.

The CPSU has outlined several strategies in order to achieve this. There should be an environment where children and young people:

- are safe from maltreatment, neglect, violence and sexual exploitation in sport
- are safe from bullying
- enjoy sporting activities
- engage in decision-making in sport.

The CPSU also outlines strategies for sports clubs, governing bodies, etc.

The club/governing body should create:

- a culture and organisation that prioritises the interests of children and young people
- the knowledge, understanding, values and commitment to promote the rights of all children and young people

- a commitment to empower children and young people by advising them of their rights and how they should be treated
- a commitment to work in partnership with parents, guardians and others to increase their knowledge of the theory and practices of safeguarding children.

(Source: www.thecpsu.org.uk/Documents/SafeguardingStrategy.pdf)

In order to achieve this, it is worth bearing in mind the following guidelines. These are just a few examples of good practice; as part of your course you will develop others.

- Always coach in an open environment; you should never have one-to-one coaching sessions with a child (under 18). That way you are ensuring there are always witnesses to your behaviour.
- Involve parents and/or carers wherever possible. In this way you are showing that, as a coach, you have nothing to hide and that your dealings with children are open and honest.
- If travelling with a mixed group of children, always ensure there is both a male and female supervisor so that a person of the opposite sex does not have to provide comfort to an athlete.
- Put the child's welfare first – before winning or even competing.
- Be a good role model.

■ The Criminal Records Bureau

In the UK, all children's coaches, teachers, health professionals and any volunteers working with children must be checked by the Criminal Records Bureau (CRB) in order to ensure they are safe to work not only with children, but also with vulnerable adults.

The CRB is an organisation that checks police records and information held by the Department of Health and the Department for Education and Skills. There are two levels of CRB check currently available: Standard and Enhanced Disclosure. They are available to any organisation whose staff or volunteers work with children or vulnerable adults.

Standard Disclosure

Standard Disclosure shows current and spent convictions, cautions, reprimands and warnings held on the Police

National Computer. If the post involves working with children or vulnerable adults, the following may also be searched:

- Protection of Children Act (POCA) List
- Protection of Vulnerable Adults (POVA) List
- information held under Section 142 of the Education Act 2002 (formerly known as List 99).

Enhanced Disclosure

Enhanced Disclosure contains the same information as the Standard Disclosure, but with the addition of any relevant and proportionate information held by the local police forces.

Assessment practice

1 As a qualified tennis coach, you have seen that there is no local club for children under 11 in your area, so in conjunction with some other qualified coaches you want to establish a junior club to help bridge this sporting gap in the local community. You need to inform prospective members and their parents what is good practice in working with the under-11s, and to devise a good practice policy for your club. You have decided the best way to do this is by compiling a PowerPoint presentation lasting around 15 minutes, which you will present at tan open meeting for new members. **P3 P4**

2 You should also produce an accompanying policy document that explains how good practice is achieved and also justifies its implementation, with particular reference to the relevant legislation and the UN Convention on the Rights of the Child. **M3 M4**

23.4 Know about signs of potential child abuse and appropriate courses of action

Before we can consider the signs of child abuse and how to deal with it, we must first define what it is. Child abuse consists of any act, or failure to act, that endangers a child's physical or emotional health and development. Someone is abusive if he or she fails to nurture the child, physically injures the child, or relates sexually to the child.

Abuse

Child abuse is generally considered to have five major types:

- neglect
- physical abuse
- sexual abuse

- emotional abuse
- bullying and/or harassment.

We consider each of these below, along with signs that might alert the coach that the abuse is happening.

Key Terms

Abuse means the cruel treatment of someone, or the wrong use of something.

Neglect

Neglect can be either physical, educational or emotional. It is considered by some authorities that more children suffer from neglect than any other type of abuse.

- Physical neglect is not providing for a child's physical needs: food, clothing appropriate for the weather, supervision, a home that is hygienic and safe, and medical care as needed.
- Educational neglect is the failure to enrol a school-age child in school, to ensure they attend school or to provide necessary special education. This includes allowing excessive absences from school (truancy).
- Emotional neglect is not providing emotional support and love: affection, attending to the child's emotional needs and providing psychological care, as needed. (This obviously overlaps with emotional abuse, see page 274).

Signs of neglect can include clothing unsuited to the weather, being dirty or unbathed, extreme hunger, apparent lack of supervision, withdrawal or attention-seeking behaviour.

Physical abuse

This is injury resulting from a physical act such as punching, kicking, shaking (usually in infants), burning or scalding. It is important to remember that this may not only be from parents or other adults, but also from other children such as siblings (brothers and sisters) and schoolmates, when it is termed as bullying.

Signs of physical child abuse can include burns, bite marks, cuts, bruises or welts in the shape of an object, resistance to going home, and fear of adults.

Sexual abuse

Sexual abuse of a child is any sexual act between an adult and a child. This includes:

- fondling – touching or kissing a child's genitals, or making a child fondle an adult's genitals
- violations of bodily privacy – forcing the child to undress; spying on a child in the bathroom or bedroom
- child pornography – using a child in the production of pornography, such as a film or magazine
- exposing children to pornography (movies, magazines or websites) or enticing children to pornographic sites on the internet
- luring a child for sexual liaisons, through the internet or by any other means
- exposing children to adult sexuality in any form (showing sex organs to a child, forced observation of sexual acts, telling 'dirty' stories, group sex)
- child prostitution or sexual exploitation (using a child to perform sex with others)
- sexual acts with a child – penetration, intercourse, incest, rape, oral sex, sodomy.

Signs of sexual abuse may include inappropriate interest in or knowledge of sexual acts, seductiveness, avoidance of things related to sexuality or rejection of own genitals or body, either overcompliance or excessive aggression, fear of a particular person or family member.

Emotional abuse

Emotional child abuse is another person's attitude, behaviour, or failure to act that interferes with a child's mental health or social development. It may include verbal abuse, psychological abuse and neglect (although this is usually considered a separate category, see above).

Some types of emotional abuse are:

- ignoring or rejection
- lack of physical affection and positive reinforcement such as hugs, praise or saying 'I love you'
- threatening, frightening or terrorising a child
- belittling and negative comparisons to others; telling the child he or she is 'no good', 'worthless', 'bad' or 'a mistake'
- shaming, humiliating or name-calling
- habitual blaming
- using extreme forms of punishment, such as confinement to a cupboard or dark room, tying to a chair for long periods of time
- child exploitation, such as child labour.

Some signs of emotional abuse can include apathy, depression, hostility, difficulty concentrating; once again, emotional abuse may come not just from adults, but from siblings, classmates etc.

▲ Cyber-bullying

Bullying is perhaps the most widespread form of child abuse, and is often perpetuated by other children. According to a 2004 KidsHealth poll of more than 1200

children conducted in the USA (www.kidshealth.org), 86 per cent of 9- to 13-year-old boys and girls said they've seen someone else being bullied; 48 per cent said they had been bullied; and 42 per cent admitted to bullying other children 'at least once in a while'.

Bullying can take many forms.

- **Cyber-bullying** – cyber-bullies send messages by email, instant messaging, internet chat rooms or electronic gadgets like camera mobile phones, to harass victims at all hours, and often among a wide circle of contacts.
- **Emotional bullying** can involve isolating or excluding a child from activities (shunning the victim in the lunchroom or on school outings) or spreading rumours. This kind of bullying is especially common among girls.
- **Verbal bullying** usually involves name-calling, incessant mocking, and laughing at another child's expense.
- **Physical bullying** often accompanies verbal bullying, and involves things like kicking, hitting, biting, pinching, hair-pulling or threats of physical harm.
- **Racist bullying** preys on children through racial slurs, offensive gestures, or making jokes about a child's cultural traditions.
- **Sexual bullying** involves unwanted physical contact or sexually abusive or inappropriate comments, from either children or adults.

Any bullying must be taken seriously, and the coach has a responsibility to stop bullying whenever it is present.

If bullying is happening, coaches may notice that the bullied child is:

- coming to the session (or going home from the session) with damaged or missing clothes, without money they should have, or with scratches and bruises
- having trouble with their activities for no apparent reason
- using a different route between home and the training/game venue
- feeling irritable, easily upset or particularly emotional.

Strategies for dealing with bullying include:

- providing good supervision for children

Case study

Budhia Singh ▶

New Delhi – The guardian of a five-year-old Indian boy who runs 50km a day denied media accusations on Wednesday he was flogging him for personal gain. Biranchi Das said he was more worried about the health of his pupil, Budhia Singh, and was seeking medical advice to study the phenomenon that has created a stir across India. 'We all know there is something wrong,' Das told reporters a day after the tiny Budhia overcame heat and humidity to run a distance of 65km in seven hours from Puri to Bhubaneswar in the eastern state of Orissa. 'I consider myself a sportsman and even I can't run 10km at a stretch. That is why I am looking for specialists to conduct tests on Budhia to see why this is happening. I want to consult as many doctors as I can,' he said.

Newspapers on Wednesday splashed pictures of the youngster on their front pages but headlines like '65km at five – isn't this child abuse?' indicated not everyone was excited by the feat. 'This is pushing the physiological limits,' said paediatrician Anupam Sibal. 'A growing body is not meant for so much wear and tear.' Others said strenuous running at such a young age could damage bones permanently, causing stunting and even deformity.

Das said he could not understand what the fuss was all about. 'If Budhia does not run, he won't know what to do,' Das said. 'All he does is eat, run and sleep. Budhia is edgy if he does not run long distance every day. I make him do it in two sessions, half in the morning and the rest in the evening.' Das said he discovered Budhia's amazing talent by chance while conducting a judo class in Bhubaneswar, the state capital of Orissa, two years ago. 'Once, after he had done some mischief, I asked him to keep running till I came back,' said Das. 'When I came back after five hours, I was stunned to find him still running.'

Budhia has already taken part in the Delhi half-marathon and other distance races across India, but Tuesday's outing was much longer than the official marathon distance of 42km. Das wants to make Budhia an Olympic star – 20 years down the line. 'He will be at his best at 25 and that is a long way off. First he needs to grow up like a normal child.'

There has been nothing ordinary about Budhia's life so far. When his father died two years ago, his mother, a dishwasher in Bhubaneswar, was unable to provide for her four children and sold Budhia to a man for $20. His new father enrolled him in a judo class run by Das. The Orissa State Government says it is keeping a close watch on Budhia and his coach and will step in if anyone misuses the boy. The State's sports minister, Debashis Nayak, has already ruled that Budhia cannot take part in long-distance races without clearance from a team of doctors.

(Source: news24.com)

1   **Do you think this constitutes child abuse?**

2   **What are the reasons for your decision?**

- providing effective consequences to bullies (e.g. exclusion from the group or team)
- using good communication between coaches and parents
- providing all children with opportunities to develop good interpersonal skills
- creating an atmosphere that is supportive and inclusive, in which aggressive, bullying behaviour is not tolerated by the majority.

Effects of abuse

The effects of abuse can be many and varied. Some of the most common are:

- academic difficulties
- aggressive behaviour
- alcohol and/or other drug abuse
- anxiety
- attention problems e.g. becoming easily distracted during conversations or while at school
- bed-wetting
- compulsive/risky sexual behaviour
- depression and introversion (isolating themselves socially)
- eating disorders
- failure to thrive
- fear or shyness
- fear of certain adults or places
- lying
- running away
- low self-esteem leading to self-neglect or even suicide attempts
- stealing
- substance abuse
- physical or mental development delay, such as failure to grow, or thumb-sucking or other age-inappropriate behaviour.

Sport-specific abuse

Sport-specific abuse usually results from the actions of the coach and/or the parents, and is often the result of the 'win-at-all-costs' mentality. Examples of sport-specific abuse include:

- overtraining
- administration of drugs (doping) such as anabolic steroids by the coach and/or parent
- excessive competition.

Courses of action

Responding to child abuse

If you suspect a case of child abuse, it is important that you inform someone (or ideally persuade the child themselves to inform someone). Useful organisations include NSPCC, which has a 24-hour helpline; your local social services department; or of course the police. Other organisations include Childline, Kidscape and the Samaritans, who all provide confidential help and advice.

www.nspcc.org.uk
www.childline.org.uk
www.kidscape.org.uk
www.samaritans.org

Recording disclosure

Any disclosure should be recorded with the following details: name of the child, date, time and location of the disclosure, and should be witnessed by at least one other adult where possible. It is important to remember that the coach has a duty of care to the child and so must report any disclosure to the relevant authority (usually social services) and/or the police. The agencies mentioned above can also be contacted by the child or coach for help and advice.

All disclosures and/or allegations must be taken seriously and treated in the strictest confidence.

In cases where no allegation has been made by the child but the coach suspects abuse, this concern should be shared not only with fellow coaches, but again with relevant agencies such as those mentioned.

These points are particularly important where either a fellow member of staff or the child's parent or guardian is the subject of the allegation or concern.

■ Dealing with bullying

Remember – bullying is also a form of abuse and should be dealt with promptly, particularly where a child is the subject of adult bullying, for example by their coach.

To show how sport can be both a benefit and a risk to

Assessment practice

For your new under-11s tennis club, you need to produce an information pack for coaches and parents which contains the following:

- how to recognise the five kinds of child abuse
- the potential consequences of child abuse if left unchallenged
- the procedure for dealing with suspected cases of child abuse
- how to recognise four different signs of child abuse in a sporting context (overtraining, etc.) **P5** **P6**

As well as the signs of child abuse, your pack should also contain explanations as to how child abuse can occur while playing sport, and how and why parents and coaches can prevent it taking place. **M5**

Your information pack should also contain an analysis of why the courses of action described above are necessary in suspected cases of child abuse. **D2**

Knowledge check

1 What document determines children's rights?

2 What Act of Parliament must coaches comply with when coaching children?

3 Give, in your own words, two points in the Coaches' Charter.

4 Name the three main effects of sport on the development of children.

5 Using the case study, describe the positive effects of the Brazil Slum Outreach Project.

6 When does the adolescent growth spurt occur in girls?

7 When do muscle fibres reach their maximum size in males?

8 What is the CPSU?

9 Give two of the child protection strategies for coaches outlined by the CPSU.

10 Name the five types of child abuse.

11 Give one sign of each type of child abuse.

Preparation for assessment

children who participate, produce a coaching manual – perhaps from the assessment tasks you have already completed – with a chapter for each element of this unit. Each chapter should be between 500 and 1000 words and meet the following requirements.

Chapter 1

Outline the needs and rights of children in sport. Include a statement of the *UN Convention on the Rights of the Child* as it relates to sport, and a statement of the social, cultural, psychological and educational needs of children. **P1**

Explain why these needs and rights are important and how sport helps to meet them. **M1**

Chapter 2

Grading tip

Grading Tip **P1** **M1**

Include in your answer some evidence as to how sport helps meet a child's needs. Use real-life examples like those used in this unit. You could also contrast children who play sport with those who don't, and discuss which group is happier and more confident, to show the importance of sports participation.

Describe for coaches the physical, social and psychological benefits to children of regular sports participation. **P2**

Explain to coaches how the benefits outlined in the above task are achieved. **M2**

Use examples of how sport has been shown to benefit children's development (social, physical and emotional) both in the UK and overseas. **D1**

Chapter 3

Grading tip

Grading Tip **P2** **M2** **D1**

Look for examples of health problems in children who do not play sport, such as obesity or asthma, and contrast these with children who play sport regularly. You can do this for things such as attendance, achievement at school, and so on.

Inform coaches about good practice in relation to child protection, and outline a general good practice policy for a sports club. **P3** **P4**

Explain to coaches how good practice in child protection is achieved through the implementation of the relevant legislation and, for example, a code of conduct for coaches. **M3**

Using a chosen sports club as an example, justify why

they need to implement the above policy/code of conduct in relation to the *UN Convention on the Rights of the Child*. **M4**

Chapter 4

Grading tip

Grading Tip **P3** **P4** **M3** **M4**

Explain why children in sport may be vulnerable to abuse, and how implementation of a child policy based on the convention can help to prevent this.

Inform coaches of the following:

- how to recognise the five kinds of child abuse
- the potential consequences of child abuse if left unchallenged
- the procedure for dealing with suspected cases of child abuse
- how to recognise four different signs of child abuse in

a sporting context (overtraining, etc.) **P5** **P6**

Also include explanations as to how child abuse can occur while playing sport, and how coaches can prevent it taking place. **M5**

This chapter should also contain an analysis of why the courses of action described above are necessary in suspected cases of child abuse, again in relation to the relevant legislation. **D2**

Grading tip

Grading Tip **P5** **P6** **M5** **D2**

This might be best done in the form of a table or flowchart to guide coaches and others through the process of recognising and reporting child abuse.

To achieve a pass grade the evidence must show that the learner is able to:	To achieve a merit grade the evidence must show that, in addition to the pass criteria, the learner is able to:	To achieve a distinction grade the evidence must show that, in addition to the pass and merit criteria, the learner is able to:
P1 describe the needs and rights of children, with respect to sport **Assessment practice page 267**	**M1** explain the needs and rights of children, with respect to sport **Assessment practice page 267**	
P2 describe the effects of sport in the development of children **Assessment practice page 274**	**M2** explain the effects of sport in the development of children **Assessment practice page 274**	**D1** evaluate the effects of sport in the development of children **Assessment practice page 274**
P3 describe good practice in relation to child protection in sport **Assessment practice page 280**	**M3** explain good practice in relation to child protection in sport **Assessment practice page 280**	
P4 produce a good practice policy, relating to child protection, for a selected sports club **Assessment practice page 280**	**M4** justify the good practice policy produced, relating to child protection, for a selected sports club **Assessment practice page 280**	
P5 describe the five kinds of abuse and potential consequences of abuse **Assessment practice page 285**		
P6 describe four different signs of potential child abuse, in sporting contexts, and the courses of action in suspected cases of child abuse **Assessment practice page 285**	**M5** explain four different signs of potential child abuse, in sporting contexts, and the courses of action in suspected cases of child abuse **Assessment practice page 285**	**D2** analyse the courses of action in suspected cases of child abuse **Assessment practice page 285**

Sport as a business

Introduction

Many people see sport as big business today, with their favourite football teams being owned by businessmen, sports events and teams sponsored by businesses, and sportswear worn as leisure clothing. Evidence of business activity can be seen across the scale of organisations in the sports industry. Freelance (self-employed) people have their own businesses as personal trainers or coaches. Next up size-wise are the many small or medium-sized enterprises (SMEs) such as private gyms and health clubs that charge membership. Some gyms and health clubs form part of a chain covering the country, such as Bannatynes and Next Generation. On a large scale are the very successful global brands, such as Adidas, Reebok and Nike, trading in sports goods around the world.

This unit aims to build your awareness of the depth of business activities in the industry, and what entrepreneurs may have to do each week to remain successful. You will find many varied examples of businesses that will help you build your understanding of organising, trading and managing the business side of sport.

After completing this unit you should be able to achieve the following outcomes:

- Understand how businesses in sport are organised.
- Understand what makes a successful sports business.
- Understand the use of market research and marketing by sports businesses.
- Understand the legal and financial influences on sports businesses.

Think it over

David Beckham's five-year contract at Los Angeles Galaxy is worth 25.6m per year (nearly £0.5 million per week). At Manchester United and Real Madrid he was reputedly earning £100,000 per week which, with endorsements and appearances, might well have risen to £5m a year. Do you think he and other players are worth these wages? Beckham is certainly a well organised businessman as well as a good player.

Sports businesses

There are many diverse types of organisation operating in the sports industry. Most have to run themselves along business-like lines to be sustainable, but not all have the same motives, purposes and structure. It is important that you are able to distinguish between them and understand how they are organised.

Public sports and leisure clubs

These are run by local authorities, and exist to provide a service to local people, not to make a profit. In fact few do, and most need a subsidy from the council to continue to operate. Club managers report to local councillors who set the rates for each year. Prices are usually set low with the aim of giving everyone in the community affordable access, but councillors must always set a rate of subsidy as well, to support the shortfall in income.

You will perhaps be a user of your local sports centre as an individual or as part of a club that is based there, such as a karate or aerobics club. Leisure clubs are often based in other premises belonging to the local authority, such as a dance or theatre group using a village hall. All clubs pay a rental or hire fee to use the premises, but these are kept to minimum to make membership affordable for all. More commercially minded organisations will charge the best rate they can get for hire.

The clubs are run along business-like lines, with a need to cover their costs and probably make a small profit, which is often ploughed back into the club. Their purpose will be simply to develop their sport or activity, while their structure is likely to be a committee that manages the club – secretary, treasurer and chairperson or captain. Although they may be business-like, these types of organisation are generally not commercially minded, and often survive on membership fees and fund-raising activities, not by trading like other businesses.

Private sports and leisure clubs

These types of club are much more commercially minded, have a different structure, and offer their services at the market rate – the highest rate at which they can continue to attract customers. Examples include golf clubs, gyms and shooting ranges. Although they may still have the motive to develop their sport, they will try to do so at a profit. This usually brings in more money to the club, which can be ploughed back, but customers will have higher expectations of what they will receive for their money. This is in contrast to public facilities, where expectations and quality of premises are usually lower to help give access for all, as opposed to access just for those better off.

Private clubs are structured in a variety of ways depending on their size and aims. They might have a management committee made up of volunteers, or they might employ a manager and small staff to run their facility and clubhouse. Some private clubs belong to organisations such as large corporations in the city, or the civil service, and are kept exclusively for their employees.

The largest chains will have a board of directors deciding on their strategies and facility managers implementing these for a profit. You will learn in more depth later what managers need to do to make their business profitable.

Theory into practice

Arrange to visit a small local sports club and ask three questions to help assess its approach to its business:

1 What is its management structure?

2 What do those running it say their main motivation is?

3 How much is it to join?

Taking it further

Now arrange to visit a local leisure centre and compare it with the organisations visited in the exercise above. Create a chart to show the differences in the two types of sports organisation – plot as many as you can.

Professional sports clubs

You will probably be more familiar with these types of organisation, as they are likely to be your favourite teams such as Sale Sharks Rugby Club, Doncaster Rovers FC or Essex County Cricket Club. These clubs are set up to compete professionally in leagues and cups, but will also have a social side including bar and facilities inside the ground, merchandising outlets for fans, and websites promoting the teams and its activities, all of which help make income. Many rich businessmen sponsor these clubs, sometimes with a view to making a profit, but often also because they have a genuine passion for the sport. The largest professional clubs are the Premiership football sides such as Manchester United, Chelsea and Liverpool. They have a board of directors and professional managers at all levels of the club. They have a global following and massive sponsorship, and can attract great sponsorship deals because of the publicity they gain and the players they can attract. You can also buy shares in these clubs on the stock market, which again provides the club with an income. (However in 2005/06 Chelsea made a business loss – see Case Study).

Theory into practice

Using a newspaper or website that gives share prices, look up the value of three Premiership clubs. Compare these with three sports retailers to see who gives the best value in share terms.

Case study

'Chelsea continue to make massive losses though are reported to be down to "only" £80.2, from £140.4 million in the previous year. The club aims to break even by 2010. The chief executive has to find ways to keep costs down to achieve the aim, such as ending contracts for expensive players.

(Source: *Leisure Opportunities* 445, 2007, p. 7.)

1   **What other measures do you think Chelsea's chief executive could take to (a) reduce costs and (b) increase income?**

Amateur sports clubs

These types of club form the backbone of British sport. It has been estimated that during a typical week as many as 8 million people will play their sport through an amateur club. They cover every sport played in this country, and vary in size from the local basketball club with three teams right up to a large tennis club with 200 members. The essence of these types of sports club is their voluntary nature and not-for-profit approach. This means people give their time freely to help run the club, coach youngsters, or play and raise funds. Sometimes expenses may be paid, for example if a secretary uses their own phone to arrange fixtures, or mails out membership forms. These clubs survive on fees and subscriptions, and maybe a small sponsor or a local sports organisation grant such as through a community sports network. You will probably have started out playing sport with a grassroots club like this. It is probably fair to say that such clubs often do not have very business-like structures, just a committee of dedicated volunteers whose reward is seeing their teams and their sport flourishing.

Think it over

What are the weaknesses of relying on such an amateur set-up to grow our sporting talent?

Coaching services

This sector of the sports industry has grown in recent years, as governing bodies of sport have developed coaching awards, and more opportunities for coaches have arisen both within and outside schools.

However, the coaching network and opportunities in this country need to grow to help talented young athletes come through. In the past, good coaches have been hard to find as wages are low and hours unsocial, so forging a career as a coach has been hard. Nowadays individuals can work for themselves, with maybe five or six schools and two or three clubs as clients. Higher-level coaching positions (such as director of coaching) exist in many professional clubs today, and also with sports governing bodies (for example Rob Andrews, 'Elite Rugby Director' for the Rugby Football Union).

One important organisation is worth a mention here – Sports Coach UK coaches the coaches and helps them improve their skills, knowledge and understanding in coaching techniques (www.sportscoachuk.org). Some issues have emerged with the broadening of coaching, such as child protection – nowadays all coaches have to have a Criminal Records Bureau check to ensure they have no adverse past history (see page 280). Most sports clubs that employ professional coaches will require them to have a recognised coaching award before they can be employed. This is a recognition of standards and quality for the club and players.

Health and fitness facilities

This sector of the industry has experienced the most growth in business terms over the past decade as people have become more aware of the need for healthier lifestyles and are willing to pay to exercise. This has been a great business opportunity for some entrepreneurs, such as David Lloyd, Sebastian Coe, Richard Branson and Duncan Bannatyne, who all have had health and fitness chains (David Lloyd Leisure, Sebastian Coe Health Clubs, Virgin Active UK, Bannatyne's Health Clubs, respectively). Health and fitness facilities of a more diverse nature also operate as businesses, such as spas, retreats and health farms.

Urban Retreat to open Heathrow day spa – the company has opened its third UK site at Heathrow Airport, which will be open to travellers from 6.30 am till 9.30 pm. Treatments vary according to the time passengers could spend there, from 15-minute facials to three-hour body treatments. Travellers can treat themselves to a shower, massage, soak or just a nap. These types of service are also found at other international airports such as Singapore.

(Source: *Leisure Opportunities* 445, 2007, p. 8.)

1 **Which type of traveller could you envisage using this service?**

▲ Time lost on a delayed flight could be spent usefully in an airport gym

Organisation

People in the business of sport organise their company in various ways to suit their business needs. Everything need not be organised within the company; some services and functions, such as printing and cleaning, are bought in from outside. Sometimes owners and managers have to assess whether they can carry out a function well, who else could do it for them and what benefits this would bring, and balance this up with whether they can pay the fees for the service.

Key Terms

Organisation – a structured arrangement of people and resources, with processes designed to achieve a particular business aim.

The processes within an organisation will cover such things as:

- tasks, roles and responsibilities
- patterns of communication
- authority and chains of command.

Let's take a look at how these occur in reality in the sports business sector.

Types of business

■ Sole trader

This type of sports business is run by a single person trading on their own. Typical examples could be a small local sports shop, someone who has a stall selling sports goods, or a self-employed coach or fitness trainer. Sole traders usually choose this route so that they can be the main decision-maker. It is a fairly straightforward process, and the tax office will provide guidance. Sole traders are responsible for any debts they incur, and their personal possessions can be taken to pay debts. On the plus side, all the profit is the trader's. Proper records must be kept of income and expenditure, and tax returns must be submitted. Perhaps one of the most famous people to start out as a sole trader is Sir Richard Branson, who began by selling second-hand records from home.

■ Partnership

A partnership is used when a few people come together to form the business. It is much the same as sole trading, except everyone shares the responsibilities. Examples would be three experts on building sports facilities forming a consultancy to advise builders and developers, such as HLL Humberts Leisure. A number of partnerships are employed in creating the new Olympic venues. At a more basic level, three university graduates might set up a partnership to run sports activity camps for children. A deed of partnership may be drawn up to ensure shares and responsibilities are clear should a dispute arise. Setting up a partnership does need legal advice, but guidance is available from Companies House, where all companies are registered.

Private limited company

A private limited company is described as being limited by shares or by guarantee. This simply means the members' liability is limited to the amount unpaid on shares they hold, or the amount they have agreed to contribute to the company's assets if it is wound up. The most common in the sports industry are those limited by shares, such as Total Fitness UK Ltd in Cheshire. You can buy a ready-made company 'off the shelf' from adverts online or in Yellow Pages, or you can form your own with legal advice. Usually the main share owners become company directors and make the decisions on strategy and operations.

Remember!

The liability aspect of having shares in a company is an important concept – liability in this case means that owners are liable for debts or obligations to pay only up to the level of the capital they have invested in the company – in other words, their liability is limited.

Public limited company

PLCs tend to be larger companies with shares offered to the general public. In this case a member's liability is limited to the amount unpaid on shares held by them. A PLC normally has many shareholders, who are the owners, but is run by directors with good business experience. Shareholders can vote on policy at the annual general meeting, and buy and sell their shares on the stock market. Accounts for these types of company have to be lodged with Companies House every year, and made public.

▲ PLCs' company accounts must be published each year

Case study

The John David Group plc (JD Sports) now has over 400 stores, but it all started when John David Sports was founded in 1981 as a partnership between John Wardle and David Makin, with one shop in Bury.

Maximum advantage was being taken from the growth in sales of international sports brands such as Adidas, Nike, Reebok and Puma, and the trend to wear sportswear more and more in everyday life.

The business continued to grow with many new outlets until 2002, and then acquired nearly 200 further stores with the acquisition of First Sport from Blacks Leisure Group plc. Most of the stores retained from this acquired portfolio have subsequently been converted to the JD Sports fascia. In 2005 JD also purchased over 70 stores from the Administrators of Allsports (Retail) Limited, thereby further consolidating its position as the leading UK retailer of fashionable sports and casual wear. The company has been 57 per cent owned by Pentland Group Plc since mid-2005, a group whose principal interests are in sports and fashion brands such as Lacoste and Speedo.

(Source: www.jdsport.co.uk/company/history)

1 Why do you think the original partnership grew so quickly? Where do you think the partners got their money to expand?

2 Why do you think they were happy to sell 57 per cent to another plc?

Theory into practice

Find details about the business activities and share prices of two other PLCs that are sports-oriented. You can do this online or in the better national newspapers. Some suggestions might be: Manchester United plc, JJB Sports plc, or a health and fitness chain.

Franchise

This is a business bought from a large company that offers resources and support for individuals to run their own version, in their own territory. Examples would be someone buying the rights to run a coaching business for kids under the banner of a well known franchisee such as Premier Sport or Football Kitz 'n' Pieces.

Case study

The Énergie franchise group is aiming to become one of the big chains of gyms in the UK over the next few years – they expect to convert many small health and fitness operations into their franchise brand. New products and a women's only approach are at the heart of their drive for growth.

(Source: *Leisure Opportunities* 446, 2007, p. 4.)

1   **Do you think this is likely to be a successful approach?**

2   **What problems can you envisage they might have?**

Nationalised industry

These organisations (sometimes called Quangos) have been set up by, and are funded by, the government. Examples include the Youth Sport Trust, Sport England, UK Sport and the English Institute of Sport. They are intended to function 'at arms length' from the government, running their respective areas semi-autonomously, but with funding guaranteed, usually

drawn from Lottery sources. In this way they are not proper companies, but they do work in a business-like manner to fulfil their role.

Structure

All sports businesses need a structure for their organisation – this can be called bureaucracy, which is meant to indicate effective working systems rather than excessive red tape! A structure gives a clear definition of titles (posts), roles and responsibilities, shows which people ought to communicate with each other, and how (lines of communication), and subordinate–superior relationships (authority). With each position and tasks come a set of procedures that help decision-making. The type of structure adopted by a sports business will depend on a number of factors, such as products and services, size, number of employees and departments, and the nature of the work.

In this section we explore some of these aspects by taking a look at managers' roles, different functions in a company, and structures that cover regional areas.

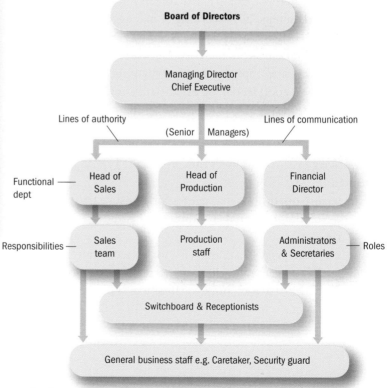

One example of a company structure

Senior management

A senior manager is next in line down from the board of management or chief executive. They tend to be put in charge of large facility, or maybe several for split-site operations. Their role is to take an overview of all operations and steer them towards the company's goals – like a ship's captain. This is a very responsible role, the senior manager may be in charge of a large work force, budget and set of buildings.

Wanted

Senior Manager for international chain of health clubs

Skills and experience:

- responsible for financial targets
- proven commercial awareness
- business acumen (ability and knowledge)
- strong leadership skills.

Management

There are many titles and types of manager in the sports industry. This may be a position you might aspire to when you qualify. The role of duty manager is described on page 299. Working at management level means making many decisions, keeping staff motivated, ensuring standards are met, dealing with complaints, and interpreting and applying new instructions. You would have to be a good leader, be organised, and certainly know your business to be effective. In many senses a manager is the link between senior staff who decide on directions for the business, and the staff who apply working practices to meet the targets set. Typical titles include:

- leisure operations manager – for a leisure trust
- development manager – for a local authority or retailer
- customer services manager – for a racecourse
- facility project manager – for a sports governing body
- manager of a golf course or health and fitness club.

Activity

Create a list of the duties you think a manager of a large tennis club might have to carry out

Functional departments

Many sports businesses are split into departments that have a specific function (see the diagram on page 297). This makes good sense as it clusters people and tasks together for ease of working and communication. Usually a specialist manager is put in charge to oversee all activities. This type of bureaucracy is favoured by larger organisations.

Theory into practice

Investigate three large sports businesses online and assess what departments they operate. Make some comparisons.

Regional structure

Sports businesses using this type of structure are usually chains or franchises. Managers are appointed to oversee a region, which may contain a number of outlets. Regions are usually quite large geographical areas such as Yorkshire or Scotland south, or they may be located in city such as Manchester or Birmingham. Managers often have a sales role to carry out, and must ensure sites are profitable. Regional managers will report regularly to the senior manager with updates on performance at each location.

Staff

Staff in sports businesses are usually split into several layers, depending on their responsibilities and job title. Whatever their level, they must work as team to meet customers' needs. The senior managers decide on the

▲ The presentation of staff reveals a lot about a business

strategy for the organisation; middle managers will decide on the tactics needed to achieve the strategy in their section; and staff dealing with customers operationalise it in reality (see diagram on page 297).

■ Chief executive

The chief executive is at the top of the company. Their role is the most important – they decide on the vision and direction for the organisation, and how the company should be run. The job advertisement below shows a list of possible roles the CE might take in a major sports business. Examples from the sport and leisure industry include Nick Varney, CE of Merlin Entertainments (the owners of Alton Towers, Legoland and Madame Tussauds among others); Brian Barwick, CE of the Football Association; and Richard Scudamore, CE of the FA Premier League.

Senior opportunity – chief executive for leisure trust

Roles:
- coordinate board meetings with other directors
- oversee product and service delivery
- contribute to marketing strategy
- generally control budgets and finance for the company
- help coordinate staffing policy and legal obligations
- present a positive image to shareholders and the public.

Taking it further

Find some advertisements in the press and/or online. Using these and the information in the advert here, design an advertisement for a chief executive for chain of fitness and health clubs.

■ Duty manager

The duty manager is further down the chain of command (see diagram on page 287). Their primary role is to oversee the daily operations of a facility, such as a pool or sports centre. There is often more than one duty manager covering shifts, as many places are open for up to 18 hours per day.

In the swim – duty manager sought for local authority leisure facility

- highly motivated and enthusiastic
- experienced
- able to work in a team
- able to act in senior role
- responsible for day-to-day operations
- know what high-quality delivery needs and means
- flexible – able to work weekends and evenings
- demonstrating leadership skills
- knowledge of swimming,
- Investors in People and Aquamark quality awards

Taking it further

Using leisureopportunities.com or magazines, identify two other duty manager positions and compare the three sets of attributes. Add any new findings to your table.

■ Sales manager

The sales manager differs from the general manager in needing specific selling skills – persuading people to join a sports club or buy equipment, for example. They are usually target-driven, and can gain bonuses for good performance. Sales managers may have a territory to manage and be quite mobile, moving from venue to venue on a daily basis to see clients, or spending a great deal of time on the phone contacting members or potential members. They will usually receive a car and travel allowance.

■ Receptionist

The receptionist is often the first point of contact for many customers, so this is a crucial role, although not always very well paid. A receptionist has to have a detailed working knowledge of the organisation – they usually operate the switchboard, take messages, and know where people are and when they will be back. The might also take bookings and answer all sorts of enquiries and complaints.

Theory into practice

Try to visit two sports facilities in your area, interview the receptionist and list the diversity of jobs they carry out. Create a job advertisement like those in previous pages – Wanted – efficient and experienced receptionist for....'.

■ Leisure attendant

This is an entry-level or starter post. A leisure attendant may work part time carrying out a range of tasks in a sports centre, such as setting up and taking down badminton nets, being a lifeguard (if qualified), cleaning, and perhaps having a health and safety award. This type of staff member might aspire to be a duty manager eventually, once they have gained a good working knowledge of the facility.

Other entry-level posts include:

- retail assistant in sports shop (dealing with customers, restocking displays, handling cash)
- junior sports event organiser (contacting clients, organisation at events, preparing press releases)
- sports promotion assistant (designing posters/ displays, assisting managers at presentations, customer liaison).

Assessment practice

Imagine you are going to form a business with some close friends. You aren't sure what is the best set-up for your company, so you decide to make some comparisons. Choose two different types of sports business and assess how they are organised. Give details of:

- the type of business and structure
- aims and purpose
- staffing levels
- products and services.   **P1 M1**

Grading tips

Grading Tip P1

Include details of the type of business and its structure, and show the staffing clearly.

Grading Tip M1

Compare and contrast the two organisations.

A sports businesses will set out with a vision of where it wants to go. This should be based on an effectively researched business plan – not just a 'gut feeling' or good idea. There is a lot more to being successful at the planning stage than people think.

Businesses try to map out a strategy based on a range of factors, such as resources, opportunities for the type of product or service they trade in, and the market they are trying to enter. Many small sports businesses will use a SWOT analysis to help them answer some of the important questions (see page 138).

Success

The key element of success is the effectiveness of a business's strategy – it should aim to use its resources well and give maximum results. It is easier to measure these results in quantifiable terms, such as profit or income. But it is also important to assess how happy customers are with the service or products they receive, and how satisfied staff are with their pay and conditions (staff often create a company's image). All the time this work is going on, the owners must try to grow the business to keep it sustainable in the long term. So success is needed at various stages of a strategy – start-up, growth and development stages, which follow on from each other to give ongoing success and good results for customers, staff, shareholders and owners.

Good research and strategy ➡ successful start-up ➡ good growth ➡ sustainable development

Remember!

Success stems from knowing where you are and what you have, having a vision and drive for where you want to be, and having a way of telling if you have arrived or are off track – this is called measuring business performance.

Think it over

What might go wrong at each stage of the strategy and development? Do you think a strategy should be fixed plan, or flexible? Why?

Let's look at some of these measures of success in little more detail. The principles established will be just as applicable to large corporations as they are to self-employed people and small businesses.

Income

This can be summed up in simple terms as the amount of money coming into an organisation. The amount of money going out of the organisation is called expenditure. To be successful, income needs to exceed expenditure by some way. Income needs to cover a whole range of expenditure or costs for a sports business:

- rent of equipment and premises
- raw goods and materials
- interest to pay back on any money borrowed
- heat, light and water bills
- taxes (such as VAT and business rates) and national insurance
- marketing of goods or services
- insurance
- wages.

Sources of income vary according to the type of business, but common sources include:

- sales of products
- membership charges
- tickets sold
- fees for services.

The excess of income over expenditure will usually be increased if the business can sell its stock of goods and services quickly and at a good profit without the costs going up markedly. This is a good measure of success. The accounting processes in a business need to be accurate and up-to-date for this measure to be of value – this is financial accounting. Once the data have been gathered, they are passed on to managers to help them run their section – this is management accounting.

Profit

This is the excess left over after all costs and liabilities (such as interest on loans or tax bills) have been covered. Owners have to decide how much of this profit they will take for themselves as earnings, how much will go to shareholders as dividends, and how much they will plough back into the business. The measure of success in profit terms is often taken through the calculation of profitability – how much profit has been made, measured against how much money (capital) was employed to make it.

Companies registered as limited or PLC (see page 296) have to publish accounts showing their profits, which helps people judge their success. (For some recent figures posted for global sports businesses, see page 303.)

Profit levels can be affected by many factors, some of which are shown in the case studies.

Case study

The sportswear firm Nike saw profits rise to $349.5 million from $305 million a year in 2004, taking full-year earnings to $1.21 billion from $945.6 million for 2005. This was mainly due to exciting new products they were able to launch very successfully around the globe. (Source: http://news.bbc.co.uk)

A price war with other sports retailers forced JJB Sports to warn of lower profits and dividends for 2006. The company said profits would come in below expectations at between £32 million and £36 million. They had to cut their prices to keep in line with the competition. (Source: *The Independent*, 7 January 2006.)

Andy McGlynn finished his sports science degree in 2005 and has been working to build his business of personal trainers for the LA Fitness chain. He has been so successful that he now employs more than 40 personal trainer staff around the country, earns a six-figure salary, and boasts of two homes in Cheshire and Cambridge and two investment properties. Andy is firmly focused on becoming a millionaire by the time he celebrates his 30th birthday. Sheer determination, hard work and a good business brain have helped Andy make a profit and be sucessful.

(Source: University of Bolton website, www.bolton.ac.uk, 8 August 2006.)

1   **Discuss with your class what other factors can affect profits.**

2   **Can you find some real examples where a lack of profit has meant that a sports business has been closed? (e.g. Scarborough Football Club in April 2007).**

Growth

Business growth is the dream of most owners and managers – it can bring more revenue, higher sales and bigger bonuses. But too rapid growth that is not thought through or resourced properly can bring a company to its knees as resources and staff are overstretched. You can't grow a business without demand for its products. Many sports businesses have experienced growth during the past decade as demand for their products has soared – such as retail outlets, as sports clothing has become mainstream fashion wear.

The Premier League and UEFA Champions League in football are worth millions in revenue to clubs that are successful. This is the case around the world for popular leagues – take a look at the statistics for American leagues in Table 24.1.

Table 24.1 Revenue and growth in US major league sports, 1990–2004 (sources: *Forbes* magazine and *Financial World* magazine, May 2005).

Sport	Revenue (US$)		Growth rate (%)
	1990	**2004**	
Major League Baseball	13bn	4.3bn	8.7
National Basketball Association	843m	2.9bn	10.1
National Football League	1.3bn	5.3bn	11.47
National Ice Hockey League	518m	2.2bn	11.9

Activity

Find out how the statistics in Table 24.1 compare with the Premier League or UEFA Champions League over the same period, or for the current year.

Key Terms

Growth is measured in business terms not just by the number of customers, but by many other means including revenue or sales, number of branches, market share, etc.

Some parts of the country see the economic value of sports-related businesses as very high, and have special development strategies, such as the North West Sports Cluster.

Case study

'The development of a sport cluster has the potential to create a virtuous circle of economic activity. For example, the existing facilities' infrastructure is state-of-the-art and gives the region the competitive advantage of being able to bid for and to host major sport events.'

(Source: www.nwda.co.uk)

1 **What do you think a 'virtuous circle of economic activity' is? Remember the north west hosts the most valuable football club in the world!**

Companies enjoying a growth phase in 2007 include:
- The Sanctuary spas (with a £50 million expansion)
- Parkwood Leisure (which operates a nationwide group of leisure centres)
- Sports and Leisure Management Limited (which manages local authority leisure contracts).

Much of the growth that sports have enjoyed is due to the exposure they get on TV – we have become something of a nation of spectators, preferring to watch our sport on a plasma screen at home, rather than live events. TV companies spend millions buying the rights to screen sports, which pushes up their value as a commodity. Indirectly, this can also be a growth factor as well, as people watch their favourite performers and are inspired to take up the sport. But sports that don't get any TV time may die out, representing a decline.

Think it over

Debate with your class whether you think sports have become too much of a commodity – they were never invented to be bought and sold, just played.

Sustainability

To be sustainable, sports businesses must set themselves up and run in such a way that that they can continue. Sustainability means 'enduring' – able to carry on whatever the circumstances. In business terms this involves a range of factors, including:
- continuing to develop an attractive product range
- having enough capital to expand and revenue to pay debts
- keeping staff, customers and shareholders happy
- being able to cope with political or legal changes
- competing with rivals and keeping market share.

Sustainability is a big issue for many SMEs in sports, as they often have limited resources to sustain them. Any organisation with few customers, staff and resources will soon become overstretched if market conditions become unfavourable. The market system operates like the law of the jungle – only the strongest survive, and responsiveness is the key.

Today, however, sustainability is not just economic – it encompasses social justice and environmental friendliness. Businesses have to be seen to be fair in their trading and green in their practices. So sweat-shop operations, paying low wages in the Far East, producing expensive sports goods for the West, are frowned upon; and organisations that do not have recycling and energy-saving schemes can also receive bad publicity.

Think it over

Suggest a range of methods for recycling and energy saving that a sport shoe manufacturer could use to become more sustainable.

The South East England Development Agency sums up this key concept of sustainable businesses as those adopting a sustainable approach to how they:
- produce, buy and sell goods
- affect the environment

- invest
- recruit, train and develop their own people
- engage with the community in which they operate
- respect the rights of people.

Customer satisfaction

There are two types of customer – internal (or staff) and external clients. Here we investigate best business practice to achieve external customer satisfaction.

First, you must ensure the business has a customer-facing approach. This is usually achieved by having good policies and procedures for staff to follow, or a customer charter; the top companies have a quality system aimed at customer satisfaction, which is applied throughout the business. Customer service is very much a team effort, and must come from the top down so that managers and owners also reflect a customer-focused approach. Good customer service leads to customer loyalty and repeat business. Many sports organisations will offer customer loyalty or incentive schemes to reward regular customers.

Remember!

The key element of good customer service is staff having a great attitude and positive behaviour – all the time, not just when they are in the mood. The important thing is consistency in meeting customers' needs.

For sports businesses with good customer service records, a number of benefits should accrue:

- customer loyalty and repeat business
- increased sales and reputation
- being recommended by satisfied customers to their friends
- a competitive edge over rivals
- a good public image – and probably more customers.

Key Terms

Good customer service – meeting customers' needs and expectations.

For someone working in a sports business, for example in a stadium booking office, best practice in customer care means applying some of the following. Most are underpinned by good communication skills:

- staff should create a good first impression every time, visually and verbally
- a dress code and appearance, so that staff are instantly recognisable
- treating all types of customer – young, old, male, female, disabled, ethnically different – with a high standard of attentiveness
- projecting a good positive attitude and confident personality
- quickly establishing a rapport with customers.

Customer care and service is not always perfect, and there will be times when complaints are made. In this case sports businesses need to have a procedure that is smooth and consistent, for the benefit of both staff and customers.

Activity

Create a flow chart showing the stages a business might use to deal with customer complaints that need the manager to help decide the outcome. Annotate each stage with what might be said to the customer so that they feel they are being treated fairly and still receiving good customer care.

Leisure Club Member Feedback

village HOTEL & LEISURE CLUB

Member Name: _____

Member Number: _____

Email: _____

Date of Visit: _____

FEEDBACK RELATES TO:

☐ Gym ☐ Pool ☐ Café Copra ☐ Other

Please make your comment here:

_____

_____

_____

_____

_____

_____

_____

_____

Please hand completed form in at reception.

Thank you

All together more.
for more information call

01482 642 422

or visit www.village-hotels.co.uk
Henry Boot Way, Priory Park, Hull. HU4 7DY.

▲ Customer care involves keeping in touch with customers' views

Taking it further

Try these short role-play scenarios with a fellow student to see how good you are.

1   At a resort, a customer has booked himself and his brother in for a windsurfing lesson. On the morning, the brother is too ill to take part. The man wants a full refund for both of them. Try to explain that no refunds are given for cancellation within 24 hours.

2   At a stadium, a new customer calls to speak to the commercial manager. You know the manager is out and about somewhere in the ground. Compose an announcement to read out over the tannoy – what would you need to know and say?

3   You are sports event organiser for a charity football match. Some of the VIPs attending are getting a bit drunk and becoming rowdy and abusive to staff. How would you deal with this to prevent it becoming an incident?

Staff satisfaction

In this section we investigate what is involved in creating a successful and satisfied staff team – the 'internal customers'. Many of the principles outlined above for external customers also apply here, for example being polite, having a good attitude, establishing a good rapport and being consistent. Perhaps this is best summed up by the phrase 'being professional'. We can add some additional pointers for staff here:

- meet deadlines for colleagues when tasks are set
- stick to rules, standards and procedures
- do your share as team member – don't be the team 'loafer'
- sometimes the little things are important, such as giving respect, keeping your area tidy and saying thank you
- use listening skills and be supportive at tough times.

From an organisation's point of view, keeping staff happy needs a blend of things that satisfy and things that motivate. There are many motivation theories you might read up on (see www.biz-ed.co.uk; also try researching

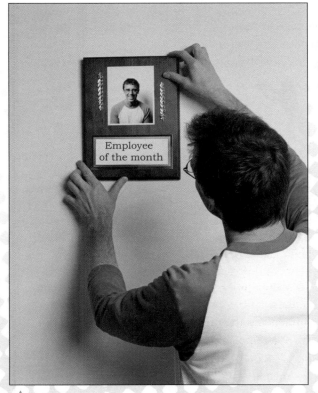

Douglas McGregor, Abraham Maslow and Frederick Herzberg). In general the following are common factors in keeping staff satisfied:

- a decent wage and clean working conditions
- chances for promotion and responsibility
- praise and incentive schemes
- a sense of value and belonging
- being trusted and respected
- not being discriminated against on any grounds
- not being overworked.

Achieving staff satisfaction will give your business a good reputation and can attract good staff as you become an employer of choice.

Think it over

Working in pairs, what other ideas could you add to the list of factors in staff satisfaction (page 305).

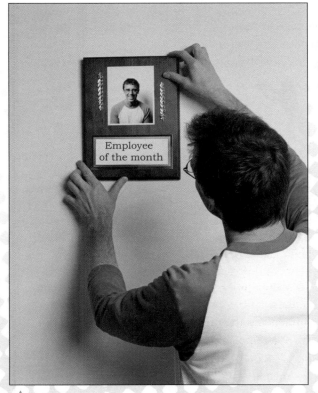

▲ **Praise and incentives improve performance**

Taking it further

There are a number of methods of assessing the quality of customer service in a business. For example, an organisation that sells customers gift experience days for special occasions (such as driving or flying activities) follows up sales with a call to clients to assess the success, service and quality of the experience. Operators who fall below their standards are taken off the list of gift experience days available. From your own research, what do the following involve?

- benchmarking
- assessing reliability
- assessing quality standards
- assessing health, safety, security and hygiene
- gaining customer feedback.

Achieving aims and targets

■ Aims

Aims are those things that a business is working towards in general terms – its vision statement or overall strategic direction.

Some examples of aims of sports businesses around the world include:

- Pitch, a public relations consultancy for sportspeople and businesses (www.pitchpr.com), aims to be 'The No. 1 communications consultancy in sponsorship and sport'
- for the 2012 Olympics in London, the British Olympic Association has vowed that Britain will be fourth in the medal tables
- Sheffield International Venues (SIV) aims 'to make Sheffield one of the top international and cultural venues for sport and leisure' – www.sivltd.com.

Smaller businesses might simply aim to make decent profit in order to stay in business. A team might aim to be in the top five of their league. Individuals with businesses might aim to sell enough products or services to make a decent living. Not all businesses can be number one!

■ Targets

Targets (or objectives) are set along the way to achieving an aim, like a staging post. For example, a potential Olympian aiming for London 2012 would need to have many objectives over the next few years to be able to peak for the Games. The same principle applies to business – many individual, group and shared objectives are set, all hopefully culminating in the achievement of the company's aims. Where targets differ from aims is in the fact that they must be readily measurable and set to a time scale.

For a business, a target might be:

- increased sales by a set amount, e.g. 10 per cent
- increased customer base, e.g. 800 new customers within six months
- greater profits, e.g. £3000 per month
- growth in market share, e.g. 1 per cent per year
- an improvement in staff productivity, e.g. 3 per cent per year.

The easiest way to remember the essence of targets is in the acronym SMART – specific, measurable, achievable, realistic, timed (see page 65).

The remit of a business is its area of authority or operations. Fulfilling the remit means reaching the targets and thus meeting the aims set, and using its resources very well, giving good returns – the perfect scenario for a business. To achieve this, many aspects of the business will have to have been managed effectively – staff, customers, raw materials, finance. This will require good systems to be in place, effective decision-making (especially when difficult situations arise), and good problem-solving skills. Many companies will reward their staff if their remit is fulfilled with an end-of-year bonus or in-kind reward.

The remit might involve:

- development, implementation and evaluation of policy against defined outcomes, as agreed with senior executives
- development, implementation and monitoring of agreed strategic and operational plans and targets
- efficient resource allocation, budgeting, financial planning and review
- effective organisational structure and review.

Grading tips

Grading Tip P2

Ensure you have a range of concepts that can be used to assess success – such as financial, growth and development, satisfaction levels, achievement of targets, etc.

Grading Tip M2

You need to be able to explain more detail for this criterion – such as profit levels, sustainability, fulfilling of remit.

24.3 Understand the use of market research and marketing by sports businesses

Marketing starts with an idea, which is then researched. The data gathered are then analysed, and out of that a plan is formed to try and create a product that people will buy. Sports businesses, just like any others, will follow this process – although many ideas never get past the early stages.

identify customers' needs and expectations

analyse data gathered about needs and wants

assess whether your company can provide the product or service for profit

set appropriate SMART objectives for a marketing plan (page 65)

develop a mix of marketing essentials (e.g. the four Ps)

keep reviewing the elements of the plan to make sure they are effective

Key Terms

Marketing is defined by the Marketing Institute as 'the management process of identifying, anticipating and then satisfying customer requirements – profitably'.

The sports industry is very competitive and often fast-moving, so it is vital to get the elements of a marketing plan right.

Remember!

A neat way to remember the principles and process of marketing is the four Ps – marketing is about getting the right **product**, **promoted** to the right people, at the right **place** and the right time, for the right **price** to satisfy their needs.

Market research

This is the first part of the marketing process, which involves sports businesses in exploring, investigating and gathering information about customers' needs and wants. Any research has to be planned and carried out very carefully as it will inform many later decisions. Most large sports businesses will have a marketing department with people whose job it is to gather and analyse this type of data, or they may employ a market research company. Examples include Lexus PR, Prescient Marketing, Comperio Research and GEM Group.

Value of market research data

■ Customer knowledge

It is important to understand the characteristics of customers and the segments they fall into, as this helps sports businesses match their products to customers' types and needs. Sports businesses may split their customers into categories like those shown in Table 24.2.

▼ Table 24.2 Market segments

Category	Examples
Socio-economic group	People classified according to their job, e.g. A and B types are managers and professionals; C types are supervisors or skilled, D and E have low skills and incomes
Age band (with some examples of products) or life stages	Under-11s – sports toys 12–18 years – sports clothing 18–24 years – sports events 25–45 years – fitness goods 45–65 years – health products
Lifestyle	Home-based sport and leisure activities Sports spectators Sports participants
Other factors, e.g.:	
Gender	Women-only products
Region	Rich areas of town
Family type	Young couple (no kids)

Analysis of preferences and sporting habits for each category can greatly help a company to know what is likely to sell, and at what price.

■ Competitors

Knowing what your competitors are doing and charging, for example, is important to sports businesses. Making comparisons, or benchmarking, is the key reason market research takes place. For large sports organisations, this can be a key factor in their pricing decisions or product range as they try to compete. For smaller operators, price may be less of an issue, but quality of goods or services will be important to know. Research may show that there are gaps in the market, or that more of the market share could be gained with a pricing change. Companies that keep a keen eye on each other are the major health and fitness clubs (Bannatynes, Next Generation, LA Fitness, Esporta, David Lloyd Leisure). Night clubs in the same district of a town will also do the same.

Theory into practice

List three other types of operator who are likely to keep a close eye on their competitors, and state what factors they will assess in their competitors' business.

■ Market environment

This describes where products and services are sold – so a sports tourism company operates in the sports tourism market; for sports clothing and equipment, the sports goods market. Sports businesses subdivide the market further into segments – such as family sectors, or 18–24-year-olds, or fans of a particular club. The market environment in the sports industry fluctuates and is subject to change, just like any other market. Changes can be caused by a range of factors (Table 24.3).

▼ Table 24.3 Factors affecting the sports business market

Change	Effect
New fashion in sportswear or clothing	Retailers have to try and stock the new range
Increase in tax by the Government	Sports businesses have to find the extra money through price increases or cost savings
Arrival of a competitor	Prices may have to go down to retain market share
Bad press, e.g. from 'bungs' or corruption, or safety concerns	Reputation and image of business may be harmed as customer confidence is damaged

Taking it further

Working with partner, add to Table 24.3 some other factors that may affect the market – think in global terms.

■ Demand and trends

Trends and changes in demand are a frequent feature of the sports market. Some recent trends give an idea of how demand can fluctuate. Demand for season tickets at Watford and Reading football clubs waned when they dropped out of the Premiership in 2007. Equally, it went up for Birmingham and Sunderland as they gained promotion. Demand for tickets to the New Wembley and Olympic venues will no doubt build up as matches take place and 2012 approaches. According to www.plunkettresearch.com, some recent trends of interest to larger sports businesses have been:

- improvements in 'smart' sports fabrics
- expansion in team merchandising
- changes in population balance towards older customers
- growth in sports media.

According to www.smallbiztrends.com, trends include:

- growth in extreme sports
- an increase in use of sports agents by professional players
- growth in women's soccer.

Think it over

Can you identify one new upward trend in sport, and one where demand has fallen? How valuable is it for a sports business to be able to predict these shifts?

■ Opportunities for development

When research is carried out, gaps in product lines or developing trends may be identified. One of the best examples is the development of football clubs offering all sorts of diverse services to their fans, such as at St James' Park, the Newcastle United ground, which offers education and IT skills classes, furniture in club colours, access to shows, concerts, venues for parties and business meetings, finance and travel clubs.

▲ Sports clubs can diversify to serve different markets

■ Pricing strategy

Market research to identify possible prices is a key factor for sports businesses. Surveys can be carried out to assess what price range new items should be in – testing 'what the customer might pay'. Price comparisons are made with competitors, or similar goods and services, to make sure the price is right. Pricing is an important part of the marketing mix, which also includes promotion and place of sale.

Strategies include:

- off-peak pricing to encourage purchases at less-busy times
- peak pricing to achieve the maximum profit at busy times
- group discounts to encourage larger numbers
- low prices for those who are young, old, or on low incomes
- price reductions for regular customers.

Low prices help companies penetrate a market, but they can't be kept low forever or the company will go out of business. High prices are used for quality products, to skim the best profit at the top end of the market.

Theory into practice

Call, email or visit a local sports business and ask if thy are willing to let you know of their pricing strategy. Are the elements of their strategy covered in the list above, or have they considered other factors as well?

Methods in market research

This section explains the research methods sports businesses can use, either themselves or through a market research agency such as Questions Answered in York (www.qaresearch.co.uk), or the Sport Industry Research Centre in Sheffield (www.shu.ac.uk/research/sirc). The larger companies such as Mintel and Deloitte charge for access to market reports.

Research can be split into two types:

- qualitative – more comment-based, showing preferences and desires
- quantitative – based on figures and statistics.

In quantitative terms, the larger the sample taken, the more likely the results are to be reliable and give a good prediction. Qualitative research is more effective with smaller groups who can go into certain aspects more deeply.

■ Primary sources

Examples of methods used to glean first-hand (primary) information from potential customers include surveys, focus groups of likely customers, and observation.

- Surveys can be carried out face-to-face, online, by telephone or by mail.
- Focus groups are discussion groups held with likely customers.
- Observation is simply that, with trained staff watching and noting customer behaviour.

Activity

Working with a partner, decide which method you would use if you were small sports shop wishing to find out what young customers thought of a new product range, and devise a plan to carry it out.

■ Secondary sources

These are usually reports or statistics that are generally available, or can be bought from specialist companies. Typically, research is carried out by an organisation and the information is published for sports businesses to use as a secondary source of information.

■ Selection of appropriate methods

Sports business people need to take care to select the right kind of method for their research (primary or secondary), and within these, whether they use a combination of surveys, focus groups, reports or official statistics. The methods selected have to suit the information needed, the time scale and cost factors. Whatever combination is used, sports businesses must ensure the data are current, accurate, reliable and easy to understand.

■ Recording

This really means how the information is collected. A range of methods can be used, again to suit time, budget, expertise and type of information being gathered. Methods that a business could consider with speed in mind are questionnaires being optically scanned, or data being collected from groups or electronically.

The second dimension of this is how the data gathered are presented – a range of different ways are commonly used, including pie charts, graphs tables, bar graphs and comparative scales.

■ Interpreting

This is the final stage of research – and the part needing the most care and expertise. Interpretation of data gathered may affect company strategy, financial plans, staffing ratios, resource requirements and product volumes, so analysis needs to be done carefully and comparisons made with other years, changes in the economic climate, social trends and labour factors. The outcome of the interpretation should guide the company forward for the next business cycle.

Think it over

Many small businesses may not have the time or finance to carry out such extensive research, nor the skill to interpret data accurately, so for some of them guesswork based on limited data or the manager's experience might be the most they can manage. What else might they do, on a small scale, to carry out some limited and inexpensive research?

Areas of research

■ Customer type

Customers are usually segmented by age, area, earnings, habits and lifestyle (see page 299). Companies need to keep effective databases of their customers' details – if they are seeking repeat business, this is the ideal way to stay in touch. But companies collecting such data must conform with the Data Protection Act and keep this information confidential.

■ Customer behaviour

Customer databases are fed by information from sales tills, check-in points and bookings systems, enabling a business to:

- track the length of visits
- log what they spend
- assess how often they visit
- keep a record of their favourite activities
- record their birthday.

Think it over

What else would be useful to know about customers that an electronic system could capture?

■ Sales trends

For retail outlets, this type of information is vital to identify which lines of sports clothing or kit are selling well. This helps outlets with restocking racks and displays, as well as telling them what is not selling well and maybe needs to be reduced in price.

■ Market share

This is the portion of the whole market that one company has. The higher this percentage, the more likely a business is to be the market leader and price-setter for that market, with others having to follow suit.

Under the Monopolies Act, one trader can't have 100 per cent of the market as this would mean no competition.

■ Market segmentation

Products and services are designed for each segment (portion of the market), so sports businesses have to carry out research to find out what each segment desires and prefers. Research helps them to achieve the matching of goods to segments, and to get the 'best fit'.

Activity

Match up the following products and services to the age segments shown (all mixed up) in Table 24.4. Now try the same for a gender segment for a partner, then swap your tables for them to try.

▼ Table 24.4 Targeting the market

Product or service	Segment	
	Age	Gender
Staging a wrestling competition	Under-9s	
A bowls tournament	Males and females in their 20s and 30s	
'Come-and-try-it' mini-rugby	Over-55s	

■ Competitor activities

In very competitive markets, knowing what other companies are doing can be very important. It might determine what price you set, what standards you have to achieve to compete, and what products or services you will need to offer to be attractive and win over customers before they spend with your competitors instead.

Market research activities

From the range of types of activity described above, the design and purpose of a few are described in a little more depth here.

Surveys

These are usually carried out based on questionnaires, which need careful design to be effective – too many open answers will give too many varied responses to be of real use. Open-ended questions do have some advantages: they allow people to explain their views; attitudes and feelings can come through more; and additional information can be gathered about the respondent. But closed questions (where people answer yes or no, or state their preference) are much easier to analyse. Multiple choice answers are popular where range of responses can be chosen. You can also use scales or ratings, as in the example below.

1	2	3	4	5
disagree	some disagreement	no opinion	agree	very much in favour

Activity

Working in groups of three, design a survey with ten questions that a sports venue could use to research players' reactions after a sports tournament had been held there. Think of the various dimensions this might need to cover.

Questionnaires

The following guidelines describe the best way to compose and present questionnaires:

- compose questions so that they are easy to understand and interpret
- don't use a lot of technical terms or jargon in questions
- ask only one thing in each question
- don't ask private or personal questions
- keep the questions brief and to the point (many people will have limited time)
- make sure the layout is clear and the sequence logical
- test it out before you use it publicly (called a pilot)

- ensure the answers are easy to record and collate into useful information
- ensure the researchers are fully trained and can answer any queries respondents may have without introducing bias.

Assessment practice

1 Compose a questionnaire that a stadium or local amateur club could use to find out what events they could stage between weekly football matches. **P3**

2 With the permission of your local stadium manager or a local amateur club, try out your questionnaire. **P4** **M3** **D1**

Product testing

This is carried out once a product has passed through the research stage and is nearly ready to be launched. It helps to iron out any last-minute hitches that the designers may not have covered. Testers may be experts, such as professional players giving feedback on a new boot or trainer, or they could be members of the public, at whom the product will eventually be aimed. Testing is usually done in secret to avoid any adverse publicity. Many sports products also have to go through stringent safety testing to ensure they are fit for purpose and safe to use.

Secondary research

Some examples of secondary research sources for sports businesses include the following.

- Commercial reports on sectors of the sports industry collected and analysed by Mintel, The Henley Centre or the Sport Industry Research Centre – might cover sales of gym memberships, spending habits for sport, or buying trends e.g. for outdoor clothing.
- General statistics freely available on various websites, such as the General Household Survey from the Office of National Statistics (www.statistics.gov.uk) or the Active People Survey from Sport England (www.sportengland.org) – cover aspects such as participation habits, spectator numbers and types of sport.
- Internal data that a business already owns can also be a secondary source – such as customer details taken during visits or transactions.
- Professional magazines such as *Sports Management* (ww.sportsmanagement.co.uk), and organisations such as the Institute for Sport, Parks and Leisure (ISPAL, www.ispal.org.uk) and the Institute of Sport and Recreation Management (ISRM, www.isrm.co.uk), also publish articles and carry out their own research, as do the sports governing bodies (see page 14).

All research has to be weighed up in terms of how it will benefit the organisation, what it will cost to create reliable data, the currency and validity of the information, plus its overall or specific usefulness.

Think it over

Working with a partner, think of five sports products you would consider dangerous, that need to go through these types of safety checks. What do you think companies have to do if their new product fails to be popular with customers who are testing it?

Theory into practice

Using the above sources, select a sports business and identify some secondary research you think is appropriate for them. After you have identified data that would be useful to the business, record your results. Say what you would analyse among the types of data, and what trends and information or recommendations you might make.

Marketing plan

Once all the data and information gathered have been analysed and conclusions drawn – sometimes this is called the marketing mix – a marketing plan is put together to guide the business's overall direction. Here we investigate some key elements of the marketing plan.

Product

The product for a sports business or customer means a tangible object or goods, such as clothing or a new racket. It is important for sports businesses to try and make their products distinctive from other similar ones, and equally to make sure the product satisfies customers' needs. Goods need to be fit for purpose, and also have some unique selling points and benefits that will help them sell well. Some examples of products with these attributes could be lightweight tennis rackets, unsinkable polypropylene canoes, or durable roller hockey boots.

Activity

What features could you add to help the following products sell better? – Trainers, replica kit, snooker cues, netballs.

Service

A sports service is different from a product – it is intangible, something that is bought and given to you, but there is no real object to take home – often it could be just memories of a great time, such as paying to watch an exciting match. The ingredients of good service are just as important as the quality of a product, for often the level of customer service helps to determine the quality of the experience. Friendly, helpful staff may be needed to complete the process, and this can even give a sports business its competitive edge.

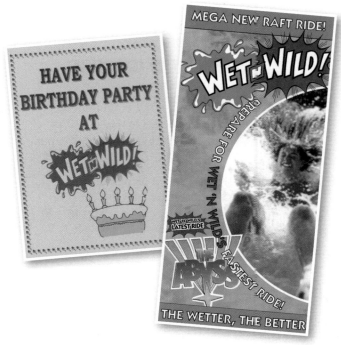

▲ Service provision is as important as tangible products to many sports businesses

Think it over

Who do you know of locally who always gives good service, making your experience satisfying? What in particular makes their service good?

Branding

Sports businesses strive to make their products and services household names – in other words, the best brand, with an image everyone recognises right away. You might say this is true of Nike or Virgin, or even Manchester United. A top brand will have high level of awareness among customers, a high market share of all similar products or services sold, and many loyal customers. The strength of a sports brand is demonstrated when the business is able to diversify, using the brand name, as Sir Richard Branson does with his many Virgin products and services.

Some Premiership football teams are such strong brand names that they have been taken over by American sports business tycoons, who see good profits to be made from global fan bases (See Table 24.5).

▼ Table 24.5 Premiership clubs buy-in. Source: *Sunday Telegraph*, 29 April 2007, page 21. 'Stripped for Action' by Simon Hart and Mark Choueke.

Club	Buyer	Amount
Manchester United	Malcolm Glazer	£790m
Arsenal	Stan Kroenke	Undisclosed amount
Aston Villa	Randy Lerner	£62.6m
Liverpool	George Gillett	£470m

Other targets are rumoured to be Tottenham Hotspur, Manchester City and Newcastle United. The massive sums from TV rights are said to be at the heart of these deals.

Life cycle

Sports products and services are said to have a life cycle, just like any other product. They go through four stages, as seen in the diagram – launch, growth, maturity and decline. Some will be reinvented and begin the cycle again. At each stage, sports businesses have to undertake marketing activities to support and grow sales until the brand is fully recognised and selling well.

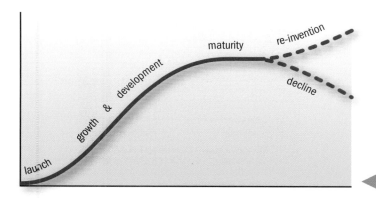

◀ The product life cycle

- Launch activities – building brand awareness (big impact/wide release tactics, such as events and TV advertising).
- Growth stage – continuing awareness, but also building loyalty.
- Maturity – working to create repeat business and further loyalty.
- Decline – adding extras to keep sales going.
- Re-invention – completely new styling and features.

Activity

Go through the product life cycle for a sports injury and physiotherapy clinic, saying what you would do at each stage.

Price

Profit targets and costs will help determine the final price for sports product or service. But the price must appear to customers to give value for money (this will have come out in market research, see page 299). For some sports businesses, such as bungee jumping or a sailing school, seasonality and weather may affect demand. Other factors might be the brand's image, and its stage in the product life cycle. Sports business where customers are on the premises for while – say a waterpark and flume ride – may be able to make enough extra income from other services (such as food and drinks) to enable them to keep entry fees low. Doncaster Dome and York Racecourse are good examples of this.

Companies have a pricing policy as part of their marketing plan. This involves planning their pricing strategy:

- trying to penetrate the market to gain a big share with a new product, by keeping prices low
- skimming the market with high prices, relying on quality and status to attract buyers (e.g. Rolex sports watches)

HEALTH & FITNESS
The Dome at Doncaster Lakeside
FITNESS VILLAGE CLASSES

Fitness Village Cycling
An intense indoor cycling class open to all levels of fitness.

Monday	6 pm – 6.45 pm & 7 pm – 7.45 pm
Tuesday	7.15 am– 7.45 am & 6 pm – 6.45 pm
Wednesday	10 am – 10.45 am, 6 pm – 6.45 pm & 7 pm – 7.45 pm
Thursday	6 pm – 6.45 pm
Friday	10 am – 10.45 am

£3.50

Healthy Heart Class
Make yours a healthy heart.

Tuesday	3 pm – 4 pm
Friday	11 am – 12 pm

£2.60 (under-50s) £3.50 (over-50s)

Teen Challenge
Supervised exercise for 13–16 year olds.

Term Time		School Holidays	
Monday–Friday	5 pm – 6 pm	Tuesday	11 am – 12 pm
Saturday	1 pm – 2 pm	Saturday	11 am – 12 pm
		Saturday	1 pm – 2 pm

£1.50

LIFESTYLE PACKAGES
Train more than twice a week? If so then the Fitness Village lifestyle packages are for you!

▲ Customer-focused services at the Doncaster Dome

- 'cost-plus pricing', used by retail chains, adding typically 60–100 per cent mark-ups based on production and delivery costs
- competitive pricing – pitching in at a level just under competitors to appear better value for money
- variable and discount pricing (more complex), adjusted to suit variables such as seasons, groups, level of service, age, times.

Activity

Devise a pricing strategy for a sports centre (with wet and dry facilities, shop and canteen), taking account of the strategies listed here.

Place

This element of the marketing plan is important for sports businesses – the method and location through which products and services are distributed (sometimes called the chain of distribution). For some sports businesses location is crucial (e.g. a high street retailer); for others it is not so important (e.g. a sports catalogue business operating over the internet). For some, the point of sale is not where the actual sport is done (e.g. a sports tourist buying a package to go diving in the Seychelles through a travel agent). Manufacturers of gym equipment sell to retailers, who have it delivered to various locations countrywide, so there is a key need to plan location and distribution carefully.

Promotion

This is a vital component of any sports business marketing plan – it is an exercise in communications, for it must convince the customer to buy. The acronym AIDA can be used to describe the stages:

- Awareness of the brand
- Interest in its benefits
- Desire to find out more
- Action – buying it.

▲ Good advertising is invaluable

Promotional activities need to be targeted at the right groups, in the right way, at the right time. Organisations can undertake a number of activities to help them promote their goods or services.

■ Advertising

This may take the form of TV and newspaper advertisements (which can be expensive), leaflets, vouchers or posters.

■ Direct marketing

This approach is more personal and is directed through the mail, by telephone, by email/internet, or posted to the home.

■ Public relations (PR)

This means creating good relations with the target groups by giving out information about the products or services, such as press releases, media sound bites, promotional events, demonstrations or interviews.

■ Sales promotions

These may be similar to PR activities, but are staged at trade shows or at actual venues, with limited discount offers, special offers, free gifts and incentives (e.g. a free hat when you buy a tracksuit). Competitions are common, such as raffles, scratchcards and phone-ins.

■ Guerilla marketing

The use of guerilla marketing has been the trend of the past decade. This involves unconventional ways of promoting goods and services – often subtle and relatively low-cost – which often appeal to smaller companies. Examples include undercover marketing (also known as stealth marketing or buzz marketing, e.g. a marketing company might pay to use a product visibly and convincingly in locations where target consumers congregate), and other high-tech and novel approaches (e.g. use of internet chatrooms and forums). It is based on understanding the psychology of potential buyers.

Theory into practice

Can you identify two such promotions that are ongoing at the moment?

■ Sponsorship activities

Many sports businesses are approached by clubs to sponsor a tournament, league or just a match. This gives the business a good image locally. Some will give not money, but sponsorship in kind, such as goods which could then be used as raffle prizes at a club night. But sponsors only want to be associated with success – so any poor performances or bad behaviour reported in the press may mean they will withdraw. The underlying aims of sponsorship are to sell more products, get good publicity for a company, and raise product awareness

Targeting customers

We have learned of the need to identify target groups and to target materials at them through relevant communication. Timing is also an important part of reaching the right customers – advertisements need to be placed in the right newspapers or magazines, or at the right times on radio and TV. Sports businesses need to position themselves in the mind of the target market as the one to choose – this creates a match between product/services and customer. Those people able to afford better sports kit, such as professional players, will buy the top brands, so marketing activities need to be delivered to them in the right dimensions (e.g. quality and superiority). Normal recreational players will buy more affordable brands, so marketing to them may focus on value for money and range of choice – targeted marketing to target customers.

Product/service process

The process of selling is a key part of the marketing mix. Staff play a large part by being polite, helpful, smart – and smiling. Good service is what we remember; bad service is what we tell our friends about. The buying process must be a pleasant experience for the customer, so staff need to be consistent in their sales techniques, regardless of the customer's age, cultural background, attitude, language or disability. The process must extend past sales to after-sales service, for example when goods are returned or repairs need to be done – this is what reinforces loyalty, recommendations and repeat business.

Assessment practice

Imagine you have recently been appointed marketing assistant for a newly established small sports business. You have been asked to contribute to the marketing strategy for the new business, which will be selling short sports breaks on the coast of the UK.

1　Identify what research needs to be undertaken and the likely sources you will use (e.g. primary and secondary) **P3**

2　How this will be done, with an indication of time scale (marketing research activities) **P6 M4**

3　Specify how you will present the data (e.g. styles and statistics, electronic or paper). **P6 M4**

4　Produce a marketing plan summarising products and services, brand name suggestions, likely life cycle (and recommendations at each stage). Remember the four Ps – price, place, promotion, product – and the importance of knowing your target markets. **P6 M4 D2**

Grading tips

Grading Tip P5 P6

The plan needs to include reasons for the research and the methods used, and you must show which product or service it relates to in the business. The research must be carried out by you, with proper records being kept.

Grading Tip M4

You must try to do most of the planning and work yourself, and give good reasons for doing it, as well as showing clear records of data collected or analysed.

Grading Tip D4

Complete all of the above, but with an analytical approach and recommendations.

24.4 Understand the legal and financial influences on sports businesses

Records show that a large percentage of companies go out of business in their first few years, mostly because they do not plan well, either financially or for the cost of trading within the law. SMEs (companies with fewer than 250 employees) are a vital area of the sports industry, perhaps representing as much as 50 per cent of sports companies. But many don't last – the DTI and Barclays estimate that as many as 65 per cent go under inside three years. In this section we investigate some of the main legal and financial aspects that cause these problems. The important thing here is not for you to know the detail of the legislation, but to understand and be aware of why the laws and regulations are there, and their main aims.

Legal influences

A number of Acts of Parliament are in place (and some have been in existence a long time) that govern how companies must be set up and run, mainly to ensure their legality and that they trade and report in an open and fair manner. Working within the law has its benefits – for sports businesses it should be seen not as a costly process, but more as a necessity. These benefits include:

- making an organisation safe for staff and customers
- ensuring that all business transactions and sales are properly conducted
- avoiding fines for bad practices

- enhancing the business's reputation
- ensuring that any accidents are properly covered and dealt with.

Companies Act (1989)

Under this Act, large companies (PLCs and those limited by guarantee) are required to register themselves and their names, and put in place procedures and systems to comply with aspects of business including the following:

- accounting records for each year, which are checked by auditors
- a director's report.

Failure to do so, or providing misleading information in these accounts, can mean an offence is committed. The Act also defines, among other things, what is permitted in terms of methods of trading, how companies must act with regard to share dealing, and how they might be inspected for wrongdoing.

The accounts and other records for larger organisations are published and lodged with Companies House in Cardiff. In 2006 an addition was made to the Companies Act, which you can read more of on the website of the Department for Business, Enterprise and Regulatory Reform (www.berr.gov.uk).

Small and medium-sized companies (which make up the bulk of the sports industry), such as Freetown Sports in Hull or OY Bikes in London, have to follow the same principles of trading but may not need to create the same type of accounts and records – they can qualify for an exception (see box).

It makes good sense to keep accurate accounts anyway, so most SMEs comply just as good business practice. Some may have to satisfy sources they have borrowed from, or the tax office.

The qualifying conditions [for an exception] are met by a company in a year in which it satisfies two or more of the following requirements:

	Small company	Medium-sized company
1 Turnover	Not more than £2 million	Not more than £8 million
2 Balance sheet total	Not more than £975,000	Not more than £3.9 million
3 Number of employees	Not more than 50	Not more than 250.

Source: www.opsi.gov.uk

SMEs can benefit from their small size and flexibility

Theory into practice

You can read more detail on the Act at www.dti.gov.uk/files/file37956.pdf. Why do you think this type of legislation is needed?

Partnership Act 1890

This Act helps to regulate and guide how partnerships must work – definitions, responsibilities of partners, liabilities, change of partners, dissolution and rights. The box gives a useful summary.

Theory into practice

You can read more on the Partnership Act at
www.hmrc.gov.uk. What could go wrong with
partnership agreements?

Partnerships can be two or more people (up to
a maximum of 20) who combine their resources
to make up a [sports] business.

They will each receive a share of the profits,
usually related in size to the amount of capital
they have invested by working on behalf of the
business. Individual members of the partnership
are responsible for any of the other partners'
debts, the partnership property. To pay debts, the
personal property of each partner can be sold off
to pay the firm's creditors.

The advantages of operating as a partnership
are:

- opportunities for sharing responsibilities in
management

- business capital sources increased

- possibility of obtaining credit.

However, partners must have confidence and
trust in their co-partners, and must make a full
and open disclosure of any matters affecting the
partnership.

Before starting in business, drawing up a legal
agreement is advisable to avoid disputes or
problems that may occur, such as differences
of opinion, death, incapacity or succession,
otherwise the Partnership Act of 1890 would be
used to resolve any tricky situations.

Source: www.businessbureau-uk.co.uk

Fair Trading Act (1973)

The Fair Trading Act 1973, among other matters,
governed merger control and inquiries into scale and
complex monopoly situations. It has now been repealed
in its entirety. Most of the Fair Trading Act 1973 was
replaced by the Enterprise Act 2002. The Competition
Act 1998 also reduced the scope of the Fair Trading Act
by establishing a system of competition law to promote
fair trading and prevent abusive practices, especially
among the larger sports businesses which can have a
dominating effect in some markets.

Theory into practice

The Competition Commission's website includes
electronic versions of the reports produced by itself
and its predecessor bodies under the Enterprise Act
2002. You can learn more of this new act at:
www.competition-commission.org.uk/rep_pub/
reports/index.htm. What are the dangers for SMEs
when large corporations dominate a sector of the
sports market?

Food and Drugs Act (1982)

The serving of food at sports events or in buildings needs
to be licensed, and premises must be inspected to protect
public health. Local authorities have the power under this
Act to carry out inspections and also to search for drugs
at sports venues or within businesses.

Health and Safety at Work Act (1974)

This is an important Act (often referred to as HASAWA)
aiming to ensure safe working practices for any
organisation. Under this Act, all companies must have a
safety policy and staff trained to ensure safety. This Act
was brought into line with other EU safety acts in 1992,
which meant that all organisations had to carry out risk
assessments. This helps them to identify hazards for all
sorts of people on their premises, and ensures they have
adequate safety measures in place to prevent or at least
minimise the chance of these hazards causing accidents
or injury. The enforcing body is the Health and Safety
Executive, which has powers to fine or close businesses

not complying with the Act, or to imprison staff and directors if they are found to be negligent. This would apply to sports businesses such as shops, stadiums, pools, clubs and gyms.

Theory into practice

You can learn more of the details of the at HASAWA www.hse.gov.uk/legislation/hswa.htm. List three possible hazards that could be found at (a) a golf driving range; (b) a go-karting venue.

Statutory requirements

Businesses must comply with regulations described as statutory requirements – they are the law, and there are no exceptions. There are now many European laws and regulations with which businesses must comply, such as the Regulations on Personal Protective Equipment and Manual Handling Operations, both of which might apply to sports businesses. There are also some other important UK statutory requirements that apply to sports businesses, such as Occupiers Liability, Working Time Regulations and Control of Substances Hazardous to Health (COSHH). Some requirements are specifically aimed at sports organisations, such as the Fire Safety and Safety of Places of Sport Act 1987, the Safety at Sports Grounds Act 1975, and the Adventure Activities Licensing Regulations 1996. There are also a number of newer types of legislation – including the Disability Discrimination Act 1995, the Data Protection Act 1998, and some consumer protection acts too. From these examples, you can see the breadth and range of regulations with which sports businesses must comply. Beneath these regulations are a range of recommended codes of practice to follow, for instance pertaining to recreation on land and water. Add to this many local byelaws that might affect sports providers (e.g. hygiene, access to land) – and we begin to see a very complex picture.

Taking it further

Working in groups, carry out some research to uncover the main issues for sports businesses relating to one of the statutory requirements. Prepare a short presentation for your class on the piece of legislation you have investigated. Show its purpose, applications and influence on a sports business.

Health and safety

It should be apparent by now that this is of paramount importance to sports businesses – it is a legal requirement, and applies to all aspects of a business. Staff must be aware of health and safety at all times – ignorance is no excuse, nor is doing nothing about a hazard. In many modern sports businesses security is also an issue – it is important to keep both customers and their possessions safe.

Failure to do so can lead to consequences (particularly now that we live in such as litigious society) such as:

- injury or death
- court cases leading to fines, being sued or imprisoned
- bad publicity
- poor reputation for potential employment
- high insurance premiums.

Employment laws

These cover situations of recruitment, working conditions, sacking and redundancy in any business. They are meant to ensure fairness and equality and prevent discrimination on the grounds of age, gender, religion, ethnicity or exploitation. Some examples also cover discipline and grievances that may occur. Employment laws help both employees and employers, as they establish the best way to act in many circumstances.

Theory into practice

Working with a partner, search for an employment law to cover the following situations:

1   Not getting a job (when ideally suited) due to being from Jamaica.
2   Not getting promoted due to being disabled.
3   Being made redundant for being too old.
4   Being sacked on the spot for swearing.
5   Not being shortlisted for new post due to pregnancy.
6   Getting caught smoking in public building.

Decide whether these cases are legal or not.

Licensing

Organisations often have to be licensed to carry out their activities, and sports businesses are no different. Typical examples include:

- a sports bar
- a casino
- an outdoor activity centre
- a stadium
- a racing circuit
- trading
- boat operators.

Activity

Using the list above, can you say which type of licence is needed for each?

Licences may be granted by magistrates, police, local authorities or specialist inspectors. Sports businesses must ensure they apply for licences in plenty of time, and that their business complies with all the requirements needed to be granted a licence.

Insurance

This is another compulsory requirement for sports businesses – it is foolish not to be insured. Premiums may seem high, but being sued for negligence could be a much higher price to pay. Insurance gives everyone peace of mind.

Examples of insurance policies that are useful to businesses include:

- when providing advice or services as a professional
- 'all-risks' cover for office contents and computers, including portable equipment
- cover for accidents to the public while on your premises
- product liability, in case products are faulty or break
- employers' liability
- business interruption (e.g. not being able to use premises)
- buildings and grounds
- legal expenses.

▲ A flash fire at the Valley Parade football stadium in Bradford in 1985 probably started when a spectator dropped a cigarette or match under the seats of the main stand, where rubbish had accumulated – 56 people died and over 200 were injured

Planning permission

Planning permission is required when you alter a building in any way, or erect a fence or hoarding, for example. The local authority planning office can help guide you, for example with plans for an extension to a gym, with coverings for pools, or a change to a shop front. This is a formal process and can take months to complete, so needs to be done before any actual work begins. The planning office will usually require you to submit accurate drawings to show what the business is planning.

Local byelaws

These are formulated to suit local conditions that might not occur elsewhere, such as those for beach or sports events, or access to and use of a park for sports. They are set by the local authority and reviewed from time to time. A sports business undertaking an event, but unfamiliar with the locality, would need to check with the council what will be required to comply with the byelaws. These are not statutory laws – just small, customised laws to suit a specific area. But failure to comply could mean an event being cancelled or fines being levied.

Theory into practice

In your local area, are there any local byelaws that apply to anyone running a sports event? (For example, consult the police, fire and council departments).

Financial influences

Here we focus on how finance influences decision-making in sports businesses.

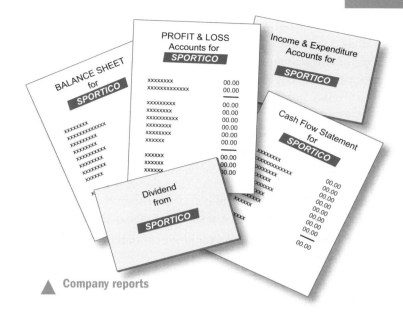

▲ Company reports

Profit

Sports businessmen and women must ask themselves profit-related questions from the outset:

- How much do I hope to make?
- How much will I plough back into the business?
- How much profit will I give to shareholders (as dividends)?
- What will my next target be?
- What will I do if I don't make my profit target?

Based on the profit a company makes, the tax office will want a proportion too. Whatever is left over after all these moneys have been allocated is termed reserves – profit kept back for development expansion or to pay future bills. Profit decisions are at the heart of business decisions.

Loss

Making a loss is a sports business's worst nightmare, for it has a negative impact on everything the company has planned. Loss-making sports enterprises have very few options:

- borrow more to cover debts
- cut costs by making staff redundant or using fewer resources
- close some outlets
- go out of business.

A business is said to be bankrupt when it cannot cover all its debts, and is not allowed to trade. This can have major consequences for individuals who are directors, for they may not be able to set up in business again. The insolvency helpline (www.insolvencyhelpline.co.uk/bankruptcy) lists the implications of bankruptcy. As noted on page 292, cash flow is vital for any business. At any one time, you need to have up-to-date records of how much you owe and to whom (these are your creditors, who may need paying quickly). To balance this, you also need to have a clear note of debtors (people who owe you money), so that you can see where the cash will flow into your business. If you cannot find cash quickly, this leaves you with low liquidity (inability to pay bills or buy new raw materials or goods to sell on). Forecasts are used to see what you need to flow in to cover these costs and other type of cost, what you will need to balance your books and provide a profit for your business.

Gross profit is the amount a business makes before taxes are deducted, while net profit is the amount left after these are all paid (which can be a lot less). Banks (who you may have borrowed from) look closely at gross profit and to see if margins (the amount you add to make profit) are being maintained or increased in line with any business plans and forecasts. You can read more on profit margins at www.biz-ed.co.uk

Shares

Shareholding affects decision-making at two stages: when setting up a company, and when deciding what dividends to pay.

Dividends are small amounts paid back to investors (shareholders) once or twice a year out of profits – it is their return for investing (buying shares) in a company. Amounts depend on how many shares are held. Companies that are not trading well, and making no or low profits, will not usually pay any dividends – this represents the risk that investors take. It is important forecasts for everything as accurately as possible, as this allows you to map out the expected path for the business – as soon as the figures don't comply with that path, you get a signal to take alternative action to correct. It's a bit like steering a ship along a course against the wind and tide – avoiding hitting other ships, running aground or springing a leak.

In order to have the benefits of limited liability and to help with raising capital, some sole traders or partnerships restructure themselves legally into a registered business (company) and issue shares. Limits are set as to how many shares and how these might be transferred, but access to new capital is very much easier.

Shares can be offered for sale and a number issued to gain the finance required. Shareholders are usually entitled to vote on company decisions.

Theory into practice

With a partner, research what the following types of shareholding are –

- ordinary   • deferred   • preference.

How might these different types be important to a new sports business?

Costs

To start up and run a business, an accurate knowledge of costs is crucial. This knowledge will feature in the feasibility stage of setting up and shaping the business as details are worked out for the company's business plan. Managers and owners need to calculate costs for many aspects, including:

- rent of premises
- cost of utilities
- equipment
- raw materials
- insurance
- wages.

Activity

Add six more costs to the list above, and say why they are important to running a company. Can you also say which costs are fixed (at the same rate most of the time), and which can be variable (change from time to time)? Businesses have to calculate these, usually on a monthly basis – how would you do this?

A regular check must be made to ensure costs are kept under control and resources are used effectively. Sports businesses need to have systems of reporting and recording in place to monitor costs. All costs have to be covered by the business's income, otherwise it will not be able to stay afloat.

Expenses

These are also costs in a sense, but are expenses incurred by staff (such as salespeople or directors) while trying to create new sales or business. Typically, they might be for travel, accommodation and maybe hospitality as potential new clients are entertained. Quite a lot of deals are struck over dinner, during a round of golf, or in a director's box at a football match, so expenses are allowed to cover this style of trading.

Interest

This is the amount that a business has to pay back in addition to any capital amounts of money it has borrowed. For example, if a sports business borrows £5000 from a bank to improve its premises, they will agree how much needs to be paid back each month plus a certain amount of interest (extra) on top (e.g. five per cent – this is called the price of borrowing or the interest rate). This is the way banks make their profit. Sports businesses must be careful not to borrow more than they can pay back, or they will get into difficulties.

Activity

Calculate what the monthly payments on borrowing £5000 would be over a period of five years with a rate of five per cent.

Dividends

Dividends are the amounts of money paid back to shareholders once or twice a year from a business's profits. This is calculated on the basis of the number of shares people hold. Usually, the more profitable a company is, the higher its dividend rate, and the more attractive its shares will be to buyers. Low or no profits can mean shareholders will sell their shares and the image of the company can go down with the share prices, which is not good for trading.

Theory into practice

Try and identify what some of the larger sports companies paid in dividends last year. You can look up their dividend rates in good quality newspapers or online, or in their published company accounts.

Credit

Credit is an allowance that suppliers make to buyers who owe them money. You are no doubt familiar with credit cards, which allow a period of time before they need paying off. When business transactions are made, money is owed. To collect this money, an invoice is sent out and usually the buyer has 30 days to pay the amount – this is how credit works. Failure to pay inside the designated time usually means that interest is added to the amount, which means the bill grows. So it is good business practice to pay on time.

Think it over

For watersports business, make a list of the fixed costs and variable costs that might have to be paid each month.

Rent

Rent is the amount a business has to pay, usually for premises. Some sports businesses (such as some sports shops) will lease their premises, which means they do not have to find large capital costs to buy or build premises, only the monthly rent. This keeps running costs down.

Mortgage

A mortgage is an amount of money borrowed to buy a building. Banks and building societies lend for this purpose. The capital and interest are usually paid back over a very long time, say 20 years, to help keep monthly payments low. This is a long-term arrangement, and reflects how most people buy their homes. A sports club might use this method to build and buy its changing rooms or club house. But failure to meet payments can mean the building is taken back by the lender.

Assessment practice

Imagine you work for a sports consultancy business, and as your first assignment you have to give two talks to two small sports businesses. They are just starting out and know very little about the financial and legal aspects of staring a new business.
Prepare two talks:

1 to cover a selection of three legal dimensions you feel they must know about

2 to cover three important financial concepts they are unsure about.

You may use slides, but should also produce a handout to leave with them for reference. **P7** **M5**

Knowledge check

1 Can you distinguish between a public, private and voluntary sports organisation – which is a business?

2 Explain what a franchise is.

3 What is a duty manager responsible for?

4 Describe two factors you feel are important to make a sports business successful.

5 Explain the difference between primary and secondary market research.

6 Give two examples each of primary and secondary market research that a sports business might carry out.

7 What is the sports product life cycle?

8 Name four Ps that should happen as part of the marketing mix or plan.

9 List three reasons why employment laws are needed.

10 Explain either credit terms or dividend payments.

Grading tips

Grading Tip P7

Make sure you have up-to-date information on any laws (Acts), as they do change.

Grading Tip M5

Your explanations need to be accurate and clear for non-specialists.

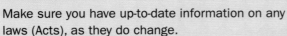

Preparation for assessment

Imagine you are a trainee sports business development consultant who advises small businesses on their strategies and planning. You have been asked to give a talk to your fellow trainees.

1 Describe and compare two different sports businesses, showing how they are organised. **P1** **M1**

2 Identify and explain what can make a sports business successful. **P2** **M2**

3 Present an example of some recent market research you undertook for a selected sports business, giving conclusions and recommendations. **P3** **P4** **M3** **D1**

4 Describe marketing activities appropriate to a sports business and show how you plan them. Prepare a sample marketing plan for circulation to your audience. **P5** **P6** **M4** **D2**

5 Explain the importance for sports businesses of three Acts of Parliament. **P7** **M5**

6 Identify why you think financial influences are key to business decisions, giving at least three examples. **P7** **M5**

Grading tips

Grading Tip **M1** **M2** **M3** **M4** **M5**

An explanation will need to use examples to help show understanding.

Grading Tip **D1** **D2**

An analysis or evaluation should do the same, but should also show a deeper understanding and make comparisons or recommendations of other approaches.

To achieve a pass grade the evidence must show that the learner is able to:	To achieve a merit grade the evidence must show that, in addition to the pass criteria, the learner is able to:	To achieve a distinction grade the evidence must show that, in addition to the pass and merit criteria, the learner is able to:
P1 describe the organisation of two different types of sports business **Assessment practice page 300**	**M1** compare and contrast the organisation of two different types of sports business **Assessment practice page 300**	
P2 describe what makes a successful sports business **Assessment practice page 308**	**M2** explain what makes a successful sports business **Assessment practice page 308**	
P3 plan market research related to, and appropriate for, a selected sports business **Assessment practice page 315**		
P4 conduct market research related to, and appropriate for, a selected sports business, with support, recording results **Assessment practice page 315**	**M3** conduct market research related to, and appropriate for, a selected sports business, recording results **Assessment practice page 315**	**D1** analyse the results of the market research, drawing valid conclusions **Assessment practice page 315**
P5 describe the marketing activities of a selected sports business **Assessment practice page 308**		
P6 produce a marketing plan for a selected sports product or service **Assessment practice page 320**	**M4** justify a marketing plan for a selected sports product or service **Assessment practice page 320**	**D2** evaluate the marketing plan identifying areas for improvement **Assessment practice page 320**
P7 describe three legal and three financial influences on sports businesses **Assessment practice page 328**	**M5** explain three legal and three financial influences on businesses in sport **Assessment practice page 328**	

Work-based experience in sport

Introduction

Sport is a growth industry, with many diverse opportunities. This unit is based on the opportunity for you to experience what it will be like to work in the sports industry and to confirm whether or not this is the industry for you.

This is an internally assessed unit. It is an opportunity for you to really experience what it is like to work in the industry. Most people do a BTEC National because they are interested in sport – but the reality of working in the sports industry can be very different. Experiencing a flavour of what particular jobs are like will give you the chance to reflect, and the opportunity to add them to your list of jobs that you are definitely interested in – or to strike them off that list.

The fundamental aim of the unit is to find your first work experience placement – this is your responsibility. An essential part of the unit is to make contact yourself with prospective placements and explore the opportunities available to you.

After completing this unit you should be able to achieve the following outcomes:

- Know about the opportunities for work-based experience in sport.
- Be able to prepare for a work-based experience in sport.
- Be able to undertake a work-based experience in sport.
- Be able to evaluate a work-based experience in sport.

Think it over

Work experience might provide you with the opportunity to get a part time job and a foot in the door of the industry, but the staff may be sceptical of your motivation and your input:

- for the management – you are another work experience student who will need looking after and training

- for the staff – you are a work experience student who will only be there for a few days.

You need to make an impression and stand out from the other work experience students. You need to excel.

- What do you think your ideal job in the industry is? Imagine yourself in that situation.

- It is your first day on work experience. What will you wear? What time will you arrive? Who will you report to? What will you take with you?

- While you are there, you want to create the right impression – how do you do this?

There are many different jobs you can do in the sports industry – it is a growth industry and the opportunities for employment are many and exciting.

The BTEC National Diploma in Sport is a vocational qualification, so work experience is a vital part of your course.

Activity

1. Think about what career or jobs you want to do in the sports industry.
2. Make a list.
3. Where can you do these locally?
4. Make a list.
5. Surf the net or go to the Yellow Pages and make a list of the name, number, address and contact at each placement you are interested in.
6. Draw up search table like the one below.

▼ **Table 25.1 Work experience search**

Organisation	Address	Telephone number	Contact name

Opportunities

Something that is common to most jobs in the sports industry is that they tend to involve irregular hours. Most people have their leisure time from 5 pm in the evening and at weekends, so these are the times when you are most likely to be required to work. If these hours and the idea of shift patterns do not appeal, you must think very carefully about whether or not you are selecting the right industry for your future employment.

There are many different sport sectors to explore. Here are some examples.

Health and fitness sector

The health and fitness sector is a particular growth area, as people's disposable income increases and their awareness grows of health, fitness and how they relate to the quality and length of life. As working hours in general reduce, and we have more leisure time, we should be fitter, but with the more sedentary nature of our work and the increase in car usage people are finding it more difficult to stay fit, and have to find ways to be active and maintain fitness. The mass media have influenced the way we eat and the exercise we do, and introduced us to a range of complementary and alternative therapies. There are now entire television channels devoted to our pursuit of the 'body beautiful', that we can watch from the comfort of our armchair – a contradiction in itself! Many of the general population now commonly own a gym/fitness membership, even if they don't always use it. Members will be tied into a contract for a year, with the gym taking the money by direct debit from the new member's account. New members often attend enthusiastically at the beginning of their membership but then drift off, making each attendance very expensive. There are many small women-only gyms offering a limited and more exclusive service, including sunbeds and vanity services, and opportunities for work in this area are increasing.

A personal trainer was once the exclusive privilege of high-ranking sportspeople or the very rich – now it is common for ordinary men and women to hire the services of a personal trainer at £25 or more per hour in a bid to find and maintain that hard-won, elusive goal of fitness.

▼ Table 25.2 A selection of jobs in the health and fitness sector

Job	Outline of role	Examples of qualifications	Clients
Sports masseur	Gives massages to sportspeople: • pre-performance massage to stimulate muscles and nervous system in conjunction with a warm-up, within one hour of performing • post-performance massage to reduce fatigue, dispose of waste products and toxins, and prevent minor injuries, within two hours of performing • injury rehabilitation to help relieve deeper injuries and prevent unidentified ones, 48 hours or more after performance	Diploma in Sports Massage	Many professional clubs have their own masseur; all sportsmen and sportswomen
Gym instructor	Most fitness suites have a gym instructor to give help, encouragement and advice to clients about their work-out, nutrition, equipment and progression on their personal exercise plan	CYQ* Level 2 Gym Instructor	People from all sections of society who use the gym
Personal trainer	Normally works one-to-one with a client, devising a personal exercise plan to suit their individual needs, and encouraging and motivating them through their personal work-out and exercise plan. They will often have a session with their client more than once a week	Premier Training† or CYQ Level 3 Personal Trainer	A range of clients, from very unfit and obese to marathon runners
Sports therapist	Works with individuals, helping to rehabilitate them following injury and to develop the best techniques to minimise injury. May work freelance from a sports centre, from home or from a club	Sports therapy degree	A wide range of sportspeople
GP referral scheme worker	The GP referral scheme was set up for GPs to refer clients who need to exercise to improve their fitness levels, such as those recovering from heart problems. The GP will write a prescription for 10 sessions at a local sports centre operating the scheme	Sports science degree; Exercise Instructor training from the British Association of Cardiac Rehabilitation‡	Those prescribed exercise by their GP

*CYQ = Central YMCA health and fitness qualifications (www.cyq.org.uk).
†Premier Training International is widely accepted as the market leader in health and fitness training in the UK (www.premierglobal.co.uk).
‡www.bacrphaseiv.co.uk

Case study

Sports masseur

Name: Emma Blake
Age: 25

What I do:

I am a masseur at a professional football club. My job involves treating players pre- and post-performance and training, as well as during stages of injury. I enjoy being part of a team that aims to rehabilitate those who are not at their baseline fitness levels. An aspect of this work is that you can see the benefits of what you are doing, and this offers lots of fulfilment.

What I enjoy:

Being able to observe athletes when they are in the first stages of injury right through to their return to fitness, partly as a result of the work that you have put in, is satisfying and rewarding. In addition, the nature of this work enables you to build close working relationships with the athletes, which makes work an enjoyable place to be.

1 **List three positive and three negative aspects of working as a sports masseur at a professional football club.**

Sport and recreation sector

▼ Table 25.3 A selection of jobs in the sport and recreation sector

Job	Outline of role	Examples of qualifications	Clients
Recreation assistant	May put out equipment, put away equipment, keep the centre clean, deal with customers, work on the poolside, deal with first aid, and keep the sports centre running smoothly. They must have a good awareness of health and safety	NVQ 2 Sport and Recreation; RLSS National Pool Lifeguard Award*; First Aid at Work†	All users of centres
Gym instructor/ fitness instructor	Most centres have a gym instructor to give help, encouragement and advice to clients about their work-out, nutrition, equipment and progression on their personal exercise plan	CYQ‡ Level 2 Gym Instructor	All users of centres
Lifeguard	Works shifts on poolside – supervise and keep users of the pool safe from accidents. Deal with accidents if they occur, tidy and clean poolside, and maintain their own lifeguard training records. Take pool tests for water clarity	NVQ 2 Sport and Recreation; RLSS National Pool Lifeguard Award; First Aid at Work	All users of centres
Leisure manager/ sports manager	Runs a sports, health or leisure centre on a day-to-day basis. Will open and close the building, deal with problems that arise, organise staffing, be responsible for cashing up; be responsible for the development and financial performance of the centre	Leisure Management Degree, HND, HNC, NVQ 3 Supervisors	All users of centres
Sports development officer	Responsible for the development of sport in a local area – encourage people who have not traditionally been involved in sport to participate (e.g. the elderly, people with mental health problems). May specialise in a particular sport (such as netball or lacrosse) and try to provide opportunities for people to participate	Degree: HND, HNC Relevant sports experience and teaching qualifications	All sections of society

Job	Outline of role	Examples of qualifications	Clients
PE teacher	Will have completed a university degree with qualified teacher status or a degree followed by a postgraduate certificate in education (PGCE) or in a school that offers the Graduate or Registered Training Programme. Has a range of knowledge and abilities in a wide variety of sports that they will be expected to teach in a secondary school (there are now also PE specialists in some junior schools, responsible for PE across the whole school)	BA, BEd, BSc, PGCE, Cert. Ed.	Children from 4½ to 19 years old
Further education and higher education lecturer	Specialises in sports lecturing at a variety of levels. Much of the teaching will be theoretical	Undergraduate degree such as BA or BSc, or postgraduate degree such as MA, or specialist knowledge from a specific industry. All lecturers would be required to complete their Certificate of Education (the teaching qualification)	Students aged 16+
Sports coach	Usually specialises in one sport, coaching it to a range of different age groups and at a range of different levels. e.g. Professional football teams will have a coach for their first team and another for the reserves, under-18s, etc.	Specialist coaching qualifications	Specific teams, group and individuals
Professional sport performer	Has a talent for a particular sport and will train, usually full-time, in that sport to achieve the highest standard possible. They will set their goal as reaching a particular event, such as the 2012 Olympics. This requires dedication and focus	Outstanding talent at a particular sport	Talented performers
Sports marketing/sports promoter	Represents a particular performer and organises their professional profile. Arrange deals with manufacturers to promote their product (e.g. David Beckham and Police sunglasses). May represent a team and arrange the team sponsorship deal; may represent an event to raise its profile (e.g. Rugby World Cup)	Marketing degree	Teams, individuals, events
Events manager	Organises sporting events (may be as large as the Olympics, Wimbledon or the FA cup; may be a smaller, more local event). Arrange the venue, hospitality, transport, staffing, promotion and advertising; coordinate everything necessary for the smooth running of the event	Sports business degree	Teams, organisers of events, sportspeople
Events worker	Assists the events manager and organises the basics of the event as directed	Sports business degree	Teams, organisers of events, sportspeople

*RLSS = Lifesavers – The Royal Life Saving Society UK (www.lifesavers.org.uk).

†First Aid at Work = Health & Safety Executive programme (www.hse.gov.uk/firstaid/index.htm)

‡CYQ = Central YMCA health and fitness qualifications (www.cyq.org.uk).

The sport and recreation sector is probably the largest, and the range and possibility for work are varied and extreme. There are many jobs based in and around leisure centres, ranging from management through to lifeguards and receptionists. Many public leisure centres are now managed by trusts, such as Greeenwich Leisure Ltd; as large organisations they are able to offer an increased range of employment such as sales and marketing, area management, events officers, training posts, sports development, outreach work in the community, and many more.

Working in education is traditionally the path many people take to working in sport – there are positions in secondary and further education, and as a new development since 2005, specialist junior school physical education teachers. This sector also includes the sports professionals, people who are paid to play their specialist sport; they may be paid from a club, sponsorship, grants, competition, or from a variety of different sources. Many sportspeople aspire to be professionals, but the dedication, financial support and self-sacrifice needed to reach such a high standard is often too difficult to attain.

Outdoor education sector

Outdoor education embraces those sports that are adventurous and often include an element of danger. There are outdoor education centres in locations all around the country, offering a range of activities to participants who might be novices or experts – they may be returning for an annual week to improve skills, or taking part in a team-building exercise to develop their ability to work together and take initiative in the workplace.

Outdoor education centres are now strictly regulated to try and prevent accidents in these high-risk activities. Participants are required to push themselves to new personal limits – this requires staff who are skilled in motivating, encouraging and controlling the safety of others. The staff will have a good level of performance in the outdoor activity.

Case study

Leisure manager

Name: Jack Noble-Evans
Age: 20

What I do:

I am responsible for opening up and locking up the centre, and for maintaining the health and safety of customers and staff. I organise staffing rosters and maintain the cashflow, ensuring the takings are banked and cashed up correctly. I take bookings, promote the centre, organise the session times, sort out the memberships, run the holiday courses, deal with customer complaints and comments, delegate duties to staff, answer the phone for enquiries, deal with emergencies and generally run the centre. The centre is attached to a school, so I have two groups of clients: school pupils and staff during the day, and members early mornings, evenings and weekends – it makes the job both more interesting and more difficult!

What I enjoy:

I enjoy working in an environment where people spend their leisure time. I like the fact that although I am only 20, I am in a management position and in charge of staff. I like working shifts, and go to the shops when it isn't busy. I like being in the position where I can make things happen and change things in the centre. I really enjoy my job!

1 **Make a list of six skills that you think someone in Jack's position would need.**

▼ Table 25.4 A selection of jobs in the outdoor education sector

Job	Outline of role	Examples of qualifications	Clients
Specialist sports instructor	Specialises in one sport (such as canoeing), and will teach it to a variety of audiences (children, people with disabilities, adults); teach on one-day, one-week or regular weekly courses	Specialist sports qualifications from governing body of specific sport (e.g. British Canoe Union level 3)	Variety of people from all walks of life
Mountain leader	Leads groups of climbers up a mountain – will have specialist qualifications and will be responsible for climbers' health and safety	BELA*	Variety of people from all walks of life
Manager	Has managerial responsibility for the staff and organisation of the outdoor centre; promote the services the centre offers, and organise day-to-day running of activities	BTEC National in Outdoor Education; outdoor education degree	Variety of people from all walks of life with an interest in outdoor activities
Sports ground maintenance	Has specialist knowledge of the physics of the ground and how to get the most from the pitches	Ground maintenance qualifications	Players, managers of teams, coaches
Sports ground manager	Ensures the planned maintenance of the ground, takes bookings, manages staff such as grounds staff, ensures pitches are ready for games in the best possible condition	Ground maintenance qualifications; management degree	Players, managers of teams, coaches

*BELA = Basic Expedition Leader Award, administered by the British Sports Trust (www.bst.org.uk).

Case study

Specialist sports instructor

Name: Joyce Smith
Age: 62

What I do:

I coach netball with school children of all ages – I go round to primary and secondary schools and give netball coaching to girls who want to learn to play and improve their netball skills. I coach in lesson time, in after-school clubs and lunchtime clubs. I umpire games in various leagues in the area, and help organise the games for the teams. I sit on two of the committees for the local leagues and I am fixture secretary for one of them.

What I enjoy:

I love watching the girls improve and go right through to become players for adult teams, and even represent the county team. I get a buzz when they come back week after week, year after year. I don't ever want to retire, I've done it all my life and can't imagine life any other way. I still play for a team now. It is great to give these girls the chance to play netball, I don't think there is enough compulsory PE in secondary schools any more.

1   **Write an account of what you might do as a specialist sports instructor. Which sport would you instruct in, what would you do, and what would you enjoy most?**

Sport and exercise science sector

This is the smallest of the sectors in the industry, and probably the most specialist, working with up-and-coming talented performers across the whole spectrum of sports. Many will specialise in a particular sport. They will have access to a laboratory and to equipment specific to a particular sport, and will work with performers to enhance and develop strength, speed, flexibility, power, nutrition, stamina and other such areas that will help to achieve differences in an athlete's ability, aiming to maximise their potential. The sports scientist will concentrate on individual areas of weakness to bring the athlete up to performance level. they will also take a holistic approach, aiming to develop them psychologically as well as physiologically.

▼ Table 25.5 A selection of jobs in the sport and exercise science sector

Job	Outline of role	Examples of qualifications	Clients
Exercise physiologist	May provide scientific support to sportspersons in a club or team setting. Works with cardiac rehabilitation patients and people with chronic diseases, setting them tests, interpreting results and providing expert advice	Sports science degree	Sportsperson, people with coronary heart disease, diabetes, coronary obstructive pulmonary disease, etc.
Bio-mechanist	Uses the scientific principles of mechanics to study the effects of forces on sports performance. Will use this information to improve, refine and develop techniques	Sports science degree	Sportspersons usually performing at a high level in their chosen sport
Sports psychologist	Helps with the mental/cognitive components of performance, helps athletes cope with anxiety and gives them the tools to evaluate personal performance. Can help coaches understand the personalities of their players in order to adapt their coaching style accordingly	Sports science degree	Sportspersons usually performing at a high level in their chosen sport
Sports nutritionist/ dietician	Most work from home on a consultancy basis, devising nutritional programmes to help sports performers reach their potential by adapting their diet to suit the needs of the sport and the individual	Sports science degree or nutrition degree	A variety of people, either a club or one-to-one with team members
Sports medicine/ injury treatment	Doctors specialising in sports-related injuries and sports-related medicine	Medical degree	Sports performers

Case study

Sports nutritionist

Name: Darren Johns
Age: 29

What I do:

I work on a freelance basis, helping people organise their eating and nutritional patterns to optimise their performance in their specialist sport. I tend to work with many long-distance runners, such as marathon runners, in their preparation for big races. I set them a nutritional diary which I expect them to adhere to, and I meet with them once a week to monitor, adapt and update it. One of my friends, who is also a sports nutritionist, is working with the England Swimming Team as they prepare for the Olympics.

What I enjoy:

I enjoy working with different people who have different needs and requirements. I really enjoy monitoring their improvements in performance as a result of a very carefully planned personal diet. I enjoy putting what I have learned into practice and sharing it with my clients. When you are freelance it can be a bit 'feast or famine', either a lot of work or very little – sometimes I will be working very hard and sometimes very little, so I have to plan my finances very carefully. I am also a freelance personal trainer, which helps to regulate my income.

1   **How does a self-employed freelance differ from a self-employed person? List three benefits and three drawbacks of each.**

Activity

For each sector described above, how many more jobs can you think of? Make a table listing them under each heading, and draw lines to indicate where jobs overlap between sectors.

Job	Sector			
	Health and fitness	**Sport and recreation**	**Outdoor education**	**Sport and exercise science**

Considerations in finding work-based opportunities

In general you will need to be fit, active and willing to undertake duties. Organise yourself, your clothing, your appearance, your transport, the cost, and the work you need to complete.

Location

As you are responsible for finding your own work experience, you need to be realistic about where it is located. It would be very exciting to have work experience at Anfield football stadium or Aintree racecourse, but if you live 200 hundred miles away it would be very difficult. Find a work experience placement where you know there are good public transport links, or where you will be able to get a lift. You might be able to stay with a relative who lives nearby for the duration of your placement. Finding somewhere within walking distance of your home would be the ideal, as you may be required to work shifts.

▲ **You don't need to travel far from home to find a challenging work placement**

Travel

You will be required to pay for your own travel to and from your placement. So do not find a placement that will incur travel expenses beyond your means, as you will soon begin to resent the cost and this will affect your performance at the organisation. Calculate the travelling time – if it will take more than a hour and a half for each journey, consider carefully whether or not you will be able to sustain it for the whole period of the placement. It is no good doing the placement and then resenting the time you spend there, as this will inhibit your ability to learn and develop your work-based skills.

Costs

The costs of work experience in addition to travel will vary according to the placement. You are likely to do your placement five days a week, for three weeks or more. If you attend college for four days a week, you might find a one-day-a-week placement during term time. No matter what the pattern of work is, you need to factor in the cost, and the effects on any existing part-time job you may have. If you are already employed, your employer may be prepared to accommodate a change for the limited time of your work experience.

You may be required to meet a code of dress. Sometimes you will be lucky enough to be given a uniform, or you will told what will be suitable to wear. If you are unsure, ask the work experience coordinator or your supervisor.

If you do not have suitable clothing, you may feel you want to buy something new.

Suitability of work

If you are injured and cannot do an active placement, select your work experience accordingly. There are plenty of placements where you will be working in the industry but do not need to be running around, such as a receptionist in a leisure centre, helping organising events, or some of a sports development officer's work.

Hours and regulations

You will be told how many hours you have to do to complete your work experience. The placement officer will tell you your hours in advance, before you start your first day, or they may tell your hours for the first day and then let you know what they will be for the rest of the placement.

There are strict rules governing the way work experience students are treated and the hours they work – if you have any concerns about the hours you are being asked to do, discuss them with your work experience officer at college.

All sections of the industry are subject to statutory regulations and laws, more information can be found in Book 1, Unit 2.

Health and safety

There are laws governing the health and safety of staff in the workplace, and these laws apply to students on work experience placements (see www.hse.gov.uk). Your place of work will not be allowed to ask you to operate dangerous machinery, or to supervise situations where specialist qualifications are required. If you are asked to supervise a swimming pool by yourself, or to take a lesson in a school without a member of staff present, this would be a breach of the health and safety regulations. But if you are asked to do either of these with qualified help or supervision, this is not in breach of the health and safety laws.

Roles and responsibilities

A good work experience placement will provide a timetable of what you will be doing, who you will be working with, and where you will be situated. You should be given a full range of experience for that placement. You may have been interviewed first, to try and ascertain what you want from the placement and to make it easier to accommodate you. But you will need to be willing to undertake menial jobs until your employer knows you better, and knows your strengths and weaknesses. Your responsibility throughout your time on placement is to act in a way that reflects well on you and on the college you are representing – you are an ambassador for your college.

In order to make a good impression you must:

- be punctual
- be reliable
- be willing to try and do everything asked of you
- if you haven't anything to do, ask if there is anything you can do to help
- be helpful
- do not sit around doing nothing – get on with your work experience diary/assignment
- if you are unsure about anything – ask.

Development opportunities

If you have a good work experience, you may be offered a job. Employers may be far more likely to offer a job to a potential member of staff who is a known quantity, rather than somebody who is unknown to the organisation. If you proved yourself to be reliable, helpful and willing, you will be remembered. You may be asked to return to do voluntary work – this may also provide you with opportunities in the future.

Progression

When you are at your placement, find out what qualifications the full- and part-time staff have. Did they all come in through the same route, or did they find their jobs through a variety of avenues? How have they progressed through the organisation, and what gave them the opportunities for progression? Did they take many additional qualifications?

Many of the people who work in the industry are quite young – there are opportunities to move into leisure centre management at quite a young age, and if you are good at your job you can progress quite quickly.

NVQs provide the chance for staff in the industry to upgrade their qualifications while working on the job. Short courses and additional qualifications, such as the governing body coaching and officiating awards, will really give you the edge over the next applicant. Seize the opportunity to complete and pass as many of these as possible. They will also help give you an insight into other sports and their needs.

Activity

1. Look at the various pathways along which staff have progressed throughout the organisation. Do you see yourself progressing through the same pathways?

2. Look at their qualifications – are they similar to each other? Are they similar to the pathway you are following, or hope to follow?

Continued development

In the sport and recreation industry, it is important to keep up to date with developments and progressions in the business. Continued professional development is ongoing training concerning various aspects of the industry, such as learning how exercises change, how equipment changes, and about new software and good practices. When you are on your placement, you can monitor developments, and the sort of courses staff are attending to develop their knowledge and skills. Many qualifications will require you to update and complete a minimum number of training hours.

Providers

Most of the sports industry is a service industry, providing a service to members, users, participants and the public. It is not an industry in which things are made (manufacturing). To be successful in the sports industry, we have to offer the best service we can so that our customers will continue to return. Sport and leisure in the UK is organised into three main sectors providing this service: the public, private and voluntary sectors.

Public sector

The public sector is the largest provider of sport in this country, and facilities are usually owned by the local authority (your borough, city council or district council). These facilities vary from one area to another. They can be run by an organisation that the council has selected, or by the council itself. Public facilities are open to all and usually are not membership-only. The council will encourage everybody to use the facilities through various marketing activities. They will have a policy of making sport accessible to all sections of the community, particularly those who traditionally have not taken part in sport. Providing a service to the local community is their primary aim. You can usually pay per visit.

Private sector

This is the sector that has enjoyed the largest growth over the past few years. These centres are usually membership-only, and aim to provide a very good service. Members usually pay a joining fee and will pay monthly membership fees by direct debit. They are usually tied into a minimum of a year's contract. Sometimes they will be specialist, such as a tennis centre, a snooker centre or a squash centre, but in the main they will provide a wider service. They aim to make a profit for the owners, many of the management team will have a performance-related pay agreement, and employees may have good terms and conditions. They also reward their investors through dividends, and are owned by shareholders (even if there is only one), who may include individuals, companies or institutions. Examples include David Lloyd Leisure, Esporta Health & Fitness Clubs and Fitness First.

Voluntary sector

The voluntary sector provides the majority of sport in this country. It is run by volunteers who enjoy sport and want to see their club or team develop. Examples include the local football teams who play on Saturdays and Sundays, hockey teams, swimming clubs, basketball teams, etc. They cover all ages, and usually cover their costs by collecting subscriptions each week. They can select who uses their club, and they run the club for its members. Often they may not have their own facilities, renting them from local councils or local private facilities. The largest voluntary organisations are the Scouts and the Guides.

Partnerships

Partnerships usually come about where more than one organisation is involved in the funding, operation or use of a facility. This can be good, as it might mean a new facility being built where there was not the opportunity in the past; but it can also be fraught with difficulty, as there is more than one organisation with a say in how things operate.

Theory into practice

Complete the following table mapping the facilities in your locality:

Sector	Name of facility	Address	Telephone number	Cost of use (e.g. membership fee)
Public				
Public				
Public				
Public				
Private				
Private				
Private				
Private				
Voluntary				
Voluntary				
Voluntary				
Voluntary				

As you can see, many of the local providers offer a different service. Go and visit some of these. Which facility do you think is best, and why?

Name of facility	Sector (public, private, voluntary)	Strengths	Weaknesses	Your overall opinion and why?

Grading tips

Grading Tip `P1` `M1`

Be logical in your approach to the work experience – set yourself targets, aims and objectives to achieve.

Assessment practice

1 Complete a table with realistic ideas of where you can complete your work experience – explain how and why it will suit you as a work experience placement. `P1` `M1`

	Health and fitness	Sport and recreation	Outdoor education	Sport and exercise
Public				
Private				
Voluntary				

2 Now put them in order of preference, evaluate each one and give reasons for your choice in a table like the one below. `D1`

	Evaluate why you want the placement	Decide on the order	Explain the reasons for your choice
Choice 1			
Choice 2			
Choice 3			
Choice 4			

25.2 Be able to prepare for a work-based experience in sport

Preparation

The key to a good work experience is to find your placement as early as possible. After you have completed your work experience search (page 334), telephone or write to the places you have identified. Be very careful how you speak to staff on the phone. Begin the conversation by saying 'good morning/good afternoon', introduce yourself and ask to speak to the person who deals with work experience. If they are not there, ask what their name is and when it will be convenient to call. They probably have a lot of enquiries for work experience, so remember to phone back and, if possible, leave a message – although do not rely on them returning your call. When you phone next, ask for them by name, make sure you introduce yourself, what course you are doing, where you are doing it, what the work experience requirement is, and what the dates are. Have a pen ready to take down any information you may need. Always be polite, enthusiastic and interested in the organisation.

First, set your aims and objectives.

Key Terms

Aim – something you want to do or achieve that is a long-term or overall goal, e.g. 'I want to be a PE teacher'; 'I want to be a personal trainer'; 'I want to be a manager of a large centre'.

Objective – something you need to do to achieve one of your aims, e.g. 'I need to pass my level 2 Gym Instructor qualification'; 'I need to achieve a degree'; 'I need to complete my UCAS form'.

Activity

What do I want to achieve from this work-based experience?

1 Aims (long term), e.g. to work in a school to understand what it is like to be a PE teacher.

2 Objectives (shorter term), e.g. what do I need to do to get my work experience as a PE teacher?

Set your targets

- Personal targets – what personal targets are you setting yourself?
- Knowledge development – how do you want to increase and improve your knowledge?
- Skills development – what new skills do you want to learn?
- Personal improvement – how do you want to improve?
- Qualifications – find out what qualifications staff at your placement have achieved. Many people move into the industry through a variety of routes; decide what might help you the most.
- Organisational development – how can I develop my organisational skills to prepare for work?
- Gathering of supplementary evidence – what evidence can I find out while I am there to help me with the National Diploma?

What do you want to get from this work experience? Your targets should be set against the SMART principles.

Specific	Your targets should relate to something you want to achieve	I want a work experience placement in a leisure centre
Measurable	They should be able to be measured	I want to find 10 contacts for work experience placements
Achievable	They have to be achievable for you to reach	Set a task and a deadline, so they will be met and not ignored
Realistic	You must set your sights on something you can achieve, otherwise you will be put off	You must have the ability to find the placement, e.g. a PE teacher in a secondary school
Time-bound	You must set deadlines that can be met	I want a placement fixed by 3 January

▲ The SMART way to identifying a placement

Application process

There are two main ways to apply for a job:

- CV and application letter
- Application form

SWOT analysis

Before you can apply for jobs confidently, you need to know more about yourself: recognise without being self-conscious what you are good at, recognise areas in which you may need development, and understand the opportunities you may want to achieve and what may be preventing you from reaching those goals.

Complete a SWOT analysis on yourself: list your strengths, weaknesses, opportunities and threats. One example is given below – but your strengths and weaknesses will be different.

Strengths	Weaknesses
▪ Communicating	▪ Voice projection
▪ Dealing with people	▪ Organisation of time
▪ IT	▪ Meeting deadlines

Opportunities	Threats
▪ To complete your National Diploma with a distinction	▪ Lack of confidence
▪ To go to university	▪ Financial
▪ To achieve FA level 2	▪ Failure to complete coursework

This information should help you to complete your CV, application forms and application letters.

Adverts

Advertisements for jobs can be found in a number of places, including:

- job centre
- local paper
- leisure opportunities
- local shops
- websites (e.g. www.jobswithballs.com, www.leisureopportunites.co.uk, www.fishforjobs.net).

The advertisements should give you a good idea of the types of jobs that exist in the sports industry, and of the skills, qualities, qualifications and experience you will need for various jobs in the industry. There is a wide selection of advertisements, with a wide variety of information and requirements. They will probably include:

- job title
- hours of work (full-time, part-time, shifts)
- location
- name of organisation
- contact number
- contact address
- contact name
- qualifications the applicant should have
- experience the applicant should have
- qualities the applicant should have
- skills the applicant should have
- short summary of organisation's aims
- what the organisation can offer the applicant
- salary
- benefits

- closing date
- how to apply (application form, CV, letter of application).

Activity

Print out or copy 10 sports profession advertisements. Go through the adverts:

1. What positions are they recruiting for?
2. Which sector are they in? (public, private, voluntary?)
3. What language do they use to attract potential employees (exciting, dynamic, etc.)
4. Identify four jobs that interest you – why do they appeal?
5. Do they show the pay on the adverts?
6. Do they ask for experience?
7. Do they ask for qualifications?
8. Do they ask for special skills or qualities?
9. Are they local?

Job description

A job description describes the duties of a particular post. It may be sent to you when you apply for a job, along with a person specification and an application form.

It may include:

- job title
- location
- who you are responsible to (e.g. assistant manager)
- a brief summary of the job
- a list of duties
- the point on the scale your salary will be based on
- holiday entitlement, shift rota, etc.

Activity

In small groups write a job description for a job as either a leisure centre manager or a fitness instructor.

Freeland Borough Council

Job Description

Department: Commercial Services Department

Division: DSD Leisure

Job Title: Leisure Attendant (Poolside)

Grade: 4 plus shift allowance and unsocial hours payment.

Accountable To: Location Manager

Duties Include:

- To patrol poolside and ensure the safety of the public.
- To undertake cleaning duties to appropriate organisation standards.
- To ensure a high level of customer satisfaction.
- To carry out teaching as necessary.
- To market and promote the Leisure Centre at all times.
- To meet the health and safety rules and regulations and adhere to health and safety laws for both staff and public.
- To undertake appropriate training as directed, such as the National Pool Lifeguard Qualification.
- To put out and put away equipment as necessary and as directed.
- To comply at all times with the Equal Opportunities Policy.
- To participate in the Staff Appraisal Scheme.
- To carry out any other duties that may be assigned commensurate with the level of the post.

Freetown FC

Employer	Freetown FC
Job Title	Strength and Conditioning Coach
Sector	Coaching, Training & Medical
Sub-Sectors	Fitness Coach
Salary	£35,000 per annum
Benefits	plus football success-related bonus of up to 50%
Town/City	Freetown
Contract Type	Permanent
Passport/Visa Required	Must be eligible to live and work in the UK

Job Description

JOB TITLE: Strength and Conditioning Coach

REPORTS TO: Club Doctor

JOB FUNCTION:

- To provide fitness conditioning services to the first team squad as required.
- To assist in the preparation of players prior to first team matches as required.
- To take responsibility for the monitoring of the progress of all players' body strength with the use of weights and body weight exercises.
- To assist as required in carrying out fitness testing.
- To explain correct use of gym equipment to players.
- To liaise with and assist in the conditioning of reserve and youth players as required.
- To provide advice and guidance to the Head of Youth and Development Coaches in respect of the conditioning and fitness of under age players involved in the Club's development system.
- Generally to provide such conditioning and fitness services as required by the Doctor, Manager and coaches.
- To liaise with all members of the sports medical and sports science team to assist in the multi-disciplinary approach.

Qualifications required — Must have relevant experience in a professional sporting environment, ideally in football!

 Job descriptions may have different styles but the main content will be similar

Person specification

A person specification is based on the personal skills, knowledge, qualities, attributes and qualifications needed to meet the job description. It will also list whether these are essential or desirable in order to do the job.

Sub-headings might include:

- personal attributes
- personal qualities
- vocational qualifications
- academic qualifications
- competence and experience.

These will be listed as essential or desirable, and the person specification should indicate whether the interviewer is going to obtain this information from the application form, the interview, or the references.

The main reason for using job descriptions and person specifications as part of the recruitment and selection process is to ensure the interviewer has a clear and objective basis to assess each candidate. Personal opinions and preferences are minimised.

Activity

Break into small groups and write a person specification for a job as either a leisure centre manager or a fitness instructor.

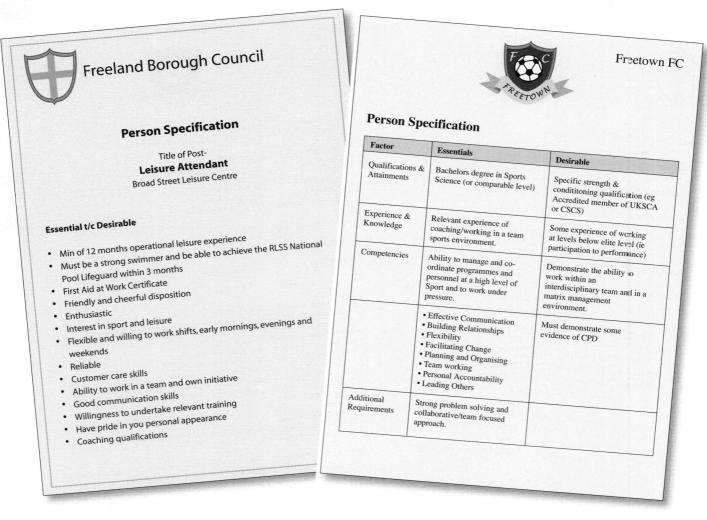

The main purpose of the person specification is to make the selection process more objective

Preparing required application documents

Your CV – curriculum vitae

Your CV is a reflection of you. How it is presented, regardless of the content, will show your prospective employer many things about you:

- your spelling
- your grammar
- your attention to detail
- your presentation skills
- your pride in your work.

A CV should be typed on a single side of A4, although as you gain more experience this will grow. There are no strict rules about layout, but it must be neat and logical, and look pleasing. Use sub-headings in bold to break up the text and help the reader find the information they need.

■ Content of the CV

The content of the CV is your decision, but as a rule it should contain the following information:

- name
- address
- date of birth
- phone numbers, including mobile
- email address
- skills, qualities and attributes

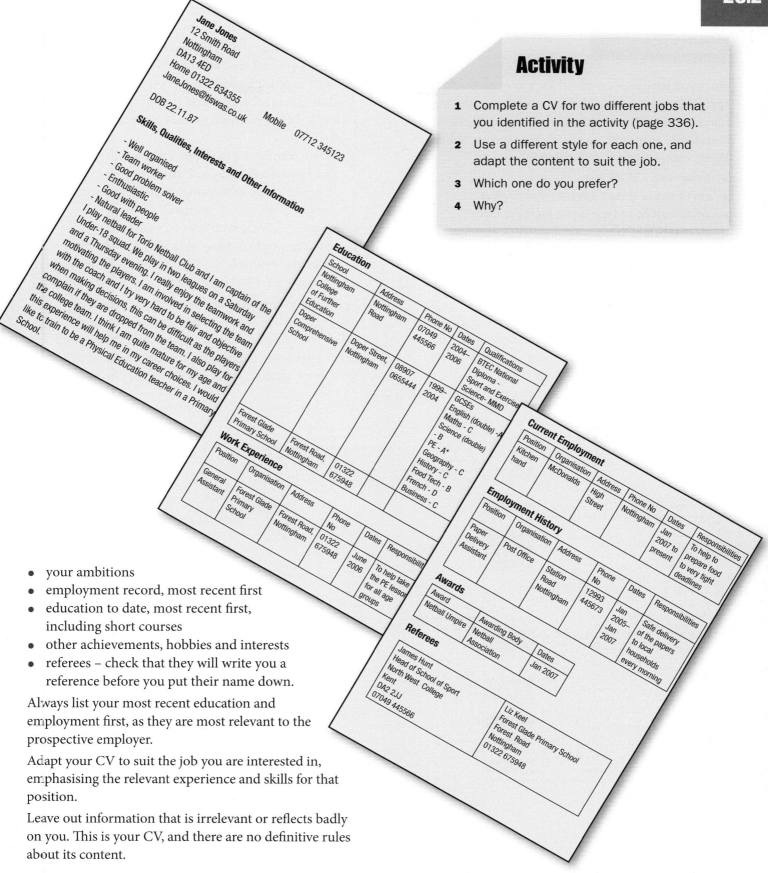

Activity

1. Complete a CV for two different jobs that you identified in the activity (page 336).
2. Use a different style for each one, and adapt the content to suit the job.
3. Which one do you prefer?
4. Why?

Jane Jones
12 Smith Road
Nottingham
DA13 4ED
Home 01322 634355
JaneJones@tiswas.co.uk   Mobile   07712 345123
DOB 22.11.87

Skills, Qualities, Interests and Other Information

- Well organised
- Team worker
- Good problem solver
- Enthusiastic
- Good with people
- Natural leader

I play netball for Torio Netball Club and I am captain of the Under-18 squad. We play in two leagues on a Saturday and a Thursday evening. I really enjoy the teamwork and motivating the players. I am involved in selecting the team with the coach and I try very hard to be fair and objective when making decisions, this can be difficult as the players complain if they are dropped from the team. I also play for the college team. I think I am quite mature for my age and this experience will help me in my career choices. I would like to train to be a Physical Education teacher in a Primary School.

Education

School	Address	Phone No	Dates	Qualifications
Nottingham College of Further Education	Nottingham Road	07049 445566	2004–2006	BTEC National Diploma – Sport and Exercise Science– MMD
Doper Comprehensive School	Doper Street, Nottingham	08907 0655444	1999–2004	GCSEs English (double) - A Maths - C Science (double) - B PE - A* Geography - C History - C Food Tech - B French - D Business - C
Forest Glade Primary School	Forest Road, Nottingham	01322 675948		

Work Experience

Position	Organisation	Address	Phone No	Dates	Responsibilit...
General Assistant	Forest Glade Primary School	Forest Road, Nottingham	01322 675948	June 2006	To help take the PE lessons for all age groups

Current Employment

Position	Organisation	Address	Phone No	Dates	Responsibilities
Kitchen hand	McDonalds	High Street, Nottingham		Jan 2007 to present	To help to prepare food to very tight deadlines

Employment History

Position	Organisation	Address	Phone No	Dates	Responsibilities
Paper Delivery Assistant	Post Office	Station Road Nottingham	12993 445673	Jan 2005– Jan 2007	Safe delivery of the papers to local households every morning

Awards

Award	Awarding Body	Dates
Netball Umpire	Netball Association	Jan 2007

Referees

James Hunt
Head of School of Sport
North West College
Kent
DA2 2JJ
07049 445566

Liz Keel
Forest Glade Primary School
Forest Road
Nottingham
01322 675948

- your ambitions
- employment record, most recent first
- education to date, most recent first, including short courses
- other achievements, hobbies and interests
- referees – check that they will write you a reference before you put their name down.

Always list your most recent education and employment first, as they are most relevant to the prospective employer.

Adapt your CV to suit the job you are interested in, emphasising the relevant experience and skills for that position.

Leave out information that is irrelevant or reflects badly on you. This is your CV, and there are no definitive rules about its content.

Application forms

Once you have seen an advert for a job you would like to apply for, and you have phoned or written expressing an interest, they will probably send you an application form. You should answer all questions fully and accurately. When completing an application form:

- write with a black pen
- check to see if they ask for block capitals
- write legibly, or type if you have the form electronically
- read each question carefully first before answering it
- most jobs will ask for a personal statement – have one prepared that you can adapt to the job (you could adapt it from your CV)
- if you have been sent a job description or a person specification, use this as a guideline to what you should include in the statement
- sell yourself – but keep it brief
- identify key statements from the advert, job

description or person specification, and talk about them – you will be shortlisted based on these
- most organisations will want you to write down your most recent education and employment first
- if you make a mistake, cross it out neatly and carry on
- ask somebody else to check it through, or read it out loud to yourself – you will soon hear the mistakes.
- do not lie – you are signing the form as a true and accurate reflection of yourself
- try not to leave it until the last minute
- post it in plenty of time, or deliver it by hand
- make sure you have the right name on the envelope – this is especially important in a large organisation

Application forms are the most common means of making a job application. They are fair because all candidates complete the same form, and the employer can't forget to ask a question. They usually have to be filled in by hand, so literacy skills can be checked.

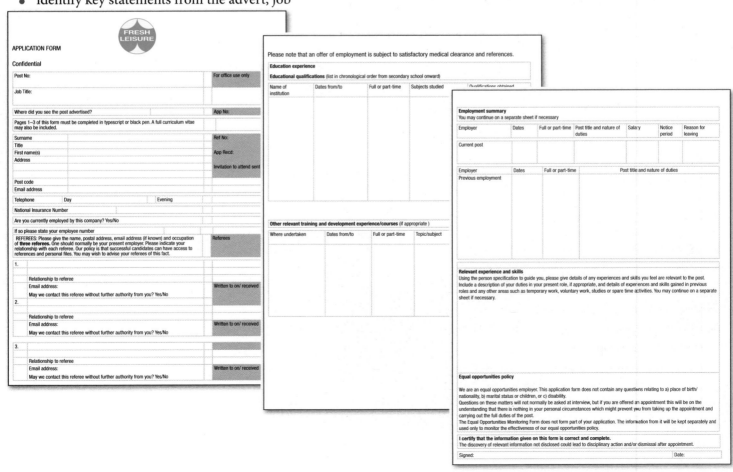

Theory into practice

In pairs, devise an application form for a hypothetical organisation. Photocopy it and hand it out to members of another small group – ask them to complete it for a job.

1. Did it work?
2. What was good?
3. What did not work?
4. Why?

Application letter

An application letter sets out all the information found in a CV, but in letter style. Some employers ask for this method of application to see if a candidate is committed enough to write a letter. And if they are committed, do they know how to write one properly? Letters will normally be completed on the computer, but some employers will ask for them to be handwritten.

Activity

Write an application letter for the same job as before. Ask your tutor to check it. Edit it, and save it electronically to use and adapt in the future.

Covering letter

When you send off a CV or application form, to be courteous you should also send a short letter with it. It should be well presented, and set out in business style (see the examples opposite).

The letter needs to be accurate and well presented. It should include:

- your name
- address
- telephone number/s
- date

---

23 John Road
Beall
Derbyshire
DE11 4RG
07889 1223456

Mrs Jones
Fresh Leisure Ltd
Leisure Design
19 Churchill Place
Derbyshire
DE44 9HT

2nd August 2007

Dear Mrs Jones

Please find enclosed my CV for the post of Leisure Assistant at Fresh Leisure Centre, advertised in the 'Derby Times' on 2 August 2007.

I am a keen sportsman and I am enthusiastic and reliable. I am at college completing my BTEC National Diploma in Sport and Exercise Science. I have certificates in FA Coaching Level 1, Community Sports Leader Award, National Pool Lifeguard Award and First Aid at Work.

I am a member at Fresh, and use the facilities regularly. I would enjoy working at such a new and exciting centre. I look forward to hearing from you in the near future.

Yours sincerely

K. J. Dixon (Mr)
Encls.

---

23 John Road
Beall
Derbyshire
DE11 4RG
07889 1223456

Fresh Leisure Ltd
Leisure Design
19 Churchill Place
Derbyshire
DE44 9HT

2nd August 2007

Dear Sir/Madam,

Leisure Assistant – Fresh Leisure Ltd

I am writing in response to your advertisement in the *Derby Times* on 2 August 2007 for the position of Leisure Assistant at Fresh Leisure Centre.

I am currently at college completing my BTEC National Diploma in Sport and Exercise Science and I am looking for my first position in the industry.

Please find enclosed my application form for your perusal and I look forward to hearing from you soon.

Yours faithfully

R. E. Jensen (Ms)
Enc.

- the job you are interested in
- why you are interested in it (very briefly)
- where and when you saw it advertised
- don't forget to sign it!

Your address
Your phone number/s

Name of contact
Company name and address
Date

Dear Sir/Madam (or Mr/Ms X)
Subheading in bold or underlined or in capitals
(e.g. **Recreation Assistant – Cascades Leisure Centre**)

Body of letter...
- Introduce yourself
- Why you are interested in this job with this company.
- What skills and experience you can offer (briefly).
- Please find enclosed my CV/application form.
- I look forward to hearing from you.

End the letter in an upbeat way – leave them on a high.
Yours faithfully (if started with Dear Sir or Madam)
Yours sincerely (if started with their name)
Your signature
Your name (typed or in handwritten capitals).

Activity

List your skills, strengths, attributes and achievements for the job you were interviewed for in class.

■ Useful skills

Useful skills to list might include:
- good communication skills
- IT skills
- customer service
- teaching and coaching skills
- common sense
- first aid
- good spoken and written English
- literacy and numeracy
- outgoing personality
- voice projection
- sense of humour
- enthusiasm
- flexibility
- stamina and good health/physical fitness
- organisational skills
- ability to work in a team
- ability to lead
- ability to deal with the public
- ability to think on your feet
- initiative.

Personal statements

Most application forms will give you a full side to complete a personal statement – this will be similar to the information you wrote for your CV, or put in your application letter. You need to outline your strengths, skills, attributes, achievements, and any other information relevant to the particular job you are applying for that doesn't appear elsewhere in the application. The employer will probably want you to handwrite it. Prepare one in advance, in rough, to minimise mistakes.

Letter accepting/declining

When you have been offered a job/work experience, you may be asked to reply in writing. Your letter should be short and well presented, thanking them for their offer and accepting or declining the job. It should be set out in business style. Two examples are given overleaf.

23 John Road
Beall
Derbyshire
DE11 4RG
07889 1223456

Fresh Leisure Ltd
Leisure Design
19 Churchill Place
Derbyshire
DE44 9HT
2 August 2007

Dear Sir/Madam,

Leisure Assistant – Fresh Leisure Ltd

Thank you for the offer of the position of Leisure Assistant at Fresh Leisure Centre. It is with regret that on this occasion I am unable to accept due to the pressure of my college work. I would like to thank you for the opportunity and wish the organization success in the future.

Yours faithfully

R E Jensen (Ms)

23 John Road
Beall
Derbyshire
DE11 4RG
07889 1223456

Mrs Jones
Fresh Leisure Ltd
Leisure Design
19 Churchill Place
Derbyshire
DE44 9HT

2 August 2007

Dear Mrs Jones

It is with great pleasure I accept the offer of the post of Leisure Assistant at Fresh Leisure Centre. Thank you for giving me this opportunity.

I will contact you to discuss my start date and shift roster.

Yours sincerely

K. J. Dixon (Mr)

Activity

In small groups, write to a hypothetical employer either a covering letter or a letter accepting or declining a post. Present your letter to the group, explaining how you decided what to include. Write your letter out on flipchart paper and display it to the room.

▼ The interview is intended for the employer to learn about you – and for you to learn about them

Interview

An interview is usually based on the job description and the person specification (see page xx). The interview panel will base their interview on these two documents and the answers you gave on your application form.

The interview

The interview should have a set format and will probably be carried out by more than one person. The format and questions should be similar for all candidates at interview, in order for the panel to compare the answers to decide who answered them the best. The interviewers should stick to a similar format.

- The panel will invite you in and introduce themselves.
- Different questions may be allocated to different panel members.
- To get the best out interviewees, the panel should not intimidate them, but should make them feel relaxed.
- The panel should understand the questions they are asking, and appear interested in the answer.
- They should listen to interviewees and be prepared with a follow-up question if necessary.
- They will ask you 'Are there any questions you would like to ask' at the end of the interview – be prepared for this and have one or two questions ready, such as 'what promotion prospects are there?'.
- They will thank you for attending the interview.
- They should tell you when you will know whether or not you have been successful.

■ Interview questions

There are a number of different types of question you could be asked. Some are easier to answer than others – try to answer in as much detail as possible without rambling, even if the format of the question was not very good in the first place. Here are some of the different styles of question you could experience.

- Closed – to find out specific information: yes/no answers (e.g. Have you worked shifts before?)
- Open – to encourage the interviewee to open up on a topic (e.g. Why do we carry out fitness tests?)
- Probing – to find out more on a particular point (e.g. Could you explain to me why you would use a Eurofit step test?)
- Clarifying – to check understanding (e.g. What do we mean by equal opportunities?)
- Scenario – to test the interviewee's ability to apply their knowledge (e.g. A child breaks their arm in your session, what do you do?)
- Rambling (e.g. When you have been at work, or not at work, what customer service or customer care

skills and tips have you developed to help you in and out of work?)
- Multiple – trying to ask more than one question at the same time (e.g. What do you see yourself doing in three years' time, what do you hope to achieve, and how are you going to achieve it?)
- Directing – leaning in the direction that the interviewer expects or favours (e.g. Don't you think football is better than going to the gym for fitness?)

Activity

Prepare 12 interview questions based on the job description and person specification you have written. Try to make them open questions. Start with the easy questions and make them progressively more difficult. Do not try and catch your interviewee out with difficult questions.

Before the interview, complete the following pre-interview checklist.

	Things you need to do before an interview
1	
2	
3	
4	
5	
6	
7	
8	
9	
10	

Activity

After the interview, complete the interview evaluation sheet.

Interview evaluation sheet	
Was I dressed appropriately?	
Did they have my application form?	
Had I sold myself on the application form?	
Did they have my CV?	
Did my CV help me sell myself to the interviewers?	
What other information could I have included on either the CV or the application form to improve my chances in the interview?	
Was my body language closed – did I have my arms folded and was I leaning back in the chair?	
Was my body language open – sitting up and looking interested?	
Did I answer the questions fully?	
Did I say' yes' or 'no' to any questions and not expand on the answer?	
Why?	
Did I answer 'I don't know' to any of the questions?	
What impression does it give to the interviewer if I answer 'I don't know' to any of the questions?	
Which was the best question I answered?	
Why?	
Did I relate any of the answers to my part-time work?	
If yes, give an example:	
If no – why not?	
Did I relate any of the answers to my sport?	
If no – why not?	
Did I relate any of the answers to other things in my life?	
If no – why not?	
Did I communicate to the interviewers that I was interested and keen to do a work placement?	
How?	
When they asked if there were any questions I would like to ask, did I have any?	
If I did the interview again today for a real work experience placement, what would I do differently?	
Why?	

Activity

In your small groups, take it in turns to be an interview panel and interview each other individually.

Interview format:

- greet the interviewee
- introduce the interviewers
- give a brief introduction to the job
- ask one or two relaxing questions to start with
- ask short, simple questions
- then ask more complex and open questions
- listen to and answer the interviewee's questions
- explain the notification system
- conclude the interview.

Film the interviews and play them back to the group. Then answer the following questions:

- how long did the interview last?
- were all the questions open?
- did the interviewee manage to make the most of the questions?
- who would you appoint to the position?
- why?

Assessment practice

1   Choose one real work-based experience post you wish to apply for, and prepare the following: SWOT analysis, your CV and covering letter, personal statement (including goals aims and objectives), and list of 10 things to do before the interview. Depending on what the organisation requests, you may need to fill in an application form or write an application letter, rather than sending your CV. **P2**

2   Extend your personal statement to justify your goals, aims and objectives, and state how this job will help you achieve them. This analysis will help you focus your application, but need not all be included in the application itself. Remember to be concise. **M2**

3   Put together your application package, have it approved by your supervisor, and send it off. **P3**

Grading tips

Grading Tip M3

To achieve this grade, put together your application package without support.

25.3   Be able to undertake a work-based experience in sport

Undertaking your work-based experience

Activities

When you find your placement – be reliable. If you are unable to attend for some reason, phone in at the earliest opportunity and explain. If you have a hospital or doctor's appointment, show your card and let your supervisor know well in advance.

■ Work experience tips

- Ensure you always turn up on time.
- If for some reason you are ill or late – phone in!
- Present yourself well – wear minimal jewellery, long hair tied back, no hat. Keep yourself clean and tidy. If you have to wear a uniform, ensure it is ironed.

- Don't complain about things you don't want to do – show that you are willing.
- Carry out tasks properly and to the best of your ability.
- Be aware of health and safety and other relevant legislation.
- Record all tasks you undertake however small, in your diary.
- Be polite and have a good attitude – you might end up with some work!
- If you have a problem with your placement, talk to your supervisor or lecturer.

Not all placements will involve actively taking part in sports ▶

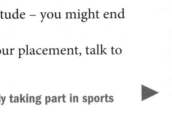

Think it over

Working in small groups, imagine yourself in a work experience placement and think of the things in your life that would be different. Make a list.

Considerations

■ Codes of practice

A code of practice is a set of rules for a specific job/activity. Make sure you stick to them.

■ Customer care

Always be helpful to customers – remember they will ultimately pay your wages! If there is something you don't know – ask.

■ Health and safety

Always be aware of your own safety in your placement. Use the equipment given and listen carefully to all information you are told concerning health and safety.

■ Legislation

You will be expected to stay inside the legal requirements for the placement. You will be told these by your work experience officer and by your placement supervisor.

■ Regulation

Follow the regulations set down by your placement officers and supervisors. If you have any doubt – ask.

■ Equal opportunities

All organisations are required by law to enforce equal opportunities for their staff and customers.

■ Quality assurance

Quality assurance aims to ensure that all customers receive the best possible service. Some organisations work to be awarded the 'Investors in People' charter mark (see www.investorsinpeople.co.uk).

■ Specific skills

If you have a specific skill to offer, try and find a placement where you can use it, for example, if you are a keen ice skater you could look for a placement at an ice rink.

Recording your work-based experience

When you are on work experience, you need to collect information for yourself about the organisation you are working for. The following outlines some of the information you will be expected to collect.

Diary of daily activities

Each day you are out on work experience, complete a diary. At the end of each week, complete a summary review and what you want to achieve the next week.

DAY 1

Date _____ **Day** _____ **Times** _____

What did you do? Evaluate your performance – where could you improve?

WEEK 1

From _____ **to** _____

Summary

Looking back over the past week, what have been the high points?

What have been the low points?

What would you like to do next week?

Information to collect

WORK PLACEMENT DETAILS

Company name: _____

Address: _____

_____

_____

Tel. no: _____

Supervisor's details:

(these details will be checked with your supervisor during placement visits)

Name	Signature	Telephone/extension number

Draw an organisational chart of your work placement. (An organisational chart usually shows the manager or head teacher at the top and the staff cascading below.) You can usually collect a diagram of this from the manager or the receptionist – include it in your assignment for submission with your diary.

Information for your assignment

1	What does the organisation do? (e.g. provide education, leisure service for the public, members, etc.)
2	Who are the customers? (e.g. students, pupils, members, etc.)
3	Give six examples of the organisation's rules and regulations (Code of Practice).
4	What is the organisation's health and safety policy?
5	When you arrive, you will be given some information about health and safety. What were you either told or given?
6	If you were not told or given anything, what information do you think you should have known regarding health and safety?
7	What is the emergency evacuation procedure? Collect a copy to submit with your assignment.
8	Where are the fire alarms and fire muster points? Draw a map to submit with your assignment.
9	What colour are the fire extinguishers? Are there different colours in different places? Why?
10	Were you told where the toilets and washing facilities were on the first day?
11	Who is the Health and Safety Officer? What is their role?
12	Who is the First Aid Officer?
13	Where is the first aid kit?
14	Where is the accident report book?
15	Attach a copy of an accident report form.
16	What are the rules about lifting heavy or large objects?
17	What have you been told about the use of cleaning substances or any other hazardous substances? What is the name of the law controlling their use?
18	What are the rules about the use of computer screens and the time spent in front of them?
19	How frequent are your breaks, and how long are they?
20	Is there equipment you are not allowed to use as you need specialist training? What is it?
21	What is a risk assessment and why are they carried out?
22	Collect an example of a risk assessment at your work experience venue to submit with your assignment.
23	What is the procedure in the following emergency situations – first aid emergency; threatened robbery; suspicious telephone calls/items/packages?
24	What is the Customer Service Policy for the organisation where you are doing your work placement?
25	What is the organisation's policy on customer complaints? Submit this with your assignment.
26	Give examples of when you have given information and advice to customers.
27	How does the organisation ensure it delivers a quality service?

An outline organisational chart ▶

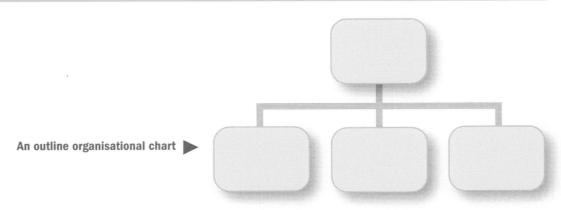

Think it over

Do you consider the organisation to be:

Public ☐

Private ☐

Voluntary ☐

How does the company fund itself?

How does the organisation meet the needs of the local community?

Achievement of goals, aims and objectives

■ Personal goals

What do I want to achieve? How am I going to achieve it?

■ Organisational goals

In your opinion, does your placement organisation treat its staff well? Is it a good place to do a placement?

■ Goals relating to qualification/study

Completing your work experience will enable you to complete this unit – aim to do it to distinction level!

Assessment practice

Carry out your assessment practice to the best of your ability, keeping a daily diary and collecting as much relevant information as possible during the time you are there. **P4 P5**

Activity

1 Write a job description for the job you are doing at your work experience placement.

2 What job title would you give yourself?

3 Describe the duties you have to do at work experience.

	Further information for your assignment
1	If you were to work at your placement full time, what qualifications would you need?
2	What skills would you need? (e.g. good communication).
3	Apart from those that you are studying, find out what other qualifications would be useful to the organisation.
4	Have you been included in any staff meetings? If yes, give details to submit with your assignment.
5	Have you been involved in any staff training or development? If yes, give details.
6	At your work experience placement, what is the marketing strategy?
7	What marketing activities are used by the organisation? (e.g. prospectuses, leaflets, email, advertising in the press; include samples of marketing to submit with your assignment).
8	What is the organisation's Mission Statement?

Grading tips

Grading Tip P4 P5

To achieve this grade, put together your assessment package without support.

25.4 Be able to evaluate a work-based experience in sport

Evaluation

You need to evaluate your performance at work experience. When you are evaluating your performance, you need to analyse critically what you have done, what you can learn from the situation, and how this will be useful in future in terms of building your skills and knowledge of the industry. If you find it difficult to evaluate, as many people do, imagine you will have to do the work experience placement again tomorrow – what could you do differently to improve your performance and your opportunity to learn new things?

Activity

Work experience – self assessment
(This report should be completed when you are near the end of your placement)

Rate your performance in the following: (poor, fair, good or excellent)

Attendance	
Punctuality	
Attitude	
Initiative	
Confidence	
Team work	
Appearance	
Competence in dealing with customers	
Competence in carrying out tasks	

Any other comments:

Your signature: _____   Date: _____

Supervisor's signature: _____   Date: _____

Activity

Work placement evaluation (To be completed at the end of your work placement)

List 10 duties undertaken.	1 2 3 4 5 6 7 8 9 10
List three elements of the work you enjoyed, and why.	1 2 3
List three aspects you didn't enjoy, and why.	1 2 3
List three new skills you have learned.	1 2 3
Would this type of work interest you as a career? Why?	
What advice would you give to a student who is about to start their work experience at your placement?	
Is there anything that could have made the placement more useful than it was?	
Were you prepared for this placement?	
Was there anything extra that you needed to know before you started?	

Taking it further

Think about your placement. Write a list of 10 different things you learned, one from each of the duties listed in the Activity on page 353. Now think about something you could have done for each one that could have improved that particular experience.

Presentation

You will need to make a presentation to your group about your work experience.

Presentation techniques

You can deliver a presentation in a variety of ways. The most common and popular way is using Microsoft PowerPoint or other presentation software. It is easy to use – you can bring in one bullet point at a time with animation, and introduce pictures, either taken by yourself or imported from the web. But as most people use PowerPoint now, in many situations, you must be careful not to administer 'death by PowerPoint'. Do not just stand and read out each slide one by one – people quickly turn off and lose concentration. Try and use a variety of methods – handouts to support your work are useful, or exhibits of work or leaflets from your placement all serve to add interest. You can use whiteboards and pens or flipcharts, which you can write on as you go along (having prepared what you were going to write beforehand). Photographs to show what you did are useful; these could be put on the computer or mounted on the wall. Posters can be used to bring a mixture of media to your work.

The most important aspect of your presentation is that you should rehearse it, so that you will stay within the time limit and so that you know and understand the words you use. Deliver it with enthusiasm!

Activities

Begin it with a slide introducing the placement, where the institution or company is, what it is, what it does, and general information pertinent to the placement. What activities did you do? List them, and use this opportunity to expand the information for the group. (Make yourself a list of information to expand the points – one postcard-sized list of expansion notes per point will help you remember what you wanted to say.) Activities could include: help lifeguard a school session; help take a dance lesson; fill envelopes full of marketing information for a summer holiday scheme; phone round a list of customers outlining the changes in membership; clean the store cupboard, etc. List even the most menial of activities you did – they all contribute to the learning experience.

Achievements

What did you achieve when you were on work experience? What did you do that you were pleased with, that was a personal achievement to you? It may be something small, such as dealing with a complaint, solving a small problem, helping a customer, or motivating a reluctant 13-year-old girl to participate in a sports session.

Don't be too hard on yourself about this – the achievements may seem quite small, as you are only there for a short time, but you should be able to list many new experiences and hopefully achievements if you had a worthwhile placement.

At the end of your presentation, evaluate your performance on the work placement and analyse what you have learned. The final question you need to answer is – would you want to do that job as a full-time career, and, if so, what would you need to do to achieve your aim? Analyse your decision using the review questions given below.

Review

Activities

Now review the activities that you did on work experience – were they what you expected?

- Did you do what you hoped you would?
- Were you given much more responsibility than you thought you would have?
- Did you feel you were used as an unpaid member of staff?
- Did you feel challenged, but not abandoned?

Achievements

- What did you achieve?
- Were you pleased with what you achieved?
- What would you have liked to have got out of your placement that you feel you missed out on?

■ Achievements of goals

Before you went on work experience, you should have listed your goals. Now analyse your achievements against those goals.

- Did you achieve them all?
- Did you achieve some?
- How many did you achieve?
- Did you achieve them fully or partially?

■ Aims and objectives

- Review the aims and objectives that you set yourself for your work experience – have you achieved them?
- Now look at your overall aims and objectives for your life – do you want to change any of them, and has the placement changed your mind about what you want to do or achieve?

■ Strengths and areas for improvement

After having completed your work experience, what do you consider to be your strengths?

Here is a list of ideas to help you:

- communications
- organisation
- customer service
- taking initiative
- dealing with problems
- solving problems
- ICT
- teamwork
- coaching and teaching.

What are your areas for improvement?

▲ Communication and teamwork may be key strengths in your placement

Activity

What could you improve in your performance on work experience that will transfer into your everyday life?

Evidence and techniques

In reviewing your work experience placement, do you wish you had collected more evidence of the work you had to do? As you reflect on it you could always return to your placement, if you got on well with the staff, and ask them to take some photographic evidence of you doing a particular activity for your diary.

■ Interviews and use of witness testimony

When you think about your interview for the work experience placement now, do you think the questions you were asked reflected the work you finally had to do? Do you think the interview was fair and appropriate?

A witness testimony is a sheet of A4 paper with space to write what you did. As you build up a relationship with the staff, you can ask them if they will complete a witness testimony for you – this should outline briefly what

Witness testimony	
Name:	
Course:	
Activity:	
What you did:	
Where (name of organisation):	
Exact location in premises:	
Time:	Date:
Statement of student's activity	
Did they complete the activity to a suitable and appropriate standard?	No/Yes
Signed:	
Date:	
Print name:	
Position:	
Student's signature:	

you did and where, and the level to which you achieved the organised activity. It should be signed both by a supervising member of staff at the work placement, and by yourself.

Now you can take the opportunity to interview the staff. Ask them if they enjoy their job; what qualifications they achieved to be appointed; what they wanted to do as a career originally; what their biggest achievement in their career has been to date.

■ Further goals

As a result of your work experience, you may now want to review your goals in life, looking not just at your overall aims and objectives, but at shorter-term goals, possibly about gaining an additional qualification such as the National Pool Lifeguard Qualification. Although you may not have considered a career as a lifeguard, for example, after work experience you might realise it is a legitimate pathway into the leisure business, and consider doing the qualification to give you a route in.

■ Experiences

The experiences you have on your work placement will not always be good, but it is valuable to have a range of different experiences even if they are not necessarily ones you want to repeat! Learning to tolerate and get on with things and people that you might not want to is for most of us, unfortunately, a necessary part of our working day. Usually this is only a small part of the job, and we all learn different techniques to deal with the less exciting and more mundane periods at work.

■ Training

You may decide after your work experience that you need extra training in the workplace. Some organisations will take you on as a volunteer assistant to improve your range and breadth of experience. As you review your goals, now is the time to review your training needs and gaps in your qualifications and experience, and address as many of them as possible.

■ Qualifications

Think about your qualifications, assess your needs, address the gaps – organise yourself to improve your qualifications.

Assessment practice

1 Review the notes on making presentations (page xx), and present your activities and achievements during your work placement to the class. **P6**

2 Review your work placement, identifying your strengths and areas for improvement, and your further goals, aims and objectives. **P7**

Grading tips

Grading Tip M4

To achieve this grade, explain why you listed these strengths, areas for improvement, and further goals, aims and objectives.

Grading Tip D2

To achieve this grade, justify your inclusion of these strengths, areas for improvement, and further goals, aims and objectives.

Knowledge check

1 What is a person specification – what is its role?

2 What is a job description – what is its role?

3 Why is it important to decide what you want to achieve in your work experience placement?

4 Why do you have to be flexible in your work experience placement?

5 What is the HSE?

6 Make a list of ten qualities an employer might be looking for during a work experience placement.

7 Why must you phone your placement if you are ill?

8 If your placement goes well, how will you benefit from it?

9 What does CV stand for?

10 What is an open question?

11 What is a closed question?

12 Which is better, an open or a closed question? Why?

Preparation for assessment

This unit is unusual in that the assessment will be based on your work-based experience. To prepare for this to be assessed, draw together the work you have completed in the four Assessment practices and produce a summary report, highlighting the main issues you have faced, and what you learned. You should include the following:

Four realistic opportunities that you identified for appropriate work-based experience in sport; with an explanation of why they are appropriate and an evaluation of the opportunities that were open to you **P1 M1 D1**

Identify your goals, aims and objectives from work-based experience and justify them, suggesting how they can be achieved **P2 M2**

Apply for your chosen work-based experience post, with support or without support **P3 M3**

Undertake your work-based experience in sport **P4**

Maintain a record of activities and achievements and present this to the class **P5 P6**

Review your experience, identifying strengths, areas for improvement, and further goals, aims and objectives, explain your conclusions and make suggestions relating to further goals, aims and objectives. Justify your explanations and suggestions. **P7 M4 D2**

Grading tips

Grading Tip **P1 M1 D1**

Look at the different jobs available – what jobs can you see yourself doing? Evaluate these opportunities.

Grading Tip **P2 M2**

What are your goals, aims and objectives? How are you going to achieve them?

Grading Tip **P3 M3**

Complete an application for a work-based placement. Have a personal statement prepared.

Grading Tip **P4**

Undertake your work experience willingly and with enthusiasm.

Grading Tip **P5**

Keep up to date with your day-to-day record of your placement.

Grading Tip **P6**

Present the content of your work experience and your evaluation of your performance while you were there.

Grading Tip **P7**

Review, explain and justify your strengths in relation to the goals, aims and objectives you set out before you went.

To achieve a pass grade the evidence must show that the learner is able to:	To achieve a merit grade the evidence must show that, in addition to the pass criteria, the learner is able to:	To achieve a distinction grade the evidence must show that, in addition to the pass and merit criteria, the learner is able to:
P1 describe four realistic opportunities for appropriate work-based experience in sport **Assessment practice page 346**	**M1** explain four realistic opportunities for appropriate work-based experience in sport **Assessment practice page 346**	**D1** evaluate the opportunities for work-based experience in sport **Assessment practice page 346**
P2 prepare for a work-based experience in sport, identifying goals, aims and objectives **Assessment practice page 358**	**M2** justify identified goals, aims and objectives of work-based experience in sport, suggesting how they can be achieved **Assessment practice page 358**	
P3 Select an appropriate work-based experience in sport and complete the application process, with support **Assessment practice page 358**	**M3** select an appropriate work-based experience in sport and complete the application process **Assessment practice page 358**	
P4 undertake a selected appropriate work-based experience in sport **Assessment practice page 362**		
P5 maintain a record of activities and achievements during a work-based experience **Assessment practice page 362**		
P6 present evidence of activities and achievements **Assessment practice page 362**		
P7 review a work-based experience in sport, identifying strengths, areas for improvement, and further goals, aims and objectives **Assessment practice page 368**	**M4** explain identified strengths and areas for improvement and make suggestions relating to further goals, aims and objectives **Assessment practice page 368**	**D2** justify identified strengths and areas for improvement and suggestions made relating to further goals, aims and objectives **Assessment practice page 368**

Index

Page numbers in **bold** type refer to key terms.